AF781907

Post-Stabilization Economics in Sub-Saharan Africa

LESSONS FROM MOZAMBIQUE

Edited by Jean A.P. Clément and Shanaka J. Peiris

INTERNATIONAL MONETARY FUND

© 2008 International Monetary Fund

Production: IMF Multimedia Division, Creative Services
Cover design: Jennifer Geanakos
Cover photographs (from top to bottom): Fishing boat, © 2007 Anzenberger Agency/Marco Moretti; primary school of Nhanpfuine, Eric Miller; Cahora Bassa Dam, João (Funcho) Costa; Woman, Steve Evans.
Figures: Choon Hwee Lee and Andrew Sylvester
Composition: Julio Prego

Cataloging-in-Publication Data

Post-stabilization economics in Sub-Saharan Africa : lessons from Mozambique / edited by Jean A.P. Clément and Shanaka J. Peiris — [Washington, D.C.] : International Monetary Fund, 2007.

p. cm.

ISBN 978-1-58906-677-9

Includes bibliographical references.

1. Mozambique — Economic conditions — 1975– 2. Mozambique — Economic policy. 3. Economic assistance – Mozambique. 4. Postwar reconstruction — Mozambique. 5. Poverty — Mozambique. I. Clément, Jean A. P. II. Peiris, Shanaka J. (Shanaka Jayanath), 1975– III. International Monetary Fund.

HC890 .P678 2007

Price: $28.00

Address orders to:
International Monetary Fund, Publication Services
700 19th Street, N.W., Washington, DC 20431, U.S.A.
Tel.: (202) 623-7430 Telefax: (202) 623-7201
E-mail: publications@imf.org
Internet: http://www.imf.org

FSC
Mixed Sources
Product group from well-managed forests and other controlled sources
www.fsc.org Cert no. BV-COC-070702
© 1996 Forest Stewardship Council

Contents

The following conventions are used in this publication:

- In tables, a blank cell indicates "not applicable"; n.a. indicates "not available"; and 0 or 0.0 indicates "zero" or "negligible." Minor discrepancies between sums of constituent figures and totals are due to rounding.

- An en dash (–) between years or months (for example, 2005–06 or January–June) indicates the years or months covered, including the beginning and ending years or months; a slash or virgule (/) between years or months (for example, 2005/06) indicates a fiscal or financial year.

As used in this publication, the term "country" does not in all cases refer to a territorial entity that is a state as understood by international law and practice. As used here, the term also covers some territorial entities that are not states but for which statistical data are maintained on a separate and independent basis.

Foreword

Mozambique, one of Africa's most remarkable success stories, has benefited from sustained aid inflows, strong and broad-based growth, and deep poverty reduction. It has grown 8 percent annually, on average, since the early 1990s and sharply reduced its poverty headcount, thanks to prudent macroeconomic policies and the implementation of two successive and well-sequenced waves of reforms. Substantial progress has also been made in the country's social sectors, including a doubling of the number of children in primary school, reduction in infant and maternal mortality, and the provision of antiretroviral treatment for HIV infection; these achievements have been financed, in part, by resources made available under the joint IMF and World Bank Highly Indebted Poor Countries (HIPC) Initiative. Endowed with abundant natural resources, Mozambique has been able to put itself on the global foreign direct investment map, attracting megaprojects worth several billion dollars. To sustain a high rate of growth and poverty reduction, it is implementing a second wave of reforms under its new Poverty Reduction Strategy (2006–09). It is also determined to avoid the natural resource curse that has plagued much of Africa in order to continue to reduce poverty.

Mozambique is well placed to achieve the United Nations Millennium Development Goal (MDG) of halving poverty by 2015. Achieving the non-income-related MDGs, however, will require Mozambique to scale up basic services. In this context, Mozambique graduated from a reform program supported by concessional financing under the IMF's Poverty Reduction and Growth Facility to one monitored, but not financed, by the IMF under a three-year Policy Support Instrument. The new program is flexibly designed to use scaled-up foreign aid to enable the country to sustain rapid, pro-poor growth and achieve the MDGs while maintaining macroeconomic stability. It is also better adapted to Mozambique's status as a post-stabilization economy that has demonstrated ownership of its economic program.

As the book notes, the collaboration between international partners and Mozambique's government can serve as a model for other countries. In addition, the authorities are determined to focus on growth-critical reforms to strengthen fiscal and financial institutions, improve the business environment, and promote transparent management of natural resources. The continuation of a stable political environment through the buttressing of this young democracy is also key to Mozambique's continued success.

The book provides technical and policy analysis from which readers may obtain insights into some of the key macroeconomic issues facing low-income countries in a post-stabilization phase. These issues are at the center of the IMF staff's work on low-income countries. They include, most notably, managing the scaling up of foreign aid, choosing the appropriate macroeconomic policy mix, undertaking financial and public finance reforms, collaborating with donors, getting on the path toward long-term sustainability and access to international capital markets, creating a virtuous cycle of natural resource use, reducing the cost of doing business, and improving competitiveness. In all these aspects, the chapters offer brief summaries of the most recent literature and draw lessons from Mozambique's experience for sub-Saharan Africa that should make the book particularly valuable to policymakers, academicians, donors, and civil society.

The book brings together material and analysis prepared by the IMF team working on Mozambique under the supervision of Jean A.P. Clément, Assistant Director in the IMF's African Department, and includes insightful articles from colleagues in the World Bank on poverty reduction, and from Mozambique's Ministry of Planning and Development on the sustainability of long-term growth. The team of authors was led by Jean A.P. Clément and included Rui Benfica (World Bank), Emmy Bosten, Felix Fischer, Louise Fox (World Bank), Julien Hartley, Sam Jones (formerly with the Ministry of Planning and Development of Mozambique), Victor Lledó, James Otto (Professor at the University of Denver Sturm College of Law), Shanaka J. Peiris (coeditor of the book), Magnus Saxegaard, and Melissa Sekkel (World Bank).

Benedicte Vibe Christensen
Acting Director
IMF African Department

Acknowledgments

The authors acknowledge the valuable support, input, and comments provided by a number of colleagues at the International Monetary Fund (IMF) and, in particular, its African Department. The authors are grateful to Asimina Caminis, for her skillful editing of the book and coordination of its production, and to Paul Gleason of the IMF's External Relations Department. They are also grateful to Messrs. Peter Gakunu and Jose Sulemane (IMF, Office of the Executive Director for Africa Constituency I) for their wise advice and to the staff of the IMF Resident Representative's Office in Maputo, in particular Massiquina Calu. They would also like to thank Eteri Kvintradze and Nienke Oomes. Larissa Leony provided research assistance. The IMF team working on Mozambique has enjoyed the support and close collaboration of colleagues from the World Bank, including, in particular, Michael Baxter, Rui Benfica, Greg Binkert, Louise Fox, Peter Moll, Peter Nicholas, and Antonio Nucifora. The team has also enjoyed close collaboration with the representatives of the international community, and an exchange of views with the representatives of civil society.

This book would not have been possible without the fruitful and open discussions with the Mozambican authorities. In particular, we are indebted to Her Excellency, the Prime Minister of Mozambique, Ms. Luísa Dias Diogo; the Minister of Finance, Mr. Manuel Chang; the Minister of Planning and Development, Mr. Aiuba Cuereneia; the Minister of Education and Culture, Mr. Aires Bonifácio Aly; the Minister of Health, Mr. Paulo Ivo Garrido; the Minister of Industry and Commerce, Mr. António Fernando; the Minister of Labor, Ms. Helena Taipo; the Minister of Energy, Mr. Salvador Namburete, the Minister of Mineral Resources, Ms. Esperança Bias; the Minister of Public Administration, Ms. Vitoria Diogo; and the Governor of the Central Bank of Mozambique, Mr. Ernesto Gouveia Gove. We would also like to thank the staff of the Ministry of Finance, in particular the Director of the Treasury, Mr. António Laíce, and the staff of the Central Bank, in particular Mr. Waldemar de Sousa and Mr. António de Abreu. The Mozambican team would like to extend its warmest thanks to the Mozambican authorities for their hospitality and openness in discussing the many challenges facing their beautiful country.

The opinions expressed herein, as well as any errors, are the sole responsibility of the authors and do not necessarily reflect the views of the Mozambican authorities, the Executive Directors of the IMF, or other members of the IMF staff.

Introduction and Overview

JEAN A.P. CLÉMENT

Mozambique, a post-conflict coastal country (see map) endowed with vast natural resources, is one of the few economic success stories in sub-Saharan Africa. It has staged a dramatic recovery from the ravages of civil war and, with the help of large and sustained aid inflows, achieved impressive and broad-based economic growth that is increasingly resilient to natural disasters, and deep and equitable poverty reduction. It now has one of the lowest levels of inequality in Africa, and the country's poverty levels declined more in rural areas, where the majority of the population lives, than in urban areas, making it only the second country in the world (after Vietnam) to see such a reduction. Nonetheless, despite Mozambique's admirable performance, absolute poverty is still more prevalent in rural areas than in urban ones, and its per capita income and human development indicators remain relatively low.

Mozambique's remarkable achievement was made possible by sound and sustained macroeconomic management, substantial official development assistance, and the launching of two successive waves of reforms tailored to the country's particular circumstances. The role of donors, including the International Monetary Fund (IMF) and the World Bank, was instrumental in promoting aid effectiveness through well-coordinated efforts. Such coordination has evolved into an institutional setup that is often praised internationally as a best practice. On the political side, Mozambique was able to successfully bring about reconciliation, and it solidified its nascent democracy through elections that were seen as generally open and fair by the international community.

Mozambique is one of the few sub-Saharan African countries that appears well placed to achieve the key United Nations Millennium Development Goal (MDG) of halving the poverty rate by 2015. Now that the post-stabilization rebound has largely run its course, however, the steady implementation of the second generation of reforms will be key to sustaining Mozambique's growth takeoff by addressing the large gaps in

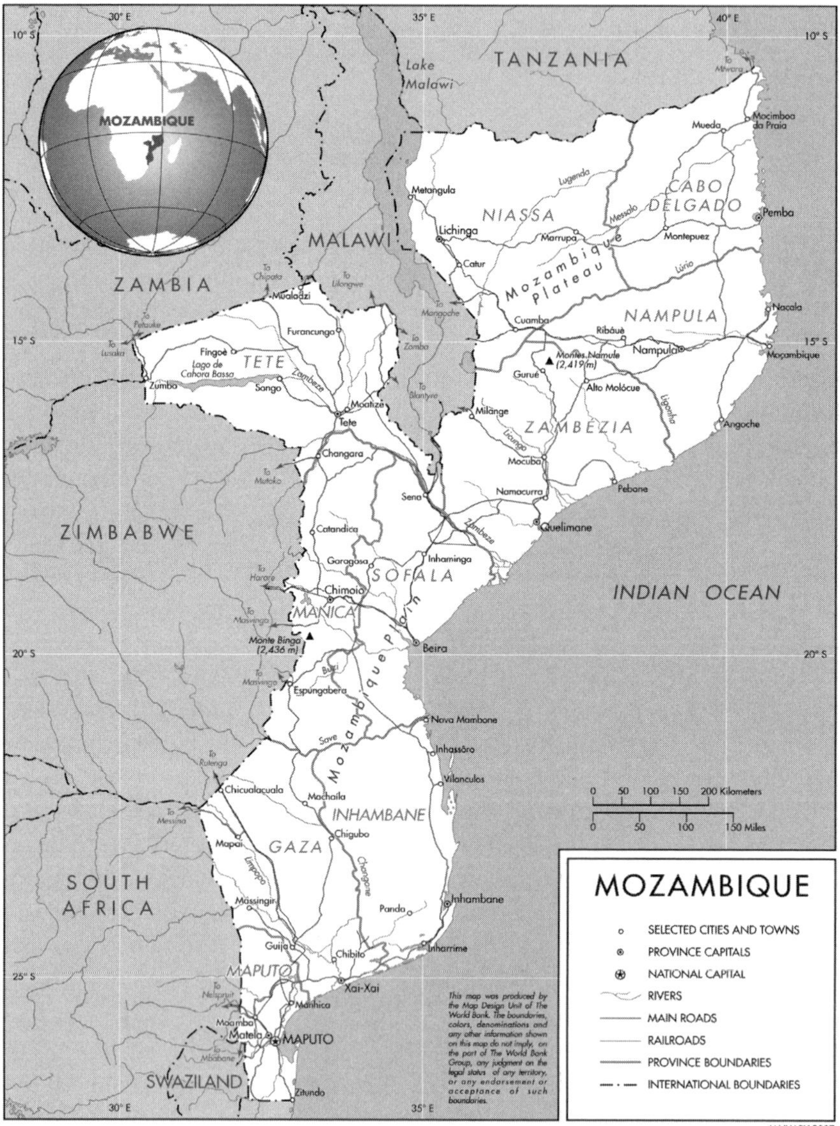
MOZAMBIQUE
TANZANIA
Lake Malawi
MALAWI
ZAMBIA
ZIMBABWE
SOUTH AFRICA
SWAZILAND
INDIAN OCEAN
NIASSA
CABO DELGADO
NAMPULA
ZAMBÉZIA
TETE
SOFALA
MANICA
INHAMBANE
GAZA
MAPUTO
Mozambique Plateau
Mozambique Plain
Mueda
Mocimboa da Praia
Metangula
Lichinga
Marrupa
Montepuez
Pemba
Catur
Cuamba
Ribáuè
Nampula
Nacala
Moçambique
Montes Namuli (2,419 m)
Gurué
Alto Molócue
Angoche
Milange
Mocuba
Pebane
Namacurra
Quelimane
Mualadzi
Furancungo
Fingoè
Lago de Cahora Bassa
Zumbo
Songo
Moatize
Tete
Changara
Sena
Catandica
Gorongosa
Inhaminga
Chimoio
Monte Binga (2,436 m)
Beira
Espungabera
Nova Mambone
Inhassôro
Vilanculos
Chicualacuala
Machaila
Chigubo
Mapai
Massingir
Panda
Inhambane
Guijá
Chibuto
Inharrime
Xai-Xai
Manhiça
Moamba
Matola
MAPUTO
Zitundo
0 50 100 150 200 Kilometers
0 50 100 150 Miles
SELECTED CITIES AND TOWNS
PROVINCE CAPITALS
NATIONAL CAPITAL
RIVERS
MAIN ROADS
RAILROADS
PROVINCE BOUNDARIES
INTERNATIONAL BOUNDARIES
This map was produced by the Map Design Unit of The World Bank. The boundaries, colors, denominations and any other information shown on this map do not imply, on the part of The World Bank Group, any judgment on the legal status of any territory, or any endorsement or acceptance of such boundaries.
JANUARY 2007

human capital and infrastructure and enhancing total factor productivity, particularly in agriculture. The achievement of non-income-related MDGs such as universal primary education, gender equality, the reversal of the incidence of malaria and HIV/AIDS, and access to safe drinking water requires that Mozambique scale up basic services without undermining macroeconomic stability. Consolidating democracy by strengthening transparency and governance, and implementing a truly participatory process at all levels of government, political life, and society will be essential steps in consolidating the country's gains.

This book analyzes the lessons for sub-Saharan Africa from the experience of Mozambique. It focuses on post-stabilization economics, including the need to choose the appropriate macroeconomic policy mix in the face of scaled-up foreign aid and a surge in revenues from natural resources. The book also discusses possible ways to respond to the challenges ahead, including how to get on the path to long-term sustainability and access to international capital markets while further reducing poverty. The lessons and challenges described in the book are likely to be of interest to policymakers, academicians, civil society, and the general public in sub-Saharan Africa and low-income countries elsewhere. Most of the chapters offer summaries of the recent literature on their respective topics.

Halving the Poverty Rate by 2015

Chapter 1 presents a brief overview of Mozambique's growth takeoff since the end of the civil war, which has been compared with the initial takeoffs of fast-growing Asian economies including Indonesia, Malaysia, the Philippines, and Thailand—the members of the Association of Southeast Asian Nations referred to in this book as the ASEAN-4—and China, India, and Vietnam. In addition to identifying the challenges ahead, which is likely to be relevant to many sub-Saharan African countries that are in the midst of growth acceleration, the chapter draws lessons from the experience of Mozambique for the rest of sub-Saharan Africa and the international community.

Chapter 2 describes Mozambique's remarkable success in reducing poverty over the past decade; the country's poverty headcount declined 25 percent between 1996 and 2002. At the micro level, average earnings per worker on smallholder farms increased by about 4 percent per year, which accounted for three-fourths of the decline in the poverty headcount. Meanwhile, growth in the higher-productivity industry and service sectors attracted workers away from the low-productivity agriculture sector. These advances were achieved through a combination of crop diversification and more extensive land use, which increased crop incomes (including from crops grown for household subsistence), and diversification into nonfarm enterprises, such as manufacturing firms based on natural resources (for example, charcoal) or agricultural products, and services. Private investment in agriculture increased demand for wage labor, which supplemented smallholder incomes. Donor-financed government spending helped bring public services closer to the population, and school enrollment rates shot up. Rural households with better market access (thanks to new or better maintained roads and other infrastructure) had a higher rate of diversification and larger incomes from nonfarm enterprises. Chapter 2 offers key lessons for other sub-Saharan African countries. First, it is important to create an enabling investment climate for private investment in smallholder agriculture that includes building market infrastructure, improving access to land, and encouraging contract grower schemes that bring new technology. Second, the development of the commercial farm sector can create wage labor opportunities that provide rural households with a source of cash income. Third, it is important to support the growth of the microbusiness sector (very small family businesses) and the development of supporting institutions, such as microcredit institutions, cooperatives, and associations.

Chapter 3, after a brief survey of the literature on sustained growth, considers the challenges and prospects for maintaining strong and sustainable rates of economic growth over the long term in Mozambique. The discussion is based on a detailed historical growth accounting analysis and a forward-looking macroeconomic projections model. In each case, it is found that high-quality growth relies on contributions from all major aggregate growth drivers—for physical investment to translate effectively into growth, it must be accompanied by continuous improvements in human capital and productivity. Thus, assuming continued access to concessionary external finance to support investment priorities, the key growth challenge identified for Mozambique will be to strengthen productivity via technological catch-up and the implementation of a second generation of reforms. The chapter concludes with a few important lessons. First, private sector investment must be stimulated via public investment in infrastructure and a strong government commitment to a stable macroeconomic environment. Second, countries with significant aid inflows need to manage them strategically to avoid unwanted macroeconomic side effects (such as Dutch disease) and to ensure that their application is aligned with domestic priorities. Third, investment in education is a vital component of a growth-conducive public policy stance. Simply expanding access to education is not enough, however; governments also need to focus on the quality of education and the development of technical skills oriented to business needs. Finally, institutional upgrading to confront the changing nature and deepening complexity of economic management challenges must remain at the forefront of development efforts.

Post-Stabilization Economics, Scaling Up of Aid, and Donor Coordination

Chapter 4 shows that the initial macroeconomic stabilization from periods of very high inflation and debt overhang, as occurred in Mozambique in the early 1990s, requires fiscal consolidation to anchor inflationary expectations and avoid recourse to unsustainable domestic financing (and public debt accumulation) to maintain a credible nominal anchor. A monetary targeting framework can be employed to maintain single-digit inflation in the face of numerous exogenous shocks. In addition, monetary and financial sector reforms, particularly those that address vulnerabilities in the banking system early on, can help consolidate macroeconomic and financial stability, set the stage for adopting a more formal inflation targeting regime, and sow the seeds for a sound expansion of the banking system that will make a growing contribution to private sector development.

Chapter 5 argues that macroeconomic conditions in Mozambique have improved markedly in the past decade, providing greater scope for an activist monetary policy geared toward minimizing macroeconomic volatility and/or achieving an inflation target. The use of monetary policy for this purpose in sub-Saharan Africa poses a number of challenges that have not been fully analyzed in the literature, which focuses mainly on the conduct of monetary policy in industrial countries. These include (1) the need to coordinate monetary and exchange rate policy with fiscal policy in order to maintain macroeconomic stability and manage the potential adverse effect on competitiveness of large and volatile aid inflows (and revenues from natural resource exploitation), and (2) the need to incorporate a realistic description of the monetary policy environment in sub-Saharan African countries. This paper attempts to incorporate these elements in a dynamic stochastic general equilibrium (DSGE) model, estimated using recently developed Bayesian estimation techniques on data for Mozambique, and to use such a model to analyze the conduct of monetary policy in Mozambique in response to aid and numerous other exogenous shocks. To the authors' knowledge, this is the first attempt to estimate a DSGE model for sub-Saharan Africa, except possibly for South

Africa. Their results confirm that a "spend and absorb" response to aid shocks is probably best in normal circumstances, although they also provide insights into why many countries seem to have been reluctant to fully absorb aid shocks owing to a desire to smooth exchange rate fluctuations. In a more realistic setting in which the economy is prone to a wider set of shocks, however, the authors' simulations suggest that a "lite" inflation targeting regime (or an exchange-rate-targeting regime if the authorities do not place a lot of weight on inflation stabilization) would perform best at minimizing macroeconomic volatility.

The model and policy rules discussed in Chapter 5 are broadly applicable to other sub-Saharan African and low-income countries. First, although it was using data for Mozambique, the DSGE model can be adapted for the purpose of policy analysis in other sub-Saharan African countries. Second, the authors' conclusions about how Mozambique should best respond to aid shocks are relevant to many countries in sub-Saharan Africa that benefit from substantial, but volatile, foreign aid. Third, the optimality of alternative monetary policy rules in terms of minimizing inflation, real exchange rate, and output volatility in a shock-prone economy is likely to be of interest to central bankers in non-CFA franc zone countries.[1] Finally, the non-CFA countries in sub-Saharan Africa are rich in petroleum and mineral resources. The effect of variations in oil and mineral export prices on revenues can be treated in a manner that is directly analogous to the authors' treatment of variations in aid. Many of the insights developed by the authors in the context of managing aid flows will therefore carry over to the monetary management of petroleum and mineral resource booms.

Chapter 6 notes that Mozambique has fully spent and absorbed most of the scaled-up foreign aid, ranging between 10 and 20 percent of GDP, it has received over the past decade or so. The additional expenditures have allowed Mozambique to scale up basic services, including doubling the number of children in primary school, reducing infant and maternal mortality, and beginning to provide antiretroviral treatment for HIV infections while sustaining economic growth of 8 percent per year, on average, and reducing the poverty headcount index from 69 percent in 1997 to 54 percent in 2003. Looking forward, illustrative scaling-up scenarios highlight the need to carefully manage a further scaling up of foreign aid. Mozambique's experience of managing foreign aid inflows and the illustrative scaling-up scenarios include a number of lessons: (1) Fully spending

[1]The 14 mostly francophone countries in the CFA franc zone system share a fixed exchange rate regime, and their economic policy decisions are taken in the context of the regional monetary arrangements.

scaled-up foreign aid could help a country make major strides in human development and poverty reduction in a short period without encountering significant macroeconomic absorption problems and microeconomic capacity constraints, although the latter may appear with a lag and would call for a coordinated approach to capacity building, particularly training of frontline workers (for example, teachers, nurses, and agriculture extension workers). (2) Prudent macroeconomic policies and well-sequenced structural reforms are key to maintaining macroeconomic stability and sustaining rapid, broad-based growth. (3) The willingness of a central bank to sell foreign exchange associated with aid inflows to mop up excess liquidity, and thus mostly absorb foreign aid, could avoid an unsustainable buildup of domestic debt and crowding out of the private sector without a significant loss of competitiveness. (4) A prudent external borrowing strategy and encouragement of foreign direct investment, particularly in the natural resource and infrastructure sectors, can help consolidate long-term fiscal sustainability and gradually reduce dependence on donors. (5) Sustained large aid inflows in the range of 10–20 percent of GDP need not result in a weaker revenue effort and reform "fatigue," including more difficult second-generation institutional reforms in, for example, public financial management, if the recipient country authorities take a longer-term perspective and the international community provides continued technical assistance.

Chapter 7 notes that enhanced donor coordination can improve aid effectiveness, as has been observed in Mozambique. Mozambique receives about US$1.2 billion per year in donor aid, which raises a number of legitimate questions about whether these funds are used well or how they could be used better. The 19 donors that provide budget support through a common financing scheme are organized in a group to support the government's poverty reduction strategy in an efficient, predictable, and less cumbersome way than other forms of donor assistance. This has helped reduce aid volatility and made donor disbursements to Mozambique among the least volatile in the region. In this chapter, Mozambique's model of donor coordination is measured against the 12 indicators specified in the Paris Declaration, which are regrouped under "ownership," "harmonization," "alignment," and "managing for results." Mozambique scores in the top 25 percent on most of the indicators, despite a number of complicating factors vis-à-vis other countries, most notably the large amount of aid it receives and the large number of donor countries. Mozambique can be considered a model for other sub-Saharan African countries in terms of donor coordination and processes that lead to continued improvements in aid effectiveness. The country's experience also confirms that budget support is superior to project aid, that increased reliance by donors on government systems increases the government's responsibility to carry out the necessary reforms, and that the role played by the national authorities has helped donors comply with the Paris Declaration. Another important lesson is that the IMF can play a catalytic role in facilitating compliance with the Paris Declaration and improving aid effectiveness.

Management of Mineral Resources

Chapter 8 recalls that some resource-rich nations that derive a large part of their export earnings from their mineral (and oil and gas) sector have seen their economies lag those in resource-poor nations. This "resource curse" affects many, but not all, mineral-led economies and has been a favorite subject of economists for the past several decades. The curse is not inevitable, and examples of nations that have avoided it are as diverse as Botswana, Chile, and Malaysia. This chapter briefly reviews the literature on the resource curse and analyzes fiscal policy elements that can assist in deflecting it. It also traces the development of the mineral industry and related policies in Mozambique from a period of domination by state enterprises through a period of foreign investment promotion, including liberal tax incentives and confidential negotiated agreements, up to today, when transparent policies are designed to harvest curse-free benefits from the sector. Mozambique is quickly becoming a minerals-led economy, with several megaprojects now in place and others being developed or in the planning process. Whether Mozambique will avoid the resource curse in the long run will be known only in coming decades, but its policy approach provides a valuable example of a nation that has recognized the risks of the curse and sought to minimize them. The chapter concludes with a few key lessons for other sub-Saharan African and low-income countries on how to support a virtuous cycle of mineral resource use.

Business Environment, Trade, and Competitiveness

Chapter 9, which draws on the basic tools and best practices described in the private sector development literature, benchmarks Mozambique's business environment relative to regional competitors and successful cases of sustained private sector–led growth with the aim of identifying reform priorities. Despite past efforts to improve the business environment, catching up with regional competitors still requires substantial improvements.

The government of Mozambique is rightfully addressing this challenge by implementing a new strategy to make Mozambique's business environment the most competitive in Africa by 2015. Mozambique is starting to emerge as a reform champion by regional standards and offers lessons on how to develop mechanisms that translate identified reform priorities into actionable, time-bound, and monitorable measures, as well on how to design implementation arrangements to promote coordination and ownership of the reform process.

Chapter 10 reviews export performance and competitiveness. Mozambique has experienced impressive economic growth, driven to a large extent by improvements in its export performance. These developments, however, reflect mainly megaproject-related exports whose impact on the economy as a whole should not be overstated. This chapter analyzes the causes underlying the comparatively lackluster performance of Mozambique's traditional export sector and makes some recommendations as to how to diversify the source of export growth to include non-megaproject exports. Although the real effective exchange rate (REER) does not suggest that Mozambique's competitiveness has been deteriorating, the chapter suggests that the REER may recently have been slightly overvalued compared with its equilibrium and thus that there may have been scope for competitiveness to improve. The author argues that evidence of REER overvaluation may have been linked to exchange rate restrictions that were in place until June 2007. The recent removal of these restrictions should contribute to improving the competitiveness of the export sector in Mozambique. In addition, there is some evidence that many of the country's traditional exports may be facing declining world demand. This, coupled with the concentration of exports, suggests that efforts should be made to diversify the export base. Doing so would require structural reforms to improve competitiveness, including improving the business climate in Mozambique and undertaking further trade liberalization.

Chapter 10 contains a number of conclusions with policy implications for Mozambique and other sub-Saharan African countries, in particular with respect to measures that may contribute to expanding the export base beyond the capital-intensive natural resource sectors while diversifying into products for which demand in the world marketplace is growing. Mozambique's experience also underlines the importance of careful monitoring of the REER to ensure that it does not become overvalued. This is particularly true in sub-Saharan Africa, where countries are prone to Dutch-disease effects and possible exchange rate overvaluation because of increased capital inflows. Finally, Mozambique's experience suggests that misalignment of the REER is typically associated with an exchange rate that is tightly managed or restricted through administrative means. This provides some justification for greater exchange rate flexibility in the face of sharp increases in capital inflows.

1

Sustaining Growth Takeoffs: Lessons from Mozambique

JEAN A.P. CLÉMENT AND SHANAKA J. PEIRIS

Mozambique is a success story in sub-Saharan Africa. It has benefited from sustained large foreign aid inflows, strong and broad-based growth, and deep poverty reduction. Since its civil war ended in 1992, Mozambique's growth record has been impressive, and its growth has especially benefited the poor: consumption among people below the poverty line has grown strongly, thanks to an expanding agricultural sector, increased nonfarm activities in rural areas, and higher wages. Today, Mozambique has one of the lowest levels of income inequality in Africa, and its absolute poverty and the poverty gap (which takes into account the distance separating the poor from the poverty line) have decreased substantially. (See Figure 1.1.) This remarkable growth performance was made possible by prudent macroeconomic policies, structural reform, and substantial donor assistance. On the political side, Mozambique has succeeded in bringing about reconciliation and solidifying its nascent democracy through three general and presidential elections.[1]

Mozambique appears well placed to achieve the United Nations Millennium Development Goal (MDG) of halving the poverty rate by 2015.[2] Its per capita income is US$303 (well below the sub-Saharan African average of US$580), however, and almost a third of the population still lives on less than US$1 a day. Sustaining Mozambique's impressive growth

[1]These elections were seen as generally open and fair by the international community.

[2]See Chapter 2.

Figure 1.1. Sustaining Growth Is Key to Poverty Reduction
(In percent)

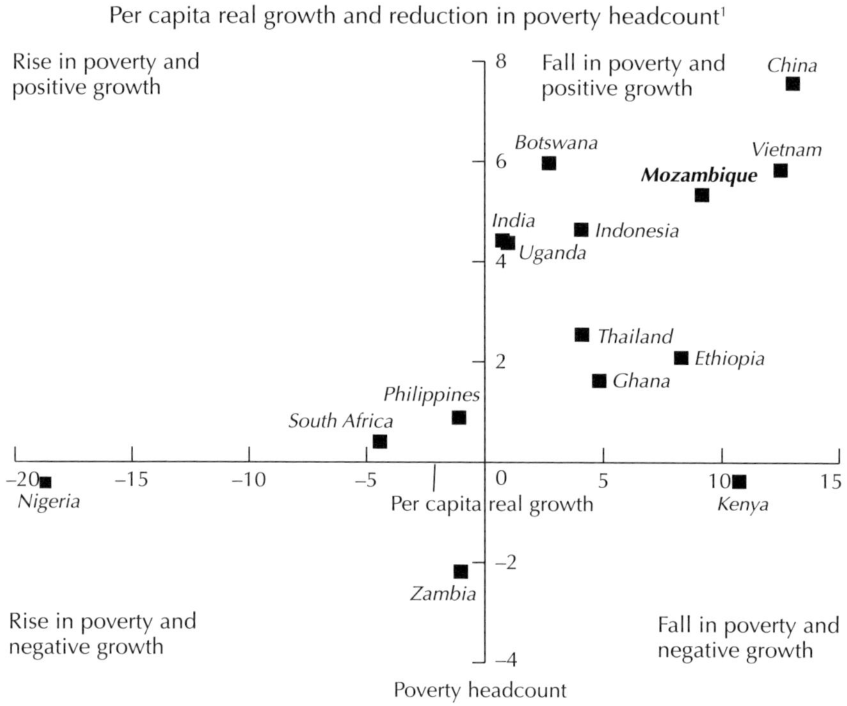

Source: World Bank, World Development Indicators database.
[1]The analysis is based on household survey data released between 1984 and 2004.

takeoff is thus key to ensuring swifter and deeper poverty reduction. This chapter, using the results of a benchmarking exercise comparing fast-growing Asian and post-stabilization sub-Saharan African countries with Mozambique, identifies potential constraints to sustaining rapid growth.[3] Although Mozambique is well placed to sustain its growth takeoff given its sound political institutions, geography (coastal location close to South Africa), and relative income equality, weaknesses in regulatory quality and law enforcement may offset these advantages to the detriment of growth.

[3]Johnson, Ostry, and Subramanian (2007) undertake a similar benchmarking exercise.

The next section provides the background to the impressive performance of Mozambique in the past 15 years, while the one that follows identifies the potential constraints to sustaining growth using the benchmarking exercise mentioned above. The third section outlines the role of the IMF in Mozambique, and the fourth and last section concludes and draws lessons about how the experience of Mozambique could be of interest to other sub-Saharan African countries.

Background

Geography and Endowment[4]

Mozambique spans more than 1,500 miles of Africa's southeast coast on the Indian Ocean. It is the world's 36th-largest country; it is nearly twice the size of California and one of the most land-abundant countries in Africa. Mozambique borders Tanzania to the north; Malawi, Zambia, and Zimbabwe to the west; and South Africa and Swaziland to the south. Mozambique has several deepwater ports and many rivers; the Zambezi River, its largest, has the greatest hydroelectric power potential in Africa. Mozambique's geography and resources offer vast potential for trade and growth, especially in agriculture, fishing, tourism, regional transportation, hydroelectricity, natural gas, oil, and minerals.[5]

Mozambique's fertile soils and favorable climatic conditions permit farmers to grow a large variety of crops, ranging from traditional subsistence crops, such as maize, cassava, and vegetables, to cash crops, such as cotton, sugar, cashew nuts, fruits, tobacco, cut flowers, and spices. The low utilization rate (15 percent) of arable land and relatively low yields suggest that the agricultural sector, which employs 80 percent of the population, could expand further. The timber industry is also very dynamic, although its resources and production should be managed in a more sustainable way. Mozambique's tourism potential is virtually untapped, despite the country's abundant marine life, coral reefs, mountains, and game conservation area. The most important trading routes, which run north-south and east-west

[4]According to a 1997 census, the spoken local languages in Mozambique are Emakhuwa, 26.1 percent; Xichangana, 11.3 percent; Portuguese, 8.8 percent (official; spoken by 27 percent of the population as a second language); Elomwe, 7.6 percent; Cisena, 6.8 percent; Echuwabo, 5.8 percent; other Mozambican languages, 32 percent; other foreign languages, 0.3 percent; and unspecified, 1.3 percent. Mozambique is divided into 10 provinces, which are subdivided into 129 districts; its capital city, Maputo, has provincial status.

[5]World Bank (2004).

along the major regional corridor, could service trade to and from South Africa and other parts of the region.

Mozambique's population, approximately 20 million, is projected to grow at about 2.4 percent annually. Since dependency rates are falling, population dynamics have not been a major driver of poverty trends; indeed, demographic dynamics have helped support rising per capita incomes and falling poverty. Nonetheless, diseases common in many parts of Africa, including malaria, tuberculosis, and HIV/AIDS, are still endemic in Mozambique. The result is low life expectancy at birth—45 years, or slightly below the sub-Saharan African average of 46. In 2005, there were 123,000 AIDS-related deaths and 400,000 children were orphaned because their parents died of AIDS, creating a tremendous loss to, and burden on, society. However, Mozambique's Human Development Index (HDI) has risen steadily over the past few years, with a score of 0.448 for 2005 and preliminary data for 2006 indicating a rise to 0.458. If improvements continue at the current rate, in 2009 Mozambique will have an HDI of 0.501, enough to propel it into the ranks of countries that have achieved medium human development.

Post-Conflict Economic History

Just 15 years ago, Mozambique was the world's poorest country. "This undesirable situation was the result of a complicated historical heritage that included a period of colonization that put little emphasis on human capital, a failed socialist economic experience, and a vicious civil war that lasted more than a decade."[6] Since signing a peace agreement in 1992 that ended 16 years of conflict, Mozambique has achieved impressive broad-based GDP growth (8 percent a year, on average) and lowered poverty (the poverty headcount index went from 69 percent in 1997 to 54 percent in 2003); this growth acceleration, more sustained than in many other post-conflict economies, has helped consolidate peace.[7] These achievements were possible because Mozambique's fairly unified government, which has a firm commitment to poverty reduction, met the preconditions for healthy growth, implementing a first wave of far-reaching institutional and structural reforms with substantial donor support.[8]

---

[6]See IMF (2007a), page 17.

[7]See Clément (2004), for a discussion of post-conflict economics in sub-Saharan Africa.

[8]Mozambique is one of the biggest recipients of concessional assistance (which amounts to about 15 percent of GDP) in Africa. This has helped improve both access to and the quality of basic services.

Economic growth has been broad-based and accompanied by a structural transformation away from primary sectors toward industrial and service sectors. (See Figure 1.2.) Growth has been sustained by an agricultural rebound, the rehabilitation of infrastructure-related sectors, construction of megaprojects, investment from neighboring countries, and buoyant foreign aid. The structural transformation is attributable partly to steady progress in liberalizing key sectors (for example, telecommunications and air transport) and the freeing up of internal trade and prices.[9] A rapid expansion in communication services and the extension of urban water and electricity services to new areas added further momentum. Though growth in the country's two most important traditional activities, agriculture (including fisheries) and commerce, has slowed recently, these sectors are still Mozambique's largest in terms of economic activity and employment; together they account for almost 40 percent of GDP.

After years of high inflation lasting into the mid-1990s, Mozambique has largely succeeded in stabilizing inflation, in part thanks to the tight money-based stabilization program, supported by prudent fiscal policies, implemented under successive IMF-supported arrangements. (See Figure 1.3.) There have, however, been bouts of inflationary episodes driven by exogenous shocks. For example, after the great flood of 2000, reconstruction necessitated a fiscal expansion. Subsequent droughts resulted in higher food prices, and a banking crisis in 2002 undermined the central bank's ability to retain monetary control. Sharp adjustments to domestic fuel prices also contributed to inflationary dynamics during the same period. More recently, monetary and financial sector reforms, together with prudent macroeconomic policies, have helped Mozambique maintain macroeconomic stability in the face of exogenous shocks, particularly higher world oil prices. (See Chapter 4.) Fiscal consolidation limited the need for the authorities to resort to monetary financing and helped reduce inflation to single-digit levels, relieving pressure on domestic interest rates. The flexible exchange rate regime helped cushion the economy against exogenous shocks and maintain competitiveness.

Mozambique has made considerable progress toward establishing a modern and effective tax system by phasing in wide-ranging reforms in a number of key areas with the support of the donor community. The first phase, which started in 1996 and focused on customs, modernized customs administration, including through the introduction of modern legislation and procedures. In a bold step, the government contracted out

[9]State-sponsored interventions in the agricultural sector were all but eliminated by the mid-1990s.

Figure 1.2. Broad-Based Economic Growth Has Been Led by Agricultural Catch-up and Industrialization

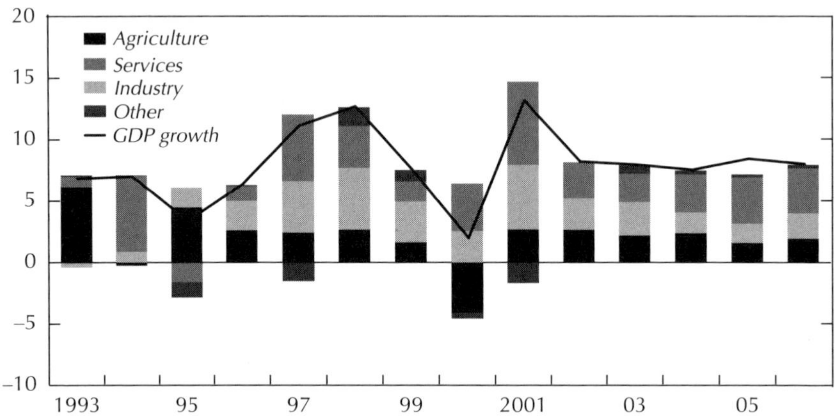

Source: IMF staff estimates.

the complete management of its customs service, with financial assistance from the U.K. Department for International Development and the World Bank;[10] it resumed managing customs administration in 2003 with continuing support from Crown Agents (the firm that originally took over administration), to prepare to integrate customs into a unified revenue authority. The second phase, the introduction of a value-added tax (VAT) in mid-1999,[11] was successful and provided the basis for shifting the focus of revenue collection from imports to domestic transactions over the medium term. The third phase of the reform, which is now under way, aims to further strengthen the design and administration of the tax system and to increase the tax ratio over the medium term. This phase draws on a comprehensive review by the IMF conducted in February 2001 and updated in March 2006, with the IMF concluding that Mozambique's tax policy regime is generally sound and appropriate for a low-income coun-

[10]Crown Agents was chosen by international tender as Mozambique's operational partner. In January 1997, under the direction of the Mozambican government, Crown Agents took over operational management of customs—the first time any government had attempted a public-private partnership of this kind.

[11]The VAT's implementation was supported from October 1996 by a technical assistance project carried out jointly by the IMF and the Swiss State Secretariat for Economic Affairs. The Fund acted as the executing agency of the project.

Figure 1.3. Prudent Monetary and Fiscal Policies Have Helped Stabilize the Economy

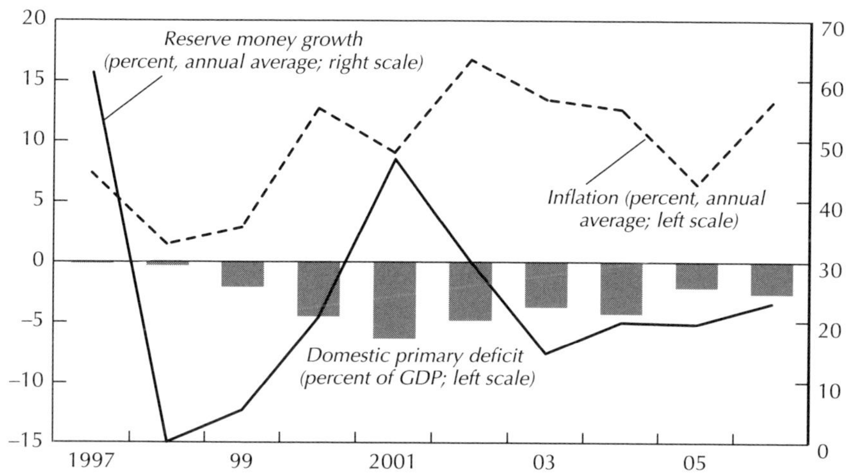

Source: IMF staff estimates.

try while noting that measures to strengthen tax administration are also moving ahead.[12] The remaining reform areas being implemented include making changes to direct taxation (for example, to reduce exemptions and rationalize income tax incentives) and establishing the central revenue authority (*Autoridade Tributária Moçambicana*; ATM) as a sustainable, semiautonomous agency and improving its operational performance, particularly in enforcing tax compliance.[13] The result is a tax regime that relies less on distortionary indirect taxes and tariff barriers. Overall, the revenue-to-GDP ratio has increased steadily, from about 11 percent in 1996 to 16 percent in 2006. (See Table 1.1.)

Government expenditures in Mozambique have generally reached the most economically and socially productive sectors (World Bank, 2005). A cohesive state apparatus and development of a consensus on how best to utilize scaled-up foreign aid that initially may have been led by the international community (including through conditionality) built a sense of country ownership over time and focused on the fight against poverty.

---

[12]See Coelho and others (2001) and Varsano and others (2007).

[13]The ATM creation law was approved by the National Assembly in December 2005, allowing for the formal creation of the ATM at the beginning of 2006.

Table 1.1. Revenue Mobilization Has Strengthened Despite Tariff Reforms
(In percent of GDP)

	1996	1997	1998	1999	2000	2001	2002	2003	2004	2005	2006
Total revenue	10.8	10.4	10.4	10.7	11.5	11.2	12.1	13.3	13.1	14.1	15.6
Tax revenue	9.9	9.6	9.6	9.9	10.5	10.0	10.7	12.3	12.1	12.2	13.4
Of which:											
Taxes on income, profits, and capital gains	1.9	2.0	1.9	1.5	1.6	1.8	2.1	2.9	2.8	2.9	3.7
Of which:											
Domestic taxes on goods and services	5.3	5.4	5.6	6.3	6.6	6.1	6.4	7.0	7.3	7.2	7.5
Of which:											
Taxes on international trade and transactions	2.1	1.8	1.8	1.8	1.9	1.8	1.9	2.0	1.8	1.9	1.9
Nontax revenue	0.9	0.8	0.8	0.8	1.0	1.3	1.4	1.0	1.0	1.9	2.1

Source: IMF staff estimates.

The Poverty Reduction Strategy Paper (PRSP) process, which resulted in the *Plano de Acção para a Redução da Pobreza Absoluta* (PARPA I) for 2000–05 and PARPA II for 2006–09, has played a positive role in this regard, particularly through the design and monitoring of a simple rule specifying that 65 percent of total spending should be in priority sectors. Good reform progress has also been achieved on public financial management (PFM) reforms since 2002, when the SISTAFE *(Sistema de Administração Financeira do Estado)* project (now in its second phase) was launched. Completed project components include the creation of a Treasury Single Account (TSA), a government-wide new organic budget law (the SISTAFE law) and its information technology component (the e-SISTAFE), which at present comprises modules for budget execution and budget preparation and has already been rolled out to all line ministries. The implementation of the SISTAFE project has helped alleviate some of the weaknesses flagged by the fiscal transparency report on standards and codes conducted in 2001 (and updated in 2004 and 2007), particularly in regard to enacting a comprehensive legal framework and strengthening the accounting and reporting system. As such, the public expenditure and financial accountability (PEFA) assessment of 2006 highlights the fact that PFM systems in Mozambique have improved greatly in recent years. (See Chapter 6, Box 6.1.) The authorities' medium-term PFM action plan and budget for 2006–09 address the remaining PFM weaknesses identified by the PEFA assessments and are financed by a multidonor common fund.

Financial sector reforms to restructure and strengthen supervision of the banking system have deepened financial intermediation. An enhanced regulatory and supervisory framework and cleaned-up balance sheets following privatization and consolidation of the banking system in the aftermath of the banking crisis of 2001–02 have restored confidence in the banking sector,[14] prompting broad money growth to outpace nominal GDP growth and credit to the private sector to almost double in just two years. These developments reflect structural factors associated with banks again becoming involved in providing consumer credit (for example, credit cards and loans to purchase durable goods) and lending for industrial activities as well as borrowing by domestic petroleum distributors related to the syndication of larger oil import transactions.

Although they are still incomplete, these reforms appear to have contributed to improvements in banking system soundness: bank profitability has recuperated, and nonperforming loans have fallen to less than 5 percent of all loans according to Mozambican accounting standards. (See Figure 1.4.)

Banks have also become more efficient. In particular, the ratios of non-interest expenses to gross income and, to a lesser extent, of personal expenses to non-interest expenses, have declined since 2004. Greater confidence in the banking system has also led to a significant decrease in liability dollarization and, thus, less financial vulnerability. Such improvements seem to have presented positive spillovers to financial intermediation. (See Figure 1.5.) Real lending rates and the spread between deposit and lending rates, on a declining trend since 2002, have been associated with a significant increase in the loan-to-deposit ratio, particularly loans denominated in domestic currency.[15] Microfinance institutions (MFIs) also proliferated: between 2000 and 2005, there was about a fivefold increase in the number of their clients and a sevenfold increase in their outstanding loans. The increase in the number of MFIs has been accompanied by a substantial improvement in their operational performance and improved recovery rates. The agriculture sector and rural areas continue to have limited access to banking services and MFIs, however.

---

[14] Following the external auditors' approval in early 2005 of the financial statements of *Banco Internacional de Moçambique* (BIM) for 2004, the enhanced supervisory regime of the BIM was discontinued.

[15] The strong decline in credit denominated in foreign currency was driven, in particular, by the implementation of a prudential measure introduced in July 2005 to provision 50 percent of foreign currency–denominated loans to non-exporters.

Figure 1.4. Banking System Soundness Indicators Have Improved . . .
(In percent)

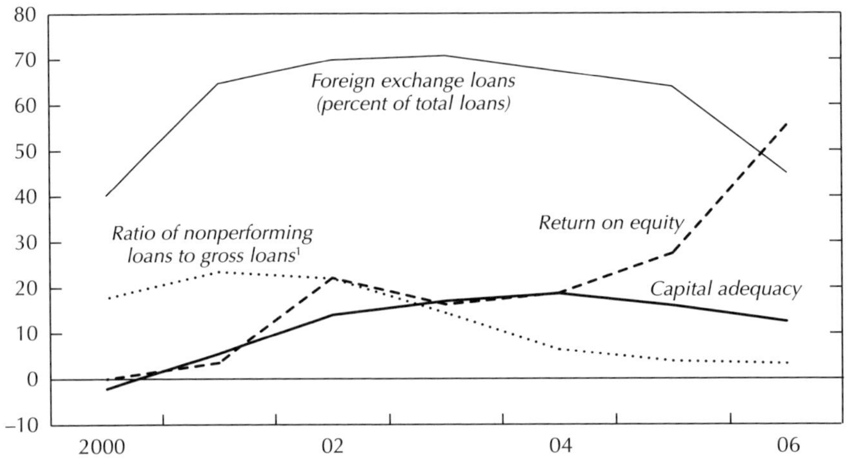

Source: Bank of Mozambique.

[1]According to Mozambican accounting standards, nonperforming loans include only part of past-due loans.

Figure 1.5. . . . Leading to an Increase in Financial Intermediation

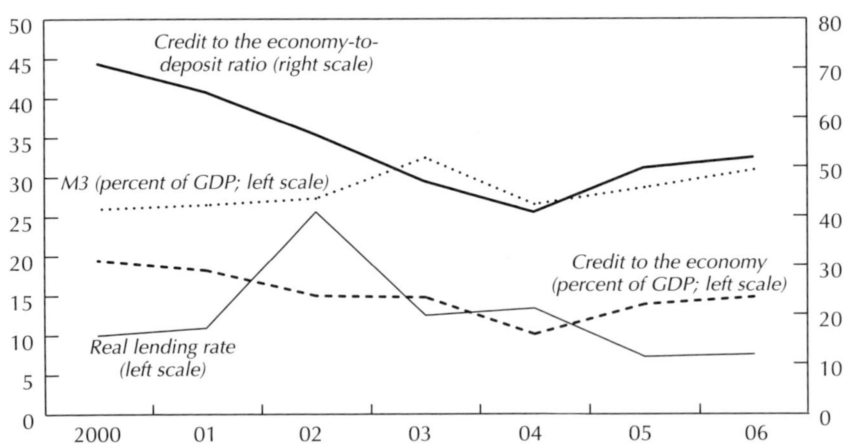

Source: Bank of Mozambique.

Trade and gradual capital account liberalization has made Mozambique one of the most open economies in sub-Saharan Africa. Successive rounds of trade reform have resulted in a tariff structure that is relatively simple: import tariffs fall into four nonzero bands (2.5, 5, 7, and 20 percent).[16] According to overall ratings of trade restrictiveness, Mozambique's trade barriers (tariff and nontariff) are lower than those of neighboring countries (Malawi, South Africa, Swaziland, Tanzania, and Zimbabwe) and most of the member countries of the Association of Southeast Asian Nations (ASEAN). (See Table 1.2.) Its trade-weighted average tariff is 9.1 percent, which is among the lowest in sub-Saharan Africa, although its simple average tariff (12.1 percent) is higher than that of most other sub-Saharan African countries, reflecting its relatively high tariffs in certain import categories with low import levels. It also belongs to only one regional trade agreement (the Southern African Development Community, or SADC) and has thus been able to avoid the confusion associated with participating in overlapping trade agreements. (See Yang and Gupta, 2005.) Mozambique's trade and foreign direct investment (FDI) patterns have been strongly influenced by favorable domestic policies for megaprojects.[17] A strong motivation for attracting large-scale FDI projects in the immediate aftermath of the conflict was to showcase the country as a location of choice for private investment, with the aim of attracting other investors. In addition to benefiting from unrestricted inflows of FDI, as well as dividend, interest, and profit repatriation, many megaprojects qualify as export-processing zones (EPZs), which allow manufacturers to import goods duty free, offer on-site customs facilities, and obtain tax incentives. For example, Mozal (one of the largest aluminum smelters in the world), which is an EPZ, is exempt not only from customs duties on imported inputs but also from corporate income, value-added, and specific consumption taxes.[18] Megaproject exports (electricity, aluminum, and gas) accounted for more than 70 percent of total exports in 2006; aluminum alone accounted for 58.6 percent of the total. The investor-friendly environment helped put Mozambique on the global FDI map and caused exports to expand sharply.[19] (See Figure 1.6.) This, together with buoyant

[16]For example, Mozambique has gradually reduced its maximum tariff rate, from 35 percent in 1999 to 25 percent in 2002, and to 20 percent in 2006.

[17]See the Appendix for an overview of megaprojects in Mozambique.

[18]Firms must employ at least 250 permanent Mozambican workers to qualify as standalone EPZs.

[19]Megaproject spillovers to the rest of the economy remain subdued because of their capital-intensive nature, profit-repatriation patterns, limited vertical and horizontal link-

Table 1.2. Tariff and Nontariff Barriers Are Low

	Trade restrictiveness		
	Overall rating (1–10)	Tariff barriers rating	Nontariff barriers rating
Comparators in sub-Saharan Africa			
Angola	1	1	1
Congo, Dem. Rep. of	2	2	1
Madagascar	2	2	1
Mozambique	**2**	**2**	**1**
Zambia	2	2	1
Mauritius	4	1	2
Botswana	5	2	2
Lesotho	5	2	2
Namibia	5	2	2
South Africa	5	2	2
Swaziland	5	2	2
Tanzania	5	2	2
Zimbabwe	6	3	2
Comparators in Asia			
Indonesia	4	1	2
Malaysia	4	1	2
Thailand	5	2	2

Source: IMF staff estimates.
Note: 1 represents lowest trade restrictiveness.

foreign aid inflows, resulted in a comfortable external position, with international reserves exceeding six months of imports at the end of 2006.

Challenges to Sustaining Rapid Growth in Mozambique

By benchmarking the experience of countries that have sustained long periods of rapid growth against conditions in Mozambique, we can identify potential constraints to sustaining Mozambique's impressive growth takeoff. (See Figure 1.7.) There is not yet a unified theory of sustained growth (Johnson, Ostry, and Subramanian, 2007), although it is well established that weak economic and political institutions are associated with economic crises and faltering growth (Acemoglu, Johnson, and Thaicharoen, 2003; IMF, 2003). Although Mozambique is well placed to sustain its growth takeoff in terms of such fundamental determinants of growth as sound political institutions (IMF, 2003), geography (coastline and proximity to South Africa (Collier and O'Connell, 2008), and low inequality (Acemoglu, Johnson, and Robinson, 2005a; Rodrik, 1999; Berg, Ostry,

ages to the economy, and reduced fiscal contribution. See the Appendix for additional information.

Figure 1.6. Exports Soared, Complementing Aid Inflows and FDI, Resulting in a Comfortable External Position

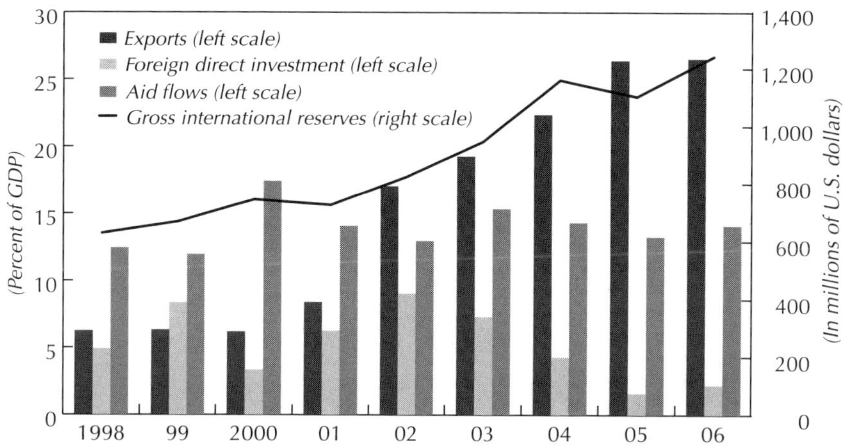

Source: IMF staff estimates.
Note: FDI = foreign direct investment.

and Zettelmeyer, 2006), its broad economic institutions remain weak.[20] (See Figure 1.8.) In addition, it has large gaps in human capital and infrastructure (see Table 1.3), which could conceivably limit returns on productive private investments (Ndulu with others, 2007). For example, a pool of skilled labor and a basic road network may be necessary to support a modern manufacturing sector. In Mozambique, initial levels of human capital may be too low to allow further human capital to accumulate (for example, it may have too few teachers and doctors to develop skills in healthy young people).

Given growth conditions in Mozambique, we seek to benchmark it against countries that started with weak economic institutions (and relatively low income levels) but were able to sustain rapid growth. Relatively few poor countries have managed to sustain rapid growth and improve their institutions; most of the successful ones are in Asia (Hausmann, Pritchett, and Rodrik, 2004; Rodrik and Subramanian, 2004). Therefore, we choose a subset of Asian successes (and a few fast-growing African economies for comparison purposes), focusing on the evolution of their

[20]Broad economic institutions are the laws, rules, and other practices that govern property rights. They also encompass the provision of law and order, and efficient bureaucracies.

Figure 1.7. Mozambique's Growth Takeoff Continues
(Growth index, 0 = 100)

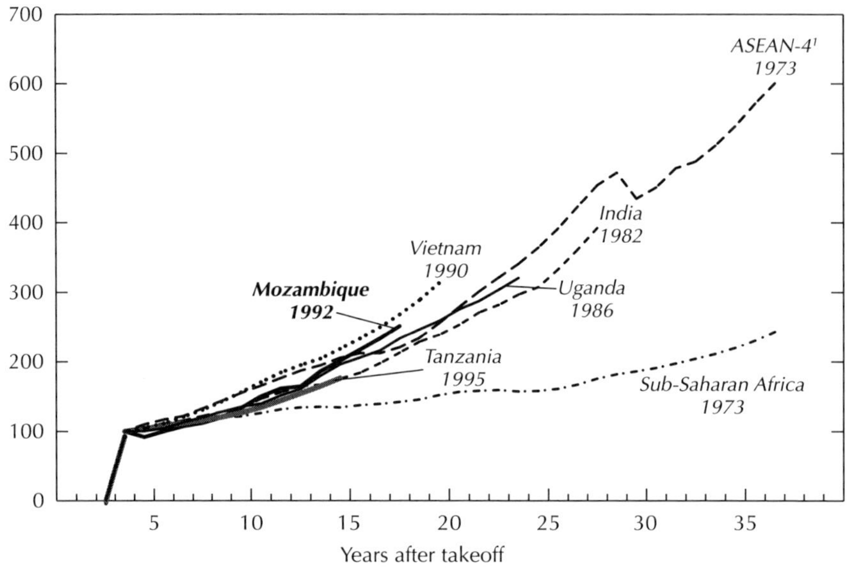

Source: IMF, World Economic Outlook database.
Note: Excludes China for presentation purposes.
[1]ASEAN-4 = Indonesia, Malaysia, the Philippines, and Thailand.

characteristics, to identify potential constraints to sustained growth in Mozambique.

Key Challenges

Productivity growth must be sustained by creating an enabling environment for the private sector through the acceleration of second-generation reforms. The analysis of Mozambique's past growth performance, based on a rigorous growth accounting framework in Chapter 3, suggests that physical capital accumulation, advances in education, and improvements in total factor productivity (TFP) have generated a relatively unbiased pattern of growth. (See Table 1.4 and Figure 1.9.) At an aggregate level, this pattern is broadly similar to the examples of sustained growth found in Asia. As has been well documented, however, measures of TFP based on Solow residuals could reflect a number of factors, including changes in capacity utilization. The results presented in Chapter 3 suggest that the Solow residual appears to have been explained largely by changes in

Figure 1.8. Benchmarking Mozambique's Governance

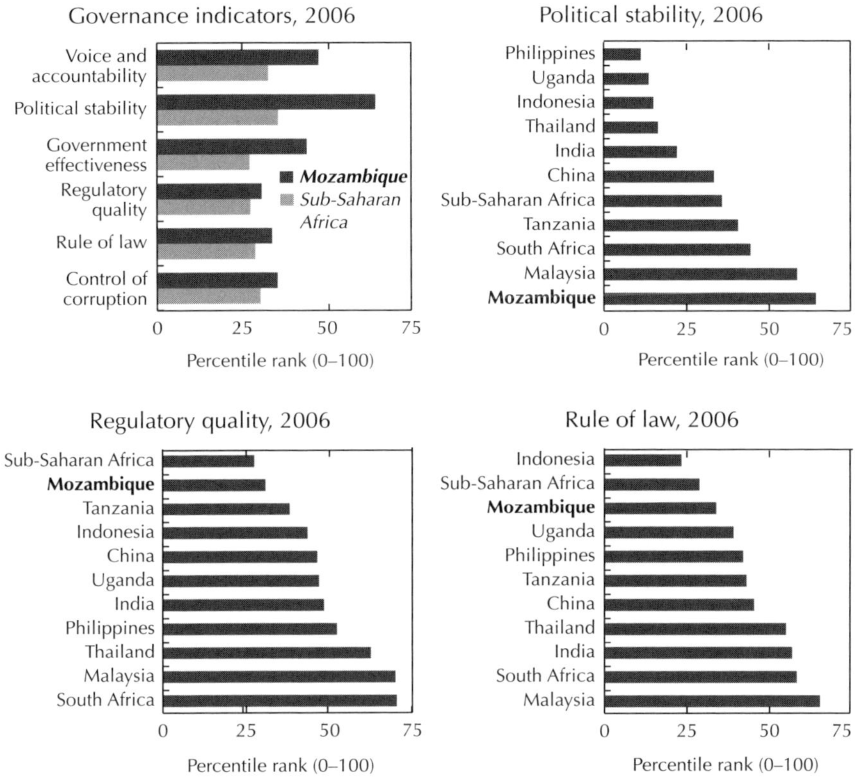

capacity utilization in Mozambique.[21] Thus, once Mozambique approaches its technological frontier, the task of sustaining strong productivity growth could become demanding. Given the country's relatively healthy level of fixed capital investment, the accumulation of factors of production alone is unlikely to be sufficient to sustain growth. Therefore, a critical challenge would be to strengthen productivity through technological advances, given the relatively low productivity in agriculture and manufacturing (see Chapter 2 and Eifert, Gelb, and Ramachandran, 2005), and to pursue second-generation institutional reforms.[22] The focus would also need to be

[21]See Krugman (1987) for an example of the view that Asia's growth "miracle" was also driven by factor accumulation.

[22]Institutional quality has been robustly associated with overall levels of productivity and economic development (see Rodrik and Subramanian, 2004).

Table 1.3. Selected Human Capital and Infrastructure Indicators

	China	India	**Mozam-bique**	Uganda	South Africa	Vietnam	Tanzania	SSA	ASEAN-4
Human development index rank[1]	81.0	126.0	**168.0**	145.0	121.0	109.0	162.0	n.a.	82.0
Life expectancy at birth *(total years)*[2]	71.4	63.5	**41.8**	48.9	44.6	70.3	46.2	46.2	70.5
Adult literacy rate[2]	90.9	61.0	**33.5**	66.8	82.4	90.3	69.4	n.a.	77.3
Reduction of infant mortality from 1970 to 2004	59.0	65.4	**63.6**	19.8	n.a.	37.6	50.6	41.4	49.0
Infant mortality *(per 1,000 live births)*[2]	26.0	61.6	**104.4**	80.2	54.0	17.4	78.4	100.5	21.0
Poverty headcount ratio at national poverty line *(% of population)*[3]	17.0	28.6	**54.0**	33.8	n.a.	37.4	35.7	n.a.	32.0
Gini coefficient[2]	43.4	37.8	**40.3**	43.0	59.3	36.1	38.2	n.a.	42.9
GDP per capita *(constant 2000 US$)*[4]	1,444.8	586.5	**291.7**	267.4	3,534.6	539.0	329.9	559.7	2,231.1
Primary completion rate, total *(% of relevant age group)*[2]	n.a.	83.6	**29.0**	61.1	95.6	100.8	55.6	61.1	96.5
Primary school enrollment ratio[2]	n.a.	89.7	**71.0**	n.a.	90.0	93.0	85.9	n.a.	89.3
Improved water source *(% of population with access)*[2]	77.0	86.0	**43.0**	60.0	88.0	85.0	62.0	56.2	90.0
Irrigated land *(% of cropland)*[2]	35.3	32.9	**2.6**	0.1	9.5	33.4	3.6	3.6	15.1
Mobile phone subscribers *(per 1,000 people)*	258.3	43.8	**36.4**	41.9	428.5	60.4	43.6	74.1	389.6
Electric power consumption *(kWh per capita)*[2]	1,378.5	435.3	**338.5**	n.a.	4,503.7	433.1	54.4	513.0	1,456.7
HIV prevalance[4]	0.1	0.9	**16.1**	6.7	18.8	0.5	6.5	6.2	0.5

Sources: United Nations Development Program, 2006, *Human Development Report;* and World Bank, World Development Indicators database.
Note: SSA = Sub-Saharan Africa.
[1]2006 data.
[2]2004 data.
[3]2000 data except Mozambique (2002).
[4]2005 data.

Table 1.4. Comparative Growth Accounting Evidence; Annual Rates of Growth
(In percent)

			Decomposition of ΔY			
		ΔY	ΔA	ΔK	ΔL	ΔH
1990–2000	Africa	2.3	–0.5	–0.1	2.5	0.4
1990–2000	East Africa	5.7	0.5	2.3	2.4	0.5
1990–2000	Latin America	3.3	0.4	0.2	2.4	0.3
1990–2000	South Asia	5.3	1.2	1.2	2.5	0.4
1992–1998	**Mozambique**	**5.22**	**1.67**	**1.84**	**1.31**	**0.4**
1999–2004	**Mozambique**	**7.4**	**1.11**	**3.84**	**1.5**	**0.92**
1980–2004	**Mozambique**	**2.6**	**–0.27**	**1.2**	**1.13**	**0.52**

Sources: Bosworth and Collins (2003) for regions; and Chapter 4 for Mozambique.

on sustaining public and private investment levels, improving average education levels, and minimizing the impact of the HIV/AIDS epidemic. In addition, although foreign aid is likely to continue to play a major role in financing government spending (about 50 percent in 2006), the level and quality of public investment will depend on the effective management of absorptive capacity pressures and public financial management systems.

Macroeconomic stability should be consolidated to help maintain growth momentum.[23] Inflation is still higher in Mozambique than in the successful Asian countries benchmarked here and in South Africa, its main trading partner. (See Figure 1.10.) The relatively high level of GDP volatility is explained mostly by weather-related shocks to agriculture, which call for better mitigation mechanisms, such as irrigation and crop diversification. (See Figure 1.11.) Fiscal policy has an important role to play in consolidating macroeconomic stability by anchoring inflationary expectations as postulated by the Sargent-Wallace framework of the so-called unpleasant monetary arithmetic, and the fiscal theory of the price level. (See Chapter 4.) In a shock-prone economy like Mozambique's, a more consistent and sophisticated management of monetary and exchange rate policy is critical, possibly through the implementation of a "lite" inflation targeting regime, as suggested in Chapters 4 and 5. Deepening domestic financial markets and building the Bank of Mozambique's credibility through greater central bank autonomy and transparency would be important in this regard. (See Chapter 4.) Real exchange rate misalign-

[23]Sustaining Mozambique's growth takeoff is dependent on avoiding a return to the high-inflation episodes that characterized much of the 1980s and the first half of the 1990s. For example, Berg, Ostry, and Zettelmeyer (2006) show that reducing inflation from 50 percent to 10 percent halves the risk of a slowdown in growth in any given year.

Figure 1.9. Gross Fixed Capital Formation Is Healthy
(Percent of GDP)

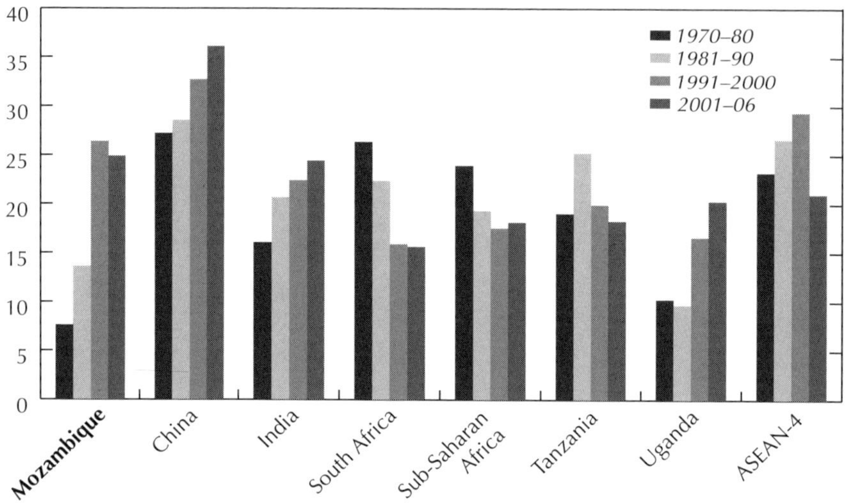

Source: World Bank, World Development Indicators database.
Note: ASEAN-4 = Indonesia, Malaysia, the Philippines, and Thailand.

ments also must be guarded against, to avoid stymieing growth.[24] In this respect, Mozambique has been largely successful in maintaining competitiveness by avoiding persistent real exchange rate overvaluations through a flexible exchange rate regime. Econometric results presented in Chapter 10 suggest that the real effective exchange rate (REER) may have been temporarily overvalued in times of tight exchange rate management in Mozambique. With a supportive fiscal stance, Mozambique should continue to aim to keep inflation in single digits through an appropriate mix of monetary policy instruments; it should also pursue greater exchange rate flexibility to cushion against exogenous shocks and avoid real exchange rate overvaluation.[25]

[24]Across a variety of methodologies, for example, overvaluation is robustly correlated with crises and derailment of growth, even when controlling for inequality and institutions (Acemoglu, Johnson, and Thaicharoen, 2003; Berg, Ostry, and Zettelmeyer, 2006; and Johnson, Ostry, and Subramanian, 2007).

[25]Since Fischer (1993), several authors have tried to identify and locate a "kink" in the relation between inflation and economic growth—associated with a maximum growth rate. Empirical studies using panels of countries have located this kink in the inflation-

Figure 1.10. Inflation Needs to Fall Further
(Average for period, percent)

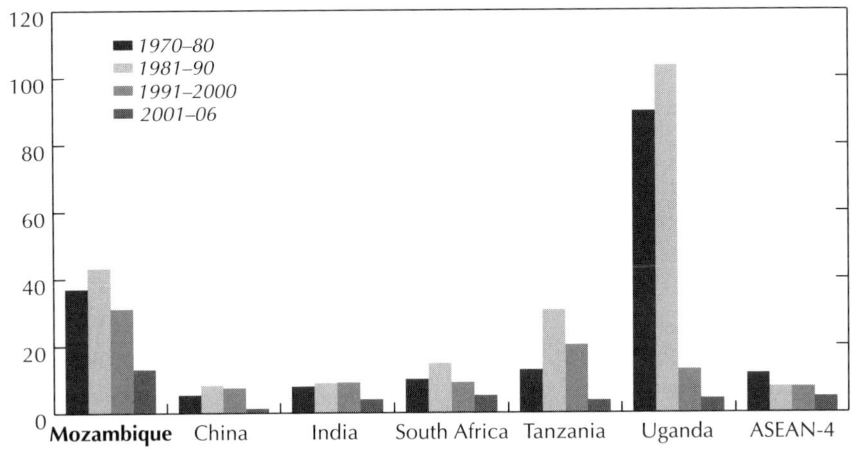

Source: World Bank, World Development Indicators database.
Note: ASEAN-4 = Indonesia, Malaysia, the Philippines, and Thailand.

Fiscal policy could continue to focus on achieving the MDGs but be carefully managed to ensure long-term fiscal sustainability and avoid a loss of competitiveness. Foreign aid inflows, amounting to about 15 percent of GDP, could continue to be fully spent and focused on priority sectors (for example, agriculture, education, health, and infrastructure, as defined in the PRSP) to help achieve the MDGs and address Mozambique's vast socioeconomic needs. The Heavily Indebted Poor Countries (HIPC) and Multilateral Debt Relief Initiatives (MDRI) have reduced Mozambique's debt levels and provided it with the fiscal space to maintain a relatively high level of expenditures (about 25–30 percent of GDP), financed mainly through concessional external borrowing and foreign grants. (See Figure 1.12.) Given the low tax-to-GDP ratio and the need to guard against aid volatility and gradually reduce dependence on donors, however, an annual average revenue increase of 0.5 percent of GDP should continue to be targeted through the Medium-Term Fiscal Framework. (See Figure 1.13.) This can be achieved by widening the tax base and improving revenue administration (Chapter 6). Beyond the PARPA II period (2006–09), strong growth and increased fiscal revenues from megaprojects—including

growth nexus at a level of inflation somewhere between 3 percent and 40 percent, with a majority suggesting a level in the 5–10 percent range (Ghosh and Phillips, 1998).

Figure 1.11. Exogenous Shocks Need to Be Better Mitigated
(GDP growth in percent; standard deviation)

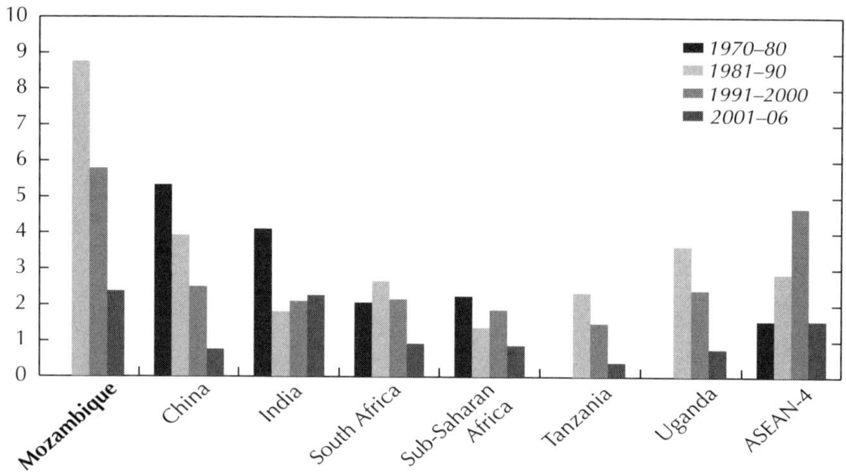

Source: World Bank, World Development Indicators database.
Note: ASEAN-4 = Indonesia, Malaysia, the Philippines, and Thailand.

the development of the multibillion-dollar Moatize coal mine project and the Pande-Temane gas project (still in its cost-recovery phase)—would help Mozambique maintain long-term fiscal sustainability and possibly allow it to start tapping international capital markets.[26] This approach would provide a strategy for exiting from aid dependence in the long run and ensure that at least recurrent spending could be financed from domestic resources. In this manner, the government can avoid recourse to unsustainable domestic borrowing to offset a decline of external assistance that could occur in the future, particularly after 2015. Mozambique has made good progress in improving aid effectiveness through enhanced donor coordination, which has recently reduced aid volatility (Chapter 7), in contrast to many other sub-Saharan African countries (Bulíř and Hamann, 2005; and Collier and Dollar, 2002), although firm donor commitments are still short term.[27] Therefore, if aid is lumpy or becomes less persistent, or

[26]Mozambique's sovereign Standard & Poor's credit rating (B) is expected to improve, especially because of the country's efforts to buttress institutional capacity and maintain debt levels closer to emerging market thresholds established by World Bank–IMF debt-sustainability analyses.

[27]A recent commitment by the United Kingdom to provide assistance over three years is an exception.

Figure 1.12. External Vulnerability Has Decreased
(External debt, percent of GDP)

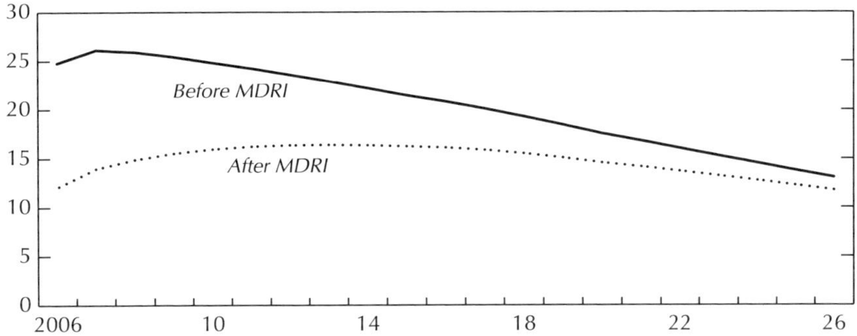

Sources: Mozambican authorities and IMF staff projection.
Note: MDRI = Multilateral Debt Relief Initiative.

microeconomic capacity constraints become binding in some sectors, the authorities may consider smoothing the expenditure pattern and saving part of the aid in international reserves to be spent and absorbed at a later date. The scaling up of spending, whether financed by donors or not, will tend to cause the real exchange rate to appreciate and, therefore, could potentially hurt the export sector and long-run growth (Chapters 6 and 10).[28] Thus, there is a need to effectively reach the most productive priority sectors to elicit a supply response and mitigate potential Dutch-disease effects by strengthening PFM systems while embarking on a public sector reform program to improve efficiency and public service delivery.[29]

Reducing the costs of business would help Mozambique diversify its export sector. Mozambique's export levels, which are similar to those of most countries in sub-Saharan Africa, are comparable to the export levels of the ASEAN-4 countries (Indonesia, Malaysia, the Philippines, and Thailand) during their initial growth takeoffs. (See Figure 1.14.) Its share of world trade has also been expanding, but that increase can be attributed to only a few sectors (Chapter 10). Mozambique's exports are dominated by capital-intensive megaprojects, though sustained growth tends to be asso-

[28]The impact on the real exchange rate and exports of spending scaled-up foreign aid explains the weak link between aid inflows and growth in developing countries, according to Rajan and Subramanian (2005).

[29]Dutch disease is defined in Chapter 6.

Figure 1.13. Revenue Mobilization Is Key to Fiscal Sustainability
(In percent of GDP)

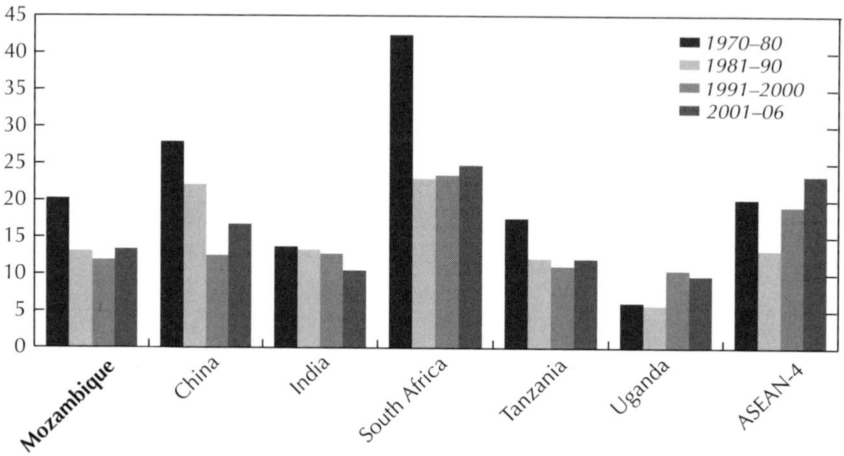

Source: World Bank, World Development Indicators database.
Notes: Data for China include grants. ASEAN-4 = Indonesia, Malaysia, the Philippines, and Thailand.

ciated with strong manufacturing exports.[30] The narrow export base and the lack of manufacturing exports may be due partly to the wide gap in business competitiveness between Mozambique, on the one hand, and the ASEAN-4 and African competitors, on the other hand, as measured by the World Bank's Doing Business and governance indicators. (See Table 1.5.) As such, lowering the costs of doing business must be at the core of the authorities' reform strategy to promote export diversification (see Chapter 9). Key priorities are to support financial sector development,[31] further liberalize trade, and reduce labor and other indirect costs, particularly costs related to trade regulations and infrastructure bottlenecks.

The cost of credit is relatively high in Mozambique, as in the rest of sub-Saharan Africa (with the exception of South Africa).[32] (See Figure 1.15.)

[30]In addition to being a labor-intensive and high-productivity growth sector, manufacturing may also support institutional development and thus improve long-term growth prospects (Acemoglu, Johnson, and Robinson, 2005b; and IMF, 2003).

[31]See Gulde and others (2006) for a comprehensive look at the financial sector challenges facing sub-Saharan Africa.

[32]Recent business surveys continue to identify the high cost of finance as the top constraint to private sector growth, and access to financial services is among the top three constraints. The lack of access to finance is also a major factor stifling firm growth in Mozambique: more than 70 percent of firms do not have access to bank lending or to

Figure 1.14. Export Growth Needs to Be Sustained
(In percent of GDP)

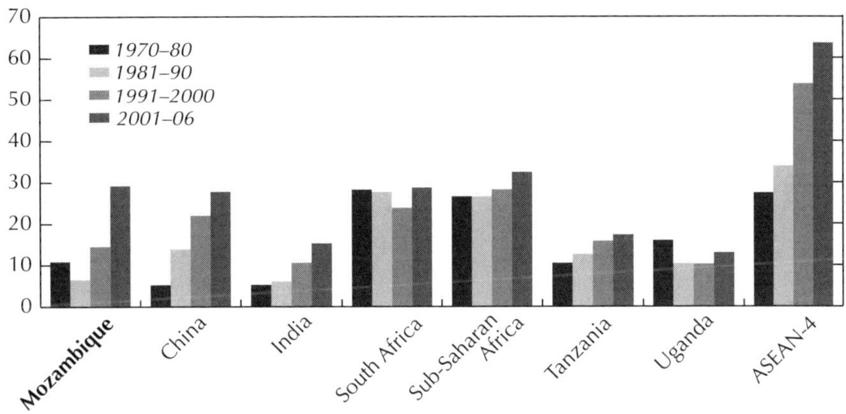

Source: World Bank, World Development Indicators database.
Note: ASEAN-4 = Indonesia, Malaysia, the Philippines, and Thailand.

Although benchmark treasury bill and deposit rates have started to come down as prices and the financial sector have become more stable, the spread between deposit and lending rates has remained stubbornly high (Chapter 4). The reasons for these large spreads, such as high credit risks and overhead costs and weak competition, also explain the low access to finance. The agriculture/rural sector's lack of access to credit is of particular concern, as indicated by this sector's shrinking share of total credit and inadequate microfinance outreach in rural areas. These problems call for a forward-looking financial sector reform strategy focused on consolidating financial stability, deepening financial markets, and improving access, particularly by addressing the institutional lending environment by such means as reducing costs of contract enforcement, enhancing credit registry coverage, and facilitating collateralized lending using property and movable assets (Chapters 4 and 9).

In the manufacturing sector, the low supply of skilled workers and labor market rigidities explain both the relatively high labor costs and low productivity (Chapter 9). In addition, high indirect costs and loss of output because of inadequate infrastructure and burdensome regulations

overdraft facilities (the percentage is even higher for small and medium-size enterprises), according to the 2003 Investment Climate Assessment (World Bank, 2003) and 2006 survey carried out by Mozambique's Ministry of Planning and Development and the Confederation of Mozambican Business Associations (CTA).

Table 1.5. Mozambique and Comparators: Distance to Top Rank in Business Environment

	Governance	Doing business
Comparators in sub-Saharan Africa		
South Africa	0.59	0.16
Mauritius	0.22	0.18
Namibia	0.37	0.23
Botswana	0.19	0.27
Zambia	0.55	0.58
Malawi	0.50	0.62
Lesotho	0.43	0.65
Mozambique	**0.53**	**0.79**
Tanzania	0.67	0.81
Madagascar	0.48	0.85
Zimbabwe	0.93	0.87
Angola	0.77	0.89
Comparators in Asia		
Thailand	0.63	0.10
Malaysia	0.34	0.14
Indonesia	0.20	0.77
Average, sub-Saharan African countries for this sample	0.45	0.48
Average, Asian countries for this sample	0.39	0.33

Sources: Kaufmann, Kraay, and Mastruzzi (2007); and World Bank (2007).

hamper the growth of manufacturers and small and medium-size enterprises, including those engaged in agribusiness/aquaculture and tourism. The focus should be on the timely implementation of the government's action plan to systematically improve on the World Bank's doing business rankings by accelerating business registration, reducing employment costs, simplifying trade regulations, and reducing the time it takes to register property (see Chapter 9). Recent progress in authorizing firms to publish their bylaws electronically and approval of a new labor law that significantly decreases the costs of hiring and firing workers are noteworthy in this regard. Infrastructure services, which are partly in the hands of state-owned or public-participating institutions, are inadequate, however.[33] This calls for clearly identifying infrastructure providers and drawing up a coherent multisector strategy to address infrastructure gaps, through such means as transparent sales of remaining public-participating enterprises and public-private partnerships (PPPs).[34]

[33]Public-participating institutions are enterprises with some private equity participation, and the remaining shares held by the state.

[34]PPPs should be carefully managed to minimize fiscal risks by transparently reporting contingent liabilities or quasi-fiscal operations in budget documents.

Figure 1.15. Financial Sector Challenges

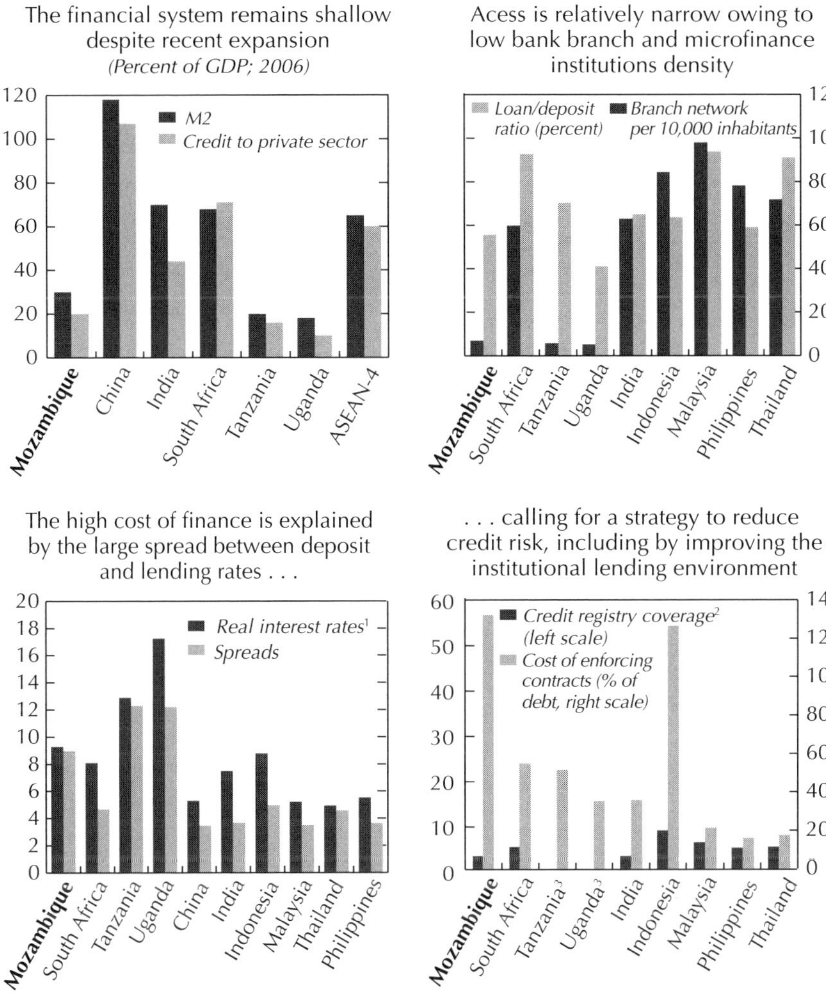

Sources: Beck, Demirguc-Kunt, and Peria (2006); IMF, International Financial Statistics; and Mozambican authorities.

Note: Average, 2000–04.

[1]Real lending rate; percent per year.

[2]Index of measures affecting scope, access, and quality of credit information.

[3]Index was zero.

The efficient and transparent management of natural resources is vital to ensure a virtuous cycle of resource use.[35] Mozambique has proven resources of coal, diamonds, gold, titanium, and petroleum and the potential to produce hydropower, but countries rich in natural resources have seldom attained sustained growth.[36] To avoid the resource curse that has plagued much of sub-Saharan Africa, Mozambique needs (1) efficient tax and regulatory regimes to attract investment while maximizing benefits to the economy,[37] and (2) more transparent management of resource revenue.[38]

Now that investors have more confidence in Mozambique (see Figure 1.16), the government recognizes that generous tax exemptions, which in the past have limited the contribution of new projects (see Appendix and Chapter 8), are not needed to attract quality investment. The Council of Ministers therefore approved both a new mining fiscal law and a new petroleum fiscal law that were in line with best international practices; both were approved by the Assembly in June 2007.[39] The government also adopted new model contracts for mining concessions, and exploration and production concession contracts (EPCCs) in the petroleum sector to complement the new laws. Since then, the government has ensured that any sizable new mineral resource projects or EPCCs in the petroleum sector adhere to the new fiscal regime. This augurs well for future revenues from the mining and petroleum sectors. The introduction of model agreements and a standardized fiscal regime is a good start, but further work remains to be done. A macroeconomic fiscal model for the extractive sector could be developed as a tool to help authorities formulate policies. A variety of taxes and fees are currently levied on the industry, and it is not always clear how they relate to each other, both in amounts and over time. The ability to forecast revenues and to understand how the ongoing reforms will affect them can aid policymakers. It is important to forecast realistic

---

[35]See Chapter 8 for a literature survey of the resource curse and strategies to address it.

[36]See Sachs and Warner (1995) and Stijns (2005). It should also be noted that the fast-growing Asian economies do not have particularly abundant natural resources.

[37]See Nellor and Sunley (1994) and IMF (2007b).

[38]In this regard, Botswana and Chile's experiences are more encouraging, although their initial economic institutions were probably stronger than Mozambique's. See Chapter 8 for an overview.

[39]The IMF and the World Bank have collaborated closely to assist the authorities in strengthening the mining and petroleum fiscal regime.

Figure 1.16. Megaprojects Have Put Mozambique on the Global FDI Map
(In percent of GDP)

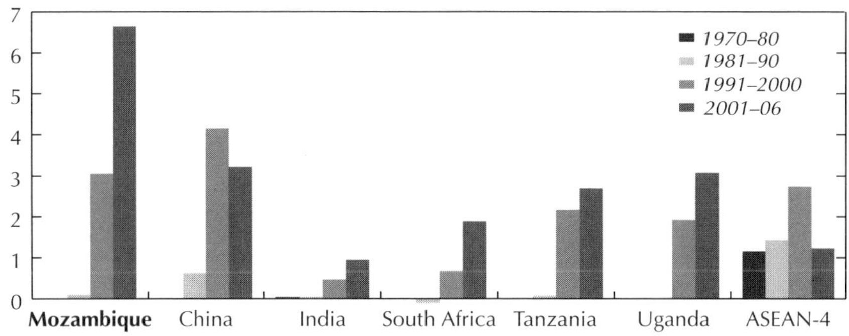

Source: World Bank, World Development Indicators database.
Note: ASEAN-4 = Indonesia, Malaysia, the Philippines, and Thailand.

fiscal revenues to ensure good budgeting practices, given the volatility of revenue flows from the sector.[40]

It is well established that revenue and expenditure transparency can play an important role in avoiding the resource curse. The Extractive Industries Transparency Initiative (EITI) is aimed directly at defeating the resource curse by improving transparency and accountability in resource-rich countries through the full publication and verification of company payments and government revenues from the oil, gas, and mining sectors. Implementing the EITI as part of a program of improved governance can help ensure that revenues from extractive industries contribute to sustainable development and poverty reduction by holding decision makers accountable for the use of those revenues. The EITI principles guarantee transparency of revenue flows to the government and can contribute to improved governance in PFM systems by using principles of revenue transparency. The Mozambican government declared in March 2008 that it will follow the EITI principles to improve transparency, revenue management, and governance in the mining and petroleum sectors, as well as to govern expansion of related megaprojects. The early adoption of the EITI principles would be a good first step in improving the transparency

[40]The Ministry of Finance currently undertakes tax projection work but does not do this yet for mineral resource projects. Because the sector is expected to grow rapidly, with several new megaprojects beginning production, there is a need to create a unit that will closely monitor these projects.

of resource revenues. The IMF (2007b) recently published its *Guide on Resource Revenue Transparency*, and government implementation of these guidelines could complement the EITI initiative. Looking forward, once revenues from natural resource use start flowing in significant amounts (for example, beyond 2010—see Appendix), the government may wish to consider the merits of a stabilization fund similar to those in Chile and Norway, for example (see Davis, Ossowski, and Fedelino, 2003), as a means to ensure fiscal stability and intergenerational equity. Finally, transparency and fiscal stability are likely to be easier to pursue in a generally applicable fiscal regime than in case-by-case negotiation, as was done in the past.

The realization of Mozambique's hydropower potential can be a future engine of growth. The transfer of ownership of the Cahora Bassa dam from Portugal to Mozambique is a historic event that, if carefully managed, can open up tremendous opportunities for exports and future infrastructure projects, including by providing access to international capital markets. An agreement to transfer majority ownership of the 2,075 megawatt (MW) Cahora Bassa hydropower plant from Portugal to a Mozambican parastatal, Hidroeléctrica de Cahora Bassa (HCB), was signed on October 31, 2006. This opens up the possibility of further hydropower development on the Zambezi, in particular the proposed Mphanda Nkuwa project (1,300 MW in the first stage, with potential for 2,275 MW), 60 kilometers downstream from Cahora Bassa, and the development of a second, 600 MW powerhouse on the north bank of Cahora Bassa itself, providing tremendous potential for export of power, energy-intensive industries, and benefits to agriculture and aquaculture from better water control. As part of the restructuring agreement signed, the government of Mozambique acquired 85 percent ownership of HCB, with the remaining 15 percent retained by the government of Portugal. In return, Portugal received payments of US$950 million, of which US$250 million was paid from retained earnings in an offshore account of HCB. The government of Mozambique decided to undertake a competitive bidding process for the selection of the lead arranger and underwriter for the financing of the remaining US$700 million and an additional US$100 million for transaction costs, relying on the A– rating of the South African power utility, Eskom (which receives most of Cahora Bassa's power output). An international banking consortium formed by Calyon and Banco BPI was selected, and commercial borrowing through a syndication of financial institutions, including hedging of exchange rate risks faced by HCB, has been secured. Importantly, the proposed project finance structure avoids any financial government guarantees through the principle of nonrecourse financing using special purpose vehicles (SPVs). Moreover, indications are that the pricing (spreads) of the borrowing is closer to emerging market levels for a tenure between 10 and 15 years. The successful conclusion of the transaction securing nonrecourse financing for the purchase of majority ownership of HCB so as not to increase the government's liabilities to commercial creditors is a historic event for Mozambique and holds promise as a means to finance future infrastructure projects while minimizing risks to debt sustainability. It would also be important to

- ensure that both the process and the final financing package are transparent, and that HCB is managed in a commercially efficient manner, is audited by external auditors, and is subject to the regular concession and tax regimes; and
- identify and incorporate into the fiscal accounts and budget documents fiscal risks and quasi-fiscal transactions, if any.[41]

Role of the IMF in Mozambique

Mozambique satisfactorily completed four IMF-supported programs during 1987–2003. These programs were instrumental in helping the country move from a centrally planned to a market-based economy, achieve macroeconomic stability, and substantially reduce its debt burden. Over this period, real GDP growth averaged close to 7 percent a year; the international reserves position was strengthened; the net present value of the public external debt was reduced from more than 500 percent of exports at the end of 1998 to less than 100 percent; and significant progress was made in implementing first-generation reforms. In addition, the share of the population living in absolute poverty declined from an estimated 80 percent during 1989–94 to 69 percent in 1997, and during 2000–03 progress was made toward achieving the objectives specified in PARPA I (2000–05). Political stability and the authorities' strong commitment to structural reform were essential to the process.

Mozambique's 2004–07 IMF-supported program under the Poverty Reduction and Growth Facility (PRGF) helped the country maintain macroeconomic stability in the face of exogenous shocks and address struc-

---

[41]Public-private partnerships, such as the one devised to carry out the proposed Cahora Bassa dam transaction, are not a panacea, however. Recognizing that such transactions carry fiscal risks because of their complex nature, the authorities see the merits of encouraging greater private participation, where possible, as the preferred mode of financing infrastructure projects to realize Mozambique's growth potential.

tural weaknesses identified in an ex post assessment (EPA).[42] The request for the program targeted fiscal consolidation in the face of an expected decline in aid inflows after the aid surge and high inflation (2000–03) that followed the floods of 2000. Fiscal consolidation limited recourse to monetary financing and helped reduce inflation to single-digit levels, relieving pressure on domestic interest rates. Mozambique's improved performance with respect to its structural program since March 2005 has also helped the authorities complete outstanding first-generation reforms identified in the EPA—in particular, strengthening revenue mobilization by creating a central revenue authority (the ATM), improving expenditure efficiency through the rollout of a government financial management information system (e-SISTAFE), and addressing vulnerabilities in the financial system.

While reiterating a commitment to improving the quality of and access to public services, the government's PARPA II (2006–09) recognizes that to sustain growth more emphasis must be placed on productivity growth and the role of the private sector. The strategy aims to achieve this by

- consolidating macroeconomic stability and maintaining competitiveness through prudent monetary and fiscal policies in the context of a flexible exchange rate regime;
- improving the investment climate and promoting employment generation by reducing the cost of doing business; and
- enhancing governance and the management of natural resources.

These near- and medium-term challenges are addressed in a three-year IMF Policy Support Instrument (PSI) designed to consolidate macroeconomic stability and sustain rapid economic growth. Given its economic stability, comfortable level of international reserves, policy performance, and lack of need for balance of payments support, Mozambique graduated to a PSI when its PRGF arrangement expired in July 2007. The government favored such an arrangement to monitor its ambitious reform program and send a signal of its commitment to donors. This approach was closely coordinated with the World Bank's new Country Partnership Strategy (2007–11) and the joint Performance Assessment Framework (PAF) of the government and donor community.

Refinements to the design of the PRGF program during its later stages allowed for a smooth transition to a PSI. The streamlining of quantitative performance criteria and adjusters at the completion of the fourth review under the PRGF program helped focus the quantitative program,

---

[42] IMF (2004).

particularly in accommodating both the spending and the absorption of foreign aid as needed.[43] The replacement of the domestic primary deficit by an asymmetric ceiling on net credit to the government with regard to external financing and the removal of the indicative target on the wage bill were particularly useful in reinforcing the management of foreign aid once it became clear that the decline in aid in 2004–05 would be reversed. Further streamlining of structural conditionality and strengthening of the interministerial committee monitoring the program helped build ownership and allowed reform priorities to be updated regularly. Given the likelihood of a further scaling up of foreign aid and Mozambique's strong performance under the PRGF program, it was decided that reform would continue under the PSI.

Close collaboration between the partners and targeted capacity building will need to continue to facilitate the realization of the reform agenda (Chapter 7). The IMF and the World Bank have worked together closely on, among other projects, the Poverty Reduction Support Credit and PRGF program content, the Cahora Bassa hydropower project, and reform of the fiscal code governing mineral resources. The practice of holding joint IMF-Bank missions has had synergistic benefits and reduced the government's burden in preparing for multiple missions. The authorities have welcomed the close coordination between the Bank, the IMF, and the donor community in Maputo. Continuous IMF technical assistance, provided in close coordination with donors (for example, in tax reform), has helped build Mozambique's administrative capacity as it takes the reform process forward. More recently, PFM reforms, on which performance lagged in the past, are progressing well. These reforms were initiated with substantial technical assistance from the IMF; the IMF has since shifted to an advisory role, and the medium-term PFM reform plan is being financed by a multidonor common fund. Mozambique's experience highlights that, by catalyzing progress early on, intensive and well-coordinated technical assistance can help build ownership and sustain the reform momentum.

Conclusions and Lessons for Sub-Saharan Africa

Mozambique's growth takeoff since the end of the civil war has been similar to that of several fast-growing Asian economies, particularly the

[43]Aid absorption is defined as the extent to which a country's non-aid current account deficit (in foreign currency terms) widens in response to an increase in aid inflows.

ASEAN-4 countries and China, India, and Vietnam. Its commitment to the stabilization effort, success in implementing first-generation structural reforms, and substantial donor assistance helped make this growth possible. The support of the international community, including the IMF, also helped Mozambique sustain its reform momentum and expand such basic services as primary education and health care. Political stability and the consolidation of democracy in three general and presidential elections, which yielded a fairly unified government with a firm commitment to stability and growth, have helped underpin growth.

Now that the post-stabilization rebound has largely run its course and first-generation reforms have been completed, however, more must be done to sustain Mozambique's growth takeoff and further ease poverty. Mozambique has relatively sound political institutions, a favorable geography, and low income inequality—conditions common to many countries that have sustained growth. What, then, may be the major constraints to sustaining Mozambique's takeoff in the years to come?

According to our benchmarking exercise, at the institutional level the country must make more progress in enhancing voice and participation at all levels, given the relatively high degree of societal fractionalization and regional disparities, so that more areas and groups benefit from growth.[44] Mozambique's economic institutions—particularly in terms of regulatory quality and the rule of law—though improving, are also relatively weak. For the latter, as our benchmarking exercise shows, it is possible to sustain growth while building institutions over the longer term, especially if efforts are made to invest in human capital and further integrate Mozambique into the global economy (Acemoglu, Johnson, and Robinson 2005a; IMF, 2005).

At the macroeconomic level, the consolidation of overall stability and a second wave of reforms would likely help Mozambique accumulate more capital and enhance its productivity growth. Inflation should be firmly anchored to single-digit levels, and real exchange rate overvaluations should be avoided. In this regard, it will be important for Mozambique to pursue a prudent macroeconomic policy mix and fine-tune its monetary policy framework.

In terms of reducing poverty, including achieving the non-income-related MDGs covering primary school completion, gender equality, and HIV/AIDS, Mozambique would need to efficiently absorb and spend addi-

---

[44]Measures of societal fractionalization are an indicator of the potential for conflict; thus, the potential for intense and disruptive conflict should not be discounted, particularly from a regional perspective (see Alesina and others, 2003; Easterly and Levine, 1997).

tional foreign aid to expand basic services.[45] This challenge would need to be carefully managed to ensure long-term fiscal sustainability, avoid a loss of competitiveness, and ease microeconomic absorptive-capacity constraints.

To promote export diversification and generate employment, Mozambique must address its relatively high costs of doing business. In particular, manufacturing exports, an engine of growth, should be promoted by deepening the financial system, further liberalizing trade and removing regulatory obstacles, and addressing human capital and infrastructure gaps.

Finally, the efficient and transparent management of natural resources is vital to ensure a virtuous cycle of natural resource use and avoid the resource curse that has plagued much of sub-Saharan Africa.

In addition to identifying the challenges ahead to sustaining Mozambique's growth takeoff, which is likely to be relevant to many sub-Saharan African countries that are in the midst of a growth acceleration,[46] we draw lessons from the experience of Mozambique for the rest of sub-Saharan Africa and the international community, including the IMF.

- Macroeconomic stability is an important prerequisite for a growth takeoff. Implementing a money-based stabilization program supported by prudent fiscal policies and first-generation structural reforms in the context of a flexible exchange rate regime can help countries sustain a broad-based growth takeoff. Reform sequencing should, in particular, pay attention to revenue-mobilization efforts and exchange system reforms, and address vulnerabilities in the financial system early on. The steadfast implementation of reform priorities tailored to particular country circumstances can be facilitated by political stability and a government commitment to focus on improving the lives of its citizens.
- A prudent external borrowing strategy combined with productive, well-governed megaproject investments can help countries consolidate long-term fiscal sustainability and gradually reduce dependence on donors. Trade and gradual capital account liberalization to attract large-scale FDI can contribute greatly to growth and spur further private investment. Consideration must be given, however, to maximizing fiscal returns and economic linkages, particularly if the

[45]Achieving the MDGs by improving education, health, and well-being will also help sustain the growth takeoff (Acemoglu and Johnson, 2006; Johnson, Ostry, and Subramanian, 2007).

[46]See Bio-Tchané and Christensen (2006) for background on sub-Saharan African countries that have experienced recent growth acceleration.

megaprojects are concentrated in natural resources or other capital-intensive sectors, which tend to have limited spillovers to the rest of the economy. The fiscal regime for mining and petroleum resources, if it is to be comprehensive, must be embodied in a country's general tax laws and supplemented by model contracts to avoid fiscal terms being negotiated on a case-by-case basis. For a country to realize its growth potential while minimizing risk, the transparency regime governing resource use and megaprojects, including public-private partnerships on infrastructure projects, should follow international best practices. Adherence to EITI principles could help ensure a virtuous cycle of natural resource exploitation.

- If scaled-up foreign aid is absorbed efficiently and deployed in productive ways, great strides in human development and poverty reduction can be made in a short time. Such quick gains create an environment conducive to sustaining growth and reform momentum. To ensure that foreign aid supports development, it seems especially important to focus on coordinating monetary policy operations with fiscal policy and to improve the efficiency and equity of spending.
- The IMF can be particularly instrumental in helping a country consolidate macroeconomic stability and complete far-reaching structural reforms that are critical to sustaining rapid, broad-based growth and poverty reduction. This requires responding rapidly to take advantage of windows of opportunity by providing balance of payments financing, technical assistance, and policy advice based on sound analysis and the lessons learned from success stories in other countries facing similar circumstances and challenges. Programs should also be designed to be flexible and responsive to the situation in each country, in particular to ensure that foreign aid is absorbed and deployed in ways that do not undermine macroeconomic stability.
- Close collaboration among development partners and the authorities, and targeted capacity building can foster authorities' sense of ownership and advance the reform agenda. Cross-fertilization of ideas, timely exchange of information, sequencing of missions, complementary technical assistance, and close coordination between bilateral and multilateral agencies are key to providing a common view to the authorities on the lessons for, and challenges facing, their country. Close coordination between the IMF and the World Bank, and with the donor community and the authorities (for example, through joint reviews and technical assistance, a common policy assessment framework matrix among donors, and alignment of missions to the country budget cycle) can build efficiency and foster country ownership.

Appendix. Megaprojects in Mozambique[47]

Oil and Gas Sector

Pande-Temane

The first contract for the exploitation of gas in Mozambique (Pande-Temane) was signed in October 2000 to develop rich gas fields near Vilanulos in Inhambane Province and to export gas to South Africa via a 900-kilometer pipeline and a central processing facility (CPF) in Temane. The gas exploration contract was granted to a joint venture between South Africa's gas giant, Sasol (70 percent); a Mozambican state-owned enterprise, CMH (Mozambican Hydrocarbons Company) (25 percent); and the International Finance Corporation (5 percent).[48] The pipeline agreement is a joint venture between Sasol (50 percent), CMH (25 percent), and IGAZ, a South African company (25 percent).

Production in 2006 amounted to 102 million gigajoules (gJs), or approximately 85 percent of total capacity. It comprised 2.4 billion cubic meters of gas (15 percent more than in 2005) and 696,000 barrels of condensed gas (31 percent more than in 2005). In value terms, US$65.6 million worth of gas and US$26.2 million worth of condensed gas were sold in 2006, implying a 25 percent rise in turnover since 2005. Although all the condensed gas is exported, approximately 4 percent of the gas produced stayed in Mozambique. (See Table A1.1.)

Pande-Temane was signed as a petroleum production agreement (PPA) under the old fiscal code, which stipulates 5 percent royalty payments on production and a tax of 17.5 percent (rising to 35 percent six years after commercial production commences) on total revenues.[49] Part of this royalty is, however, paid in kind. Total royalties paid to the authorities in 2006 comprised 1.3 million gJs of gas paid in kind, and another US$2.4 million paid in cash. The contractor is exempt from paying any withholding tax on dividends or interest payments under the PPA. Simulations done by Daniel and others (2007) suggest that the end of the cost-recovery phase and a ramping up of production from existing fields will dramatically

---

[47]Information in this section is based on discussions with the authorities and background work undertaken by Julien Hartley and Magnus Saxegaard.

[48]The International Finance Corporation, the private sector arm of the World Bank Group, may decide to sell its stake in the joint venture company to CMH (80 percent) and a private Mozambican company (20 percent).

[49]As with current petroleum contracts, tax concessions are made on expenditures relating to exploration, operating expenditures, and capital expenditures.

Table A1.1. Pande-Tehmane and Sasol Projects, 2004–06

	2004	2005	2006
Gas			
Production *(million gJs)*	52.6	88.9	102.1
Exports *(million gJs)*	49.6	86.0	98.0
Royalties in kind *(million gJs)*	0.09	0.14	0.14
Royalties paid *(million US$)*	1.5	2.3	2.4
Sales *(million US$)*	30.4	57.2	65.6
Condensate			
Production *(thousand barrels)*	294.5	531.1	696.0
Sales *(thousand barrels)*	211.5	532.8	539.5
Exports *(million US$)*	5.7	16.3	26.2
Royalties *(million US$)*	0.3	0.8	1.3

Source: National Petroleum Institute of Mozambique.

raise the contribution of Pande-Temane to the budget, to approximately US$130 million (including taxes and dividends) by 2027, the most conservative estimated date for resource exhaustion, and excluding expansion and finds from prospective fields (see Figure A1.1).

In 2005, Sasol and ENH (National Hydrocarbons Company of Mozambique) signed a production-sharing agreement (PSA) to develop two new fields in the Temane area (Inhassorio and G East).[50] The project, which is expected to expand capacity from 120 million gJs to 183 million gJs, also includes the expansion of the existing pipeline to South Africa and the CPF. The fiscal terms of the Pande-Temane PSA differ somewhat from those of the PPA. In particular, the contractor is subject to withholding tax on interest payments to nonresidents (20 percent), while the rate of corporate income tax is fixed at 35 percent throughout. The two new gas fields are currently in the development stage, whereas INP (National Petroleum Institute of Mozambique) is awaiting the development plan for the pipeline.[51]

[50]PPAs are signed if there are proven gas resources, as was the case initially in Pande-Temane, whereas PSAs are signed if exploration is necessary. In both cases, Sasol produces on behalf of CMH, which owns the concession by virtue of its being a public company. (CMH is a subsidiary of ENH.) Since 2001, the trend has been toward signing exploration and production concession contracts whereby the producer is granted a concession and pays royalties to the government.

[51]The development stage comes after the exploration stage, in which drilling and seismic surveys are conducted to find gas reservoirs and determine their commercial viability. After the development stage, a field enters the production stage. Given that there is no concession fee, Mozambique's government receives no revenue until the production stage.

Figure A1.1. Projected Government Revenue from Pande-Temane Project
(In millions of U.S. dollars)

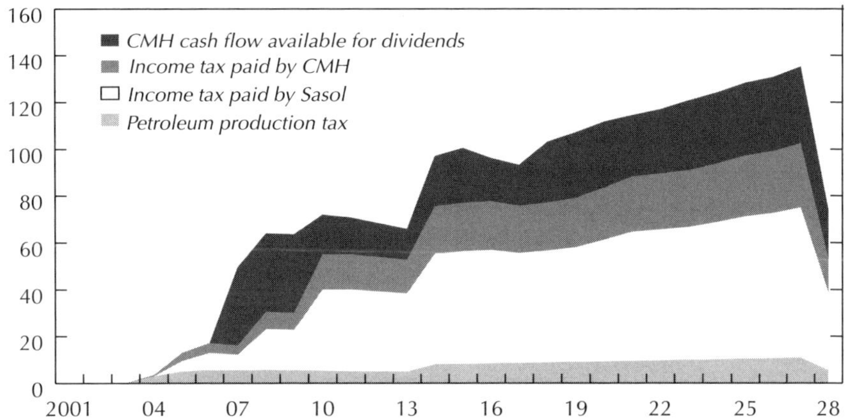

Source: IMF staff estimates based on World Economic Outlook database oil prices until 2012 and constant real terms thereafter.

Note: CMH denotes the Mozambican Hydrocarbons Company, a state-owned enterprise and a subsidiary of ENH (National Hydrocarbons Company of Mozambique).

Zambezi offshore

An EPCC was signed in June 2002 with Petronas (Malaysia) to explore for oil in the Zambezi basin. The project is currently in the exploration phase; three possible sites are being explored. Drilling started in June 2007 at one of the sites (at a cost of US$47 million), while seismic surveys are being conducted at the other two sites before a decision is made as to whether to start drilling there as well. Note that current legislation allows companies eight years to explore a site before deciding whether or not to develop it.

Inhaminga onshore

An EPCC was signed in June 2003 with DNO (Norway). Thus far, two dry wells have been drilled. A third well is scheduled to be drilled this year.

Zambezi onshore

An EPCC was signed with Zambezi Onshore (a subsidiary of BANG) in November 2006 to explore for oil. The company, which is confident that the area possesses oil reserves, has committed to drill one well in 2007.

Rovuma basin

A total of six EPCCs have been negotiated for the exploration of offshore and onshore oil in the Rovuma basin, in northern Mozambique (see Figure A1.2), by the following companies:

- Norsk Hydro (Norway) and ENH—January 2006;
- Anadarko (United States)—December 2006;
- Ente Nazionale Idrocarburi (ENI) (Italy)—December 2006;
- Artumas (Canada)—contract has been signed; and
- Petronas (Malaysia)—under negotiation.

Except for the concession awarded to Norsk Hydro, which was negotiated directly, all other concessions were awarded after a competitive bidding round. All these concessions are covered by the old fiscal code. The government has committed not to sign any new agreements before the new fiscal regime is in place. It is expected that bidding will start on a new set of concessions in 2008.

Petroline

Petroline is a joint venture between Petromac (a state-owned petroleum distributor in Mozambique) and Gigajoule International (South Africa) that was established to set up a pipeline for the reexportation of petroleum products from Maputo to Nelspruit in South Africa. The petroleum will be delivered to Matola harbor by oil tankers; it will then be pumped into the proposed pipeline and on to South Africa.

Based on the development plan submitted by Petroline at the end of 2006, demand for the pipeline will be between 700 million and 1.4 billion liters of petroleum product over the next eight years. Demand is then expected to rise by 3.5–4 percent a year. The direct capital investment required for the project is estimated at US$180 million.

The company has been granted a license to operate in Mozambique and is currently awaiting a license to sell fuel in South Africa.

Hydropower

Hidroeléctrica de Cahora Bassa (HCB) is the concession company for the Cahora Bassa dam and the 2,075 MW hydroelectric power plant in Tete Province of Mozambique and the electric current transmission line from Cahora Bassa to the border with South Africa and certain other lines in Mozambique. Construction of the dam started in 1969; its commercial operation started in 1977. The company was established in 1975 as a joint

Figure A1.2. Oil and Gas Exploration in the Rovuma Basin

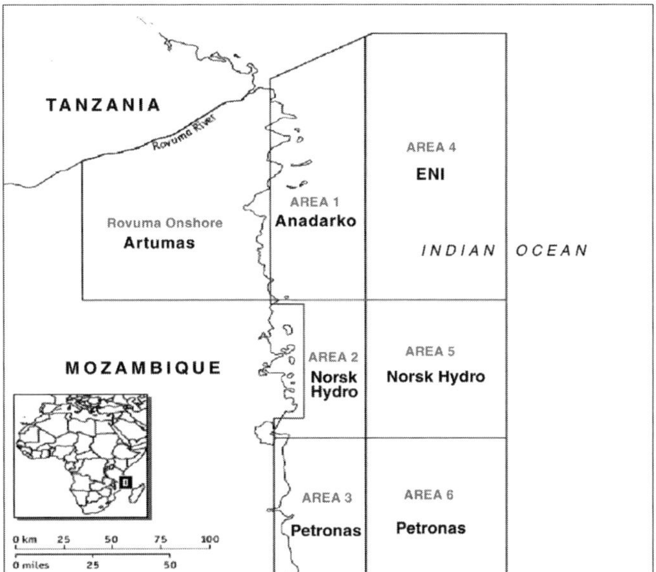

Source: Empresa Nacional de Hidrocarbonetos.

venture between the government of Mozambique, with a share of 18 percent, and the government of Portugal, with a share of 82 percent.

As part of the restructuring agreement signed in October 2006, the ownership of HCB changed, with Mozambique holding 85 percent and Portugal holding 15 percent. In return, the government of Portugal received payments, with all figures in U.S. dollars, of $950 million, $250 million of which was paid in November 2006 by HCB, as repayment of debt.[52] The balance of $700 million was paid in 2007.

As part of the restructuring agreement, HCB has been awarded a new 25-year concession to operate the existing facilities. The agreement entitles the company to the revenues generated. In return, Mozambique will receive 10 percent of HCB's gross revenues and will impose normal company taxes. This contrasts with the 1975 concession agreement under which the government of Mozambique made the dam and the power station available to HCB free of charge and levied no taxes in an attempt to expedite amortization of

[52]HCB's initial debt to the government of Portugal was US$500 million. Under the 1975 concession, all free cash flow was used to repay this debt. Under the new restructuring plan, the remaining debt will be converted to equity.

the debt to the government of Portugal.[53] The new concession also includes the right to develop the north bank of the Lake Cahora Bassa, where plans are under way to develop a second power station with a capacity of 850 MW. Plans are also under way to construct a second dam at Mphanda Nkuwa, 70 kilometers downstream from Cahora Bassa, with a capacity of 1,300 MW. Increased capacity to generate electricity is a requirement for several other industrial projects being considered in Mozambique, such as the phase 3 expansion of Mozal, an aluminum smelter (see below), and the proposed titanium and zirconium mine at Chibuto.

HCB sells its electricity under two long-term PSAs and one-short term PPA. The PSA with Eskom (the national electricity utility of South Africa) provides for the supply of up to 1,450 MW under a tariff formula that was renegotiated in 2004 and is designed to reflect a gradually increasing percentage (reaching 100 percent in 2007 from 50 percent in 2003) of Eskom's full avoided cost for the generation and transmission of the electricity. Increasing demand for power in South Africa and the region is expected to raise tariffs (and thus Eskom's avoided cost) at a rate greater than inflation over the next 10–15 years.[54]

The electricity sold to Eskom includes 300 MW allocated to EDM (Electricidade de Moçambique) under the second PSA. The EDM tariff was set at 55 percent of the Eskom tariff in 2005 and 2006 and will rise to 70 percent in 2007. In addition, HCB provides 150 MW of electricity to ZESA (the national electricity utility of Zimbabwe) under a contract underwritten by Eskom. The terms of this contract are confidential. In the event of excess capacity, HCB has the opportunity to sell its excess power to the Southern Africa Power Pool. Newspaper reports also suggest that negotiations may be under way to sell electricity to Malawi.

Over the past five years, HCB's revenues have more than doubled, while earnings before interest and taxes (EBIT) have increased threefold. Owing to high interest payments and the effect of exchange rate fluctuations on the company's foreign currency debt to the government of Portugal, the company's after-tax profits have been negative every fiscal year since 2001, except for fiscal year 2004 (when exchange rate appreciation contributed to an increase in profits).[55] After the rescheduling, total sales are projected

[53]In fact, the debt was not serviced, owing in part to civil disturbances in Mozambique, and it has now grown beyond the cash-flow capabilities of HCB. This provides part of the rationale for the decision to restructure HCB.

[54]Eskom's avoided cost estimates are not very transparent, however, giving it an advantage in overall negotiations.

[55]Mozambique's fiscal year runs from January 1 to December 31.

Table A1.2. HCB Projections
(In millions of U.S. dollars)

	2006	2007	2008	2009	2010
Total sales	202.6	247.0	254.0	268.7	282.7
Operating costs	79.0	92.5	95.6	99.7	103.9
Of which, salaries	28.3	30.0	31.8	33.7	35.7
Of which, amortization	29.1	27.9	27.9	27.9	27.9
Operating result	123.6	154.5	158.3	169.0	178.8

Source: HCB.

to average US$251 million annually for 2006–10 while operating results (after tax) are projected to average US$156 million annually over the same period. (See Table A1.2.) Concession fees and taxes are expected to rise to nearly US$12 million by 2010.

Minerals and Mining

Mozal[56]

Mozal's production of aluminum has grown steadily over the past three years, from 532 thousand tons in 2004 to 557 thousand tons in 2006. This is close to the current capacity of the Mozal smelter, whose capacity doubled in 2003 as part of the Mozal II expansion. Reports from various sources suggest that BHP Billiton is considering expanding the capacity of the Mozal smelter by another 250 thousand tons (Mozal III expansion). This expansion, which, it has been speculated, may come online in 2009, will make the Mozal smelter one of the biggest in the world. A feasibility study for the expansion has already been completed, according to BHP Billiton, and the key aspect of the project agreement is the agreement of a power contract.

Although production has remained relatively steady, profits have increased dramatically in line with the rise in world aluminum prices. BHP Billiton's profits derived from Mozal increased by 42 percent (from US$130 million to US$185 million) between Mozambique's fiscal years 2005 and 2006. Indications from the first half of fiscal year 2007 (up 105 percent relative to the first half of fiscal year 2006) suggest that profits will be substantially higher next year.

[56]The information in this section is based mainly on reports from the BHP Billiton Group, which has a 47 percent stake in Mozal.

Moma

Kenmare Resources announced in April 2007 that mining operations had commenced at the Moma Titanium Minerals Mine, which is estimated to contain one of the largest deposits of titanium-bearing mineral sands in the world (accounting for approximately 8 percent of global titanium feedstock). In addition, recent drilling has increased the mineral resources within the concession by more than 60 percent, which should enable Kenmare to significantly increase production while maintaining a long-life mine. (Financing for this project is based on a 20-year life for the mine.)

Production is estimated to reach 389 thousand tons in 2007, although Kenmare expects to reach 800 thousand tons per year once it starts operating at full capacity. Expansions are already being planned that would raise annual production to 1.2 million tons per year by the end of 2009. Market agreements covering more than 60 percent of the first five years of revenue have been concluded. Kenmare expects that the world market for titanium, driven by strong demand and tight supply, will continue to perform well.

Kenmare also has an active uranium exploration program in northern Mozambique in Tete and Niassa Provinces. Initial results have been promising, with some deposits of uranium identified. Further exploration work is under way.

Moma benefits from substantial fiscal benefits by virtue of its status as an industrial free zone (IFZ). Projects with IFZ status can be exempted from VAT, excise duties, customs duties on capital goods, and real property transfer tax, and can benefit from a reduced corporate income tax rate (12.8 percent).

Moatize coal mine[57]

The Moatize coal mine project is located in western Tete Province and is being developed by the Brazilian mining firm Companhia do Vale do Rio Doce (CVRD), the world's largest iron ore miner. In November 2004, CVRD won the bid, for US$123 million, for the rights to explore and develop the deposit; to undertake feasibility studies to develop a 1,500 MW coal-fired power plant, port facilities, and a rail link to the port; and to assess other domestic industrial projects linked to the mine. The feasibility study, which was submitted to the government in November 2006, indicates that by 2010 the project will mine about 26 million tons of coal a year, of which about 11 million tons will be marketed for export and 4 million tons will be made available to the planned domestic power

[57]See Chapter 8.

plant. The area around Moatize is considered by some to be the largest unexplored coal province in the world, with reserves estimated at 2.4 billion tons, allowing the extraction of metallurgical and thermal coals. Total investment is estimated at US$2 billion.

Bibliography

Acemoglu, Daron, and Simon Johnson, 2006, "Disease and Development: The Effect of Life Expectancy on Economic Growth," NBER Working Paper No. 12269 (Cambridge, Massachusetts: National Bureau of Economic Research).

———, and James A. Robinson, 2001, "The Colonial Origins of Comparative Development: An Empirical Investigation," *American Economic Review*, Vol. 91 (December), pp. 1369–401.

———, 2005a, "Institutions as the Fundamental Cause of Long-Run Growth," in *Handbook of Economic Growth*, Volume 1, Part A, ed. by Philippe Aghion and Steven Durlauf, pp. 385–472. Also available as NBER Working Paper No. 10481 (Cambridge, Massachusetts: National Bureau of Economic Research).

———, 2005b, "The Rise of Europe: Atlantic Trade, Institutional Change, and Economic Growth," *American Economic Review*, Vol. 95 (June), pp. 546–79.

Acemoglu, Daron, Simon Johnson, and Yunyong Thaicharoen, 2003, "Institutional Causes, Macroeconomic Symptoms: Volatility, Crises and Growth," *Journal of Monetary Economics*, Vol. 50 (January), pp. 49–123.

Alesina, Alberto, Arnaud Devleeschauwer, William Easterly, Sergio Kurlat, and Romain Wacziarg, 2003, "Fractionalization," *Journal of Economic Growth*, Vol. 8, No. 2, pp. 155–94.

Beck, T., A. Demirguc-Kunt, and M.S.M. Peria (2006), "Banking services for everyone? Barriers to bank access and use around the world," Policy Research Working Paper No. 4079 (Washington: World Bank).

Berg, Andy, Jonathan D. Ostry, and Jeromin Zettelmeyer, 2006, "What Makes Growth Sustained?" (unpublished; Washington: International Monetary Fund).

Bio-Tchané, Abdoulaye, and Benedicte Vibe Christensen, 2006, "Right Time for Africa," *Finance & Development*, Vol. 43 (December), pp. 8–13.

Bosworth, B.P., and S.M. Collins, 2003, "The Empirics of Growth: An Update," Brookings Discussion Paper in International Economics No. 2/2003 (Washington: Brookings Institution).

Bulíř, Aleš, and A. Javier Hamann, 2005, "Volatility of Development Aid: From the Frying Pan into the Fire?" paper presented at IMF Seminar on Foreign Aid and Macroeconomic Management, Maputo, Mozambique, March 14–15.

Clément, Jean A.P., ed., 2004, *Postconflict Economics in Sub-Saharan Africa: Lessons from the Democratic Republic of the Congo* (Washington: International Monetary Fund).

Coelho, I., P. Dos Santos, A. Teixeira, J. Tomás, and R. Varsano, 2001, *Moçambique: Para una reforma do sistema tributário e sua administração* (Washington: International Monetary Fund).

Collier, Paul, and David Dollar, 2002, "Aid Allocation and Poverty Reduction," *European Economic Review*, Vol. 46 (September), pp. 1475–500.

Collier, Paul, and Stephen A. O'Connell, 2008, "Opportunities and Choices," in *The Political Economy of Economic Growth in Africa, 1960–2000*, Volume 1, ed. by B. Ndulu, P. Collier, R. H. Bates, and S. O'Connell (Cambridge: Cambridge University Press).

Daniel, Philip, Ana Paula Dourado, Diego Mesa Puyo, and Alistair Watson, 2007, "The Petroleum Sector: Fiscal and Economic Terms," Aide-Mémoire of the IMF's Fiscal Affairs Department mission (unpublished; Washington: International Monetary Fund).

Davis, Jeffrey M., Rolando Ossowski, and Annalisa Fedelino, 2003, *Fiscal Policy Formulation and Implementation in Oil-Producing Countries* (Washington: International Monetary Fund).

Easterly, William, and Ross Levine, 1997, "Africa's Growth Tragedy: Policies and Ethnic Divisions," *Quarterly Journal of Economics*, Vol. 112 (November), pp. 1203–50.

Eifert, Benn, Alan Gelb, and Vijaya Ramachandran, 2005, "Business Environment and Comparative Advantage in Africa: Evidence from the Investment Climate Data," Working Paper No. 56 (Washington: Center for Global Development).

Fischer, Stanley, 1993, "The Role of Macroeconomic Factors in Growth," *Journal of Monetary Economics*, Vol. 32 (3), pp. 45–66.

Ghosh, A., and Stephen Phillips, 1998, "Warning: Inflation May Be Harmful to Your Growth," *Staff Papers*, International Monetary Fund, Vol. 45, No. 4, pp. 672–710.

Gulde, Anne-Marie, Catherine Pattillo, Jakob Christensen, Kevin Joseph Carey, and Smita Wagh, 2006, *Sub-Saharan Africa: Financial Sector Challenges* (Washington: International Monetary Fund).

Hausmann, Ricardo, Lant Pritchett, and Dani Rodrik, 2004, "Growth Accelerations," NBER Working Paper No. 10566 (Cambridge, Massachusetts: National Bureau of Economic Research).

Hernández-Catá, Ernesto, Stanley Fischer, and Mohsin S. Khan, 1998, "Africa—Is This the Turning Point?" IMF Paper on Policy Analysis and Assessment 98/6 (Washington: International Monetary Fund).

International Monetary Fund (IMF), 2003, *World Economic Outlook, April 2003*, World Economic and Financial Surveys (Washington).

———, 2004, *Republic of Mozambique: Ex Post Assessment of Mozambique's Performance Under Fund-Supported Programs*, IMF Country Report No. 04/53 (Washington).

———, 2005, *World Economic Outlook, September 2005*, World Economic and Financial Surveys (Washington).

———, 2007a, *Republic of Mozambique: Poverty Reduction Strategy Paper*, IMF Country Report No. 07/37 Washington).

———, 2007b, "Guide on Resource Revenue Transparency" (Washington).

Johnson, Simon, Jonathan D. Ostry, and Arvind Subramanian, 2007, "The Prospects for Sustained Growth in Africa: Benchmarking the Constraints," IMF Working Paper 07/52 (Washington: International Monetary Fund).

Kaufmann, Daniel, Aart Kraay, and Massimo Mastruzzi, 2007, "Governance Matters VI: Aggregate and Individual Governance Indicators for 1996–2006," Policy Research Working Paper No. 4280 (Washington: World Bank).

Krugman, Paul, 1987, "The Myth of Asia's Miracle," in *Pop Internationalism* (Cambridge, Massachusetts: MIT Press).

Levine, Ross, 2005, "Finance and Growth: Theory and Evidence," in *Handbook of Economic Growth*, ed. by P. Aghion and S. Durlauf (Amsterdam: Elsevier North-Holland), pp. 865–934.

Mozambique Ministry of Planning and Development (MPD), 2006, "Enterprise Development in Mozambique: Results Based on Manufacturing Surveys Conducted in 2002 and 2006," Discussion Paper No. 33E, (Maputo: National Directorate of Studies and Policy Analysis). Available via the Internet: http://www.mpd.gov.mz/gest/documents/33E_Enterprise_Developing.pdf

Ndulu, B. J., with L. Chakraborti, L. Lijane, V. Ramachandran, and J. Wolgin, 2007, *Challenges of African Growth: Opportunities, Constraints, and Strategic Directions* (Washington: World Bank).

Nellor, David, and Emil Sunley, 1994, "Fiscal Regimes for Natural Resource Producing Developing Countries," IMF Paper on Policy Analysis and Assessment 94/24 (Washington).

Rajan, Raghuram, 2006, "The Persistence of Underdevelopment: Constituencies and Competitive Rent Preservation" (unpublished; Washington: International Monetary Fund).

———, and Arvind Subramanian, 2005, "What Undermines Aid's Impact on Growth?" NBER Working Paper No. 11657 (Cambridge, Massachusetts: National Bureau of Economic Research).

Rodrik, Dani, 1999, "Where Did All the Growth Go? External Shocks, Social Conflict, and Growth Collapses," *Journal of Economic Growth*, Vol. 4 (December), pp. 385–412.

———, and Arvind Subramanian, 2004, "From 'Hindu Growth' to Productivity Surge: The Mystery of the Indian Growth Transition," IMF Working Paper 04/77 (Washington: International Monetary Fund).

Sachs, J., and A. Warner, 1995, "Natural Resource Abundance and Economic Growth," NBER Working Paper No. 5398 (Cambridge, Massachusetts: National Bureau of Economic Research).

Stijns, J.-P. C., 2005, "Natural Resource Abundance and Economic Growth Revisited," *Resources Policy*, Vol. 30 (2), pp. 107–30.

Varsano, R., Odette de Oliveira, R.M. Villela, and Irene Yackovlev, 2007, "Mozambique: Evaluation of the Post-Reforms Tax System," IMF Technical Assistance Report,

Fiscal Affairs Department (unpublished; Washington: International Monetary Fund).

World Bank, 2003, *Mozambique Industrial Performance and Investment Climate 2003* (Washington: World Bank).

———, 2004, *Removing Obstacles to Economic Growth in Mozambique: A Diagnostic Trade Integration Study* (Washington: World Bank).

———, 2005, "Mozambique: Country Economic Memorandum" (unpublished; Washington: World Bank).

———, 2007, "Doing Business in 2008" (Washington).

Yang, Y., and S. Gupta, 2005, "Regional Trade Arrangements in Africa: Past Performance and the Way Forward," IMF Working Paper 05/36 (Washington: International Monetary Fund).

2

Halving the Poverty Rate by 2015

LOUISE FOX, RUI BENFICA, AND MELISSA SEKKEL

Mozambique has been remarkably successful in reducing poverty over the past decade. Sustained, broad-based growth resulted in a 25 percent decline, equivalent to 4 percentage points a year, in the poverty headcount between 1996 and 2002. Mozambique's impressive poverty reduction performance was driven not only by the high rate of economic growth but also by the character of this growth. At the macro level, achieving growth without an increase in inequality was key, since this allowed a modest private consumption growth to efficiently reduce poverty, leaving room for a strong increase in investment to generate future growth. At the micro level, broad-based, labor-intensive growth in the nonagricultural sectors diversified household incomes, which underpinned the pro-poor growth performance. This chapter draws lessons on the linkages between growth and poverty reduction and analyzes the major factors associated with poverty reduction in Mozambique during 1996–2002. It uses both macro-level and nationally representative expenditure and income household survey data to illustrate those relationships in recent years and project future performance. The case of Mozambique also offers important lessons for other low-income sub-Saharan African countries, and we summarize these in our conclusions.

The chapter is structured as follows. First, it looks at the poverty and growth record over 1996–2002, paying special attention to relative trends across space and sectors of activity in the economy. Second, it analyzes the micro-level determinants of consumption growth and poverty reduction. Third, given the importance of rural poverty reduction over the period, particular attention is given to the sources of rural income growth, including the continued role of crop income and the increased importance of income diversification. Fourth, using assumptions with respect to sectoral growth and employment structure, we project the incidence of poverty for the years 2007 and 2015.

In spite of the progress, more than 50 percent of Mozambique's population remains poor. We conclude that although agricultural growth was crucial for poverty reduction, particularly in rural areas, diversification of livelihoods away from agriculture was also important in reducing vulnerability and improving welfare. If economic growth supporting increases in the productivity of labor and other factors is sustained over the next decade, and is coupled with continued expansion of social services to the poorest, Mozambique is likely to make good progress toward achieving the United Nations' Millennium Development Goals (MDGs), in particular, the goal of halving absolute poverty by 2015. Efforts will need to be made to ensure that growth and poverty reduction continue to be achieved without increased inequality. This will primarily involve achieving continued increases in labor productivity and income for smallholder farmers.

Poverty and Growth Record

Between 1996 and 2002, Mozambique's growth performance contributed to reducing the number of people in abject poverty by nearly 30 percent, from 69 percent to 54 percent, according to its own national measure of the minimum living standard.[1] The reduction was relatively more accentuated in rural areas (Figure 2.1). As expected, growth was efficient at poverty reduction because it raised incomes in the areas and sectors where the poor were concentrated. The 15 percentage point decline in poverty can be disaggregated into component parts, indicating the importance of particular regions or sectors of activity (Table 2.1). Incomes and consumption per capita increased rapidly, leading to an 11.1 percentage point decline in the poverty headcount for households engaged primarily in agriculture—the main activity of the poor—and this accounted for 75 percent of the decrease in poverty. Regionally, poverty fell sharply in the center of the country, which is not the poorest part but is relatively populous.

Urban poverty fell by less than rural poverty, but since the share of the population in urban areas is low, the *total* poverty impact of this develop-

[1]For a description of the methodology, see MPF, IFPRI, and Purdue University (2004).

Figure 2.1. Poverty Rates in 1996 and 2002
(Pecent of total population)

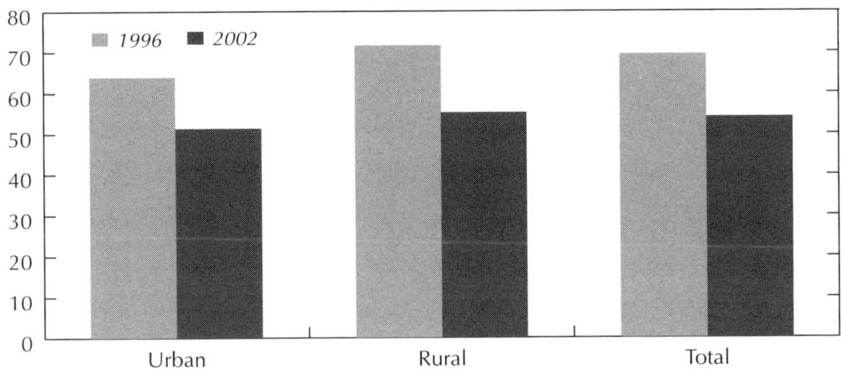

Source: National Expenditure Surveys, 1996 and 2002.

ment was small. Key reasons for the slower pace of urban poverty reduction were inflation and a depreciating currency, which contributed to the increased costs of imported goods and of urban services such as transportation (owing, among other things, to higher fuel costs). Since these items are important in the consumption basket of the urban poor (rice is a staple food in urban areas), real consumption growth was slower in those areas.[2] Migration was not a factor in poverty reduction, but the shifts in livelihoods were: the shift of some households out of agriculture as their main source of income and into other sectors reduced poverty by 10 percent.

Households used the increased income to diversify their consumption toward nonfood items (Table 2.2). Since households had more income, meeting basic needs took up proportionally less of it, and the share of food in total expenditures fell in both rural and urban areas in favor of nonfood items. The additional income was increasingly spent to buy consumer durables and to fix up dwellings. By 2002, the majority of households in both rural and urban areas had radios; rural households also acquired bicycles, while in urban areas households bought TVs, clocks, and a few motorbikes. The vast majority of households in 2002 were able to afford housing with durable walls, and in urban areas the majority of residential buildings had durable roofs.

[2]See MPF, IFPRI, and Purdue University (2004) for a further discussion of the observed increase in urban poverty.

Table 2.1. Decomposition of Changes in Poverty by Location and Sector, 1996–2002

	Levels and changes (*In percent*)	Population shares		
			1996	2002
Mozambique				
Poverty in 1996	69.4			
Poverty in 2002	54.1			
Total change in poverty from 1996 to 2002 *(percentage points)*	–15.3			
Regional decomposition		**By region**[1]		
Change in poverty in north	–3.7	North	32.3	32.3
Change in poverty in center	–11.7	Center	41.9	41.9
Change in poverty in south	0.12	South	25.7	25.7
Total intraregional component *(percentage points)*	–15.3			
Population shift (*regional migration*)	0.0			
Interaction component (*residual*)	0.0			
Urban-rural (*consistent 2002 definition*)		**By area of residence**		
Change in urban poverty	–3.6	Urban	29.0	32.0
Change in rural poverty	–11.6	Rural	71.0	68.0
Total intrasectoral component *(percentage points)*	–15.2			
Population shift (*urban-rural migration*)	–0.22			
Interaction component (*residual*)	0.11			
Aggregate sectors (by head of household)[2]		**By sector of employment of head of household**		
Change in agriculture poverty	–11.1	Agriculture	78.7	71.3
Change in industry poverty	–0.8	Industry	7.6	5.3
Change in Service 1 poverty	–0.9	Service 1	9.4	17.5
Change in Service 2 poverty	–0.9	Service 2	4.1	5.8
Total intrasectoral component *(percentage points)*	–13.9			
Population shift (*sector shift*)	–1.5			
Interaction component (*residual*)	0.1			

Source: National Expenditure Surveys, 1996 and 2002.

Note: Table entries are changes in the incidence of poverty, in percentage points, that are attributable to the group. A negative number indicates a reduction in poverty.

[1]North includes Niassa, Cabo Delgado, and Nampula; center includes Sofala, Tete, Manica, and Zambezia; and south includes Gaza, Inhambane, Maputo Province, and Maputo City.

[2]Individuals are assigned to the sector where the household head is employed. If the head is not employed, they are assigned to the sector of employment of the other oldest adult. If nobody is employed (fewer than 5 percent of all cases), they are assigned to agriculture. Service 1 includes trade, transport, and services; Service 2 includes health, education, and public administration.

During the same period, national inequality (measured by consumption per capita) remained about the same (Table 2.3). In other words, the growth process helped the poor as much as the rich and, as a result, growth

Table 2.2. Nonmonetary Measures of Welfare

	All		Urban		Rural	
	1996	2002	1996	2002	1996	2002
Food share	68	61	63	50	71	66
Durable goods						
Radio	29	65	43	65	24	65
TV	5	9	12	23	2	1
Clock	24	43	36	60	20	34
Motorbike	1	2	2	3	1	1
Bicycle	13	40	11	23	15	50
Housing						
Durable wall	31	85	50	87	22	85
Durable roof	16	25	40	56	7	11

Source: National Expenditure Surveys, 1996 and 2002.

was efficient in reducing poverty.[3] At about 0.40 on a per adult equivalent basis, and 0.42 on a per capita basis, Mozambique's Gini coefficient is moderate.[4] It is above those of South Asian countries China and Indonesia, and of African countries Tanzania and Malawi, but is one of the lowest in Africa and in the developing world as a whole. In sub-Saharan Africa, the Gini coefficients of Kenya, Uganda, and Zambia are all higher, as are those of most countries in Central America, Central Asia, and the Middle East.[5] There was a modest increase in inequality in Mozambique's urban areas, which helped account for the lower poverty reduction observed there. By contrast, rural inequality was not a factor in poverty reduction, nor was the rural-urban gap—which, in any case, is also quite low in Mozambique compared with other countries in the region—important.

Why was Mozambican economic growth pro-poor? One reason was the growth of labor productivity in agriculture. The rate of annual growth of production in agriculture was only about half the growth rate of GDP overall, but the sector shed labor into other sectors so that average labor productivity rose, fueling income growth for households whose main source of income was in this sector (Table 2.4) as well as for households that depended on this sector for subsistence and food security.

Labor in both rural and urban areas moved into the services sectors, and growth in these sectors was pro-poor as well. Primarily private sector services, such as retail trade, transport, food preparation, financial services, and telecommunications, saw their share of the labor force more

[3]For further details, see Fox, Bardasi, and Van den Broeck (2005); and James, Arndt, and Simler (2005).

[4]The Gini coefficient is defined as a ratio of the areas on the Lorenz Curve.

[5]Comparison number from the World Bank's POVCAL database.

Table 2.3. Measures of Inequality, 1996/7 and 2002/3

	Gini coefficient		Theil index	
Area of residence	1996	2002	1996	2002
Urban	0.434	0.463	0.373	0.462
Rural	0.350	0.363	0.231	0.256
All	0.381	0.403	0.286	0.343

Decomposition of the Theil index in within- and between-group inequality (groups defined by urban/rural)

	1996	2002
Within-group inequality	0.280	0.335
Between-group inequality	0.006	0.008
Percent of within-group inequality	97.9	97.7

Source: National Expenditure Surveys, 1996 and 2002.

than double. Primarily public services also increased as a share of the labor force, but this sector remained small. Incomes grew very rapidly in the public sector, however, so the growth of income brought the poverty rate for households headed by a public sector employee down to only 33 percent. Even though it accounted for only a very small percentage of the labor force, this sector contributed to poverty reduction as well. Average earnings were higher in the service sectors than in agriculture, and earnings growth was strong despite falling productivity.[6]

The industrial sector suffered net job destruction owing to the closing or downsizing of a number of parastatal manufacturing enterprises. The layoffs, combined with increased private investment, led to a strong growth in value added and major improvement in productivity per worker. The construction sector boomed during the period, contributing to the high rate of economic growth overall in the industrial sector. Construction doubled its share of total employment to 2.0 percent, and average earnings in this sector rose. A number of new businesses started up as well.

A key development behind rising labor productivity was the withdrawal of youth labor from the labor force. This involved primarily youth between the ages of 10 and 18, who mostly either did not enter the labor force or were able to leave the labor force to go to school. The share of those aged 10 years and above who reported being in school as their primary activ-

[6]Falling productivity, often viewed negatively, is a mathematical certainty for a sector that experiences a rapid growth in the labor force without a similar growth in physical capital or technological change. In the nonagricultural sectors of a country with incomes as low as Mozambique's, such an outcome is normal and positive from a poverty-reduction standpoint.

Table 2.4. Summary Statistics on GDP, Poverty, and Consumption by Sector, 1996–2002
(In percent)

	1996	2002	1996–2002
	Share of GDP		Annual average growth rate
GDP	100.0	100.0	9.2
Agriculture[1]	34.4	26.9	4.8
Industry	16.0	26.1	18.6
Services (private)	40.9	38.2	8.0
Services (public)	8.7	8.8	9.3
	Share of labor force		Annual average growth rate
Labor force	100.0	100.0	0.8
Agriculture[1]	89.7	81.7	–0.8
Industry	3.4	3.1	–0.6
Services (private)	5.0	12.3	17.1
Services (public)	1.8	2.9	8.7
	Average labor productivity		Annual average growth rate
Total	4.0	6.5	8.4
Agriculture[1]	1.5	2.1	5.6
Industry	18.2	54.1	19.9
Services (private)	31.6	20.2	–7.2
Services (public)	19.3	19.8	0.4
	Poverty headcount		Annual change in poverty rate
Household	69.2	54.1	–4.0
Agriculture[1]	72.6	58.2	–3.6
Industry	65.4	54.0	–3.1
Services (private)	54.6	44.4	–3.4
Services (public)	56.0	32.9	–8.5

Sources: International Monetary Fund; and National Expenditure Surveys, 1996 and 2002.
[1]Agriculture includes domestics.

ity increased from 17 percent to 22 percent, and many in this group were girls, who were no longer required exclusively to stay home and help with domestic tasks. The ability of households to support these dependents while they are in school is another indication of the strength of the improvements in household welfare. As noted later, this has led to major improvements in human capital formation in Mozambique and should contribute to stronger economic growth in the future. It has also led to a strong increase in employment in the education sector.

In sum, the overall productivity increase and the structural changes in Mozambique's economy strongly supported poverty reduction. Most sectors with strong growth in output (for example, construction, trade, and education) had an even stronger growth in employment. The exceptions were in the industrial sector (Figure 2.2). In agriculture, where the majority of the population works, the decline in employment was pro-poor. By the end of

Figure 2.2. Average Annual Growth Rates of Output and Labor Force by Sector, 1996–2002
(In percent)

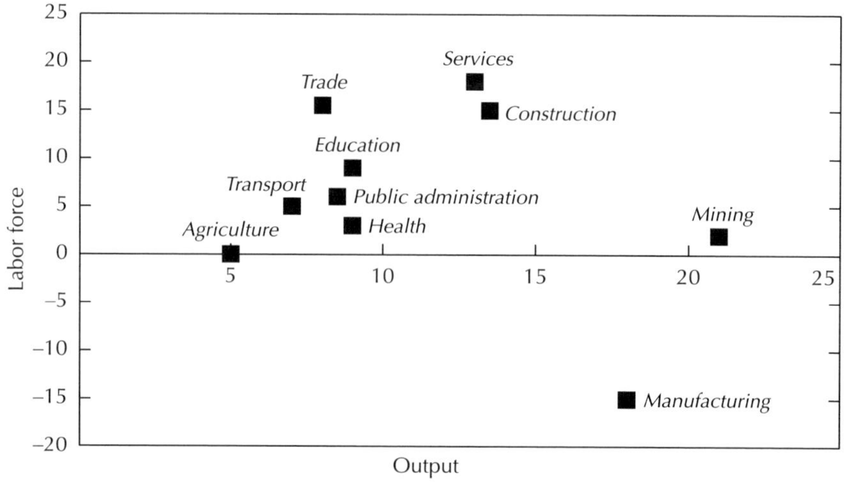

Source: National Expenditure Surveys, 1996 and 2002.

the period 1996–2002, agriculture accounted for only about one-fourth of Mozambique's GDP.

Looking forward, Mozambique needs to sustain the pattern of labor-intensive growth in the nonagricultural economy, as more shifts in the structure of the labor force out of agriculture will be required in the future to continue the improved poverty-reduction performance. This is because in 2002, 80 percent of the labor force was still working in the agricultural sector despite its low and falling share in GDP. To get a clearer picture of this structural shift and its implications for households, we now turn to the micro foundations of this poverty and growth performance and focus on how households, and their livelihoods, have changed over the decade of poverty reduction.

Behind the Numbers: Micro-Level Determinants of Poverty Reduction

Household Livelihoods and Employment Patterns

Aggregate growth and structural change affect households through changes in a complex set of factors known as livelihoods. Livelihoods, as conventionally defined, comprise "people, their capabilities and their means of living, including, food, income, and assets," where assets refer to both tangible (such as productive resources and household goods) and intangible assets (such as rights, claims, and access to such resources).[7] The livelihood strategies that individuals and households adopt tend to reflect the opportunities and assets (natural, physical, financial, human, and social) available to them; their remuneration (monetary or otherwise) from these activities determines the economic changes in household welfare. Poorer households, with smaller asset bases, tend to have fewer livelihood options. Changes in livelihood strategies represent the response of households to the macro events analyzed previously; livelihood changes in households feed back into sectoral and aggregate economic performance.

Relative monetary poverty or wealth is a condition of the household at a given moment in time and results from the demographic structure of the household, its assets, and its income (including income in kind). In Mozambique, the dominant factors behind poverty reduction were the changes in the structures of both urban and rural livelihoods, which, especially in rural areas, were associated with improvements in welfare. By contrast, during 1996–2002, the demographic structures of households changed very little. The number of dependents did increase by 20 percent on average, however, owing to the withdrawal of household members from the labor force. The increase in dependents was greatest in the poorest households, where the number of dependents per worker (economic dependency ratio)[8] rose from about 1.1 to 1.5 in 2002. It is an indication of the strength of the Mozambican recovery that such a large increase in dependents in the poorest households did not result in increasing inequality.

The dominant labor force trends during the period between the two surveys were the growth of *private* wage employment and of *nonagricultural self-employment* (Table 2.5). Overall, wage employment grew modestly, as public sector wage employment fell by 3 percent per year, on average. Private wage employment more than made up for this loss, however, growing at 18 percent a year for six years. This trend was most evident in urban areas, which averaged 19 percent growth; but even in rural areas, private wage jobs grew by 10 percent (from a very small base). The contraction in government jobs hit rural areas hardest, since the cashew-processing plants were shut down and the growth in private wage jobs was slower. In urban areas, the share of private wage jobs increased from one-third to two-thirds of total

[7]Chambers and Conway (1991).

[8]The economic dependency ratio is the ratio of the number of people not working to the number of people working.

Table 2.5. Growth Rate of Labor Force (Ages 10 and Higher), by Type of Employment (Rural/Urban), 1996–2002
(In percent)

Type of employment	Share of all workers 1996/97	Share of all workers 2002/03	Growth rate 1996/97–2002/03	Rural 1996/97	Rural 2002/03	Growth rate 1996/97–2002/03	Urban 1996/97	Urban 2002/03	Growth rate 1996/97–2002/03
Agriculture (all)[1]	88.8	81.5	–0.6	94.8	93.1	–0.3	71.3	53.5	–1.9
Self-employed, nonagriculture	3.8	8.1	14.3	2.0	3.6	10.6	9.0	19.0	16.5
Wage employment	7.4	10.4	6.7	3.2	3.3	0.7	19.6	27.5	8.9
Public	4.8	3.8	–3.2	2.1	1.3	–6.9	12.8	9.7	–1.7
Private	2.6	6.6	17.7	1.1	2.0	9.8	6.8	17.8	20.9
All economically active	100.0	100.0	0.8	100.0	100.0	0.0	100.0	100.0	2.9

Source: National Expenditure Surveys, 1996 and 2002.
[1]Agriculture excludes those employed in the public sector.

wage employment. Most of the private wage jobs are in the industrial sector (including mining and construction), but a growing share are in the services sector. The growth in wage jobs appears to have contributed to poverty reduction, since, for the most part, workers employed in private wage jobs were overrepresented in upper-income households.[9]

The growth of nonagricultural self-employment was widespread, since it occurred in both rural and urban areas. Nearly two-thirds of this employment was in urban areas, however. Although the source of demand for the products and services of rural nonfarm self-employment was most likely the growth in agricultural sector incomes, the shift of the labor force into this sector—which grew overall by 16 percent a year—was a major factor in rural poverty reduction, since average incomes in this sector are 50 percent above those in agricultural self-employment. In urban areas, 95 percent of self-employment was in the services sector in traditional informal sector activities such as wholesale and retail trade, transport (taxis, small buses), catering and restaurants, repairs, lodging, and gardening. In rural areas, the sector is more diverse, including manufacturing based on natural resources (for example, charcoal, small wood furniture) or agricultural products (for example, milling, brewing), as well as services similar to those provided in the urban sector.

[9]It is possible that those employed in wage jobs in 2002 were living in high-income households in 1997, so, in the absence of panel data, we cannot be sure about the total effect this had on poverty. If wage jobs had not been created, however, the increase in labor income surely would have been lower.

Table 2.6. Educational Distribution of Labor Force, by Gender
(In percent)

Highest level of education	Share of labor force						Average annual growth 1996–2002		
	1996			2002					
	All	Male	Female	All	Male	Female	All	Male	Female
Never attended or completed EP1	80.5	70.8	88.4	78.1	68.0	85.6	0.3	–0.2	0.2
EP1	13.1	19.0	8.2	13.4	18.4	9.3	1.1	–0.1	2.7
EP2	4.7	7.3	2.6	5.3	7.6	3.4	2.7	1.1	5.3
SG1	1.0	1.7	0.4	1.8	3.0	0.8	11.0	10.4	12.2
SG2	0.4	0.6	0.1	0.9	1.6	0.4	18.9	17.8	21.8
Technical	0.3	0.5	0.1	0.5	0.8	0.1	6.9	8.9	–1.5
Post-secondary	0.0	0.1	0.0	0.1	0.2	0.0	18.7	16.6	26.6
Total	100.0	100.0	100.0	100.0	100.0	100.0	0.8	0.4	0.7

Source: National Expenditure Surveys, 1996 and 2002.

Notes: EP1 denotes primary education, Grades 1 through 5; EP2 denotes primary education, Grades 6 and 7; SG1 denotes secondary education, First Cycle/Grades 8 and 9; SG2 denotes secondary education, Second Cycle/Grades 10 through 12.

Women continued to participate actively in the economy. As a result of the trend of increased school enrollment for girls, the educational level of women in the labor force rose (Table 2.6). But still, in 2002, 86 percent of economically active women reported having not attended school or completed EP1 ("Primary Education 1"—the first 5 years of formal education). The distribution of women in the labor force by type of job did not change much between 1996 and 2002. Women's access to paid jobs was about the same between the two years—the growth rate was higher in 2002, but it had increased from a tiny base. Women have expanded into self-employment, especially in urban areas. Nonetheless, the dominant sector of employment for women remains agriculture, either as self-employed persons or as family workers (Table 2.7). By remaining in agriculture, women facilitate the diversification of sources of income for the household while ensuring food security. This pattern of household income generation may have advantages, but it may also be reducing women's access to cash income relative to men's. This may support the maintenance of gender inequities and may have implications for future efforts to shed labor and raise labor productivity in agriculture.

A Closer Look at Rural Income Structure and Growth

The increase in rural incomes was a major force behind Mozambique's poverty-reduction performance. Yet rural poverty is still severe and widespread. Sustaining rural poverty reduction may prove to be a serious chal-

Table 2.7. Type of Employment, by Gender and Sector, 1997–2003

Type of employment	Share of sector, by gender (In percent)		Number of employed (Thousands)		Percentage change	Total share of labor force (In percent)	
	1997	2003	1997	2003	1997–2003	1997	2003
Agriculture, female	58.7	61.2	4,344	4,283	−1.4	52.7	49.9
Agriculture, male	41.3	38.8	3,056	2,717	−11.1	37.1	31.7
Self-employed nonagriculture, female	31.9	41.5	99	287	189.4	1.2	3.3
Self-employed nonagriculture, male	68.1	58.5	212	405	91.4	2.6	4.7
Public sector wage, female	15.4	20.7	50	66	34.0	0.6	0.8
Public sector wage, male	84.6	79.3	272	254	−6.7	3.3	3.0
Private sector wage, female	11.8	16.8	25	95	276.8	0.3	1.1
Private sector wage, male	88.2	83.2	189	472	149.7	2.3	5.5
All economically active, female	54.8	55.1	4,492	4,737	5.5		
All economically active, male	45.2	44.9	3,708	3,863	4.2		
Total						100.0	100.0

Source: National Expenditure Surveys, 1996 and 2002.

Notes: Agriculture includes domestic and unpaid family workers in agriculture. Self-employed workers in other sectors include unpaid family workers if the industry they work in is different from agriculture.

lenge in years to come. Therefore, it is important to develop a better understanding of how rural households generate their incomes and what changes have occurred in the structure of that income over time, which justifies taking a closer look at the changes in production patterns and sources of income growth for households. We use income data from nationally representative rural household income surveys for the same years, 1996 and 2002. Although mirroring the trends described previously, these data provide details on households' income-earning strategies, showing the structure of rural household incomes and how it has changed over time.

The main source of agricultural growth in Mozambique has been production of basic food crops, but export-oriented cash crop production is also expanding. Between 1997 and 2002, basic food crop production grew at an average rate of about 3–4 percent annually. Maize and millet production showed the greatest increases, followed by sorghum, beans, rice, and cassava. The number of households engaged in production of export crops and the total cash crop production for export have also increased; particularly important are sugarcane (for larger enterprises), cashews, copra, cotton, and tobacco. Within the crop sector, production was considerably more diversi-

Figure 2.3. Average Annual Growth Rates of Rural Household Income per Adult Equivalent, by Income per Adult Equivalent Quintiles, 1996–2002
(In percent)

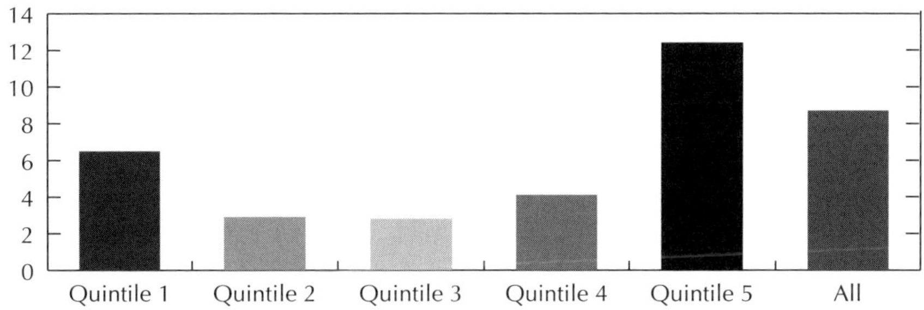

Source: Mozambique, National Rural Income Surveys, 1996 and 2002.

fied in 2002 than in 1996, as the mean number of crops grown per household increased from fewer than five crops in 1996 to almost eight crops in 2002.

The shift into a more diverse crop mix and into higher-value crops has resulted in improvements in crop incomes for all income groups. Rural household income—defined as the value of crop production and sales, and earnings from nonfarm self-employment and wage income—showed a pro-poor trend similar to that of rural consumption growth (Figure 2.3). Rural households are overwhelmingly smallholder farms. Crop income is the most important income source, especially for poorer households, and growth in income from this source explains a great deal of the increases (nearly 80 percent) in mean income for the poorest groups (Table 2.8).

Although it is not obvious from national consumption data, analysis of rural income data shows that differences between richer and poorer households in rural areas widened between 1996 and 2002. Rural households in all income groups increasingly relied on nonagricultural sources such as livestock, wage labor, and nonfarm enterprise income (Tables 2.9 and 2.10). The probability of a household engaging in wage labor and nonfarm enterprises increased over the period and was directly correlated with income levels in each year. Increased crop income from export crop sources is also correlated with income. Households in areas with better infrastructure were more likely to have noncrop income sources. Regression analysis shows that a shorter distance to a paved road increases the size of a household's noncrop income as well.

Most of the increase in crop income has been achieved through extensive agricultural practices, such as area expansion. Yet the area cultivated

Table 2.8. Structure of Rural Household Income, by Source and Income Quintile, 1996 and 2002
(Percentage of income by source, quintile, and year)

Quintiles of net household income/adult equivalents	Survey years	Crop income	Livestock sales	Wage labor	Nonfarm enterprise	Total
Quintile 1	1996	92.5	1.6	2.8	3.1	100.0
	2002	85.3	4.4	2.1	8.3	100.0
Quintile 2	1996	87.5	2.0	1.7	8.8	100.0
	2002	84.4	3.6	1.8	10.2	100.0
Quintile 3	1996	81.9	1.4	1.8	14.9	100.0
	2002	75.8	3.8	6.3	14.1	100.0
Quintile 4	1996	78.2	1.1	2.4	18.4	100.0
	2002	61.0	3.9	14.6	20.5	100.0
Quintile 5	1996	74.8	1.0	2.1	22.0	100.0
	2002	38.7	2.9	25.9	32.5	100.0
All rural households	1996	83.0	1.4	2.1	13.4	100.0
	2002	70.9	3.8	9.1	16.2	100.0

Source: Mozambique, National Rural Income Survey (TIA), 2002.

(averaging 1.4 hectares) is still too small for income maximizing. One reason farms remain small is that current agriculture practices—most Mozambican farmers make very little use of technologies such as improved seeds, or of chemical inputs such as fertilizers, pesticides, and herbicides—do not support larger farm sizes as labor shortages emerge. Failure to modernize means that basic food crops widely grown by smallholder farmers, predominantly for subsistence, have exhibited relatively stagnant yields (output per hectare) (Walker and others, 2004; Benfica, 2006; Benfica, Tschirley, and Boughton, 2006; and Boughton and others, 2006a). The conundrum for Mozambican agriculture is that although land area expansion is still important to achieving the needed returns through larger-scale production, the ability of households to expand that area may be limited under the currently available technology. There will have to be gains in productivity at the farm level, including the use of labor-saving technologies, if agricultural growth is to be sustained and to continue contributing to rural poverty reduction.

Smallholders can increase land productivity and crop income through diversification into profitable cash crops, production of many of which is tied to contract farming schemes. The use of productivity-enhancing technologies (particularly fertilizers) in Mozambique (where rural credit and input markets are poorly developed) is generally associated with such

Table 2.9. Sources of Rural Household Income (All and Major), by Quintile, 1996 and 2002
(In percent)

Quintiles of net household income/ adult equivalents	Survey year	Households earning income from source				Households earning highest proportion of income from source				
		Crop income	Livestock sales	Wage labor	Nonfarm MSE	Crop income	Livestock sales	Wage labor	Nonfarm MSE	Total
Quintile 1	1996	98.8	9.1	15.8	9.1	95.0	0.9	1.2	2.9	100.0
	2002	100.0	20.2	6.5	27.9	89.5	2.8	1.2	6.5	100.0
Quintile 2	1996	99.6	14.8	19.0	21.8	93.0	0.2	0.7	6.1	100.0
	2002	100.0	29.5	7.0	34.4	89.4	1.6	1.4	7.6	100.0
Quintile 3	1996	99.8	14.3	18.6	34.3	82.1	0.8	2.1	15.0	100.0
	2002	100.0	32.9	14.3	40.6	79.2	2.1	6.4	12.2	100.0
Quintile 4	1996	99.7	16.1	27.2	49.8	81.3	0.3	1.0	17.4	100.0
	2002	100.0	36.2	24.4	51.6	59.5	2.6	16.6	21.3	100.0
Quintile 5	1996	100.0	15.2	24.2	61.8	76.5	0.7	0.6	22.2	100.0
	2002	100.0	36.1	36.7	61.5	34.3	1.6	28.6	35.5	100.0
All rural households	1996	99.6	13.9	21.0	35.4	85.6	0.6	1.1	12.7	100.0
	2002	100.0	30.6	16.5	42.0	72.7	2.2	9.7	15.4	100.0

Source: Mozambique, National Rural Income Survey (TIA), 2002.
Note: MSE denotes medium-size and small enterprises.

crops and schemes.[10] If expansion of production takes place with improved technologies, particularly labor-saving ones involving animal traction and irrigation and chemical inputs capable of increasing yields, the effects can be significant for increasing both households' food security and their ability to market their crops, and invest, off the farm. Furthermore, the contribution of agricultural growth to rural poverty reduction can be maximized if roads and access to markets are improved, resulting in better market integration across subregions. Evidence suggests that access to markets (both domestic and regional cross-border) improved over the period, and prices have tended to converge in domestic markets, indicating increased market integration, but further progress is needed.

Finally, off-farm income, particularly from wage labor and nonfarm self-employment, has played an important role in income growth and poverty

[10]Households engaged in the cultivation of those crops tend to either apply them to food crops or follow rotation recommendations that contribute to increased yields in those crops. In addition to that, nongrowers of those crops in growing areas also tend to apply them to their food crops (Benfica, 2006; Benfica, Tschirley, and Boughton, 2006).

Table 2.10. Sources of Growth in Rural Household Income, by Quintile, 1996–2002

Annual quintiles of net household income/adult equivalents	Annual growth rate in income, 1996–2002	Change in mean total income attributable to each source, 1996–2002[1]				
		Crop income	Livestock sales	Wage income	Nonfarm enterprise	Total
Quintile 1	6.5	77.2	5.0	–3.0	20.0	100.0
Quintile 2	2.9	77.0	6.0	5.0	12.0	100.0
Quintile 3	2.8	79.2	7.9	13.9	–1.0	100.0
Quintile 4	4.1	39.4	9.1	38.4	13.1	100.0
Quintile 5	12.4	–8.0	4.0	55.0	49.0	100.0
All households	8.7	9.9	5.0	46.5	38.6	100.0

Sources: Mozambique, National Rural Income Survey (TIA), 2002; Boughton and others (2006a).

[1]Percent of the total change attributable to the source. Calculated as a share of each source change in the total change.

reduction. Lack of opportunities in this sector may jeopardize sustainable poverty reduction over the longer run. Therefore, efforts to increase households' access to those opportunities, in both the agricultural and the nonfarm sectors, are important. Increased wage-earning opportunities would come about through expanding the activity of larger farming households, such as commercial smallholders (predominantly in export cash crops), capable of generating employment. Increasing the availability of nonfarm wage-employment opportunities through public investment (for example, on public works) could generate direct and indirect poverty-reduction effects through increased effective demand in the local economy. Participation in nonfarm businesses is important for all income groups. It will, therefore, be important to promote the development of a more diversified nonfarm business sector in rural areas to achieve sustained rural income growth and poverty reduction. Focusing on business with backward and forward production linkages capable of generating multiplier effects can have a much more substantial and broad-based impact on rural poverty. Past experience shows that continued public investment in rural infrastructure is key.

Overall Determinants of Consumption Levels in Mozambique

After the structural changes described above, what are the key factors that determined the levels of consumption in Mozambican households in 2002/03? To answer this question, we ran a regression, using as the dependent variable the log of household consumption per adult equivalent.[11] We used a broad set of independent variables in the analysis, and our results can be interpreted as the household production function for consumption.[12] We included some variables that may be partly endogenous, such as household composition, because we still wanted to control for the independent part so that it did not pollute the other coefficients. We also included the gender of the head of household; the presence of any disabled adults or children; and the marital status, education, and sector of activity of the head. We estimated separate regressions for urban and rural areas, since we found the structures were quite different. To control for regional effects, we used dummy variables for districts (which show up as district fixed effects).[13]

With the exception of those for older household members, most variables on household composition are significantly negative—the more people in the household, the lower the consumption per capita. It is noteworthy that the effect of different demographic groups on household consumption is roughly the same in rural and urban areas (Table 2.11). The only exception is for the number of men between 15 and 59 years old. This suggests that men in rural areas may not bring in as much in terms of household consumption as they take out, but that men in urban areas do. Possibly there are better opportunities for men in urban areas to add to household consumption, corrected for all other variables that may affect opportunities. Having disabled children in the household does not seem to affect household consumption, but the presence of disabled adults has a negative effect on household consumption in rural areas.[14] This is as expected, since it adds to the dependency burden of the household. In rural areas, the age of the household head has a negative effect on household consumption. A widowed head (regardless of gender) significantly reduces consumption in urban areas. In rural areas, we find that living in a household with a married female head results in higher consumption. We suspect that these households have a husband who could be a migrant worker sending remittances to his family or that they are actually polygamous households.

---

[11]A log specification (1) reduces the effect of outliers on the variables, thus producing a normally distributed variable; and (2) allows the coefficient to be interpreted as the marginal percentage effect of the independent variable on household consumption.

[12]The analysis of the determinants of poverty in Maximiano, Arndt, and Simler (2005), using the same data but slightly different variables or variable specifications, leads to broadly the same results. Especially with respect to the importance of education, the results strongly confirm each other.

[13]The survey covered 128 districts in 1996 and 144 districts in 2002.

[14]In 1996/97, disabled adults had a negative effect on consumption only in urban areas.

Table 2.11. Consumption Regressions with District Fixed Effects, 2002

Dependent variable: log consumption	Urban Coefficient	Urban Significance	Rural Coefficient	Rural Significance	Significance of difference
Household demographics					
Number of children aged 0–5	–0.061	***	–0.045	***	
Number of children aged 6–9	–0.093	***	–0.076	***	
Number of children aged 10–14	–0.106	***	–0.108	***	
Number of men aged 15–59	–0.003		–0.064	***	***
Number of women aged 15–59	–0.021	**	–0.028	***	
Number of adults>60	0.025		–0.028		
Any disabled adults	–0.052		–0.100	***	
Any disabled children	0.020		–0.052		
Age head of household	0.006		–0.007	**	**
Age head square	–0.000		0.000	**	**
Head female	0.092		–0.186		
Head's marital status[1,2]					
Married	–0.027		–0.141		
Polygamous	0.001		–0.024		
Divorced	0.030		–0.058		
Widowed	–0.277	**	–0.127		
Added effect of female head on marital status					
Female and married	0.102		0.385	**	
Female and polygamous	0.036		0.199		
Female and divorced	–0.209		0.057		
Female and widowed	0.237		0.171		
Head's education[3]					
Some education	0.129	***	0.062	***	*
Completed EP1	0.234	***	0.131	***	**
Completed EP2	0.451	***	0.298	***	**
Completed SG1	0.715	***	0.695	***	
Completed SG2	1.142	***	0.542	***	***
Head's employment sector[4]					
Mines	0.231	***	0.174		
Manufacturing	0.014		0.275	***	**
Construction	0.036		0.038		
Transport	0.293	***	0.660	***	***
Trades	0.304	***	0.296	***	
Services	0.113	***	0.158	***	
Education	–0.072		0.283	***	***
Health	0.267	***	0.341	***	
Public administration	0.156	***	0.132		
Constant	9.049	***	10.174	***	
District fixed effects[5]	Yes		Yes		
Observations	4,001		4,695		
Adjusted R-squared	0.364		0.374		

Source: National Expenditure Survey, 2002.

Notes: Three asterisks (***) denote significance at 1 percent; two asterisks (**) denote significance at 5 percent; and one asterisk (*) denotes significance at 10 percent. EP1 denotes primary education, Grades 1 through 5; EP2 denotes primary education, Grades 6 and 7; SG1 denotes secondary education, First Cycle/Grades 8 and 9; SG2 denotes secondary education, Second Cycle/Grades 10 through 12.

[1]Head's marital status. We included interaction terms with the gender of the household head. The first set of coefficients on marital status represents the total sample effect. The interacted terms represent the marginal effect for female-headed households. If the interaction terms (head female*X) are significantly different from zero, the total effect for female heads is the effect obtained from the first set of coefficients plus the interaction effect.

[2]Base category = single male.

[3]Base category = no education.

[4]Base category = head I agriculture.

[5]In 1996, 128 districts were covered; in 2002, 144 districts.

Education of head of household has the expected positive signs, with rising returns, reflecting the relative scarcity of secondary and post-secondary education (in rural areas the number of post-secondary observations is very low, as is demand for this level of education, which may account for the declining returns). Returns are higher in urban areas for all levels of education. For upper secondary, the return shoots up in urban areas—the growing industrial and service sectors need more skilled labor than is being produced. Controlling for education, having the head work in mining (urban), manufacturing (rural), transport, trade, services, education (rural), health, and public administration (urban) increases household consumption compared with work in agriculture. The premiums are significantly lower in urban areas for manufacturing, transport, and education. Working in education seems to be equal to working in agriculture (controlling for education) in urban areas, which seems to suggest an emerging teacher pay issue in urban areas.

In sum, the conditions appear promising for continued poverty reduction in Mozambique. Structural change in the economy is translating into higher standards of living at the household level. Education, a key determinant of household living standards, is expanding rapidly. Even with disappointing results on completion in poor households, the levels of education of both males and females in the labor force will rise. In rural areas, though, the low completion rates will slow down the progress in poverty reduction, since the returns to acquiring just a few years of lower primary education are very low. Economic activity and employment are expanding in areas that are labor intensive and provide a strong boost to consumption (for example, trade, transport, publicly financed services), since there is a significant increase in effective demand. In addition, some of the expanding activities, particularly manufacturing (food processing), have important forward linkages with agriculture that may help boost growth in that sector. Although this regression does not allow for many inferences to be drawn about prospects in the agricultural sector, analysis by Walker and others (2004) has indicated that increased access to markets and land; productivity-enhancing inputs and technologies; and improved education, which can help sustain and increase labor productivity, will be important for future growth in the agricultural sector.

Prospects for Future Poverty Reduction

Mozambique has made good progress to date in reducing poverty and is likely to achieve the Millennium Development Goal of halving the poverty headcount by 2015. As stated in previous sections, sustained economic growth in various sectors and the diversification of the household economy through labor-force migration away from agriculture have been important in this process. In this section, we undertake simulations under alternative scenarios regarding GDP growth and sector migration to assess the prospects for future poverty reduction. We divide the households into two groups according to sector of employment of the head: agriculture and nonagriculture. We assume that household consumption per capita grows at the same rate as GDP in the sector of employment of the head of household[15] and that growth is distribution neutral—that is, there is a constant elasticity of poverty with respect to growth (Fox, Bardasi, and Van den Broeck, 2005).

As presented in Table 2.12, we make assumptions on sector GDP growth and sector migration to describe three alternative scenarios and the respective projections with respect to poverty reduction. Under all scenarios, nonagricultural GDP grows faster than agricultural GDP, but different assumptions are made regarding the actual pace and rate of mobility of households across sectors, particularly from agriculture to nonagriculture. The following scenarios are assumed:

(1) *Optimistic sector GDP growth with sector migration.* Under this scenario, we assume that agricultural GDP grows at an average annual rate of 7.3 percent in 2002–06,[16] and 3.2 percent in 2007–15, while nonagricultural GDP grows at 7.5 percent and 5.7 percent, respectively, during the same periods. It is assumed that employment in the agricultural sector grows at 0.8, and employment in the nonagricultural sector at roughly 5.1 percent a year, implying that labor migrates into nonfarm employment over the projected period.

(2) *Optimistic sector GDP growth without sector migration.* Under this scenario, we keep optimistic assumptions regarding sector GDP growth. Regarding sector employment over the period, we assume the unlikely outcome that it grows at the same pace in both the agricultural and the nonagricultural sectors (by an annual average of 2.4 percent for 2002–07 and 2.2 percent for 2008–15)—that is, sector migration does not occur. Since diversification was a great deal of the past poverty-reduction story, we want to test the consequences of no diversification on poverty-reduction prospects.

---

[15]We are grateful to Maria Teresa Benito-Spinetto for the GDP growth rate projections.

[16]GDP growth rates for 2004, 2005, and 2006 for the nonagricultural sector are estimated/projected to be 8.5 percent, 6.6 percent, and 8.6 percent, respectively; GDP growth rates for the agricultural sector (including fisheries) are 8.0 percent, 6.6 percent, and 6.7 percent, respectively.

Table 2.12. Assumptions and Poverty Projections, by Sector of Employment

	Assumption on sector GDP and employment				Poverty projections		
	Annual sector GDP growth rates		Annual sector population growth rates[1]		Poverty headcount		
Scenarios	2002–06	2007–15	2002–07	2008–15	2002	2007	2015
Scenario 1	Optimistic GDP growth with sector diversification						
Agriculture	7.3	3.2	0.8	0.8	58	40	29
Nonagriculture	7.5	5.7	5.1	5.1	44	40	37
					54	40	31
Scenario 2	Optimistic GDP growth without sector diversification						
Agriculture	7.3	3.2	2.4	2.2	58	45	40
Nonagriculture	7.5	5.7	2.4	2.2	44	33	20
					54	42	34
Scenario 3	Pessimistic GDP growth without sector diversification						
Agriculture	6.3	2.2	2.4	2.2	58	48	48
Nonagriculture	6.5	4.7	2.4	2.2	44	36	26
					54	45	42

Sources: World Bank GDP estimates; National Expenditure Surveys, 1996 and 2002.
[1]Based on the 2002 population; the growth rates assumed here result in the National Institute of Statistics of Mozambique's projected total population for 2007 and 2015.

(3) *Pessimistic GDP growth without sector migration.* This is the worst-case scenario overall. It assumes that GDP growth in both sectors is slower (1 percent less than in the other scenarios), with nonagricultural GDP still growing faster than agricultural GDP, and that sector migration does not occur—that is, employment in both sectors grows at the same pace.

The poverty projections for 2007 and 2015 under each of these scenarios are presented in the last columns of Table 2.12 (by sector and aggregate) and in Figure 2.4 (aggregates only).

Overall, the results of the simulations emphasize the importance of sustaining economic growth and creating an enabling environment for the continued transformation of the economy. Sustained economic growth rates in Scenarios 1 and 2 result in significantly lower overall poverty rates—31 and 34 percent, respectively—in 2015.

As described in Scenario 1, if people move out of agriculture, as they have in the past decade, and growth continues, poverty overall, and particularly among those staying in agriculture, will decrease faster than if diversification does not occur. As stated previously, that has, in part, to do with the fact that labor productivity will increase rapidly in the sector. It should be noted, however, that increased productivity of labor (output per worker) has been made possible owing to a simultaneous expansion in the land area, and not to technological innovation, which has resulted

Figure 2.4. Poverty Headcount Projections Under Alternative Scenarios of Sectoral Structure and GDP Growth, 2007 and 2015
(In percent)

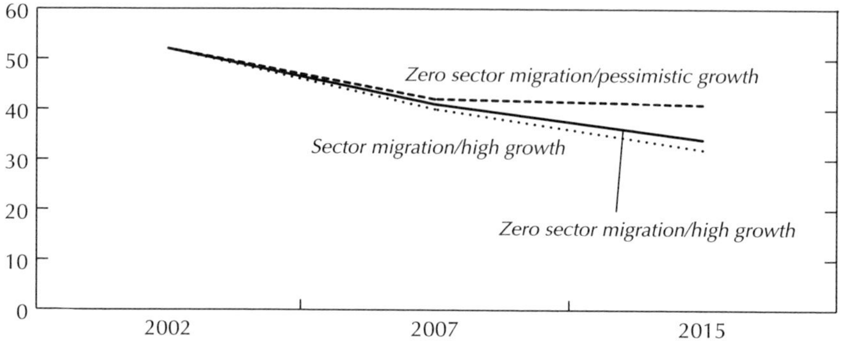

Source: Mozambique, National Expenditure Surveys, 1996 and 2002; and GDP projections.

in stagnant yields (output per hectare). Continued progress will depend, therefore, on the degree of intensification in the sector in years to come. Likewise, continued expansion in output in the nonfarm sector, which would have important effects on poverty reduction, is more likely to occur and be sustained if labor is more productive.

The conclusion here is that if growth can be sustained and inequality remains at more or less the same level, it should be possible for Mozambique to reach the Millennium Development Goal of halving the poverty rate by the year 2015.

Conclusions

Poverty in Mozambique has declined by both monetary and nonmonetary measures. The national headcount ratio was reduced from 69 percent to 54 percent over 1996–2002. The drop was more substantial in rural areas than in urban areas. Overall, inequality increased only slightly over the period. What elements of Mozambique's growth and development process were most important? We have identified the following factors.

First, growth was faster in nonagricultural labor-intensive sectors. This growth structure allowed households to become less dependent on low-productivity agriculture, gaining a larger share of income from private wage jobs and nonfarm enterprises. Although most households with at least two earners have agriculture as a primary or secondary activity, agriculture is usually engaged in by women (with 90 percent of women working in it) and less often by men. The absolute size of the agricultural labor force fell, and labor productivity (output per worker) increased, contributing to Mozambique's strong poverty-reduction performance.

Second, increased employment in higher-productivity activities increased all incomes, not just those at the top. In rural areas, subsistence agriculture still provides more than half of total income, but the rest comes primarily from sales of agricultural products and employment income. In urban areas, the fastest-growing sectors of employment were trade and private services, which were fast-growing sectors of GDP as well. Third, the quality of the labor force increased. Younger labor force participants left the labor force to go to school, and potential labor force participants stayed out of the labor force, and in school, longer. Education is still important for increased consumption, regardless of household size or location.

What are the prospects for continued pro-poor growth and poverty reduction? Rural income growth was crucial to the relatively bigger reduction of poverty in rural areas, and sustainable growth in crop income through productivity increases and crop diversification remains important for pro-poor growth. Smallholders can increase land productivity and crop income through diversification into profitable cash crops; policy and programs should be directed toward this goal. Continued access to land and improved access to markets, both domestic and foreign, and technology will be important in transforming Mozambican agriculture from low-productivity/subsistence to high-productivity/commercial and taking households out of poverty. Improvements in rural infrastructure are a crucial piece of the puzzle.

Second, promotion of self-employment opportunities and the creation of private sector wage jobs are important in both rural and urban areas. Off-farm income, particularly wage labor, played an important role in income and consumption growth, particularly for the highest-income households. Although wage labor jobs may not be available to the majority of households in the near future (the growth of formal sector jobs is still expanding from a low base), income diversification is crucial for rural poverty reduction. Investments in human and physical capital that increase the productivity of the self-employed sector will be critical to future success. Future growth may depend as well on the development of supporting institutions (for example, micro credit, savings cooperatives, and associations).

Our projections suggest that if Mozambique is able to sustain strong economic growth over the next 10 years, the poverty-reduction MDG can be met. Labor-intensive growth in the nonagricultural sector, which allows labor to continue to shift out of agriculture, is important in reducing poverty. Poverty reduction strategies should focus on the following: (1) expanding access to education (along with improving the quality of education); (2) achieving a growth performance balanced between agriculture and nonagricultural sectors; (3) expanding income-earning opportunities for poor households in the nonagricultural sector, allowing them to continue to diversify their sources of income outside agriculture; and (4) improving agricultural productivity through sustained intensification and increased access to markets.

Mozambique remains a very poor country—still one of the poorest in Africa. It offers important lessons on pro-poor growth, primarily for the low-income sub-Saharan African countries. The main lesson is that there is no substitute for a balanced growth strategy. Growth in the nonagricultural sector allows households to diversify income sources, while improvements in average labor productivity in crop agriculture support smallholder incomes. Within this context, four other lessons stand out.

- First, it is important to create a good investment climate for private investment in smallholder agriculture. This means improving market infrastructure, increasing access to land, and encouraging contract-grower schemes that bring new technology into the sector. Unless smallholders are allowed to diversify and modernize, there is a risk they will be left out and inequality will increase.
- Second, by encouraging the parallel development of a larger commercial farm sector, wage-labor opportunities arise that provide rural households with a source of cash income that they can invest or use for household needs.
- Third, supporting the growth of the microbusiness sector (very small family businesses) is critical to pro-poor growth. In Mozambique, this happened by default—the government did not try to interfere in this sector.
- Fourth, education pays off and is a critical building block for any poverty reduction strategy. But households need to have enough income security to send their children to school. Once Mozambican households had this security, young people began to stay in school longer.

Bibliography

Benfica, Rui, 2006, "An Analysis of Income Poverty Effects in Cash Cropping Economies in Rural Mozambique: Blending Econometric and Economy-Wide Models" (unpublished; Ph.D. dissertation; East Lansing, Michigan: Michigan State University, Department of Agricultural Economics).

———, David Tschirley, and Duncan Boughton, 2006, "Interlinked Transactions in Cash Cropping Economies: The Determinants of Farmer Participation and Performance in the Zambezi River Valley of Mozambique," paper presented at the 26th International Association of Agricultural Economists Conference, Gold Coast, Australia, August 12–18.

Boughton, Duncan, David Mather, David Tschirley, Thomas Walker, Benedito Cunguara, and Ellen Payongayong, 2006a, "Changes in Rural Household Income Patterns in Mozambique, 1996–2002, and Implications for Agriculture's Contribution for Poverty Reduction," MINAG/DE/DAP Research Report No. 61E (Maputo: Ministry of Agriculture, Directorate of Economics/Department of Policy Analysis). Available via the Internet: http://www.aec.msu.edu/fs2/mozambique/wps61e.pdf

Boughton, Duncan, David Mather, Christopher B. Barrett, Rui Benfica, Danilo Abdula, David Tschirley, and Benedito Cunguara, 2006b, "Market Participation by Rural Households in a Low-Income Country: An Asset-Based Approach Applied to Mozambique," forthcoming in *Faith and Development*. Available via the Internet: http://www.aem.cornell.edu/faculty_sites/cbb2/Market%20Participation%20Mozambique%20Dec2006.pdf

Chambers, R., and G. Conway, 1991, "Sustainable rural livelihoods: practical concepts for the 21st century," IDS Discussion Paper No. 296 (Brighton: IDS).

Fox, L., E. Bardasi, and K. Van den Broeck, 2005, "Poverty in Mozambique: Unraveling Changes and Determinants," Africa Region Working Paper Series No. 87 (Washington: World Bank).

James, Robert C., Channing Arndt, and Kenneth R. Simler, 2005, "Has Economic Growth in Mozambique Been Pro-Poor?" (Maputo: Mozambique Ministry of Planning and Finance, Direcção Nacional do Plano e Orçamento; Purdue University; and International Food Policy Research Institute).

Maximiano, Nelson, Channing Arndt, and Kenneth Simler, 2005, "Qual foi a Dinâmica dos Determinantes da Pobreza em Moçambique" (Maputo: Mozambique Ministry of Planning and Finance, Direcção Nacional do Plano e Orçamento).

Mozambique Ministry of Planning and Finance (MPF), International Food Policy Research Institute (IFPRI), and Purdue University, 2004, "Poverty and Well-Being in Mozambique: The Second National Assessment" (Maputo).

Walker, Thomas, David Tschirley, Jan Low, Maria Tanque, Duncan Boughton, Ellen Payongayong, and Michael Weber, 2004, "Determinants of Rural Income in Mozambique in 2001–2002," MINAG/DE/DAP Research Report No. 57E (Maputo: Mozambique Ministry of Agriculture, Directorate of Economics/Department of Policy Analysis). Available via the Internet: http://www.aec.msu.edu/fs2/mozambique/wps57e.pdf

3

Sustaining Growth in the Long Term

SAM JONES

The question of how to achieve rapid and sustained growth has challenged economists for generations. As Robert Lucas (1988) has famously remarked, "the consequences for human welfare involved in questions like these are staggering: once one starts to think about them, it is hard to think about anything else." The potential contribution of economic growth to well-being has been demonstrated by the achievements of various East Asian countries over recent decades. At the same time, it is patent that not all countries have been able to replicate these successes, with economic performance in sub-Saharan African countries being of particular concern. The World Bank, for example, remarks that global poverty is increasingly coming to assume an African face owing to the "slow and erratic" rates of economic growth across the continent over the last thirty years (Ndulu, 2007). Thus, although experiences of individual countries have been diverse, the importance of understanding what may be required to promote robust economic growth in Africa cannot be overstated.

After achieving independence from Portugal in 1975, Mozambique rapidly became embroiled in a prolonged and complex civil war. The conflict period was marked by severe economic decline. This was accompanied by substantial internal dislocation and structural changes in the economy related to attempts at achieving socialist control (until 1985), followed by gradual market liberalization (from 1985 onward). Following the attainment of peace in 1992, which was confirmed by democratic elections in 1994, Mozambique has witnessed rapid economic growth and poverty reduction. Aggregate real income grew at an average annual rate of 7.7 percent from 1993 to 2005 with improvements evident across a wide range of development indicators. (See Chapters 1 and 2 for further discussion; see also Mozambique Ministry of Planning and Development, 2006b.)

Despite these impressive achievements, the long-term nature of the development challenge cannot be ignored. The country ranks 168 out of 177 countries in terms of overall human development; the poverty headcount remains above 50 percent; and average life expectancy—about 42 years[1]—is among the lowest in the world. The Mozambican authorities recognize the central importance of economic growth, considering it to be a necessary condition for both poverty reduction and the achievement of broader development targets such as those incorporated in the United Nations Millennium Development Goals (MDGs). Rough estimates, however, indicate the extent of the future growth challenge. If Mozambique were to maintain real per capita growth of 6 percent per year, a higher rate than has been achieved by China during recent decades, it would take almost 40 years for it to attain South Africa's 2003 per capita income of US$10,346.[2]

Despite the central role accorded to output growth, there is no consensus as to how it can be increased or sustained over the long run (Easterly, 2007). This is clear from the continued controversy over the determinants of rapid growth in the newly industrialized economies (NIEs) of East Asia (see Sarel, 1995), and, more recently, in India and China.[3] As a point of departure for this chapter, however, it is useful to highlight the conceptual distinction between proximate and "deep" determinants of growth. The latter refer to the microeconomic causative processes behind output growth, focusing on dynamics in specific markets over time as well as political economy influences on policy choices. The former take a broader perspective, looking at the patterns of change in macroeconomic aggregates, including overall efficiency. Although the two approaches are complementary, an aggregate focus is essential to developing a coherent overall framework for understanding past dynamics and, thus, identifying core processes of interest. This is the objective of this study. More specifically, the following questions are asked:

---

[1]Figures from UNDP (2006).

[2]Calculations are based on purchasing-power-parity (PPP) measures of income using estimates from World Bank (2005c).

[3]The NIEs include Hong Kong SAR, Korea, Singapore, and Taiwan Province of China.

- What have been the aggregate determinants of Mozambican growth to date;
- What are the challenges to sustaining growth over the long run; and
- What might other low-income countries learn from the Mozambican experience?

To enable this study to provide an evidence-based response, rigorous quantification of the past (proximate) sources of economic growth is undertaken using a growth accounting methodology. This tells us that the rapid rates of growth achieved since the early 1990s, averaging 7.5 percent per year, have been based on strong contributions from all principal growth drivers, namely accumulation of physical capital (public and private), improvements in human capital quality, and productivity gains. The pattern of growth can thus be described as having been relatively "unbiased," in the sense that no single aggregate determinant of growth appears to have been dominant.[4] At the same time, however, there is evidence to suggest that overall productivity growth has been supported largely by stabilization and adjustment gains related to postwar recovery. Consequently, prospects for sustaining productivity growth over the long term are uncertain. These issues are considered further, based upon an understanding of past growth dynamics, via a simple macroeconomic growth projections model. The results from this exercise confirm the importance of maintaining an unbiased growth pattern in which sustained productivity improvements play a central role. They also show that institutional strengthening, strategic management of foreign aid, and continued expansion of access to education at all levels will be critical.

In pursuing the analysis, a number of specific research contributions are made. First, rather than focusing only on aggregate factors of production, an index decomposition technique is used to quantify the contributions of both labor and physical capital stock subfactors. With regard to labor, this involves elaborating new estimates of changes in human capital quality via education for the period. Second, rigorous (cointegration) techniques are applied to assure the quality of the growth accounting estimates. Third, in order to understand observed changes in total factor productivity, the part explained by movements in capacity utilization is estimated. Fourth, with respect to the projections model, this study employs a new proxy for absorptive-capacity constraints associated with foreign aid. Moreover, the

[4]There is an intricate vocabulary surrounding patterns of growth. Thus, the term "unbiased" is used to avoid confusion with terms such as "balanced" or "complementary."

inclusion of this proxy and the specification of the model are validated by calibration on historical data.

The remainder of this chapter is structured as follows: the next section gives a brief review of the academic growth literature, concentrating on insights into the question of sustaining growth in developing countries; the third section describes the technique of growth accounting, reviewing its basis in economic theory before moving to a description of the empirical method and data sources adopted here. The growth accounting results are presented in the fourth section, starting with a review of previous studies for Mozambique, followed by the findings and analysis of this exercise. The fifth section presents the macroeconomic-growth-projections model that is used to quantify the aggregate impact of emerging policy challenges. The sixth section reflects on these findings to provide some general lessons for sub-Saharan Africa; the final section presents some conclusions. Note that to enhance readability technical aspects are reserved for separate appendixes.

By way of a caveat, this analysis does not make specific reference to the economic impact of a handful of large industrial projects (known as megaprojects) initiated in the postwar period. Close consideration also is not given to the potentially large output contribution from future natural resource extraction initiatives. This is not to deny their economic importance. To date, however, these activities have been foreign owned, have enjoyed generous fiscal benefits, and have shown only minimal backward linkages. As such, their contribution to past domestic (national) income growth has been limited. Their future role also raises a range of specific policy issues that are more appropriately treated separately, as in Chapters 1, 8, and 9.

Understanding Sustained Growth

Previous research that has sought to identify how public policy can promote sustained growth typically employs cross-country econometric methods. On the one hand, these are used because growth accounting, which focuses on proximate growth determinants (see the next section), is not suited for quantifying the contributions of individual microeconomic policy choices to growth. On the other hand, there is an absence of counterfactual evidence at the country level that can be used to estimate a robust relationship between growth outcomes and policy choices. Although cross-country econometric methods can be extremely powerful, their limitations have been noted widely and particularly in relation to growth dynamics (for example, Durlauf, Johnson, and Temple, 2005; Temple, 2000). Observing a significant correlation between a given policy variable and output growth does not signify a robust one-way causative relationship. Moreover, if policies can be understood as rules mapping states of the world to actions (World Bank, 2005a, Chapter 8), one can hardly expect average regression results for an aggregate policy measure to indicate the best conditional rules (policies) and implementation measures for a specific country to follow. There is also, of course, the separate matter of how cross-country differences in these policies should be measured.

Both in light of these concerns and in recognition of the endogeneity surrounding policy choices, much recent scholarship views generic policy prescriptions with skepticism. Past growth is traced to specific aspects of geography, political-institutional history, and factor endowments. Thus, as set out in Rodrik (2004), policymakers are advised to focus on specific distortions at the country level. This is not to say, however, that the cross-country regression literature has nothing to offer. Perhaps its clearest advice applies to how economic growth can be undermined. Research indicates numerous factors that weaken growth in a quantifiable way across countries over time. These include armed conflict, extreme economic and political polarization, unsustainable management of public finances (for example, high fiscal deficits), hyperinflation, and political instability, to name just a few. For exchange rate valuation, although there is some evidence that undervaluation can boost growth via export competitiveness, a clearer empirical result is that substantial exchange rate volatility undermines growth (Berg, Ostry, and Zettelmeyer, 2006). Of course, the origins of these growth-inhibiting factors are often in deeper political economy processes; even so, the historical record suggests that many countries have failed to achieve the minimal political and economic preconditions needed to support sustained growth.

A second insight derives from economic theory. This tells us that the proximate determinants of economic growth are enhancements in factor productivity and the accumulation of stocks of physical and human capital. These variables, described here as aggregate growth drivers, provide a consistent framework for thinking about growth. In other words, policies to enhance growth must be expected to have an impact on at least one of them. On this basis, a noteworthy characteristic of sustained growth episodes has been the realization of consistent gains across each of these growth drivers. Recent research on East Asia, for example, interprets the "remarkable" growth rates achieved in some countries as being precisely due to the combination of rapid factor accumulation with sustained productivity enhancements (IMF, 2006, Chapter 3). Simply put, as long as we accept some form of diminishing returns to factor accumulation, aggregate productivity must be integral to sustained growth. This point is supported by scholarship that investigates the specific factors associated with sustained, as opposed to temporary, growth episodes. A broad finding is that consistent productivity gains are present in the former episodes but absent in the latter. Hausmann, Pritchett, and Rodrik (2005), for example, find that the partial impact of positive terms of trade shocks is confined to temporary growth spurts. In contrast, deeper institutional reforms that hold implications for market functioning (efficiency) are associated with sustained growth episodes, although these are highly idiosyncratic in nature. These arguments are confirmed by the considerable weight of research that posits a strong relationship between high-quality institutions and rapid productivity growth (for example, Bosworth and Collins, 2003; IMF, 2006).

The preceding should not be taken to weaken the case for factor accumulation. Investment in physical capital is one of the few variables robustly and positively associated with growth in cross-country regressions (for example, Levine and Renelt, 1991).[5] From a developing country perspective, sustained investments in core public goods (for example, infrastructure) may be necessary to reduce private transaction costs, resolve coordination problems, and thus stimulate private sector growth. Also, referring once again to the experience of the NIEs, investment in export-related industries has been a characteristic feature of their growth success. Without these sector-specific investments, it is hard to envisage how these countries would have been able to move up the global value-chain (IMF, 2006). Although private and public investment can be critical, the experience of many African countries shows that accumulation is not sufficient, in itself, to generate growth (Easterly, 1997). Indeed, recent improvements in African growth rates since the late 1990s have been ascribed to productivity growth linked to improved macroeconomic stability and the quality of public financial management (Carey, Gupta, and Pattillo, 2005).

With respect to the accumulation of human capital, even scholars who question the nature of the link between growth and education do not hold that improvements in human capital quality via education are irrelevant. As Pritchett (1996) argues, the education puzzle is more about finding a consistent relationship between the (weak) macro and (strong) micro evidence for the productivity-enhancing effects of education. Part

[5]Interpretation of this relationship, however, is not straightforward, given the potential simultaneity between investment and output growth (see Durlauf, Johnson, and Temple, 2005).

of this puzzle is methodological. Especially at the cross-country level, it has not been resolved how to adjust for either differences in the quality of education outcomes, on which there is only poor information, or the match between labor supply and employment demand. These difficulties echo those encountered in identifying a robust relationship between foreign aid and growth. Relevant here is Tarp's (2006) reminder of the iron law of regressions—that with a "dirty" dependent variable (growth), noisy data, and weak proxies, results are biased toward zero. Michaelowa's (2000) survey of evidence for returns to education in Africa confirms the depth of these methodological difficulties, concluding that there are no reliable estimates of the effect of education on growth. Findings from growth accounting exercises that include adjustments for education also must be interpreted with caution. The relative volatility of growth rates compared with the smoother but slower rate of change in human capital quality means that these types of results provide no clear basis on which to derive benchmark estimates of the elasticity of income with respect to education.

In sum, although a policy blueprint for sustained growth cannot be expected, the literature does provide guidance in a number of areas. First, a broad set of preconditions must be in place for growth to "stick." Second, activities that generate a relatively unbiased pattern of growth should be encouraged. For developing countries with large aid inflows, the binding constraint in this regard may not be aggregate investment. Rather, combining human capital improvements with continued productivity gains in strategic sectors may be the fundamental challenge.

Growth Accounting

Theoretical Framework

The central idea behind growth accounting, which finds its origins in the work of Solow (1957), is to explore the proximate determinants of economic growth based on an aggregate production function. In general terms, aggregate output is expressed as a function of accumulated factor inputs and their use-efficiency; that is, $Y = F$ (factors, efficiency). A key empirical problem underlying any growth accounting exercise is how to move from a general functional form to a valid, workable representation of this relationship. For this, it is standard to make two core assumptions: efficiency changes are taken to be Hicks-neutral, in the sense that they apply equally across all factors of production; and factor prices are used as proxies for factor marginal social products. (For elaboration, see Barro, 1998.) Of course, these are not necessary simplifications and a range of other approaches have been used in the literature (see Caselli, 2005). Relaxation of these assumptions, however, generates considerable empirical complications that fall beyond the scope of this study and, therefore, are not considered.

It should be emphasized that growth accounting typically focuses on real changes on the supply side of the economy. As such, it does not quantify movements in nominal prices or terms of trade in either international or intersectoral terms. This means that various microeconomic determinants of accumulation and reallocation of resources may not be identifiable. For example, the effect of macroeconomic policies pertaining to exchange rate management or inflation control are not captured under this framework and therefore are necessarily excluded from the analysis for Mozambique. In recognition of their importance, however, these issues are discussed in depth in other chapters in this volume, including the contributions in Chapters 6 and 10.

Among the theoretical and empirical difficulties involved in growth accounting, two particular issues are relevant to this study. First, calculation and interpretation of factor efficiency remain controversial. This dimension is often directly associated with technical innovation and is described as total factor productivity (TFP). As set out in Hulten (2001), however, it is more appropriate to understand this term as reflecting a broad range of efficiency effects, including those deriving from differences in organization, institutional quality, and technical innovation. Moreover, since growth-accounting methods generally calculate TFP as a residual, it also captures errors arising from bias or mismeasurement in the other variables. As such, residual TFP (the term used hereinafter) may be little more than a "measure of our ignorance" (Abramovitz, 1956). What this means is that interpretation of movements in residual TFP can be ambiguous, necessitating additional analysis outside the aggregate growth accounting framework.

Second, methodological choices are important, since growth accounting results are sensitive to both measurement techniques and underlying assumptions (Jorgenson, 2005; Sarel, 1995). For this reason, accounting methods have been elaborated in numerous ways, with particular effort being focused on the measurement of labor and capital as well as how they enter the production function. Numerous studies have shown that the role of residual TFP growth typically falls once one accounts for movements in the quality or productivity of factor inputs. To put it another way, since factor inputs can embody technological and efficiency gains, the inclusion of quality-adjusted factors, as opposed to only their raw amounts, tends to considerably boost the estimated growth contribution of factor accumulation, with a corresponding reduction in residual TFP. This result has been shown to hold for both developed economies (see the references and estimates in Jorgenson, 2005) and cases of sustained growth in developing countries. For example, both Young (1994) and Bosworth, Collins, and Chen (1995) conclude that East Asian growth successes can be attributed principally to significant and sustained investments in human and physical capital rather than "miraculous" productivity growth alone.

Empirical Implementation

From the preceding review, an important message is that growth accounting must pay careful attention to measurement, making adjustments for factor quality where possible. The methodology adopted here permits the disaggregation of physical and human capital into various subcomponents via an index-decomposition approach. This technique is used to aggregate the effects of unequal changes in raw inputs (quantities) and marginal productivities (returns) into a meaningful composite growth measure for a given set of factors. The first step is to define real output in standard fashion as:

$$Y = A(K)^{a}(W)^{1-a}, \tag{1}$$

where Y denotes real output, A a measure of TFP, K physical capital, W a measure of economic services from human capital, and a the marginal social product of capital. When $0 \leq a \leq 1$, this is a Cobb-Douglas function, a special case of the translogarithmic function for which changes between two periods can be estimated by:

$$\ln(Y_t / Y_{t-1}) = \ln(A_t / A_{t-1}) + \bar{\theta}_K \ln(K_t / K_{t-1}) + \bar{\theta}_W \ln(W_t / W_{t-1}), \tag{2}$$

where $\bar{\theta}_i$ gives the average share of factor i in total factor payments over the two periods (Young, 1994). This equation forms the core of the methodology applied in this study. It represents a Tömqvist-translog index employed widely in the growth analysis literature as a discrete time approximation of the Divisia index.[6] The chain properties of the Tömqvist index are attractive, meaning it can be used as an aggregator for both physical and human capital subinputs. In other words, one can apply equation (2) in a hierarchical fashion to build up a detailed understanding of the contributions

[6]For discussion of index number theory with reference to economic growth, see Dean and Harper (1998).

of subfactors, such as different categories of labor and capital, to output growth. At the highest level of aggregation shown here, TFP is calculated as a residual, assuming that all other variables are known.

Although this represents a robust framework to estimate the contribution of various subfactors to aggregate growth, construction of the required indices can be problematic. Where data are inadequate, dirty, or unreliable, it is common for analysts to employ raw factor inputs and ignore quality adjustments. Although this has been true of the majority of previous growth accounting exercises for Mozambique (see subsection "Previous Studies" in the section "Accounting for Mozambican Growth" below), this study does not conform to that pattern. Rather, the required data series are constructed from a wide range of official Mozambican sources, including census, household survey, educational enrollment, and macroeconomic information. The relevance of this effort is underlined by the considerable socioeconomic changes that have swept Mozambique over the past 30 years. With respect to the quality of human capital, for example, education of the indigenous population was neglected during the colonial period, and on the eve of independence, approximately 93 percent of the population was illiterate. In response, education has remained a major policy priority, and considerable advances have been made in the educational profile of the population. Thus, these changes should be addressed within the growth accounting analysis.

Details of the methods used to estimate both the human capital and the physical capital stock series are summarized in Appendix I. For the former, the stocks of workers are split into three education categories (unskilled workers, those with primary education, and workers with at least a secondary education). For physical capital stocks, the disaggregation is between the public and the private sectors. At this point, it is worth highlighting four specific challenges encountered in constructing the required growth accounting data series. These are deriving robust estimates for (1) the starting value used to initialize the physical capital stock series; (2) the depreciation rate to apply to the physical capital stock; (3) the shares of aggregate factors in total output; and (4) the impact of changes in capacity utilization. Although it is known that decomposition results can be sensitive to different assumptions for these unknowns, numerous studies resort to standard rules of thumb (for example, cross-country averages) rather than rigorous, country-specific estimates. For Mozambique, the former tactic is not likely to be reliable, given the nature of the period in question. For example, the standard assumption of a constant annual rate of physical capital depreciation of about 5 percent is not coherent owing to the long-term effects of civil conflict as well as relatively rapid structural changes to the economy. In addition, although capacity utilization is often taken to be a cyclical phenomenon, and thus immaterial to long-term growth accounting, changes in usage may be particularly important in Mozambique given the previously mentioned events.

In keeping with the emphasis of this paper on measurement quality, econometric techniques are used to estimate the above unknowns. For the first three, an iterative process is employed to select values that optimize the overall fit of the relationship described in general form by equation (1). Details of the procedure, which requires the relevant variables to be cointegrated, are given in Appendix II, Cointegration Technique. With respect to capacity utilization, no direct adjustments are made to the growth accounting data. As a result, the effect (if any) of variations in capacity usage is incorporated in the overall estimate of residual TFP. The method adopted thus involves attempting to isolate the changes in residual TFP explained by variations in capacity utilization. To do so, changes in capacity utilization are proxied by movements of the output-capital ratio around its long-term trend. This derives from the assumption of a stable long-run (trend) relationship between output and the capital stock under competitive conditions. Further details of this technique are set out in Appendix II, Capacity Utilization.[7]

Accounting for Mozambican Growth

Previous Studies

Before presenting the results of this study, it is useful to review previous growth accounting exercises for Mozambique. As shown in Table 3.1, findings from these studies do not tell a consistent story. Even the contribution of labor force growth, perhaps the most straightforward factor input to measure, differs considerably between the studies. Clearly part of this variation derives from differences in the periods covered, data sources used, and methodologies applied. With regard to the underlying data, where Mozambique features as part of a multicountry study, it is common to employ secondary sources, such as international data sets, rather than original data. These differences underline the sensitivity of growth accounting results to methodological choices. Perhaps the only tenta-

[7]Studies employing similar methods include Young (1994) and Schwerdt and Turunen (2006); see also Kamps (2004) for discussion of disaggregation of the public sector's physical capital stock.

Table 3.1. Comparative Growth Accounting Evidence
(Annual rates of growth, in percent)

Period	Region /Country	Source	ΔY	Decomposition of ΔY			
				ΔA	ΔK	ΔL	ΔH
1960–96		(a)	1.7	0.9	0.8	0.1	
1960–2000		(b)	0.5	0.3	0.1		0.1
1960–2002	**Mozambique**	**(c)**	**3.6**	**0.3**	**2.3**	**1.0**	
1995–2000		(b)	4.9	3.7	1.1		0.1
1997–2002		(d)	8.6	3.5	3.2	1.3	0.6
1960–2000	Africa	(e)	3.2	–0.1	0.5	2.5	0.3
	East Asia	(e)	6.7	1.0	2.3	2.9	0.5
	Latin America	(e)	4.0	0.2	0.6	2.8	0.4
	South Asia	(e)	4.6	1.0	1.0	2.3	0.3
1990–2000	Africa	(e)	2.3	–0.5	–0.1	2.5	0.4
	East Asia	(e)	5.7	0.5	2.3	2.4	0.5
	Latin America	(e)	3.3	0.4	0.2	2.4	0.3
	South Asia	(e)	5.3	1.2	1.2	2.5	0.4

Sources: (a) Sulemane (2001); (b) Ndulu and O'Connell (2003); (c) Aka and others (2004); (d) Benito-Spinetto and Moll (2005); and (e) Bosworth and Collins (2003).

Notes: Estimates for East Asia exclude China; for source (e), regional estimates are GDP weighted; where labor (L) contribution is absent, all figures are in per worker terms; and where ΔH is absent, no adjustment is made for human capital quality.

tive conclusion one might make is that residual TFP growth has been an important feature of Mozambique's recent growth success. Over the long run, however, there is no unambiguous evidence for a consistent upward trend in this productivity measure.

Referring to international comparisons, which are shown in the bottom portion of the table, low-productivity growth appears to have been typical of African growth experiences over the last forty years. This point is made by Aka and others (2004), who argue that the disappointing growth seen across most of sub-Saharan Africa since 1960 can be traced to a bias toward factor accumulation (capital investment) and an absence of productivity gains. As shown in Table 3.1, the only aggregate growth driver for which Africa records a reasonable comparative performance (excluding labor growth) is human capital improvement. Following the discussion in the section "Understanding Sustained Growth," differences in regional growth experiences indicate that where one or more growth drivers records a relatively weak performance, sustained output also tends to be poor. This is evident for both Latin America and Africa. These estimates support the argument that successful periods of sustained growth typically depend on robust (unbiased) contributions from all growth drivers.

Results

Turning to the present growth accounting analysis, statistical tests confirm that it is appropriate to employ the optimization procedure based on the cointegration framework described in Appendix II, Cointegration Technique.[8] The results from this exercise are summarized in Table 3.2. As expected, the model gives an extremely strong overall fit, and the cointegration measure is highly significant, as desired. The aggregate factor shares are plausible and corroborate estimates based on social accounting matrices for Mozambique (Arndt and others, 1998; Arndt, Jensen, and Tarp, 2000; and Tarp and others, 2002) that put the share of capital in output at approximately 30 percent. Also, consistent with the impact of civil war, the depreciation rate is estimated to have followed a declining trend, falling from 18 percent to 6 percent over the period, with the midpoint coinciding exactly with the peace agreement reached in 1992.

Employing these results to finalize the growth accounting series, the decomposition technique allows us to split the contribution from human capital (W) either into the three education-based categories or into the separate effects of changes in labor force quantity (L) and quality (H). Table 3.3 gives the latter presentation, while Table 3.4 splits the capital and labor contributions into more detailed subfactor components. In both tables, the growth decomposition is given for the overall period (1980–2004) as well as for specific subperiods bounded by points of structural change (for example, civil war and immediate postwar reconstruction). Figure 3.1 shows the evolution of indices of the major growth components over the full period based on the annual rates of growth used to estimate equation (2).

With respect to residual TFP, Table 3.3 distinguishes between its estimated trend component, taken from the regression results, and remaining noise. Since residual TFP measures tend to capture numerous efficiency effects, however, the methodology described in Appendix II, Capacity Utilization, is applied. Table 3.5 summarizes these results, decomposing residual TFP into three components: the part explained by changes in capacity utilization, a remaining deep trend, and unexplained noise. From these decompositions, and as plotted in Figure 3.2, movements in residual TFP appear to be explained almost entirely by changes in capacity utilization. As discussed in the same appendix, however, where TFP changes are lumpy in nature owing to, among other things, large foreign direct invest-

[8]In other words, augmented Dickey-Fuller tests do not reject the null hypothesis that the variables in equation (A2) have unit roots, while a linear combination of them is stationary.

Table 3.2. Estimation of Long-Run Production Function

	Coefficients	Standard error
Capital stock *(K)*	0.28	(0.08)
Quality-adjusted labor *(W)*	0.72	(0.08)
TFP trend (1980–91)	–0.02	(0.00)
TFP trend (1992–2004)	0.03	(0.01)
Postwar dummy	–0.71	(0.13)
Constant	–2.60	(0.31)
Observations	25	
Log likelihood	53.65	
Average depreciation rate (1980–91)	15.25	
Average depreciation rate (1992–2004)	9.00	
Cointegration test†	–4.07	

Source: Author's calculations

Notes: All coefficients are significant at the 1 percent level; † denotes the value of the *t*-statistic calculated as per Engle and Granger (1987). TPF denotes total factor productivity.

ment (FDI) inflows and/or structural changes, this decomposition methodology may not accurately separate utilization changes from productivity effects. Given the tumultuous economic changes in Mozambique over the period, the strength of this finding must be treated with caution. Even so, micro evidence supports the view that capacity-utilization changes have broadly followed the trajectory indicated in Figure 3.2. According to Biggs, Nasir, and Fisman (1999), for example, firm-level capacity usage was less than 30 percent in 1989, rising to 48 percent in 1998. More recent surveys (Byiers and Rand, 2007) confirm that utilization rates have continued to rise, climbing to around 59 percent by 2005. Thus, these results can be regarded as indicative, but not precise, estimates of underlying determinants of residual TFP.

Civil War Decline

Reflecting on the results, output decline from 1980 to 1992 can be understood primarily in terms of physical capital contraction and productivity losses. With respect to the former, although the value of the public sector capital stock remained broadly stable in real terms during the period, private sector stocks suffered significant real reductions (see Table 3.4). This derives principally from the fact that public sector investment continued at a moderate pace through the war years, averaging 8 percent of GDP. In contrast, private sector investment was negligible, averaging only 1.3 percent. This differentiated pattern clearly indicates the higher sensitivity of private sector investment to economic stability and structural conditions.

Table 3.3. Aggregate Growth Decomposition

	ΔY	ΔTFP Trend†	ΔTFP Noise‡	ΔK	ΔW ΔL	ΔW ΔH
1980–91 (civil war)	–1.72	–2.13	–0.12	–0.66	0.81	0.38
	(100)	(124.1)	(6.9)	(38.3)	(–47.1)	(–22.3)
1992–98	5.22	2.62	–0.95	1.84	1.31	0.40
	(100)	(50.2)	(–18.2)	(35.2)	(25.1)	(7.7)
1999–2004	7.37	2.62	–1.51	3.84	1.50	0.92
	(100)	(35.6)	(–20.5)	(52.2)	(20.3)	(12.4)
1980–2004 (full)	2.58	0.44	–0.71	1.20	1.13	0.52
	(100)	(17.1)	(–27.6)	(46.4)	(43.8)	(20.3)

Source: Author's calculations.

Notes: Figures in parentheses are in percent; † is derived from the results shown in Table 3.2; and ‡ denotes remaining, unexplained residual TFP movements. TFP denotes total factor productivity.

Declines in productivity during the civil war are evident in both overall and trend estimates for residual TFP. In broad terms, this accords with evidence for the period that documents major shortages of primary inputs, electricity blackouts, and transportation difficulties (Arndt, Jones, and Tarp, 2007). As was to be expected, much of this is captured by the capacity-utilization component, suggesting that the remaining trend decline in factor productivity (efficiency) was less intense, at only –0.6 percent per year (versus –2.3 percent overall). Illustrated in Figure 3.2, the capacity-utilization component shows an extremely sharp decline during 1980–85, followed by a period of relative stabilization through 1990. The former result is consistent with a rapid tightening of production constraints during the early 1980s owing to the deteriorating conflict and foreign exchange shortages, which were compounded by extensive price controls. The flatter trend of the latter period coincides with the introduction of economic stabilization and adjustment measures beginning in 1985 that are likely to have eased certain production constraints.

Changes in capacity utilization, however, are not the entire story, given the remaining trend decline in deep TFP. A number of effects may be behind this. First, the pervasive disruption caused by conflict, including internal displacement, is likely to have generated substantial (heightened) inefficiencies in market functioning. This may be particularly the case in labor markets despite (slow) expansion of access to education during the civil war. The trend decline in deep TFP therefore may reflect the negative productivity spillovers from market inefficiencies associated with the war. Second, the civil war was marked by a series of natural disasters, including both floods and droughts (Hall and Young, 1997). Given the residual nature of TFP and the high frequency of these disasters, it is plausible that

Table 3.4. Subfactor Growth Decomposition

	ΔY	ΔTFP	ΔK		ΔW		
			ΔK_g	ΔK_p	ΔU	ΔEP	ΔES
1980–91 (civil war)	–1.72	–2.25	0.22	–0.88	0.26	0.78	0.16
	(100)	(131.0)	(–13.0)	(51.3)	(–15.0)	(–45.3)	(–9.1)
1992–98	5.22	1.67	0.58	1.26	0.58	0.79	0.34
	(100)	(32.0)	(11.2)	(24.0)	(11.1)	(15.2)	(6.5)
1999–2004	7.37	1.11	1.33	2.52	0.25	1.31	0.85
	(100)	(15.0)	(18.0)	(34.2)	(3.4)	(17.8)	(11.6)
1980–2004 (full)	2.58	–0.27	0.60	0.59	0.35	0.92	0.38
	(100)	(–10.4)	(23.5)	(22.9)	(13.5)	(35.6)	(14.9)

Source: Author's calculations.

Notes: Figures in parentheses are in percent; only residual total factor productivity (TFP) is shown; K_g and K_p denote government and private sector capital stocks; U denotes unskilled workers; EP and ES denote workers with primary and secondary school qualifications, respectively.

the negative TFP trend may also be capturing the harmful impact of these events on total output.

Postwar Recovery

Turning to the period beginning in 1992, accumulation (rehabilitation) of the physical capital stock consistently explains a large part of output growth (around 45 percent). The breakdown of physical capital's contribution into private and public sector components (Table 3.4) reveals the comparatively larger role of private capital accumulation in the postwar phase, for which it explains two-thirds of capital's overall contribution to growth. Echoing the dominance of private sector capital stock contraction during the war, this highlights the central role of private sector recovery in Mozambique's postwar success. In comparison with the more stable public sector savings, private sector savings have grown rapidly in the postwar phase, reaching an average rate of 12.8 percent of GDP during 1999–2004. In particular, private sector investment has been boosted by inflows of new (as opposed to returning) foreign investment. According to Bank of Mozambique statistics, FDI was almost zero during the civil war and grew only negligibly in the immediate postwar phase. Recently, however, Mozambique has experienced a comparative FDI boom, receiving an average of around US$250 million per year, which is equivalent to 6 percent of its GDP, in such investments. While a large portion of this refers to a small number of large, capital-intensive industrial projects, one should not discount the considerable number of smaller investors in tourism and other industries that have provided a stimulus to the construction sector, employment creation, and, thus, output growth. That this has occurred

Figure 3.1. Indices of Major Growth Components Based on Growth Accounting Results
(Indexed at 1990 = 100)

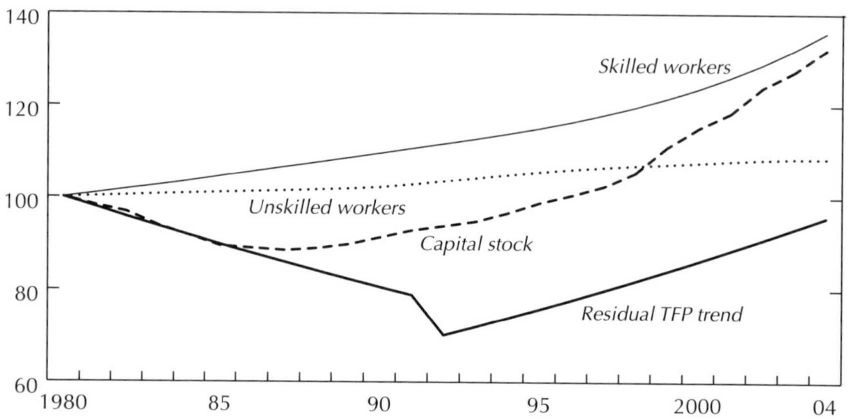

Source: Author's calculations.
Note: TFP = total factor productivity.

primarily in the later postwar period attests to the need for economic and political stability to be credible before external investors are willing to move. In turn, these findings underline the essential contributions of enhanced macroeconomic stability and institutional reforms in improving the business environment.

This is not to negate the critical contribution of public sector investment to postwar growth. In this context, it should be highlighted that foreign aid to Mozambique has financed, on average, the totality of government investment both during and after the civil war (Arndt, Jones, and Tarp, 2007). With recent increases in net aid to the government, deriving in part from considerable bilateral and multilateral debt cancellation, the estimated contribution of public sector investment to aggregate output growth has risen to 18 percent for 1999–2004 (see Table 3.4). These estimates, however, do not fully capture the positive spillover effects (externalities) from investments in both public infrastructure and education. Given the paucity of these goods at the end of prolonged conflict, the magnitude of social returns to public investments (and, by association, foreign aid) is likely to have been significant for Mozambique. Of course, and as is discussed further in the next section, this statement should not be taken as arguing that one can expect high returns from aid in the future.

Table 3.5. Decomposition of Overall Residual TFP Growth

	Δ*TFP*	ΔCapacity†	Trend‡	Noise††
1980–91 (civil war)	–2.25	–2.25	–0.59	0.59
	(100)	(100.0)	(26.0)	(–26.0)
1992–98	1.67	1.44	0.57	–0.33
	(100)	(86.0)	(34.0)	(–20.0)
1999–2004	1.11	1.38	0.57	–0.84
	(100)	(124.7)	(51.3)	(–76.0)
1980–2004 (full)	–0.27	–0.27	0.04	–0.04
	(100)	(100.1)	(–14.7)	(14.6)

Source: Author's calculations.

Notes: Figures in parentheses are in percent; † denotes the component explained by changes in capacity utilization; ‡ denotes the deep trend in total factor productivity (TFP) growth after adjusting for capacity utilization; and †† denotes the remaining unexplained (short-term) variation.

Changes in the quality of human capital are also an important part of the growth story. If one focuses on the pure gain associated with changes in education (ΔH in Table 3.3), it will become apparent that its relative and absolute contribution to output growth has risen consistently throughout the postwar period. When expressed in terms of a percentage point contribution to growth, the 0.92 estimate for 1999–2004 is also extremely impressive by global standards (see Table 3.1).[9] This figure reflects the extremely low educational base, even by African standards, from which Mozambique has progressed. For example, according to the estimates developed here, in 1980 a staggering 93 percent of the economically active working population had no formal educational qualifications. This had declined to 85 percent by 1992 and then to 74 percent in 2004, a fall of 11 percentage points in the postwar period alone. Thus, sustained investments in education, which were in large part financed by foreign aid, have made a central contribution to postwar growth.

A review of the structure of changes in the workforce is of further interest. First, there has been a distinct upward shift in the overall rate of growth of the active labor force compared with the civil war period (Table 3.4), reflecting not only the absence of conflict but also more general improvements in health and incomes since 1992. This growth has not been equally distributed across all labor categories, however. Even in terms of pure numbers (that is, ignoring productivity differences), the cohort of skilled workers has grown much more rapidly than the unskilled cohort. Table 3.4 shows that the growth contribution of unskilled workers has followed a declining trend in the postwar period, explaining less than

[9]Of course, this estimate for Mozambique refers to a relatively short time frame; the challenge, as discussed in the next section, will be to maintain this performance.

Figure 3.2. Decomposition of Residual Total Factor Productivity
(Indexed at 1980 = 100)

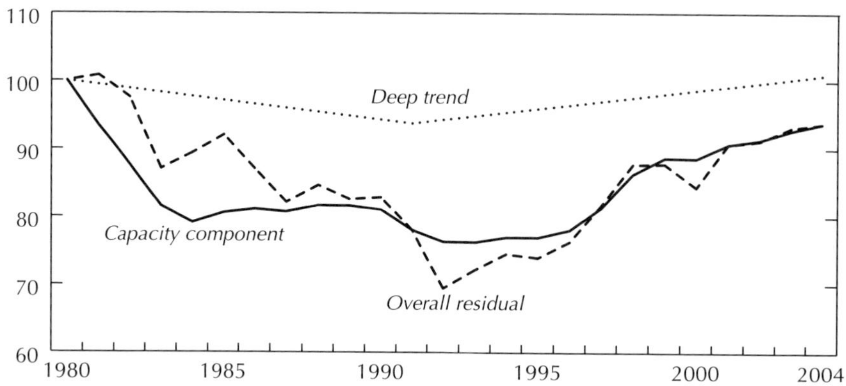

Source: Author's calculations.

5 percent of aggregate growth since 1999. Consistent with the government's emphasis on expansion of the primary education sector, workers with a primary education have made the largest contribution of all labor categories to total value added in the postwar period. The cohort with a secondary school education, however, has witnessed the fastest expansion since 1992, explaining 11.6 percent of total value added for 1999–2004, against 6.5 percent for 1992–98. As such, the contribution of skilled labor to growth is being increasingly driven by secondary-level education, suggesting that further expansion at this level and beyond will be necessary to support future employment demands.

Turning to residual TFP, Table 3.4 shows that this measure has made a 1.4 percentage point (or 23 percent) annual average contribution to postwar output growth. Although this recovery is somewhat lower than the rate of decline during the civil war (–2.3 percentage points a year), the size of the TFP residual should be interpreted with caution. As noted previously, the civil war years were affected by a series of natural disasters. In contrast, and aside from notable exceptions, the postwar period has been more benign, on average. In fact, this point helps explain the substantially higher trend rate of residual TFP growth in the postwar period (2.6 percent), compared with the overall residual (1.4 percent). The lower value reflects the large shocks attributable to severe droughts in 1992 and massive floods in 2001. To put it another way, the effects of these disasters are captured by the negative noise term in Table 3.3. Despite this difference, the overall rate of residual TFP growth is far from disappointing by international standards. As shown in Table 3.1, East Asian countries achieved an average annual rate of residual TFP growth of about 1 percent for 1960–2000. The detailed tables in Ndulu and O'Connell (2003), based on the same approach and period, not only confirm this result but also reveal that of all sub-Saharan African countries in the sample, only Mauritius achieved an average rate of residual TFP growth exceeding 1 percent. Furthermore, if the larger underlying trend in residual TFP growth is used as a comparator, Mozambique's performance since 1992 ranks alongside the residual TFP growth rates achieved by both India (1.6 percent) and China (3.8 percent) since the late 1970s (as estimated in Bosworth and Collins, 2006). In sum, postwar growth has been supported by sustained gains in factor productivity as measured by residual TFP.

A fundamental question for Mozambique, however, is whether this pattern of TFP growth can be sustained as opposed to being a temporary, post-conflict phenomenon. Three arguments warn against an overly optimistic interpretation of the recent Mozambican TFP record. First, the capacity-utilization decomposition suggests that postwar changes in the TFP residual have been driven largely by an improvement in utilization rates. As such, deep postwar TFP growth may have been more modest, at about 0.57 percent (trend).[10] Notably, however, the component of residual TFP growth associated with capacity utilization does not indicate an immediate postwar recovery (see Figure 3.2). Sustained gains were evident only after 1995, following the consolidation of peace by means of multiparty elections in 1994, and continued through 2005, albeit at a slower rate more recently. This reveals that post-conflict recovery is long term in nature and remains an ongoing process.

Second, complementary evidence supports the general argument that productivity has not shown unambiguous aggregate gains in recent years. In contrast to an expected trend increase in the output-capital ratio owing to productivity improvements, Figure 3.3 shows that this ratio has followed a declining path during the postwar period, indicating a bias toward capital accumulation rather than (intensive) productivity enhancements. At the sectoral level, research summarized in Benito-Spinetto and Moll (2005) for the agricultural sector suggests that yields for many crops have remained stagnant since the mid-1990s and, in many cases, have remained below prewar levels. Although this is not to ignore isolated cases of relative success, such as in the tobacco sector, postwar growth in smallholder farm-

[10]Of course, although this growth rate is inferior to those of East Asian countries, it is far superior to the African average, as may be seen in Table 3.1.

Figure 3.3. Scatter Plot of Output-Capital and Output-Labor Ratios, by Year

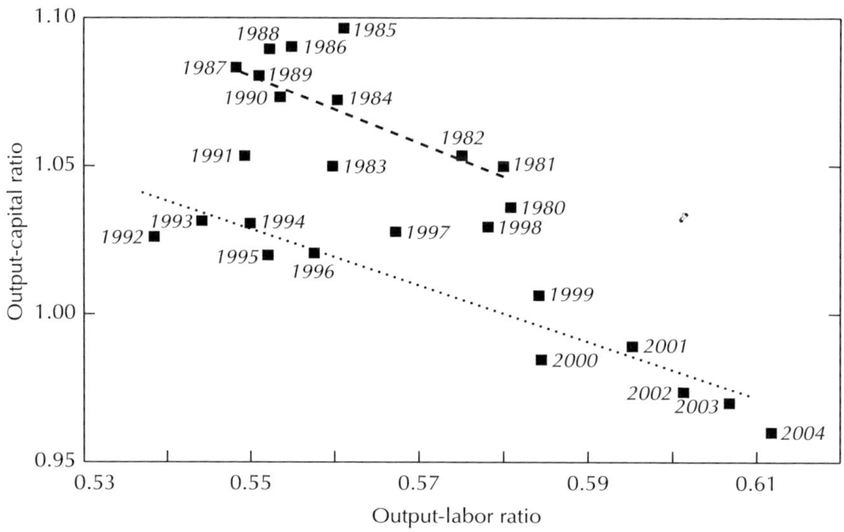

Source: Author's calculations.

ing, which accounts for the vast majority of agricultural output, appears to have been based on the return of populations to rural areas and trend expansion in land use, rather than robust productivity jumps. Finally, and taking a longer-term view, none of the TFP measures suggest that there has been an unambiguous upward shift in aggregate productivity (efficiency) since 1980. For 1980–2004, the growth rate of overall residual TFP is estimated to have averaged –0.27 percent; the underlying trend in the same residual has averaged 0.44 percent; and the deep trend has averaged only 0.04 percent. These results imply that any long-term productivity improvements have been moderate at best.

In summary, postwar growth in Mozambique has been founded on robust (unbiased) contributions from all principal growth drivers. Solid improvements in the quality of the human capital stock have accompanied significant capital deepening and residual TFP growth. Even so, the sustainability of observed productivity gains remains in doubt. Evidence suggests that during the civil war Mozambique was producing at a point well within its production-possibilities frontier. Postwar growth in residual TFP appears to have been dominated by movement toward this hypothetical frontier rather than outward movements of the frontier itself. Although recovery of this nature is a necessary foundation for future productivity gains, maintaining growth rates at their recent high levels may become increasingly difficult as easy gains from postwar recovery diminish.

Toward Sustained Growth

Quantitative Model

Based on the preceding analysis of past growth patterns, this section considers the challenges of future growth. Taking an aggregate production function as a starting point, simple behavioral dynamics are added in order to specify endogenous and exogenous sources of growth over time. Described formally in Appendix III, the model focuses on the relationship between output growth, productivity, and factor investment for 2005–30. In this respect, it has a broad affinity with World Bank "investment gap" models (for an overview, see Tarp, 1993, Chapter 4) although, in this case, variables referring to external accounts are not included. A critical assumption underlying this exercise is that necessary growth preconditions hold over the long term. Thus, referring back to the discussion in the section "Understanding Sustained Growth" above, these imply that macroeconomic policies are not highly distortionary and achieve reasonable stability across key policy targets such as the real exchange rate. In sum, the model aims to highlight aggregate challenges that may differentiate between episodes of sustained rapid growth and disappointing low-growth performances.

Adding simple behavioral functions to the growth accounting framework allows the relationship between growth and specific policy challenges to be illuminated. Two particular issues are reflected in the model echoing concerns identified in the government's recent Poverty Reduction Strategy Paper (Mozambique Ministry of Planning and Development, 2006b). First, the prevalence of HIV/AIDS in the working population is assumed to affect (negatively) labor force growth, investment, and human capital quality as suggested in the literature.[11] Second, foreign aid is included as a core source of funds to finance public investment. This reflects Mozambique's historical dependence on aid, the low (current) rates

[11]See the contributions in Haacker (2004) and, for Mozambique, Arndt (2006). Note that the model does not account for some of the more complex dynamics associated with HIV/AIDS, such as the lag between infection and symptom onset, or the role of antiretroviral therapies.

of domestic saving, and the sheer scale of the development challenge. The baseline assumption, discussed later on, is that aid is stable at 12 percent of GDP, versus almost 25 percent of GDP in the postwar period. In light of both Mozambique's macroeconomic record and international moves toward the scaling-up of external aid, this is not wholly unreasonable.

It would be naïve, however, to assume that foreign aid is always growth enhancing. Two further variables are therefore introduced to capture some of the more complex effects surrounding foreign aid. The first is the government investment share *j*. Assuming, for simplicity, that aid directly enhances growth only via government investment (see equation (A11) in Appendix III, Behavioral Dynamics), *j* reflects the point that where aid finances recurrent consumption, its long-term growth effects may be reduced. As discussed in Yang, Gupta, and Powell (2005), use of aid to fund domestic recurrent expenditure, as opposed to investment, may undermine growth via Dutch disease effects. The second variable is a measure of aid-related absorptive capacity *f*, proxied by the ratio of external aid to total investment.[12] The hypothesis is that a relatively high level of aid may generate negative side effects. While formal modeling of absorptive capacity is in its infancy (for a discussion, see Bourguignon and Sundberg, 2006), and no comprehensive treatment is attempted here, numerous scholars argue that returns to aid may be diminishing after some saturation point is reached or even turn negative at high levels (Lensink and White, 2001). In the model, absorptive-capacity pressures operate through private investment and improvements in the quality of human capital. The former is intended to reflect investment efficiency and incentive effects, while the latter reflects labor market effects, including the challenge for Mozambique of maintaining educational quality in the face of rapid, aid-financed expansion of the school network. (See Arndt, Jones, and Tarp, 2007.)

The model is employed to examine growth scenarios generated from different assumptions. As a starting point, it is helpful to set out a "base case" against which other scenarios can be compared, the objective being to create a plausible but positive growth path that follows smoothly from current conditions. The values chosen for the exogenous variables under this scenario are summarized in Table 3.6. The majority of these are based on recent trends in the Mozambican data and need little justification. Of note is the choice of 1.4 percent growth in exogenous TFP, which is equal to the average value of overall residual TFP growth during the postwar

[12]Note that this should not be confused with the national accounting concept of absorption; see also Yang, Gupta, and Powell (2005).

Table 3.6. Sensitivity of 2030 Income per Worker to Simulations of Individual Changes in Calibrated Parameters and Base Case Exogenous Variables

Description		Label	Value†	SE	ΔY/L by 2030‡ −%	+%
Variables	Labor force growth	*n*	2.55		5.6	−4.2
	HIV/AIDS prevalence	*v*	15.60		10.9	−12.6
	Government revenue in GDP	*r*	15.00		−17.8	19.2
	Aid in GDP	*x*	12.00		−10.1	11.3
	Government investment share	*j*	0.40		−31.3	35.8
	FDI in GDP	*z*	5.00		−8.2	8.0
	TFP growth	*a*	1.00		−21.1	27.0
Parameters	*p* (lag growth)	ρ_0	0.50	0.00	−0.1	0.1
	p (government investment)	ρ_1	0.33	0.00	−0.2	0.2
	p (absorptive capacity)	ρ_2	−0.11	0.02	−0.1	0.1
	p (inflation)††	ρ_3	0.00	0.02	.	.
	Δ*H* (government investment)	η_0	0.19	0.02	−5.7	6.1
	Δ*H* (private investment)	η_1	0.02	0.01	−2.1	2.2
	Δ*H* (absorptive capacity)	η_2	−0.58	0.06	−1.7	1.7

Source: Author's calculations.

Note: † denotes base case values for exogenous variables (top) and calibrated parameter estimates (bottom) as explained in the text; ‡ denotes the percentage change to per worker income in 2030 versus the base case: simulations for variables represent shifts of ±50 percent; simulations for parameters are equal to ±2 standard errors (SE); †† denotes that a parameter is not simulated, since it is excluded from the model.

period. Clearly, this is higher than the trend rate of deep TFP growth and remains relatively strong in comparison with long-term estimates for many developing regions, including East Asia (see Table 3.6). The plausibility of this assumption is discussed later on.

Model Calibration

To validate the model and to enhance its realism for Mozambique, the model parameters are calibrated econometrically. Specifically, a Seemingly Unrelated Regression (SUR) technique (Zellner, 1962) is employed based on the growth accounting data set and additional historical data. Equations (A12) through (A14) in Appendix III, Behavioral Dynamics, are estimated in this manner and the results are summarized in Table 3.6, giving both the estimated values and the standard errors for each of the parameters.[13]

[13]Although the final TFP equation includes no parameters, it is added to the SUR system as a form of control, including only a constant plus a postwar dummy variable on the right-hand side. In no case is adjustment made for HIV/AIDS prevalence *v* owing to its limited impact in the past. To remove noise, variables are smoothed using a Hodrick-Prescott filter. Estimation of equation (A10) is discussed in Appendix III, Behavioral Dynamics.

Excluding inflation, which is subsequently dropped from the model, all parameters are significant at the 1 percent confidence level. All significant parameters are also of the expected sign, being negative for absorptive capacity and positive otherwise.[14] Of note are the strong positive results relating to government investment in both the private investment and the human capital growth functions. The latter underlines the key role of (public) education in boosting labor productivity; the former indicates the complementarity between public and private investment in Mozambique as discussed above in the subsection "Postwar Recovery." In sum, the calibration method provides empirical support for the specification.

Confirmation of the suitability of the calibrated parameters is given by sensitivity tests. Employing the base case values for the exogenous variables, a variation of two standard errors (negative and positive) in each of the parameters is simulated. For each simulation, the impact is measured as the percentage change in per worker income in 2030 versus the base case level. As indicated in Table 3.6, the average absolute impact of the simulation yields a very small (1.7 percent) change in 2030 income. The largest impact from the simulation is 6 percent (parameter η_0), reflecting the key role of government investment in human capital growth in the model. Note, however, that the calibration is based on historical trends, which saw extremely rapid growth of human capital, particularly in the postwar period. Thus, this same parameter is adjusted by a factor of 0.75 under the base case scenario, reflecting the arithmetic logic behind the assertion that as average education levels rise, maintaining a constant rate of human capital growth will become increasingly difficult. Despite this adjustment, the sensitivity tests indicate the model is stable with respect to moderate measurement error in the parameters.

Policy Results

Insights regarding the opportunities and threats to sustained growth are given by the sensitivity tests applied to the exogenous variables (Table 3.6). These simulate the impact on per worker income in 2030 of a 50 percent variation in the base case values. The scenarios given in Table 3.7 go further, showing the impact on the overall pattern of growth of different (combined)

---

[14]Although the negative sign on the absorptive-capacity parameters is based on past trends, this principally reflects the fact that, at the height of the civil war, foreign aid was the only major source of investment finance. The value for *f* peaked at the end of the war, declining consistently thereafter to a fourth of its peak value by 2004.

Table 3.7. Long-Term Growth Scenario

Scenario	Period	ΔY	$\Delta Y/L$	ΔTFP	ΔK	ΔH
Base case	2005–15	5.34	3.57	1.31	1.67	0.59
	2016–30	4.76	3.04	1.30	1.16	0.58
Zero HIV/AIDS	2005–15	7.33	4.78	1.41	2.40	0.97
	2016–30	6.50	3.95	1.41	1.58	0.96
Weak education	2005–15	4.66	2.90	1.31	1.54	0.05
	2016–30	3.97	2.25	1.30	0.90	0.04
Negative	2005–15	2.67	0.96	0.65	0.22	0.09
	2016–30	2.66	0.94	0.65	0.21	0.08
Positive	2005–15	7.26	4.93	1.66	2.39	0.88
	2016–30	5.82	3.97	1.63	1.55	0.79

Source: Author's calculations.

Notes: Projections are based on the model set out in Appendix III; contribution of labor force growth is given by the difference between ΔY and $\Delta Y/L$; scenarios are described in the text; all figures are average annual growth rates.

assumptions for both the exogenous variables and parameter values. The main policy issues revealed by these two exercises are discussed below.

Base case potential

The base case holds inherent interest, projecting average annual real output growth of 5.3 percent (3.6 percent per worker) through 2015, followed by a slightly slower rate from 2016 to 2030.[15] This scenario reflects trends in the recent data and suggests that prospects for sustained economic growth are good, in turn confirming the World Bank's (2005b) baseline forecast of a 5 percent annual potential growth rate for the country over the long term. This upside potential can be traced to various features of the Mozambican economy (discussed further later on), including the valuable demonstration effect of successful growth and poverty reduction since 1992. Under this scenario, the relative composition of growth is highly comparable to the country's postwar experience, indicating a continuation of an unbiased growth pattern. Even so, with diminishing returns to new investments and moderate expectations of productivity growth, the base case suggests that the 7.5 percent average growth rate achieved over 1992–2004 may not be sustained easily. Moreover, this scenario presumes that the government is able to facilitate a successful graduation from postwar recovery to ongoing economic transformation. As already indicated with regard to productivity growth, this task may become increasingly demanding as the nature of the growth challenge evolves.

[15]Unless otherwise indicated, references to output growth are stated in aggregate, rather than per worker, terms.

Productivity growth

A salient result from the sensitivity tests is the comparatively large impact of movements in the exogenous component of TFP growth. A 50 percent increase in this component generates a 27.0 percent increment in income per worker by 2030 compared with the base case. Slightly smaller contractions derive from a 50 percent reduction, with the difference owing to the dynamic structure of the model. Even under the base case, the contribution of TFP growth to total output growth remains around 25 percent. It is recognized that to the extent that such strong rates of TFP growth are realistic for Mozambique, the potential for catch-up is enormous. This is quantified by estimates in Eifert, Gelb, and Ramachandran (2005) based on firm-survey data, which suggest that Mozambican TFP is not only less than a third of China's but also one of the lowest in their sample of African and Asian countries. The potential for technological enhancement is clear in the agricultural sector, where use of irrigation technology, fertilizer, and improved seeds remains minimal (see Arndt, Jones, and Tarp, 2007; and World Bank, 2005b). Scope for significant TFP gains also comes from second-generation reforms aimed at strengthening public institutions and regulatory structures. As was discussed above, institutional quality has been robustly associated with overall levels of productivity and economic development (see also Rodrik and Subramanian, 2004). Institutional upgrading is consistently highlighted as a key policy priority for Mozambique. For example, a recent review conducted by the main foreign donors (jointly with the government) singles out justice sector weaknesses as a major preoccupation (Mozambique Ministry of Planning and Development, 2006a). In addition, an effective regulatory structure pertaining to land access and use is likely to become increasingly essential, given the considerable growth potential of agriculture and tourism. This point is well understood by the Mozambican government, and numerous institutional reforms are envisaged under the current poverty reduction strategy. Although these are likely to be challenging, the model indicates that failure to achieve institutional reform could seriously jeopardize future growth potential.

Capital investment

Both the sensitivity tests and the growth scenarios underline the need to maintain high levels of investment in fixed capital. Under the base case, effective investment averages approximately 18 percent of GDP, of which about half is from the private sector. To achieve this, the policy focus evidently falls on raising domestic savings—for example, via financial deepening—and continuing to attract foreign investment. Given Mozambique's reasonable natural resource base and strategic location close to South Africa, prospects for foreign investment remain good. The growth challenge, however, will be to ensure strong backward linkages from new investments. With respect to the public sector, the model confirms the importance of maintaining a robust investment share *j*. A dramatic cut in this share to 20 percent of total available public funds generates a 31 percent fall in 2030 income per worker (Table 3.6) or a decline of almost 2 percentage points in annual output growth compared with the base case. Evidently, results of this size assume that social returns to public investment will remain high and that public and private investment will continue to be complementary. This is certainly plausible, given the relatively limited coverage of public services and infrastructure (for example, potable water and roads) throughout the country; however, ensuring public investments are well targeted and effectively maintained will be vital to achieving sustained output growth.

Public financial management

As discussed previously, the sustainable financing of public investment will be a key challenge. This, in turn, raises the question of the appropriate mix of foreign and domestic contributions to public funds. Although the sensitivity tests indicate a sizable response of final output to changes in both domestic revenues and external aid, they also indicate that domestic revenue is a preferred financing mechanism, given the potential absorptive-capacity problems surrounding external aid (discussed later in this chapter). In comparison with the base case, this suggests that a gradual replacement of external aid by domestic revenue would generate small growth gains over the long term. The validity of such a scenario, however, depends on how any disincentive effects arising from increases in the overall tax burden compare with gains from reductions in reliance on external aid. Evidently, such questions go beyond the scope of the model. The more general policy message, however, is that fiscal policy choices are highly relevant and must be based on an understanding of critical growth constraints and opportunities. Careful management of the overall aid portfolio and ongoing development of the government's technical capacity in these areas are therefore relevant priorities.

Absorptive capacity

As is well understood, the final impact of fiscal policy depends on the combination of revenue and expenditure effects. Thus, aid management must embrace the efficiency and effectiveness of aid-financed expenditure. The pertinence of this observation is underlined by simulations of large increases in the absorptive-capacity parameters. For example, a tripling of η_2 in the human capital growth function (equation (A13)) generates a 0.5 percentage point fall in annual output growth compared with the base case. Alternatively, the sensitivity tests for the investment share j indicate that a reduction of the share of aid devoted to investment goods logically reduces average public investment, generating a corresponding decline in output growth. As a result, paying close attention to the intertemporal mix of investment and consumption in government expenditure is advised. This is particularly relevant where there are increasing demands on recurrent expenditures linked to the cumulative impact of (aid-financed) public investments.[16]

HIV/AIDS

The model clearly shows that the HIV/AIDS epidemic has considerable potential to weaken future growth. The base case employs official government estimates that put the current prevalence at 15.6 percent of the working population, growing to 16.8 percent in 2010, at which point it stabilizes. Although these rates are high in global terms, the task of containing prevalence below 20 percent is critical in light of the experiences of other countries in southern Africa (for example, Botswana). The potential growth impact of the epidemic can be gauged from Tables 3.6 and 3.7. The latter shows that under a hypothetical scenario of 0 percent prevalence (zero HIV/AIDS), annual growth would be approximately 2 percentage points greater than in the base case. In support of the model, these orders of magnitude are highly consistent with alternative estimates for both Mozambique (for example, Arndt, 2006) and other countries where prevalence is relatively high. Thus, effective actions to reduce the spread and nefarious economic effects of the epidemic will be crucial to realizing sustained economic growth.

Education

Consistent with the analysis of past sources of growth, the modeling exercise confirms that continued improvements in labor force quality via education will be necessary to sustain future growth. This is indicated by the role of human capital in the base case scenario, which explains about 11 percent of output growth to 2030. In comparison with the estimates given in Table 3.1, such a long-term return to education would be at the upper end of international experiences. Even so, prospects for achieving this must be considered reasonable, given the comparatively low average

---

[16]A clear example of this challenge may be found in the Mozambican education sector (among others) during recent years, as discussed in Arndt, Jones, and Tarp (2007).

levels of education in the workforce and the substantial external funding available to the sector. Additionally, and as implied by the growth accounting results, a core challenge will be not only to expand access but also to ensure a high quality of education that meets the needs of modern businesses. It follows that enhancements to labor market efficiency would also contribute to the subsequent allocation of improved human capital to productive employment. The risks to output growth associated with only weak improvements in the quality of human capital are demonstrated by the "weak ΔH" scenario (Table 3.7), which shows negligible growth in human capital quality over the forecast period, simulated by large reductions in the investment parameters within the human capital function. Although this ignores possible wider spillover effects on private investment and productivity growth, the result remains marked: a reduction in annual growth of around 0.7 percentage point compared with the base case is forecast. Thus, continued education and worker training will be a key part of any future growth success.

Unbiased growth

The previous scenario brings into focus an important general point—improvements in any single growth driver are unlikely to sustain rapid growth. This is supported by the final two scenarios in Table 3.7. In each case, they combine a range of moderate changes in relevant directions to the exogenous variables and parameters. The "negative" scenario results in an annual growth rate of 2.7 percent (or 1.0 percent per worker), equivalent to a real increase of only 27 percent in real income per worker during 2004–30. As depicted in Figure 3.4, this would fall far short of a sustained rapid growth trajectory and demonstrates that the policy challenges involved in achieving long-term growth are hardly trivial. In turn, this scenario affirms that the government's target of sustaining annual real growth at 7 percent through 2009 (Mozambique Ministry of Planning and Development, 2006b) cannot be achieved by "business as usual." By the same token, however, there are plausible grounds for optimism. With moderate improvements across the base case exogenous variables and selected parameters, the model shifts into a higher gear that enables the achievement of rapid, sustained growth (also Figure 3.4). Under these positive assumptions, absolute real income per worker is projected to rise more than threefold by 2030, which is equivalent to an annual aggregate growth rate of 7.3 percent (or 4.9 percent per worker). Moreover, the scenario confirms that sustained growth will depend on improvements across all aggregate growth drivers, reaffirming the need for second-generation institutional reforms, sustained public investment, and educational strengthening.

Figure 3.4. Scenarios of Tendencies in Real Income per Worker
(Constant 1980 prices indexed at 2004 = 1; projections cover 2005–30)

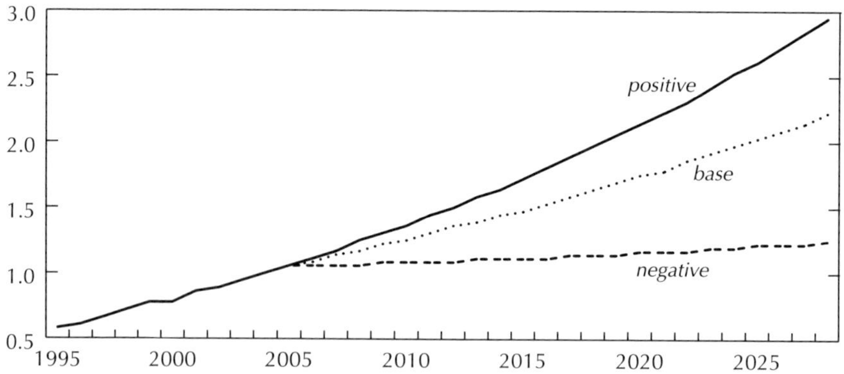

Source: Author's calculations.

Lessons for Sub-Saharan Africa

Before concluding, it is relevant to consider what lessons we might draw from this analysis for other sub-Saharan African countries. Despite the difficulty of making meaningful generalizations from country-specific studies, the Mozambican case is relevant from the point of view of illuminating the dynamics of sustained post-conflict growth from an extremely low base. Various sub-Saharan African countries, including the Democratic Republic of the Congo, Liberia, and Sierra Leone, fit this broad description and may wish to replicate certain features of the Mozambican growth experience.

A basic question, however, is whether the Mozambican pattern of growth should be held up as a positive example. If one refers only to the analysis of proximate growth determinants, the response from this study is favorable. The analysis has shown that the pattern of growth in Mozambique has been relatively unbiased, with robust contributions from all growth drivers deriving from both private and public sector activity. At a highly aggregated level, this growth pattern is comparable to episodes of sustained growth observed in other countries, such as the NIEs as well as China and India more recently. This is not to say that at a deeper microeconomic level, Mozambican growth shares similar features with growth in East Asia. Profound differences in industrial structure, export composition, and institutional conditions suggest that such an argument cannot hold. The message of this study is straightforward but bears repeating: to achieve sustained growth, physical capital accumulation must be accompanied by productivity gains and educational improvements.

A few specific lessons can also be taken from this analysis. First, although there can be high social returns to sustained investments in public goods in settings such as Mozambique, private sector initiative is essential. Thus, raising domestic private savings and attracting foreign investors may be appropriate public policy priorities, as long as backward linkages can be assured. Second, this study has underlined the importance of effective, growth-oriented management of aid-financed public investments. Absorptive-capacity constraints and Dutch disease effects are not immaterial to long-term growth prospects in high-aid settings. Third, early investments in the education system, in both conflict and post-conflict situations, are essential to sustain growth over the long term. Expanding access to education should not, however, be undertaken without paying attention to educational quality or the structure of demand for educated workers. Indeed, the recent evidence for Mozambique indicates that there has been a relatively large contribution from highly skilled workers in particular. Finally, the importance of maintaining the necessary preconditions for growth, such as macroeconomic stability and sound public financial management, cannot be overemphasized. Here the argument for "good" institutions is strongest—promoting a virtuous circle linking institutional improvements to productivity to economic growth may, indeed, be the linchpin of sustained growth.

Conclusion

This chapter has discussed the challenge of sustaining growth in Mozambique. A review of cross-country evidence suggests that, at the policy level, there are no simple rules to follow. Even so, the starting point must be to avoid large-scale economic distortions and political errors that undermine incentives to pursue long-term output growth. Sustained growth episodes are unlikely to depend on one growth driver alone; rather, accumulation of raw factors of production must be accompanied by enhancements in their quality and overall productivity levels. The analysis of Mozambique's past growth performance, based on a rigorous growth accounting framework, suggests that physical capital accumulation has played a fundamental role. Sustained advances in education and improvements in overall factor productivity (residual TFP), however, have generated a relatively unbiased pattern of growth. At a very aggregate level, this pattern has broad similarities with episodes of sustained growth that have occurred in other countries, such as the NIEs of East Asia. Even so, the estimated gains in Mozambique's factor productivity appear to have been driven largely by postwar recovery in capacity-utilization rates. Consequently, as Mozambique approaches its technology frontier, the task of sustaining strong productivity growth may become more demanding.

Realistic long-term growth scenarios for Mozambique show the sensitivity of future growth rates to current policy challenges. These include sustaining public and private investment, improving average education levels, and minimizing the impact of the HIV/AIDS epidemic. Although foreign aid is likely to continue to play a critical role in support of public spending, the quality of investment will depend on effective management of absorptive-capacity pressures. This means that strengthening government capacity in aid management and expenditure analysis should be given priority. Furthermore, the accumulation of (high-quality) factors of production alone is unlikely to be sufficient to sustain growth. A critical challenge is thus to enhance productivity via technological catch-up and second-generation institutional reforms. Actions to address binding constraints in these areas will be essential to ensuring that the Mozambican success story continues.

Appendix I. Data Series

Human Capital Series

For the human capital series, economically active persons are subdivided into three categories based on their highest level of completed education.[17] These are (1) primary school (either EP1 or EP2); (2) secondary school (ES1 or above); and (3) no formal education. The focus on educational categories takes as its point of departure the assumption that education represents a long-term economic investment; that is, this study assumes a positive relationship among education, economic productivity, and wages (income). International microeconomic evidence generally supports this proposition (for example, Harmon, Oosterbeek, and Walker, 2003), which is confirmed for Mozambique by poverty studies showing a consistent association between higher levels of education and a lower incidence of

[17]This section draws on the human capital stock data in Jones (2006), where the estimation procedure is described in finer detail.

poverty (Fox, Bardasi, and Van den Broeck, 2005; Maximiano, Arndt, and Simler, 2005).

Annual student matriculation figures for the primary and secondary levels (taken from Instituto Nacional de Estatística (INE), 2005) are used to construct perpetual inventory-type stocks similar to those used in estimation of the fixed capital stock. Although methods of this kind are found in the literature for both single- and cross-country studies (for example, Ahuja and Filmer, 1995; Barro and Lee, 1993), they typically require long time-series data on repeat and dropout rates. Although these data are available for recent years in Mozambique, they are not sufficient for the time horizon of interest. Instead, survival probabilities implicit in the data are used, such as the ratio of EP2 to EP1 students,[18] as well as information in education transition matrices estimated in Arndt and Muzima (2004). The latter can be used to determine the likelihood that a given student will repeat, progress beyond, or exit a given scholastic level. Finally, in order to fix the series for each category, concrete data points from the 1997 census and the 2002/2003 household survey are used. These are sufficient to build a consistent time series that reflects the gradual improvements in educational efficiency (lower dropout and repetition rates) recorded over time.

To move from raw stocks to quality-adjusted inputs, it is necessary to focus on value added. The flow of services from a given worker can be described as a function of wages and hours worked. Ignoring the latter for the time being, and following Nehru, Dhareshwar, and Development Economics Department (1994), an aggregate quality-adjusted human capital measure can be defined as the product of the size of the labor force and an index of human capital quality. Formally,

$$W = LH = L\sum_{i=1}^{r} (p_i\varphi_i), \tag{A1}$$

where p_i denotes the share of the total active labor force in category i and φ_i denotes a measure of their average wage relative to a base (unskilled) category. Note that the contribution to changes in this aggregate measure owing to each category can be estimated via a Tömqvist decomposition described in equation (2) in the text.

---

[18]The abbreviations EP1 and EP2 refer to the two cycles of primary school (Escola Primária); ES1 and ES2 refer to the first of two cycles of secondary school (Escola Secundária) in Mozambique.

In the absence of time-series wage data, household survey evidence is used to measure the consumption premiums associated with different levels of education. Given the existence of numerous nonsalary forms of income, as well as diverse earnings sources, consumption data are generally seen to be a reliable guide to well-being in developing countries (Ravallion, 1992). One can further assume that consumption is a good proxy for differences in hours worked; in other words, consumption is a final outcome variable that is, among other things, a function of hours worked and income earned. On this basis, the productivity increment owing to education can be estimated from a Mincerian-type regression in which consumption is regressed on the level of education and a vector of control variables.[19] Although time-series data are not available to evaluate whether these consumption premiums have moved over time, the household survey undertaken in 1996/97 indicates that, at least through 2002, they have remained broadly stable. Also, during the 1980s, despite greater scarcity of educated workers, socialist wage and price controls are likely to have dampened wage differentials. As a result, it is reasonable to assume that relative productivity differences owing to education have remained stable over time. This refers only to the relative increment and not the wage rate per se.

Physical Capital

The total physical capital stock is disaggregated into government and private sector components. Consistent with other studies, real capital stocks are estimated by means of the perpetual inventory method, which requires estimates of gross investment, the rate of stock depreciation, and a starting value. Investment data are taken from official government statistics at an economy-wide level, while government budget execution accounts give the public sector component (INE, 2005). Gross private sector investment can thus be calculated as the residual. Note, however, that government investment has been largely dependent on external aid throughout the period, and a substantial portion of this aid has not been

[19]The results are based on the most recent nationally representative household survey (2002/03) and are highly comparable to findings from similar regressions on the same data set (for example, Fox, Bardasi, and Van den Broeck, 2005). Note that the consumption indicator is available only for households, while the education measure is available for individuals. This represents a source of bias in the results for which no adjustment is attempted. The estimates used here are given by the simple average of results from individual- and household-level regressions. See Jones (2006) for further discussion.

registered in the government accounts. Estimates in Arndt, Jones, and Tarp (2007) suggest that, even in recent years, official figures for aid to the public sector are underestimated by at least 10 percent and, further, exclude the investment (activities) of the large number of nongovernmental organizations (NGOs) that support public service provision. To adjust for these errors, official investment figures are therefore inflated by a factor of 10 percent.

To estimate the share of these sectoral stocks in capital's total value added, social accounting matrices (SAMs) developed in the postwar period (see the subsection "Results" under "Accounting for Mozambican Growth" above) indicate that private sector profits constitute about 40 percent of total payments to capital. On this basis, the capital series is initialized assuming the weights of the public and private sectors in total capital are both 50 percent. This is a plausible assumption, given the adoption of socialist central planning at that time and, thus, the widespread nationalization of economic production. Over time, these weights are adjusted according to the respective size of each stock in total physical capital. This results in a private sector share of about 42 percent for the postwar period, which is consistent with the SAM findings.[20] Appendix II, Cointegration Technique, describes the method used to complete the physical capital stock series.

Appendix II. Estimation

Cointegration Technique

To estimate the critical parameters needed to complete the physical capital stock series (namely the starting value, the rate of depreciation, and its aggregate share in value added), the cointegration technique applied to Uganda in IMF (2005) is followed. This is based on the two-step cointegration procedure set out in Engle and Granger (1987). As an extension to the former study, however, the depreciation rate is not fixed but rather is permitted to follow a time trend (slope).

Formally, an iterative procedure is run to select values for d, d_0, and K_0 that maximize the significance of the Engle and Granger test statistic calculated from the residual series e_t, defined from

$$\ln Y_t = \ln A_0 + ct + a \ln K_t + (1 - a) \ln W_t + e_t, \tag{A2}$$

[20]Simulations indicate that the growth accounting results are largely insensitive to moderate changes in these underlying assumptions.

$$K_t = I_t + K_{t-1}(1 - d_0 + dt). \tag{A3}$$

In estimating equation (A2), trend TFP growth is allowed to vary between the civil war and postwar periods. The resulting error series e_t thus gives short-term variations in output unexplained by either trend TFP growth or changes in the other variables.

Capacity Utilization

Capacity utilization can be defined generically as the ratio of actual output (Y) to potential output (Y^*). An economic definition of Y^* is the level of output that corresponds to competitive equilibrium, assuming that technology and the capital stock are (quasi-)fixed inputs (Berndt and Fuss, 1989). Thus, when the ratio Y/Y^* is unity, the firm faces no incentives to alter its fixed capital stock, since both short-run and long-run marginal costs are tangential. Given that this definition focuses on new investment (or divestment), at an aggregate level it is plausible to use movements of the output-capital ratio around its long-term trend as a proxy for changes in capacity utilization. This derives from the well-known property of a stable output-capital ratio in neoclassical growth models under steady-state growth, which is also reflected in the projections model described in Appendix III. Even where productivity is improving, consistent with an upward trend in Y^*/K_t, short-run variations around the trend can be interpreted as indicative of changes in capacity utilization rather than in productivity. Obviously, this assumes that competitive conditions prevail and that changes in productivity (or TFP) are relatively gradual, thus generating a smooth underlying trend in the output-capital ratio.

Two steps are required to estimate the contribution of changes in capacity utilization to changes in residual TFP. First, define

$$\Delta u_t - (Y_t/K_t) - \psi_t, \tag{A4}$$

where u_t denotes a proxy measure of capacity utilization and ψ_t refers to the long-run (optimal) output-capital ratio calculated by applying a Hodrick-Prescott filter to the observed historical series.[21] Second, undertake a simple regression of the relationship

$$\Delta A_t = c_0 + \gamma_0 \Delta u_t + e_t, \tag{A5}$$

[21]The smoothing parameter is chosen as $\lambda = 400$, which is 25 percent of the default value for quarterly data.

where c_0 denotes the intercept and e_t the residual error. Assuming the coefficient on Δu_t is positive and significant as desired (and the overall model is meaningful), the null hypothesis of no relationship between TFP and capacity utilization can be rejected. In turn, the remaining unexplained variation in ΔA can be interpreted as indicative of deep movements in TFP arising from technological innovation and other factors. Finally, as with the overall residual TFP series, changes in deep TFP can then be split into civil war and postwar trends as well as remaining noise.

Appendix III. Projections Model

Macroeconomic Framework

For the projections model, a behavioral side is added to a growth accounting framework. Thus, consider the standard Cobb-Douglas aggregate production function where A denotes a Hicks-neutral efficiency parameter, K denotes physical capital, L denotes the labor force, and H a labor force quality (education) index. Ignoring prices, real output per worker is given by

$$Y/L = y = A(k)^{a}(H)^{1-a}, \tag{A6}$$

where k denotes the capital-labor ratio (K/L). Thus the growth rate of per capita income, Δy, is defined as:

$$\Delta y = \Delta A + a\Delta k + (1 - a)\Delta H. \tag{A7}$$

Recognizing that $\Delta k = \Delta K - \Delta L$, and following the standard practice of defining the net change in capital as the sum of government and private sector investment *minus* depreciation, that is, $(g + p)Y - dK$, one can restate the model as

$$\Delta y = \Delta A + \Delta H + a[(g + p)\psi - d - \Delta L - \Delta H], \tag{A8}$$

where g denotes government investment as a ratio of GDP, p denotes the investment ratio of the private sector (including FDI), d denotes the rate of capital depreciation, and ψ denotes the aggregate output-capital ratio.

Behavioral Dynamics

To add a behavioral side, the following variables are added: the natural rate of labor force growth (n); the proportion of the labor force infected with HIV/AIDS (v); the level of foreign aid in GDP (x); domestic government revenue as a ratio of GDP (r); the government's investment share (j), representing the proportion of total government revenue channeled to investment activities; foreign direct investment in GDP (z); inflation (i); an exogenous component of TFP growth ($\bar{\Delta A}$); and a proxy for absorptive-capacity constraints related to external aid (f). Ignoring time subscripts for the current period, the following relationships are then defined:

$$f = x/(g + p) \tag{A9}$$

$$\Delta L = \min(n, n^*) \tag{A10}$$

$$g = j\,(r + x)(1 - v) \tag{A11}$$

$$p = (z + \rho_0 \Delta Y_{t-1} + \rho_1 g + \rho_2 f + \rho_3 i)(1 - v) \tag{A12}$$

$$\Delta H = (\eta_0 g + \eta_1 p + \eta_2 f)(1 - v) \tag{A13}$$

$$\Delta A = \bar{\Delta A} - 0.5 v \Delta A_{t-1}. \tag{A14}$$

Econometric calibration of the model is discussed in the text section "Toward Sustained Growth" in subsection "Model Calibration." Note that the inclusion of HIV/AIDS effects in equations (A11) through (A14) essentially follows the empirical approach set out in Haacker (2002). Note that growth in human capital quality is affected, both directly and indirectly, by HIV/AIDS prevalence—the indirect effect occurs through changes in investment, while the direct effect refers to the productivity loss owing to increased illness and reduced average experience in the workforce. The impact of HIV/AIDS prevalence on labor force growth in equation (A10) is modeled as the lower value of the labor force growth rate unadjusted for HIV/AIDS effects (n) and an estimated adjusted rate (n^*). For the latter, an econometric estimate of the relationship $n^* = \beta_0 v + \beta_1 n$ is made (for 1998–2010), taking the dependent variable as the official forecast for labor force growth adjusted for the base case HIV/AIDS prevalence. Both parameters are significant at the 1 percent level, with $\beta_0 = 0.15$ and $\beta_1 = 1.6$.[22] Note, however, that since this is not a formal economic relationship, these parameters are not included in the sensitivity tests (also the section "Toward Sustained Growth"). Two further fixed modeling assumptions can be noted. First, physical capital depreciation d

[22] Since the model is implemented in discrete time, the increment to capital in time t refers to savings made in the previous period.

is set at 7 percent, which is the average rate for the past 5 years estimated in the cointegration exercise. Second, the share of physical capital in total product *a* is estimated at 35 percent; this is slightly higher than the historical growth accounting estimate, but reflects the substantial capital deepening that has accompanied postwar growth (see the subsection "Postwar Recovery" in the text).

Bibliography

Abramovitz, M., 1956, "Resource and Output Trends in the United States Since 1870," *American Economic Review,* Vol. 46, No. 2, pp. 5–23.

Ahuja, V., and D. Filmer, 1995, "Educational Attainments in Developing Countries: New Estimates and Projections Disaggregated by Gender," Policy Research Working Paper No. 1489 (Washington: World Bank).

Aka, E.B., B. Akitoby, D. Ghura, and A. Tahari, 2004, "Sources of Growth in Sub-Saharan Africa," IMF Working Paper 04/176 (Washington: International Monetary Fund).

Arndt, C., 2006, "HIV/AIDS, Human Capital, and Economic Growth Prospects for Mozambique," *Journal of Policy Modeling,* Vol. 28, No. 5, pp. 477–89.

———, A. Cruz, H.T. Jensen, S. Robinson, and F. Tarp, 1998, "Social Accounting Matrices for Mozambique: 1994–95," Trade and Macroeconomics Division Discussion Paper No. 28 (Washington: International Food Policy Research Institute).

Arndt, C., H. T. Jensen, and F. Tarp, 2000, "Structural Characteristics of the Economy of Mozambique: A SAM-Based Analysis," *Review of Development Economics,* Vol. 4, No. 3, pp. 292–306.

Arndt, C., S. Jones, and F. Tarp, 2007, "Aid and Development: The Mozambican Case," in *Theory and Practice of Foreign Aid,* ed. by S. Lahiri, Vol. 1 of *Frontiers of Economics and Globalization* (Amsterdam: Elsevier), pp. 235–88.

Arndt, C., and J. Muzima, 2004, "Estimating Efficiency Trends in Education: A Minimum Cross Entropy Approach with Application to Mozambique," Discussion Paper No. 2E (Maputo: National Directorate of Studies and Policy Analysis, Ministry of Planning and Development, Republic of Mozambique).

Barro, R.J., 1998, "Notes on Growth Accounting," NBER Working Paper No. 6654 (Cambridge, Massachusetts: National Bureau of Economic Research).

———, and J.-W. Lee, 1993, "International Comparisons of Educational Attainment," *Journal of Monetary Economics,* Vol. 32, No. 3, pp. 363–94.

Benito-Spinetto, M., and P. Moll, 2005, "Mozambique: Macroeconomic Developments, Economic Growth, and Consequences for Poverty" (unpublished background paper for the 2005 Mozambique Country Economic Memorandum; Washington: World Bank).

Berg, A., J.D. Ostry, and J. Zettelmeyer, 2006, "What Makes Growth Sustained?" (unpublished: Washington: International Monetary Fund).

Berndt, E.R., and M.A. Fuss, 1989, "Economic Capacity Utilization and Productivity Measurement for Multi-Product Firms with Multiple Quasi-Fixed Inputs," NBER Working Paper No. 2932 (Cambridge, Massachusetts: National Bureau of Economic Research).

Biggs, T., J. Nasir, and R. Fisman, 1999, "Structure and Performance of Manufacturing in Mozambique," Regional Program on Enterprise Development (RPED) Paper No. 107 (Washington: World Bank).

Bosworth, B.P., and S.M. Collins, 2003, "The Empirics of Growth: An Update," Brookings Discussion Paper in International Economics No. 2/2003 (Washington: Brookings Institution).

———, 2006, "Accounting for Growth: Comparing China and India" (unpublished; Washington: Brookings Institution).

———, and Y. Chen, 1995, "Accounting for Differences in Economic Growth," Brookings Discussion Paper in International Economics No. 115 (Washington: Brookings Institution).

Bourguignon, F., and M. Sundberg, 2006, "Absorptive Capacity and Achieving the MDGs," UNU-WIDER Research Paper No. 2006/47 (Helsinki: United Nations University–World Institute for Development Economics Research).

Byiers, B., and J. Rand, 2007, "Enterprise Development in Mozambique: Results Based on Manufacturing Surveys Conducted in 2002 and 2006," Discussion Paper No. 33E (Maputo: National Directorate of Studies and Policy Analysis, Ministry of Planning and Development, Republic of Mozambique).

Carey, K.J., S. Gupta, and C.A. Pattillo, 2005, "Sustaining Growth Accelerations and Pro-Poor Growth in Africa," IMF Working Paper 05/195 (Washington: International Monetary Fund).

Caselli, F., 2005, "Accounting for Cross-Country Income Differences," in *Handbook of Economic Growth*, ed. by P. Aghion and S. Durlauf, Vol. 1 (Amsterdam: Elsevier), Chap. 9, pp. 679–741.

Dean, E.R., and M.J. Harper, 1998, "The BLS Productivity Measurement Program, in *Conference on New Directions in Productivity Analysis, March 20–21, 1998* (Washington: United States Department of Commerce, Bureau of Labor Statistics).

Durlauf, S.N., P.A. Johnson, and J.R. Temple, 2005, "Growth Econometrics," in *Handbook of Economic Growth*, ed. by P. Aghion and S. Durlauf (Amsterdam: Elsevier), Vol. 1, Chap. 8, pp. 555–677.

Easterly, W., 1997, "The Ghost of Financing Gap: How the Harrod-Domar Growth Model Still Haunts Development Economics," Policy Research Working Paper No. 1807 (Washington: World Bank).

———, 2007, "Was Development Assistance a Mistake?" in American Economics Association, *Annual Meeting 2007 Conference Papers* (Chicago). Available via the Internet: http://www.aeaweb.org/annual_mtg_papers/2007/conference_papers.php.

Eifert, B., A. Gelb, and V. Ramachandran, 2005, "Business Environment and Comparative Advantage in Africa: Evidence from the Investment Climate Data," CGD Working Paper No. 56 (Washington: Center for Global Development).

Engle, R.F., and C.W.J. Granger, 1987, "Co-Integration and Error Correction: Representation, Estimation, and Testing," *Econometrica*, Vol. 55, No. 2, pp. 251–76.

Fox, L., E. Bardasi, and K. Van den Broeck, 2005, "Poverty in Mozambique: Unraveling Changes and Determinants," Africa Region Working Paper No. 87 (Washington: World Bank).

Haacker, M., 2002, "The Economic Consequences of HIV/AIDS in Southern Africa," IMF Working Paper 02/38 (Washington: International Monetary Fund).

———, ed., 2004, *The Macroeconomics of HIV/AIDS* (Washington: International Monetary Fund).

Hall, M., and T. Young, 1997, *Confronting Leviathan: Mozambique Since Independence* (Athens, Ohio: Ohio University Press).

Harmon, C.P., H. Oosterbeek, and I. Walker, 2003, "The Returns to Education: Microeconomics," *Journal of Economic Surveys*, Vol. 17, No. 2, pp. 115–56.

Hausmann, R., L. Pritchett, and D. Rodrik, 2005, "Growth Accelerations," *Journal of Economic Growth*, Vol. 10, No. 4, pp. 303–29.

Hulten, C., 2001, "Total Factor Productivity: A Short Biography," in *New Developments in Productivity Analysis*, ed. by C.R. Hulten, E.R. Dean, and M.J. Harper (Chicago: University of Chicago Press).

International Monetary Fund (IMF), 2005, *Uganda: Selected Issues and Statistical Appendix*, IMF Country Report 05/172 (Washington).

———, 2006, *World Economic Outlook, September 2006*, World Economic and Financial Survey (Washington).

Instituto Nacional de Estatística (INE), 2005, "30 anos de Independência nacional: Um retrato estatístico," technical report (Maputo).

Jones, S., 2006, "Growth Accounting for Mozambique (1980–2004)," Discussion Paper No. 22E (Maputo: Mozambique Ministry of Planning and Development, National Directorate of Studies and Policy Analysis).

Jorgenson, D. W., 2005, "Accounting for Growth in the Information Age," in *Handbook of Economic Growth*, ed. by P. Aghion and S. Durlauf (Amsterdam: Elsevier), Vol. 1, Chap. 10, pp. 743–815.

Kamps, C., 2004, "New Estimates of Government Net Capital Stocks for 22 OECD Countries, 1960–2001," IMF Working Paper 04/67 (Washington: International Monetary Fund).

Lensink, R., and H. White, 2001, "Are There Negative Returns to Aid?" *Journal of Development Studies*, Vol. 37, No. 6, pp. 42–65.

Levine, R., and D. Renelt, 1991, "A Sensitivity Analysis of Cross-Country Growth Regressions," Policy Research Working Paper No. 609 (Washington: World Bank).

Lucas, R. J., 1988, "On the Mechanics of Economic Development," *Journal of Monetary Economics*, Vol. 22, No. 1, pp. 3–42.

Maximiano, N., C. Arndt, and K.R. Simler, 2005, "Qual foi a Dinâmica Dos Determinantes da Pobreza em Moçambique?" Discussion Paper No. 11 (Maputo: Mozambique Ministry of Planning and Development, National Directorate of Studies and Policy Analysis).

Michaelowa, K., 2000, "Returns to Education in Low-Income Countries: Evidence for Africa," paper presented at the annual meeting of the Committee on Developing Countries of the German Economic Association, Hamburg, June 30.

Mozambique Ministry of Planning and Development, 2006a, "Aide-Mémoire of the 2005 Joint Review (with Programme Aid Partners)," technical report (Maputo). Available via the Internet: http://www.pap.org.mz

———, 2006b, "Plano de Acção para a Redução da Pobreza Absoluta 2006–2009 (PARPA II)," technical report (Maputo).

Ndulu, B., ed., 2007, *Challenges of African Growth: Opportunities, Constraints, and Strategic Directions* (Washington: World Bank).

———, and S. A. O'Connell, 2003, "Revised Collins/Bosworth Growth Accounting Decompositions," Explaining African Economic Growth Project, African Economic Research Consortium. Available via the Internet: http://www.swarthmore.edu/SocSci/soconne1/aercgrth.html

Nehru, V., A. Dhareshwar, and Development Economics Department, 1994, "New Estimates of Total Factor Productivity Growth for Developing and Industrial Countries," Policy Research Working Paper No. 1313 (Washington: World Bank).

Pritchett, L., 1996, "Where Has All the Education Gone?" Policy Research Working Paper No. 1581 (Washington: World Bank).

Ravallion, M., 1992, "Poverty Comparisons: A Guide to Concepts and Methods," Living Standards Measurement Paper No. 88 (Washington: World Bank).

Rodrik, D., 2004, "Rethinking Growth Strategies," World Institute for Development Economics Research (WIDER) Annual Lecture No. 8 (Helsinki: United Nations University).

———, and A. Subramanian, 2004, "From 'Hindu Growth' to Productivity Surge: The Mystery of the Indian Growth Transition," IMF Working Paper 04/77 (Washington: International Monetary Fund).

Sarel, M., 1995, "Growth in East Asia: What We Can and What We Cannot Infer from It," IMF Working Paper 95/98 (Washington: International Monetary Fund).

Schwerdt, G., and J. Turunen, 2006, "Growth in Euro Area Labour Quality," ECB Working Paper No. 575 (Frankfurt: European Central Bank).

Solow, R., 1957, "Technical Change and the Aggregate Production Function," *Review of Economics and Statistics*, Vol. 39, No. 3 (August), pp. 312–20.

Sulemane, J., 2001, "Economic Decline: A Study with Reference to Mozambique" (Ph.D. dissertation; Notre Dame, Indiana: University of Notre Dame, Department of Economics).

Tarp, F., 1993, *Stabilization and Structural Adjustment: Macroeconomic Frameworks for Analysing the Crisis in Sub-Saharan Africa* (London: Routledge).

———, 2006, "Aid and Development," Discussion Paper No. 06-12 (Copenhagen: University of Copenhagen).

———, H.T. Jensen, C. Arndt, S. Robinson, and R. Heltberg, 2002, "Facing the Development Challenge in Mozambique," Research Report No. 126 (Washington: International Food Policy Research Institute).

Temple, J., 2000, "Growth Regressions and What the Textbooks Don't Tell You," *Bulletin of Economic Research*, Vol. 52, No. 3 (July), pp. 181–205.

United Nations Development Program (UNDP), 2006, *Human Development Report* 2006: *Beyond Scarcity: Power, Poverty and the Global Water Crisis* (New York).

World Bank, 2005a, *Economic Growth in the 1990s: Learning from a Decade of Reform* (Washington).

———, 2005b, "Mozambique Country Economic Memorandum: Sustaining Growth and Reducing Poverty," Report No. 32615-MZ (Washington).

———, 2005c, *World Development Indicators 2005* (Washington).

Yang, Y., S. Gupta, and R. Powell, 2005, "The Macroeconomic Challenges of Scaling Up Aid to Africa," IMF Working Paper 05/179 (Washington: International Monetary Fund).

Young, A., 1994, "The Tyranny of Numbers: Confronting the Statistical Realities of the East Asian Growth Experience," NBER Working Paper No. 4680 (Cambridge, Massachusetts: National Bureau of Economic Research).

Zellner, A., 1962, "An Efficient Method of Estimating Seemingly Unrelated Regression Equations and Tests for Aggregation Bias," *Journal of the American Statistical Association*, Vol. 57, No. 298 (June), pp. 348–68.

4

Monetary and Financial Sector Policies: The Road to Price and Financial Stability

Shanaka J. Peiris and Victor Lledó

After years of very high inflation prior to the mid-1990s, Mozambique has succeeded in stabilizing inflation, albeit with some lapses. A key factor in bringing inflation under control has been the implementation of a firm money-based stabilization program supported by prudent fiscal policies under successive IMF-supported arrangements. Financial liberalization and bank restructuring at early stages were also important in this regard. There have been, however, bouts of inflationary episodes driven by both domestic shocks (for example, droughts, floods, and banking crises) and external shocks (for example, inflows of foreign aid and fluctuations in oil prices). Thanks to monetary and financial sector reforms, Mozambique's financial system, once government owned, has come a long way since the end of the civil war, evolving into a full-blown market-based system.

The challenges for Mozambique—a post-stabilization economy—are to continue implementing an appropriate macroeconomic policy framework to consolidate macroeconomic stability, and to pursue a reform agenda aimed at deepening financial intermediation in a sound manner. The literature points to a number of areas that need to be considered. First, one must choose a consistent macroeconomic policy mix to consolidate macroeconomic stability (Sargent and Wallace, 1981; and Woodford, 2001), and a monetary policy framework to maintain inflation at single-digit levels (Fischer, 1993; Ghosh and Phillips, 1998; and IMF, 2005).[1] Therefore, the

[1]Alternatively, the central bank could tie its currency to another country's currency to maintain price stability, but that option is not under consideration for Mozambique, which

next section begins by evaluating the role of macroeconomic stabilization policies and the monetary transmission mechanism in Mozambique, with the latter focusing on evaluating the appropriateness of the Bank of Mozambique's (BM) current monetary targeting framework and mapping a way forward. Second, one must implement reforms that ensure the sound development of the financial sector. Financial development is recognized as important for economic growth (Levine, 2005), and it could also help promote price stability (Posen, 1995). Banking system distress and crises are also economically very costly (Frydl, 1999; and Noy, 2005). Thus, the section "Monetary and Financial Sector Reforms" examines Mozambique's experience with these reforms as the country moves toward price and financial stability. The last section concludes by identifying the remaining challenges for Mozambique and lessons for other countries in sub-Saharan Africa at a similar stage of financial development and with a similar macroeconomic environment.

Stabilization Policies and the Monetary Transmission Mechanism

Macroeconomic Policy Mix

The effectiveness of monetary policy in controlling inflation depends critically on its coordination with fiscal policy. It is well established that governments running persistent deficits will, sooner or later, be forced to finance those deficits through money creation (seigniorage), thereby producing inflation (Sargent and Wallace, 1981). While this theory does not rule out the importance of other mechanisms that can fuel inflation and cause it to become persistent, fiscal imbalances have remained central to most models.[2] The "fiscal view" of inflation has been especially prominent in the developing country literature, which has long recognized that less efficient tax collection, political instability, and more limited access to external borrowing tend to lower the relative cost of seigniorage and increase dependence on the inflation tax (Alesina and Drazen, 1991; Cukierman, Edwards, and Tabellini, 1992; and Calvo and Végh, 1999). As

aims to maintain a flexible exchange rate regime (to absorb shocks and maintain a comfortable level of international reserves), and is, therefore, not discussed here.

[2]A similar line of reasoning lies behind the fiscal theory of the price level (Canzoneri, Cumby, and Diba, 2001; and Woodford 2001). This theory posits that increased government debt adds to household wealth and, hence, to demand for goods and services, leading to price pressures.

such, Catão and Terrones (2005) find that the higher the ratio of the fiscal deficit to narrow money, the higher the rate of inflation in developing countries, including those with moderate levels of inflation.[3] Estimating ordinary least squares from the first quarter of 1996 to the third quarter of 2006, we find that, for an average M1/GDP ratio of about 7 percent in Mozambique, a 1 percent reduction (increase) in the ratio of the budget deficit to GDP lowers (raises) inflation by about 2½ percentage points on average, all else constant.[4] This value lies at the low end of the range of the impact of deficits on inflation in low-income countries estimated in Catão and Terrones (2005) and is closer to the values reported for emerging markets. The result may reflect the short time span, which captures mostly the post-stabilization phase in Mozambique and the absence of nontraditional channels of fiscal influence on inflation—namely monetization expectations and the wealth effects of public debt—which can be formed independently of the size of the budget deficit (Kwon, McFarlane, and Robinson, 2006).

To account for the different channels of fiscal policy effects on inflation, one could focus on the role of public debt—instead of the fiscal deficit—in determining inflation and inflation expectations. Using a simplified forward-looking model of inflation following Castro, De Resende, and Ruge-Murcia (2003), Kwon, McFarlane, and Robinson (2006) establish a linear relationship between inflation and increases in money supply and public debt (both domestic and external) so that the relationship can be tested empirically. Given the limited time-series data for individual countries, Kwon, McFarlane, and Robinson (2006) employ panel data techniques to allow for the variability of individual countries while preserving the dynamics of adjustment within countries. The regression results show that debt growth has a strong and stable positive effect on inflation in low-income economies and the smaller advanced economies.[5] The coefficient for public debt is nearly 0.2 for the short term, implying that a 1 percent increase in public debt leads to a 0.2 percentage point increase in inflation.

[3]However, they do not detect a strong positive connection between deficits and inflation in low-inflation advanced economies, which may be explained in part by the greater autonomy and credibility of these economies' monetary policy, their deeper financial markets, and other institutional constraints that link public borrowing more closely to tax and spending smoothing.

[4]The relationship between deficits and inflation was robust to the inclusion of other explanatory variables, such as oil prices and degree of trade openness, as in Catão and Terrones (2005).

[5]In contrast, in 13 major advanced economies, none of the explanatory variables, except lagged inflation, show significant short-term associations with inflation.

The coefficients are lower than those of money growth but are significant at the 5 percent level. The strong debt-inflation linkage, after controlling for money growth, is consistent with the significant positive relationship between fiscal deficits and inflation only during high-inflation episodes in low-income countries (Catão and Terrones, 2005; and Fischer, Sahay, and Végh, 2002). Kwon, McFarlane, and Robinson (2006) also undertook a simple vector autoregression (VAR) to trace the transmission channels of the fiscal influence on inflation. The panel VAR outcomes lend additional support to the prediction of the fiscal-monetary model of inflation—that the debt-inflation link is affected by institutional and structural factors. Impulse responses for low-income countries show a strong and positive response of money supply and inflation to fiscal shocks, whereas the impulse responses for major advanced economies do not. This suggests that increases in public debt in developing countries are more often than not accommodated by monetary easing—a phenomenon known as fiscal dominance.

We apply a VAR to Mozambique as in Kwon, McFarlane, and Robinson (2006) to identify the transmission channels of the fiscal influence on inflation and to test whether the cross-country debt-inflation relationship identified from the panel regressions holds for Mozambique. Our VAR consists of inflation and growth of public debt (both domestic and external), money, and real GDP from the first quarter of 1996 to the fourth quarter of 2006. Impulse responses are based on the Cholesky decomposition of the structural shocks in the order of output, public debt, money, and prices (see Figure 4.1).[6] The choice of lag length is determined by the Schwarz criterion and the Akaike information criterion. The VAR outcomes confirm the significance of public debt dynamics in determining inflation in Mozambique. The impulse response functions show that the price level is positively affected by money supply and public debt but that the latter has a longer-lasting effect on inflation. The variance decompositions suggest that money plays a greater role in explaining inflation dynamics over the first two quarters but that fiscal shocks start to play a similar role thereafter (see Figure 4.2). Also, expansionary fiscal shocks have expansionary effects on money supply while the opposite does not hold. These results are similar to those from the panel VAR estimates for low-income countries in Kwon, McFarlane, and Robinson (2006) and robust to changes in

[6]The exchange rates are also included in the robustness test to control for possible biases from exchange rate volatility on the debt dynamics. The directions of the impulse responses remain unchanged in an alternative VAR that includes the exchange rate as an endogenous variable.

Figure 4.1. Public Debt, Money, and Inflation

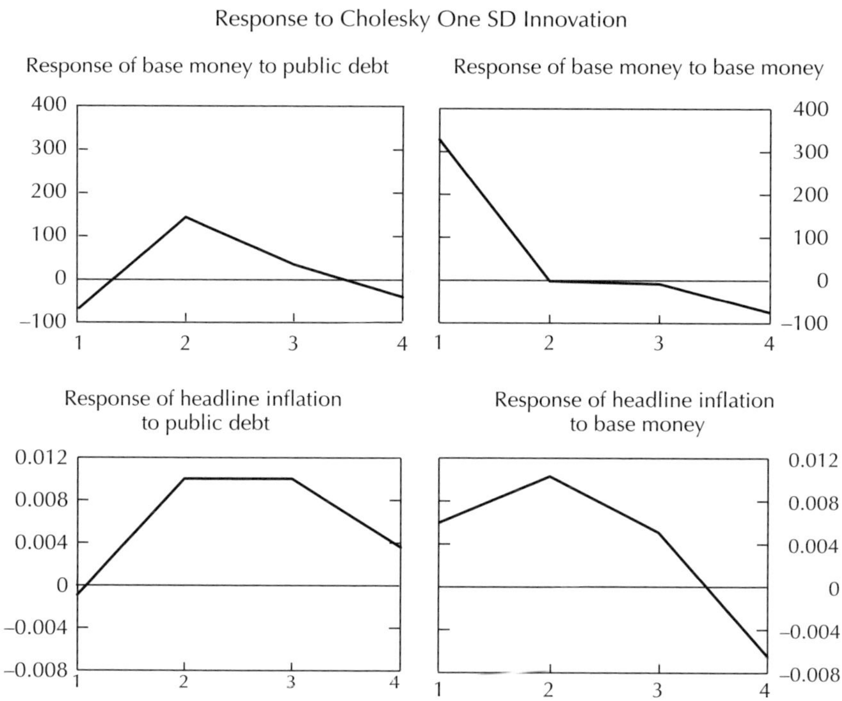

Source: Authors' calculations.

the ordering of the shocks. The impact of only domestic debt shocks on headline inflation and base money follows a similar pattern (and is thus not reported here) but is stronger than total public debt, highlighting the important role played by net domestic credit to the government.

Caution is needed, however, in interpreting these results. The implications of rising public debt for inflation are observationally similar in the Sargent-Wallace framework (1981) and the Fiscal Theory of the Price Level (FTPL). Nonetheless, there is an important theoretical distinction between the two (Leeper and Yun, 2005). Under the FTPL, an increase in public debt raises the wealth of the holders of government bonds without reducing the wealth of others. As bond prices rise, aggregate demand for goods and services increases, pushing up prices in the general economy. Under the Sargent-Wallace framework of the so-called unpleasant monetarist arithmetic, an increase in government debt that is not fully backed by a future real primary surplus will increase concerns about the moneti-

Figure 4.2. Public Debt, Money, and Inflation

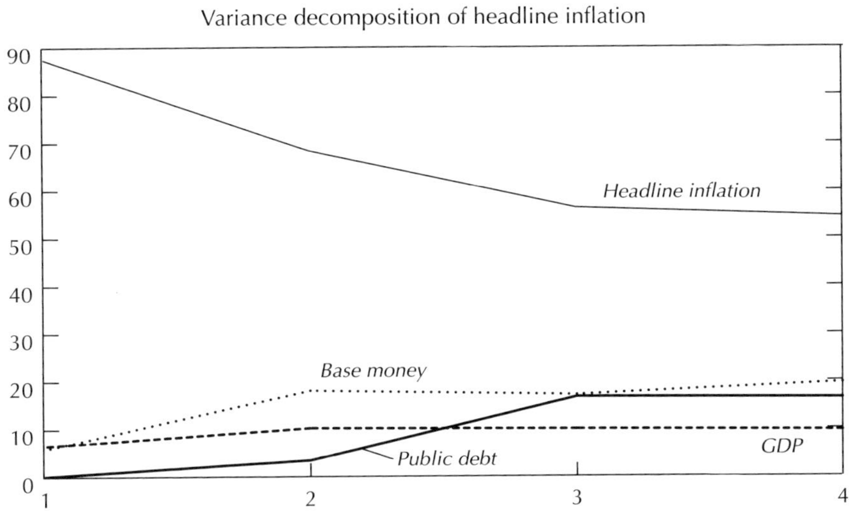

Source: Authors' calculations.

zation of public debt and raise inflation expectations, thereby reducing demand for government bonds and boosting interest rates. With both models predicting higher prices in response to rising public debt, and underdeveloped bond markets providing little information on market-determined interest rates, it is difficult to infer which is the dominant force in Mozambique. Notwithstanding, thc VARs confirm that movements of public debt (particularly domestic debt) do matter for inflation dynamics in Mozambique, providing scope for fiscal consolidation and reduction of public debt, including limiting net issuance of domestic debt for sterilization purposes to further support a disinflation program.

By the same token, the credibility of a given fiscal path is also important. For example, in a highly aid- and resource-dependent economy like Mozambique's, in the absence of institutional mechanisms that ensure rapid fiscal adjustment in the event of declines in foreign aid (or the country's inability to lock in high aid levels through firm medium-term commitments by donors) or resource revenues, it may be impossible to rule out the expectation of an increase in future required seigniorage. In such a situation, the literature indicates that fiscal rules that limit the size of budget deficits or public debt could, under appropriate circumstances, be an important institutional means of safeguarding price stability (see

Chapter 6). The independence of the central bank could also help reduce monetization concerns, and the development of the financial sector could help promote price stability, as the financial sector tends to support the central bank's policy autonomy (Posen, 1995).

Monetary Transmission Mechanism and Appropriate Policy Framework

The easing of concerns regarding fiscal dominance and the removal of distortionary controls over domestic interest rates and liberalization of the financial sector provide scope for a more activist role for monetary policy.[7] The domestic financing requirement of the central government budget in Mozambique has been falling and negative in recent years, particularly credit from the central bank.[8] As indicated above, this helped Mozambique reduce inflation to single digits and is likely to have mitigated concerns about the monetization of public debt.[9] In fact, the medium-term fiscal framework, which was approved for the first time by the Council of Ministers in 2006, explicitly avoids recourse to domestic financing. In such an environment, many view the current monetary policy setting in sub-Saharan Africa as an interim stage in a move toward wider adoption of formal inflation targeting practices in which inflation (more precisely, expected inflation) is the intermediate target, instead of either some monetary aggregate or the exchange rate, and where the interest rate rather than base money is the operational instrument (see Adam and O'Connell, 2005).[10] Thus, while elements of this debate will necessarily reflect themes in the current literature on monetary policy in emerging market countries (for example IMF, 2005; and Hakura, 2005), to the extent that post-

---

[7]See the section "Monetary and Financial Sector Reforms."

[8]Across sub-Saharan Africa—but particularly outside the CFA zone—there has been a steady decline in domestic deficit financing. The overall decline was similar for post-stabilization economies, with central bank credit showing the biggest decline.

[9]According to Adam and O'Connell (2005), the contraction in domestic credit since the 1990s has been associated with a steady decline in inflation in sub-Saharan Africa. Outside the CFA zone, inflation has been consistently in the single digits, although the averages mask a number of cases where fiscal dominance persisted and inflation remained out of control—for example, Angola, the Democratic Republic of the Congo (until 2002), and, more recently, Zimbabwe—and a number of countries where inflation remained at persistently high levels, at least by contemporary standards (Nigeria, The Gambia, Ghana, Malawi, and Zambia).

[10]It is now widely accepted that the primary role of monetary policy is to maintain price stability (IMF, 2005; and Batini and Yates, 2003), which is defined by many as an annual rate of inflation in the low single digits in industrial countries (Bernanke and others, 1999) and in the single digits in low-income countries (Fischer 1993; and Ghosh and Phillips, 1998).

stabilization economies like Mozambique are free of fiscal dominance, current policy arrangements are inflation targeting frameworks in the broad sense of being centered on maintenance of a nominal anchor (see Adam and O'Connell, 2005). In this respect, therefore, the relevant policy questions are not only how, and over what horizon, countries may make the move toward formal inflation targeting but also whether and how the operation of monetary policy can be improved given current monetary frameworks.[11] To consider this issue, we turn to an empirical evaluation of the monetary transmission mechanism, followed by a look at the monetary and financial sector reform process in Mozambique.

There has been a burgeoning literature on the transmission mechanism of monetary policy in many countries. Typically, this strand of research has been conducted in the context of a VAR framework pioneered by Sims (1980). Notable examples using VAR to identify transmission of monetary policy for advanced economies include Christiano, Eichenbaum, and Evans (2000) for the United States; Kim and Roubini (2000) for the G-7 economies; and Peersman and Smets (2003) for the euro area. A few recent papers have also studied the monetary transmission mechanism for a number of countries in sub-Saharan Africa. For example, Saxegaard (2006) uses a threshold VAR model for a number of sub-Saharan African countries and finds that excess liquidity in the region weakens the monetary transmission mechanism and, thus, the ability of the monetary authorities to influence demand conditions. Aron and Muellbauer (2001) analyze different aspects of the transmission mechanism in South Africa, including the degree of exchange rate pass-through and the impact of openness. However, there has been little analysis of the monetary transmission mechanism in Mozambique and other post-stabilization economies in sub-Saharan Africa, leaving a number of unanswered questions and somewhat of a vacuum of knowledge in this area. We will therefore examine the monetary transmission mechanism in Mozambique and explore the following questions:

- What role do monetary aggregates (and credit) and interest rate shocks play in transmitting monetary impulses through the economy?
- What is the degree of exchange rate pass-through?

[11]There is also the question of how the instruments available for conducting monetary policy should be deployed in shock-prone post-stabilization economies in sub-Saharan Africa such as Mozambique, while these economies maintain a commitment to low and stable inflation (and reduced macroeconomic volatility, more generally). This question is discussed in Chapter 5.

- Are there measures of core inflation that are better controlled by monetary policy?

Structural VAR Modeling

Following Kim and Roubini (2000) and Sims and Zha (2006), we assume the economy is described by a structural-form equation:

$$G(L)Y_t = C(L)\,X_t + \varepsilon_t,$$

where $G(L)$ is an $n \times n$ matrix polynomial in the lag operator; $C(L)$ is an $n \times k$ matrix polynomial in the lag operator; Y_t is an $n \times 1$ vector of endogenous Mozambican variables; and X is a $k \times 1$ vector of exogenous foreign variables; ε_t is an $n \times 1$ vector of structural disturbances, with $\mathrm{var}(\varepsilon_t) = \Lambda$, where Λ is a diagonal matrix and the diagonal elements are the variances of structural disturbances; therefore, structural disturbances are assumed to be mutually uncorrelated.

Corresponding with this structural model we can estimate a reduced-form VAR:

$$Y_t = A(L)Y_t + B(L)X_t + \mu_t,$$

where $A(L)$ and $B(L)$ are matrices polynomials; μ_t is a vector of reduced-form disturbances, with $\mathrm{var}(\mu_t) = \Sigma$.

There are many ways of recovering the parameters in the structural-form equations from the estimated parameters in the reduced-form equation. Some methods give restrictions on only contemporaneous structural parameters. A popular and convenient method is to orthogonalize reduced-form disturbances by Cholesky decomposition (as in Sims, 1980, among others). However, in this approach to identification, we can assume only a recursive structure. Sims (1986) suggests a generalized method (structural VAR) in which nonrecursive structures are allowed while still giving restrictions only on contemporaneous structural parameters.

We assume the exogenous vector X_t contains a terms of trade index for Mozambique (*TOT*), foreign aid inflows (*AID*), and the U.S. federal funds rate (*USR*):

$$X_t' = [TOT\ AID\ USR].$$

These variables are included to control for changes in the overall global economic stance (*USR*) and fluctuations in the prices of Mozambique's main exports and imports (*TOT*). We also include foreign aid (*AID*) since it is found to improve the fit of the model—not surprisingly, given the magnitude of aid in Mozambique, which is consistently above 10 percent of GDP.

Since the monetary authority follows a feedback rule—it sets monetary policy in response to economic news—it is important to control for the systematic component of the policy rule in order to identify exogenous monetary policy changes. If the monetary authority tightens monetary policy in response to a negative and inflationary supply shock, the ensuing recession and price inflation are due not only to the monetary contraction but also to the original negative supply shocks. To identify the part that is due to monetary policy alone, we include the price of oil (*GAS*), a proxy for negative and inflationary supply shocks. The other endogenous variables include real GDP, the headline consumer price index (*CPI*), the domestic treasury bill interest rate (*R*), the base money stock (*M*), and the nominal exchange rate against the U.S. dollar (*E*):

$$Y_t' = [GAS\ GDP\ CPI\ R\ M\ E].$$

The system encompasses the key sources of inflation identified by Loungani and Swagel (2001) and Barnichon and Peiris (2007) in their analysis of the sources of inflation in developing countries, particularly in Africa. First, as discussed by Agénor and Montiel (1999), inflation in developing countries is often linked to underlying fiscal imbalances. Such imbalances can lead to an increase in inflation by causing excessive money creation, as in Sargent and Wallace (1981), or by triggering a balance of payments crisis and resulting in an exchange rate depreciation, as in Liviatan and Piterman (1986). Another source of inflation may be due to macroeconomic overheating—that is, an excessive expansion of aggregate demand over potential output supply—as examined by Coe and McDermott (1997) for 13 Asian economies, estimated by the influence of an activity variable such as GDP. A third source of inflation, examined by Ball and Mankiw (1995), is supply-side "cost shocks"—movements in the prices of particular goods, such as oil, that lead to persistent changes in the aggregate price level. Finally, as discussed by Chopra (1985), inflation may have a substantial inertial component arising from the sluggish adjustment of inflationary expectations or the existence of staggered wage contracts (see Calvo, 1983; and Christiano, Eichenbaum, and Evans, 2001). There may also be inflationary shocks coming through shocks to marginal costs as postulated by the more recent literature on New Keynesian Phillips Curves (see Galí and Gertler, 1999).

Estimations based on other interest rates (rediscount rate); monetary aggregates (M2, M3, and domestic credit to the private sector); exchange rates (nominal effective exchange rate and exchange rate against the South African rand); real activity measures (exports); and consumer price indices (for nonfood items and energy) were also examined but are not presented here as the results were largely similar to the baseline model.

Identification scheme 1: Recursive VAR

The first identification scheme is the standard approach that imposes a recursive structure of the VAR, with the ordering of variables given by Y_t'. Intuitively, it assumes that GDP has no contemporaneous effect on oil prices (*GAS*); prices (*CPI*) have no immediate effect on output (*GDP*); interest rates (*R*) have no immediate effect on prices; monetary aggregates (*M*) have no immediate effect on interest rates; and the nominal exchange rate (*E*) has no immediate effect on monetary policy. This amounts to estimating the reduced form, then computing the Cholesky factorization of the reduced-form VAR covariance matrix.

Identification scheme 2: Non-recursive structural VAR

Unlike the recursive identification, we assume a contemporaneous relation between interest rates, money, and the exchange rate, following Kim and Roubini (2000) and Sims and Zha (2006). Interest rates are allowed to respond contemporaneously to shocks to output, prices, and the exchange rate. Money responds to interest rates and the exchange rate but does not respond immediately to contemporaneous output and price shocks. Following previous work by others (for example, Sims, 1986), we use as an identifying restriction the idea that monetary policy cannot respond contemporaneously to disturbances in the general price level or the level of GDP. The argument for this restriction is based on the absence of contemporary data on these variables at the time policy decisions have to be made. This assumption gains some credibility in the current paper relative to previous applications of it, however, because we allow the contemporaneous response of monetary policy to global oil prices. The nominal exchange rate responds immediately to all other variables.

The VAR models are estimated using quarterly data between 1996 and 2006.[12] All variables are in log-differences, except interest rates, which are in percentage terms.[13] This is likely to result in the loss of information on long-run relationships between the variables in the system, which is a weakness in the approach. However, given the short time span of the sample, we do not consider that an explicit analysis of the long-run behav-

[12]Quarterly GDP series were only recently made available in Mozambique. However, the series is still not short and subject to revisions; therefore, a quarterly GDP proxy was constructed statistically by estimating the correlates of real annual GDP and using predictions based on the quarterly explanatory variables.

[13]An analysis of the time-series properties of the variables revealed that the variables are integrated of order one or I(1). Therefore, the series are first-differenced for estimation purposes to avoid the spurious and inconsistent regression problem (Hendry, 1995).

ior of the economy would have been fruitful or essential to answering the questions at hand.[14] Standard information criteria are used to select the lag lengths of the VARs, which turn out to be two quarters.

Results

The results of the baseline model under the two identification schemes were broadly similar; therefore, only the impulse responses and variance decomposition of the non-recursive structural VAR are shown in Figure 4.3. The first set of graphs in Figure 4.3 display the impact (the impulse response) of a one standard deviation oil price, GDP, headline inflation, interest rate, monetary policy (base money), and exchange rate shock (defined as an exogenous, unexpected, temporary rise at $t = 0$) on GDP, headline inflation, and the nominal exchange rate. The relative importance of the exogenous and monetary policy shocks for fluctuations in output, prices, and the nominal exchange rate at different forecast horizons can be gauged through the forecast error variance decompositions.

The key insights are as follows:

- The effect of monetary impulses on GDP appears to be insignificant, while oil price and exchange rate shocks possibly have a modest impact on the real economy. This could be due, in part, to measurement problems with the constructed GDP series, although the impact on alternative real activity variables such as exports and non-megaproject exports also does not seem significant; the impact of exchange rate shocks on non-megaproject exports is more discernible.
- A monetary policy shock has a significant impact on prices. For example, the percentage change in the price level over an initial percentage change in base money is 0.21 for headline inflation and 0.12 for core (nonfood and energy) inflation after two quarters. The pass-through of M2 and M3 is also significant, albeit less pronounced, while the impact of interest rate shocks on prices is insignificant. Monetary aggregates do not have a more discernible or larger impact on measures of core inflation. There is also no evidence of a significant credit channel (shocks to domestic credit to the private sector) to prices.
- The exchange rate pass-through to headline inflation is greater than measures of core inflation.[15] The cumulative impulse response to an exchange rate shock of one standard deviation (or 8 percent) gives an exchange rate pass-through elasticity (percentage change in price

---

[14]Instead, see Piñón-Farah (1998) for analysis of the long-run demand for money in Mozambique.

[15]This may be explained by the greater share of nontradable goods in core inflation.

Figure 4.3. Effects of Exogenous and Monetary Shocks (Recursive VAR), 1996–2006

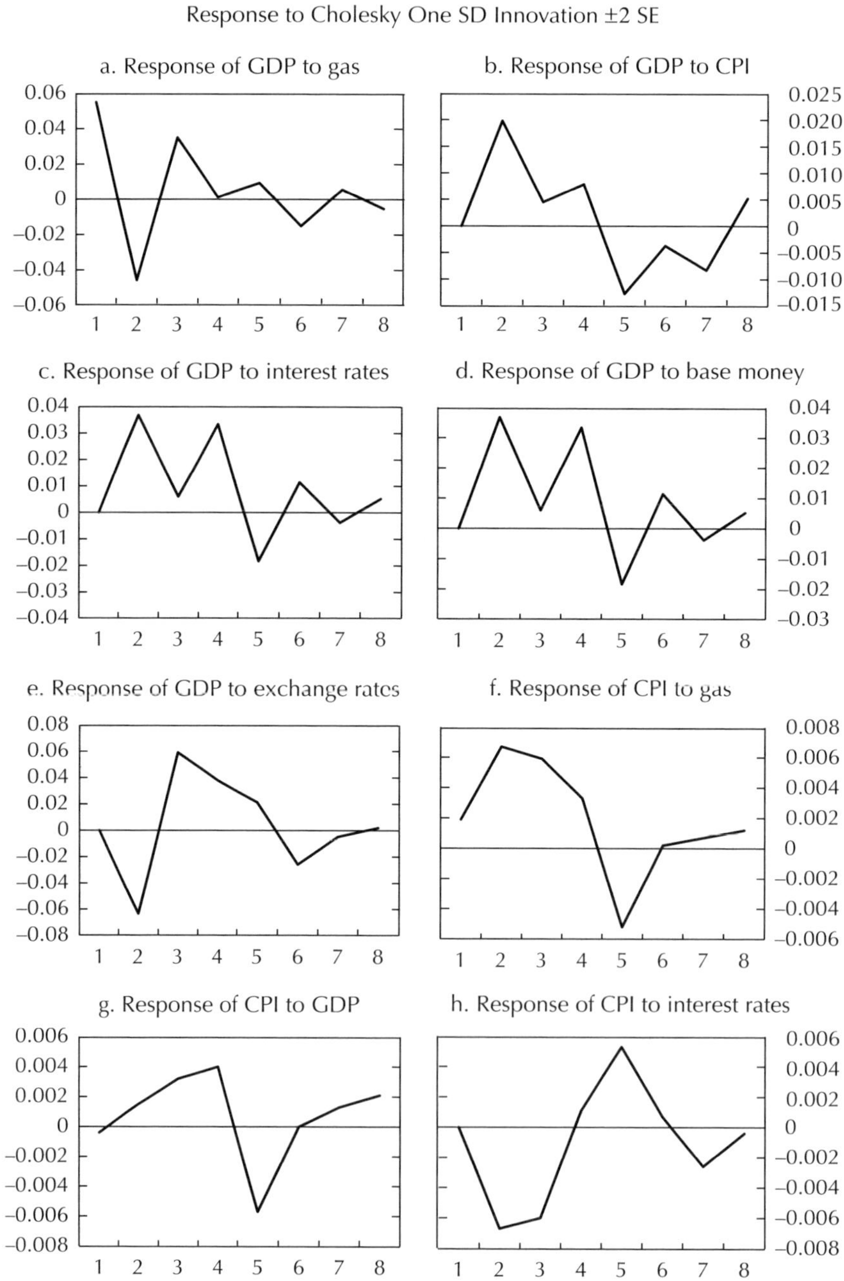

Figure 4.3 *(continued)*

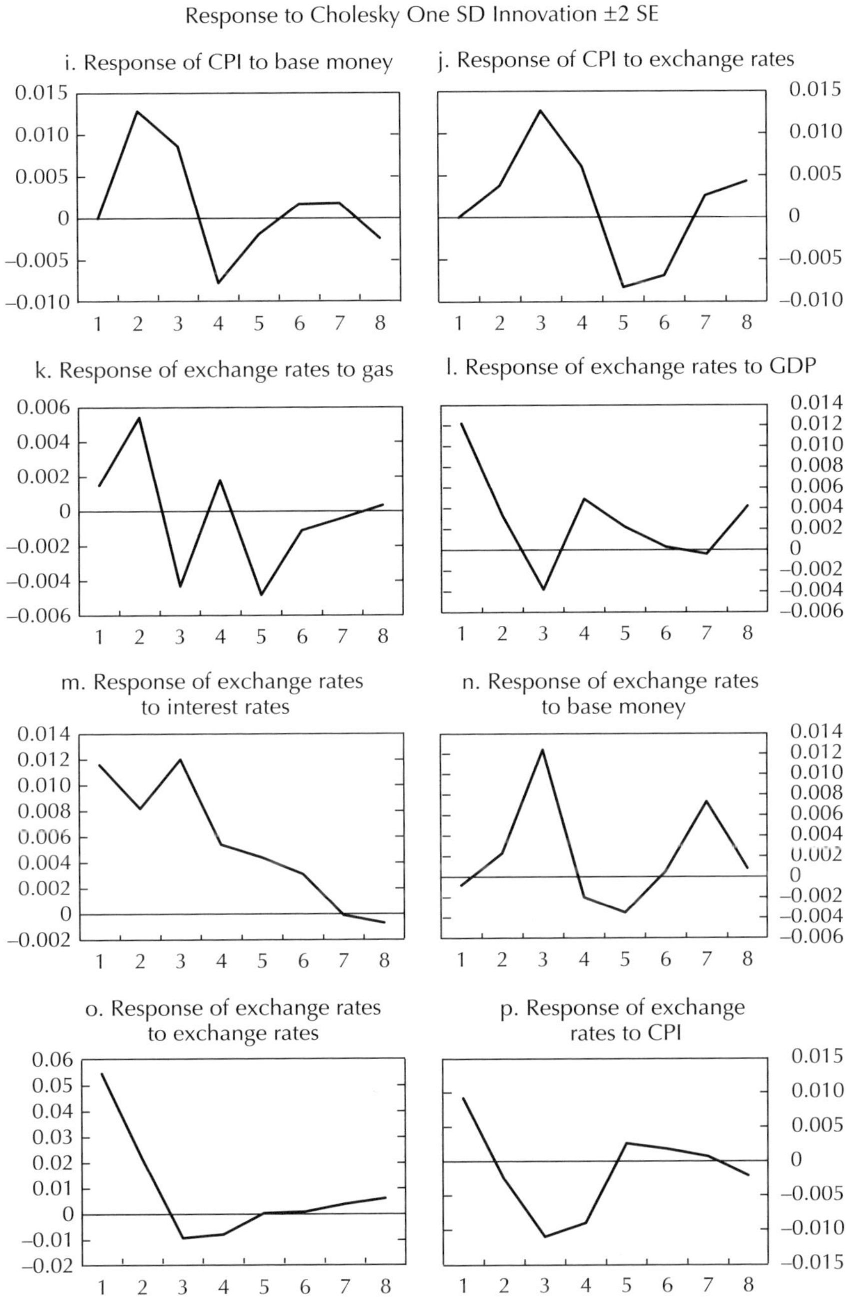

Figure 4.3 ***(concluded)***

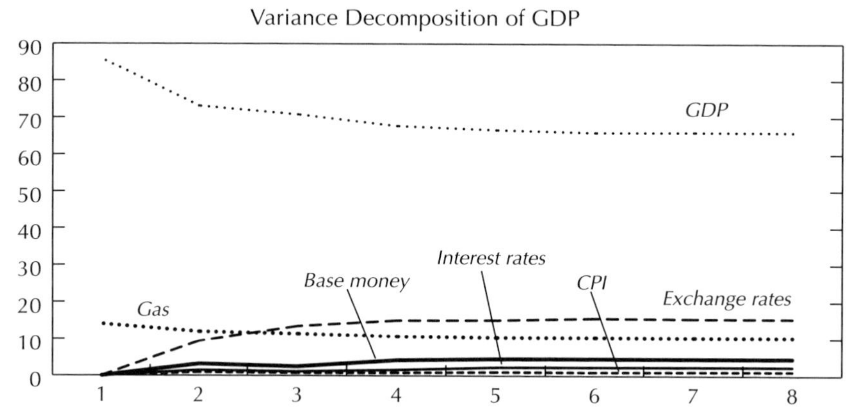

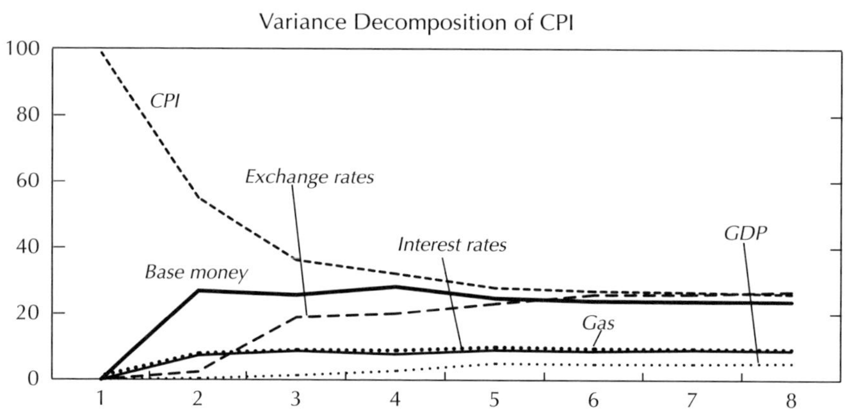

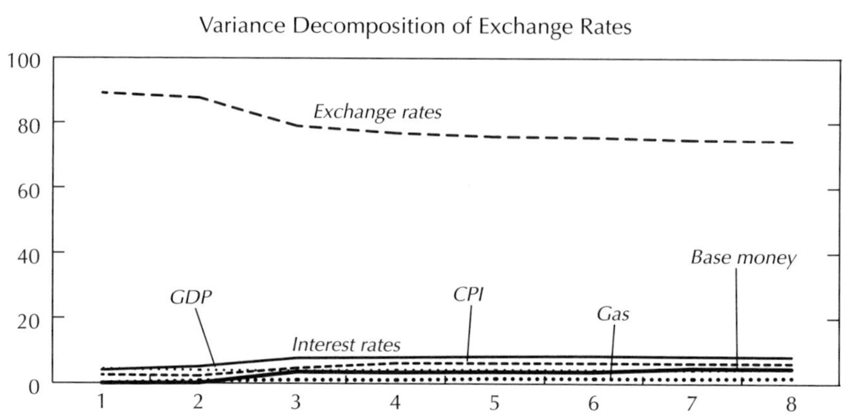

level t periods after the shock over an initial percentage change in the exchange rate) of 0.36 for headline inflation after four quarters. The pass-through to core inflation is negligible. This suggests that the exchange rate pass-through to headline inflation takes place almost exclusively through food prices. The less than one-to-one exchange rate pass-through may be explained by the degree of openness and strategic behavior in the form of pricing-to-market under imperfect competition.

- The nominal exchange rate does not appear to be susceptible to monetary and interest rate shocks. The latter suggests a somewhat low degree of capital mobility in Mozambique, although one should not be too surprised to find it hard to explain nominal exchange rate movements (see Engel, Nelson, and West, 2007).[16]

Economic Interpretations of the Econometric Results

The empirical findings suggest that headline inflation in Mozambique is significantly influenced by monetary policy (base money). Therefore, the results confirm that firm base money control has played an important part in bringing inflation under control. But they also show that times of lax monetary policy owing to weaknesses in the monetary and liquidity management framework and to events such as the banking crises that undermined monetary control have contributed to greater price instability (see "Monetary and Financial Sector Reforms" below). In addition, headline inflation is explained largely by its own innovations and, with food items weighted heavily in the CPI basket, is no doubt susceptible to wild swings in food prices caused by weather-related shocks to agriculture. Moreover, monetary aggregates and interest rates seem to have little impact on real output. This may be the result of structural weaknesses in the financial sector, which, at least until recently, are likely to have hampered the transmission mechanism of monetary policy. These weaknesses are likely to have made it difficult to cushion exogenous shocks in a systematic and credible way, on occasion causing substantial volatility in both prices and nominal interest rates. Volatility was also probably further exacerbated by Mozambique's shallow foreign exchange and public debt

[16]It should be noted, however, that Chapter 6 reports that foreign exchange intervention operations have a significant impact on the nominal exchange rate, indicating that the central bank's actions could have an impact on the exchange rate, even though their impact on base money is not discernible, possibly because of sterilization operations.

markets, with exchange rates and interest rates responding to numerous shocks not under the control of the central bank.

The base money–targeting approach seems to have been an appropriate policy framework, and the existence of the target appears to have anchored inflationary expectations and provided some discipline to discourage overly inflationary policies, albeit with some lapses. The BM has been targeting the monetary base—currency and bank reserves—as a way to achieve its longer-term goal of price stability. For an operational target to succeed in achieving a price objective there should be an identifiable transmission mechanism from the target to the price objective so that policymakers can determine the level they should seek. Our results show that base money does well on this count, similar to the findings in Barnichon and Peiris (2007), where the money "gap" appeared to contain significant information regarding the evolution of inflation in sub-Saharan Africa, although the transmission of monetary impulses through the real economy—and particularly to output—is less clear. Also, interest rates do not have an identifiable transmission mechanism to prices, making them unsuitable as instruments of monetary policy for now. In addition, policymakers need an active market in the target instrument that is not dominated by the central bank. In Mozambique, secondary debt markets have limited activity, with no overnight trades at all on some days. Targeting a rate in a market that barely trades would be difficult or impossible. Even if enough trading developed to make such targeting mechanically possible, it is not clear that achieving the targeted interest rate would result in the desired outcomes for the broader market structure or the economy.

Looking forward, the pursuit of a "lite" inflation targeting regime (Stone, 2003) could be seen as a transition to a full-fledged inflation targeting regime. The BM conducts monetary policy in a difficult setting characterized by a high propensity to transact in cash, shallow domestic financial markets, and an economy prone to numerous exogenous shocks. This is further complicated by large foreign exchange inflows in the form of grants and loans to finance the country's large fiscal deficit and poverty reduction strategy, which injects vast amounts of liquidity into a thinly monetized economy. Against this background, Chapter 5 shows that a judicious mix of foreign exchange sales and domestic debt issuance to mop up excess liquidity and target inflation could help the monetary authorities maintain a low level of macroeconomic volatility. Such a regime, which employs less market-oriented monetary targets, is close to the current base money–targeting regime in terms of its operational framework, can be implemented gradually, and can serve as an intermediate step toward a full-fledged inflation targeting regime.[17] In the next few years, by putting in place some of the preconditions for implementing a full-fledged inflation targeting regime (see Carare and others, 2002, and Box 4.4), Mozambique may gradually transition to such a regime.

Monetary and Financial Sector Reforms

First Wave of Reforms (1992–2000)

Liberalization of the financial system was one of the main objectives of Mozambique's successful post-conflict reform program during the 1990s and was an important element in IMF-supported programs during the period.[18] In 1993, the BM moved to a market-determined exchange rate system and established an interbank foreign exchange market. Interest rates were fully liberalized in 1994, but real interest rates were not consistently positive until 1997 owing to structural obstacles, including state ownership of the two dominant banks. Monetary management gradually evolved from a reliance on credit ceilings on individual banks to the use of reserve requirements and, starting in 1997, indirect instruments of monetary control. These measures have enhanced monetary control, helping to bring inflation down from very high levels and substantially decrease its variance (Figure 4.4). In line with economic theory and previous country experiences (McKinnon, 1973; Shaw, 1973; and Mirakhor, 1990), interest rate liberalization has also jump-started financial savings (Figure 4.5).

Financial sector reforms during this period also focused on developing the legal framework and establishing a basic supervisory regime for a more competitive market-based banking system. Several theoretical and empirical studies have shown that increasing banking competition by reducing government ownership as well as by removing obstacles to foreign entry are an important trigger to the subsequent development of sound, deep, and more efficient financial systems (Shleifer and Vishny, 2002; La Porta, Lopez-de-Silanes, and Shleifer, 2002; Barth, Caprio, and Levine, 2004; and Claessens and Laeven, 2004).

[17]Stone (2003) defines inflation targeting "lite" regimes as ones where the central bank "announce[s] a broad inflation objective but owing to [its] relative low credibility [it is] not able to maintain inflation as the foremost policy objective. Their relatively low credibility reflects their vulnerability to large economic shocks and shallow financial markets and a weak institutional framework."

[18]See IMF (2004) for a more detailed account of reforms undertaken in the context of IMF-supported programs during this period.

Figure 4.4. Mozambique: First-Generation Reforms and Inflation Dynamics, 1996–2000
(In percent)

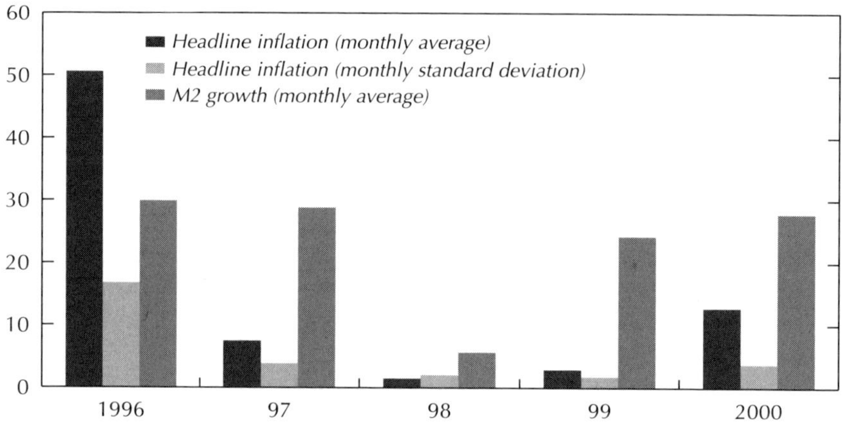

Source: IMF, International Financial Statistics.

Mozambique's reform experience appears to corroborate this hypothesis while emphasizing the importance of complementing it with a well-managed privatization process and appropriate regulatory and supervisory practices. The Financial Institutions Law and the Central Bank Law were passed in 1991, introducing banking supervision rules that were later supplemented by prudential regulations and the introduction of on-site and off-site inspections. Institutional reforms focused on separating the commercial and central banking functions of the BM. These reforms were accompanied by the restructuring and cleanup of the commercial arm of the BM, which was renamed Banco Comercial de Moçambique (BCM) in 1992. BCM was partially privatized, along with Mozambique's other main government-owned bank, Banco Popular de Desenvolvimento (BPD, renamed Banco Austral, BA), between 1996 and 1997. Obstacles to private and foreign ownership of banks were removed, leading to a marked increase in the number of banking institutions, most of them foreign owned. On balance, foreign bank entry has brought Mozambique the knowledge and skills required to establish a proper market-based financial system, as well as additional resources for financial intermediation. The partial sale of BPD and BCM to a foreign investor of dubious quality, on the other hand, demonstrates the shortcomings of a poorly managed privatization compounded by weak supervisory practices, as described below.

Figure 4.5. Mozambique: First-Generation Reforms and Financial Intermediation
(In percent)

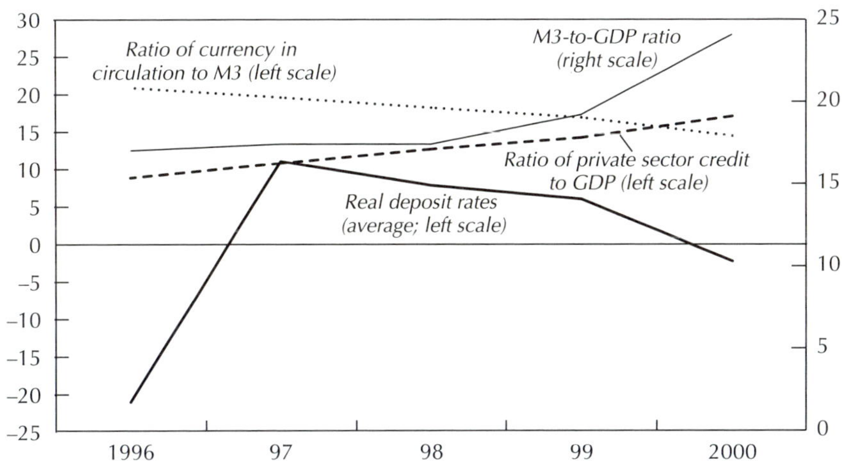

Source: IMF, International Financial Statistics.

Remaining Weaknesses in the Monetary and Financial System in 2002

Notwithstanding initial advances brought by the first wave of financial sector reforms, a number of structural problems with a direct impact on the stability, soundness, depth, and efficiency of the financial system remained.

Despite improvements in monetary management, inflation rates remained relatively high and volatile (Figure 4.4). Although this outcome was due, in part, to Mozambique's vulnerability to significant supply shocks (for example, related to weather and terms of trade), the volatility of prices and nominal interest rates highlighted weaknesses in the monetary framework and public debt management (Box 4.1). Such weaknesses prevented monetary authorities from cushioning largely fiscally induced demand shocks (that is, the unanticipated influx of external grants and loans, and costly recapitalizations described above) in a systematic, credible, and transparent way, causing, at times, substantial volatility in prices, as well as in nominal interest and exchange rates. Shallow foreign exchange and public debt markets exacerbated this volatility, prompting the government to adopt temporary measures to tightly manage interest and exchange rates—an action that reversed some of the original gains from financial liberalization and further compromised the transparency of the monetary framework.

Box 4.1. Weaknesses in Monetary Policy Management

Before Mozambique's banking crisis in 2000–02, effective monetary policy and public debt management in Mozambique were compromised by weaknesses in the monetary framework and in the Bank of Mozambique's (BM) net financial position.

The monetary framework lacked transparency. Market participants did not fully understand the goals or operational framework of the country's monetary policy, in part because of insufficient efforts by the BM to communicate with market participants, and also because of inconsistencies in the use of instruments that sent conflicting signals on the monetary policy stance.

BM's fragile financial position put the central bank's operational independence at risk. While the BM reported positive capital and declared operating profits, its net worth and profits became negative once valuation adjustments were properly accounted for. The BM's losses originated mainly from (1) accumulated foreign exchange valuation losses on its external liabilities to foreign lenders, and (2) operating losses stemming from sterilization (costs of monetary policy) not transferred to the budget.

Although a basic supervisory framework for the banking system had been put in place, the government did not have the capacity to effectively implement the new regulations; this problem was compounded by the absence of adequate reporting standards for monitoring the soundness of bank lending. The soundness of the financial system was further undermined by an increasing degree of liability dollarization, with foreign currency–denominated loans accounting for 70 percent of total loans in 2002. Moreover, despite their partial privatization, the two main state-owned banks remained subject to political interference, and a weak legal environment for lending (Box 4.2) translated into a rising level of nonperforming loans (especially for BCM and BA), high lending rates, and a poor level of financial intermediation even by regional standards, as reflected in Mozambique's low credit-to-GDP and loan-to-deposit ratios (Table 4.1).

Mozambique's high lending rates and poor financial intermediation were a result of numerous structural factors. Real lending rates in meticais during 1999–2002 averaged 17.5 percent. Such high and rigid rates were due primarily to very large intermediation spreads, which, according to a decomposition exercise conducted in Mozambique's 2003 Financial

Box 4.2. Weaknesses in the Institutional Lending Environment

Mozambique's high credit risk was attributed partly to its lack of institutional capacity to help lenders make informed decisions by disseminating information on borrowers' creditworthiness or to enable lenders to collect from borrowers upon default. Debt enforcement for unsecured loans through the courts was inefficient, and the country lacked both comprehensive laws for enforcing the collection of the collateral for secured loans and efficient bankruptcy laws.

Days to Resolve Business Dispute, 2002

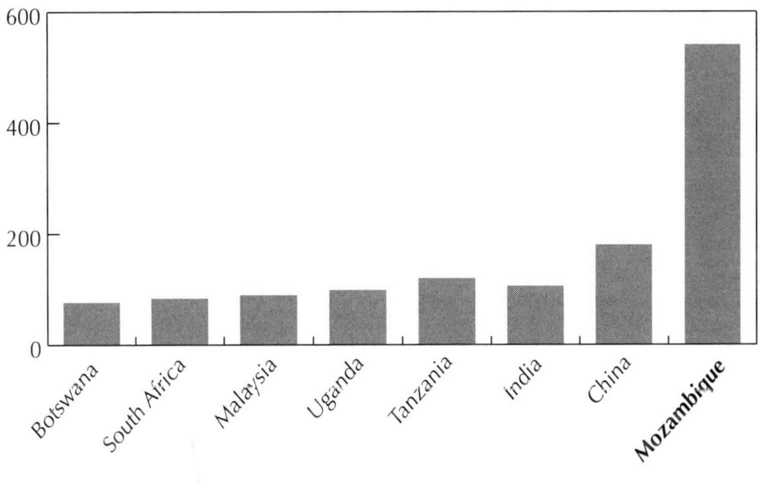

Source: World Bank (2003).

In the absence of institutions that could facilitate loan recovery and contract enforcement, banks were compelled to adopt a conservative stance toward smaller borrowers, restricting access to credit and charging higher rates. Lack of information on borrowers' creditworthiness further aggravated this problem; indeed, it increased uncertainty regarding nonperforming loans, forcing banks to increase their loan loss provisions (which made credit more costly), impose stringent collateral requirements, or simply refuse credit to applicants with no previous credit history.

Table 4.1. Mozambique and Comparators: Financial Intermediation, 2002

	Private credit	Deposits	Deposit dollarization (*Percent of total deposits*)	Bank concentration (*Percent of largest five banks*)
	(*Percent of GDP*)			
Mozambique	**14**	**23**	**57**	**96**
Sub-Saharan Africa	26	27	42	83
Low-income countries	18	21	49	71

Sources: IMF, International Financial Statistics; and Barth, Caprio, and Levine (2004).

Sector Assessment Program (FSAP)[19] (Figure 4.6), were caused partly by high levels of nonperforming loans made to state-owned enterprises and other noncompliant borrowers in the aftermath of the bank privatization process in the mid-1990s and banking crisis of 2000–02. Other factors included (1) high overhead costs that reflected, in part, the small size of the Mozambican financial system and credit risks; (2) high reserve requirements; and (3) generally substantial profit margins, reflecting high bank concentration and limited competition.

Weaknesses in Mozambique's financial system became particularly apparent during the costly recapitalization operations that took place in the aftermath of the bank privatization process. The privatized banks performed poorly because of continued insider lending and lending to parastatals, and the weak regulatory environment. As a result BA became insolvent. It was renationalized in 2000 and then reprivatized when it was sold to Amalgamated Banks of South Africa (ABSA) in 2001. ABSA accepted only 20 percent of BA's loans, so the Mozambican government had to provide bonds to cover the remaining 80 percent at a cost of approximately US$107 million. Likewise, BCM also continued to report losses after its privatization and was recapitalized by its shareholders in late 2000 and early 2001 at a total cost of US$130 million, half of which was paid by the government. This amount turned out to be insufficient, and an additional bailout of US$11 million (of which US$2.5 million came from the government) was necessary once the merger of BCM with Banco Internacional de Moçambique turned the new bank (currently referred to as BIM) into a market leader considered "too big to fail."

[19]The FSAP is a joint IMF–World Bank initiative introduced in 1999. FSAPs are undertaken at the request of a member country for the purpose of identifying the strengths and vulnerabilities of the country's financial system, determining how key sources of risk are managed, ascertaining the financial sector's development and technical assistance needs, and helping the country prioritize its policy responses.

Figure 4.6. Mozambique: Decomposition of Interest Rate Spreads in Meticais

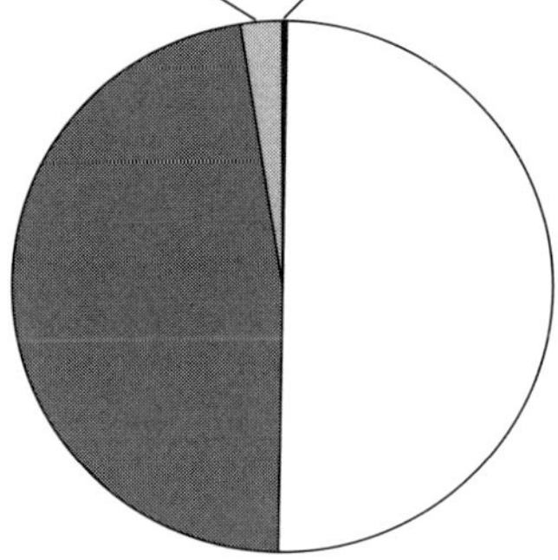

Source: Bank of Mozambique.
Note: 2002 data.

Lessons from the 2000–02 Banking Crisis and Subsequent Reform Efforts

Benefiting from recommendations from Mozambique's 2003 FSAP and with technical assistance from the IMF, the World Bank, and other donors under the program known as the Financial Sector Technical Assistance Project (FSTAP), the Mozambican government initiated well-sequenced reforms aimed at strengthening banking supervision, prudential regulations, and financial reporting in line with international best practices.[20] To limit the volatility in prices and interest rates, it made refining monetary policy formulation and deepening monetary and public debt markets top priorities. The government also initiated a more gradual program of reforms directed toward improving the legal and institutional environment for lending and then toward promoting the sound development of nonbank financial institutions (NBFIs), initially by enhancing the regulatory and supervisory framework.[21]

[20]See IMF (2007) for details on the Mozambican authorities' forward-looking financial sector strategy.

[21]NBFIs in Mozambique were deemed small, nontransparent, and subject to limited institutional and regulatory oversight. As such, they could mask sizable contingent fiscal liabilities. The situation was particularly critical in the insurance and pension sectors, where supervisory capacity was diluted and, in the case of pensions, weak. In particu-

Box 4.3. Strengthening Banking Supervision and the Regulatory Environment

Measures adopted over the past four years included the following:

1. Comprehensive diagnostic reviews of the major banks by international firms according to International Financial Reporting Standards (completed in 2005).
2. The implementation in 2004 of the new Financial Institutions Law, strengthening the central bank's supervisory powers and introducing stricter penalties for noncompliance.
3. Strengthening banking supervision in line with the Basel Core Principles by building on- and off-site supervisory capacity, requiring financial institutions and corporations to prepare financial statements in compliance with international accounting standards, and adopting prudential regulations that reflect international best practices.
4. Adoption of International Financial Reporting Standards by the BM in 2006 and by commercial banks in 2007.

Mozambique's reform effort has been noticeable. Over 2004–06, the government demonstrated its commitment to returning banks to private ownership; it has announced its intention of withdrawing from the one bank in which it remains a minority shareholder. Reform efforts have been pronounced in the area of banking supervision and reporting standards (Box 4.3). A new law strengthening the BM's supervisory and enforcement mandates was implemented in 2004. To dispel uncertainties about the overall condition of the banking system following the restructuring, the government allowed international firms to carry out comprehensive diagnostic reviews of the major banks according to international financial reporting standards (IFRS). These reviews, which were concluded in 2005, endorsed the overall soundness of the banking system. The authorities also continue to make progress in aligning on- and off-site banking supervision practices and accounting standards with international best principles.

While there has been some recent progress in improving the monetary policy framework, important measures to enhance monetary policy

lar, supervisory capacity in the insurance sector was shared by the Ministry of Finance (insurance) and the National Social Security Institute (INSS). Supervision of pensions was weakened by the fact that the Ministry of Finance had both an administrative and a prudential mandate.

operations and public debt management have yet to be implemented. The BM has already taken important steps to strengthen its monetary policy operations by increasing the use of foreign exchange sales and issuance of treasury bills to sterilize excessive liquidity, and it is currently working to improve liquidity management, ensure its operational independence, and deepen foreign exchange, money, and debt markets (Box 4.4). Over time, these measures should set the stage for the BM to gradually transition to a "lite," and subsequently to a full-fledged, inflation targeting regime.

Reforms in the institutional lending environment have followed but have lagged behind other reforms. Among the few achievements on the legal front have been the implementation of the new Commercial Code and the establishment of the commercial sections of the judicial tribunals in the cities of Maputo, Beira, and Nampula. The Commercial Code will help relieve the overburdened judicial system by making commercial disputes less likely. The commercial sections of the judicial tribunals became operational in 2007, and are expected to accelerate the recovery of unsecured loans once they have received appropriate equipment, facilities, and technical assistance. Debt recovery is expected to be accelerated even further once a revised Civil Procedure Code with streamlined judicial procedures is enacted. However, despite these encouraging steps, significant measures are still required to improve the lending environment (Box 4.5).

The government has taken initial steps to support a sound expansion of NBFIs. The BM has started to license and supervise deposit-taking MFIs. A new law on social protection recently approved by the National Assembly will help strengthen the social security and supplementary pension systems. As part of the restructuring of the INSS, an actuarial study to determine whether the current level of contributions is capable of sustaining the benefits covered will be completed in 2008. The government is also enhancing the regulatory and supervisory framework for the pension and insurance sectors. The Insurance Law is being reviewed in line with international best practices, and revised prudential and solvency requirements for Mozambican insurers are being developed, while a new IFRS-compliant Chart of Accounts for insurers will also be designed. New regulations are also being prepared for supplementary pension funds. Looking ahead, the focus will need to shift to strengthening the capacity of industry regulators.

Gauging the Impact of Reform

Financial sector reforms, while still incomplete, have contributed to marked improvements in the soundness and efficiency of the banking

Box 4.4. Strengthening Monetary and Public Debt Management

Monetary policy framework. The BM has adopted a money targeting framework using base money as the operational target. In order to improve the BM's transparency and communication vis-à-vis market participants, the BM has approved a long-term monetary policy strategy document clarifying the money targeting framework, defining a new format for the monetary policy committee, and specifying the BM's communication policies. The central bank has also made good progress in increasing its analytical capacity through the development of databases and the use of standard monetary models in assessing the appropriateness of the monetary policy stance. Work is ongoing to translate the annual and quarterly monetary targets into a liquidity management plan that separates the management of short-term "temporary" and long-term "structural" liquidity resulting from government domestic expenditures financed mainly through foreign donor inflows. The BM introduced repos in 2007 to fine-tune temporary liquidity variations and is working to ensure an appropriate mix of foreign exchange sales and net treasury bill issuance for the purpose of sterilizing structural liquidity so as to facilitate absorption of foreign aid, with clear signaling of sterilization and intervention actions in the foreign exchange market. The deepening of debt and foreign exchange markets will also be needed to avoid undue movement in interest rates and exchange rates.

Central bank independence. The central bank's operational independence in conducting sterilization operations has been secured through a more comprehensive agreement to shift the corresponding costs to the Ministry of Finance. Further reforms are also needed to clarify that the central bank's sole objective is price and financial stability while legally ruling out the possibility

system. Bank profitability has recovered, and the share of nonperforming loans has fallen to less than 5 percent of all loans since 2005, according to Mozambican accounting standards (Figure 4.7). Greater confidence in the banking system has led to a significant decrease in liability dollarization and thus less financial vulnerability.[22] Banks have also become more efficient. In particular, the ratio of noninterest expenses to gross

[22]The strong decline in credit denominated in foreign currency was driven, in large part, by a prudential measure introduced in July 2005 that required loan loss provisioning to cover 50 percent of foreign currency–denominated loans to nonexporters. This decrease was, however, accompanied by an increase in applications for private external financing.

of financing the fiscal deficit, to further enhance central bank autonomy and credibility.

Central bank liquidity management. The BM is in the process of refining its liquidity monitoring and forecasting with technical assistance from the IMF. Additional technical assistance is needed to enhance the BM's capacity to accurately forecast short-term liquidity flows in the financial system and manage temporary fluctuations in liquidity using appropriate instruments. Of critical importance are improvements in the information provided by the Treasury on its daily cash flows and use of repos to fine-tune temporary liquidity variations (see previous page).

Public debt management. Reform is still in its early stages. The government needs to develop a strategy for the management of domestic debt, and the public debt department at the Ministry of Finance will need to be restructured and its staff trained.

Treasury bill and money markets. While recent progress was achieved with the removal of interest caps on T-bill auctions, more needs to be done to promote an active and liquid market for government securities. At the top of the list would be improving the enforcement of the legal framework governing the transfer of securities and the implementation of a real-time gross settlement system to foster the development of a secondary market. On the latter, the government has just submitted a draft law on a new national payment system.

Foreign exchange markets. Important steps have recently been taken regarding the interbank foreign exchange market (MCI) with the elimination of exchange rate bands in foreign exchange auctions and the MCI, and measures to promote the practice of firm quotations among market participants. Further MCI reforms are needed with the adoption of an appropriate collateral system.

income and, to a lesser extent, the ratio of personal expenses to noninterest expenses have been declining since 2004.

Mozambique's financial sector reforms have also had positive spillovers to financial intermediation. The enhanced regulatory and supervisory framework and cleaned-up balance sheets—especially at BIM—have restored confidence in the banking sector, causing broad money growth to outpace nominal GDP growth and credit to the private sector to almost double in just two years (Table 4.2, Figure 4.8). These developments reflect structural factors associated with banks again taking on consumer credit (for example, credit cards and loans for the purchase of durable goods) and lending for industrial activities, as well as borrowing by domestic petroleum distributors related to the syndication of larger oil-import transactions. Lending to the

Box 4.5. Strengthening Mozambique's Lending Environment

Framework for secured transactions. Additional measures include updating the legal framework for secured transactions. The recent enactment of a decree on urban land use and corresponding regulations was a first step in this direction; it is expected to facilitate the use of urban land as collateral by reducing the time and costs involved in transactions. Next steps in this area would be to tackle the modernization and linking of property registries and to implement a new Bankruptcy Law.

Enhancement of the scope and reliability of the credit registry. Reform is just starting in this area with assistance from the International Finance Corporation (the private sector arm of the World Bank Group) and the Millennium Challenge Corporation. With assistance from the IFC, the BM will conduct a feasibility study to examine options for increasing the scope and reliability of its credit registry.

agriculture and rural sectors remains minimal, however. Real lending rates and spreads have also been on a declining trend since 2002.[23]

MFIs have grown significantly in the past decade. During 2000–05 there was a fivefold increase in the number of clients and a sevenfold increase in outstanding loans (Figure 4.9). Consolidation also seems to be under way: 3 institutions out of about 35 control more than 68 percent of the active loan portfolio. However, MFI outreach is very limited. Rural areas account for less than 12 percent of total borrowers. Nonetheless, growth has been accompanied by a substantial improvement in performance. The percentage of MFIs with recovery rates considered acceptable (90 percent or above) increased from 16 percent in 1997 to about 30 percent in 2005. The access of the agriculture and rural sectors to banking and MFIs remains limited, however.[24]

[23]Issues related to financial depth are discussed further in Chapter 9 in the context of reforms in the business environment designed to improve the access of small and medium-size enterprises and rural areas to financing.

[24]About 62 percent of MFIs and 50 percent of micro borrowers are concentrated in the Maputo-Matola urban corridor; rural areas account for less than 12 percent of borrowers and only 5 percent of the total active portfolio. To some extent, this disparity in microfinance provision seems to reflect the large concentration of nonagricultural informal activities in the province of Maputo or Maputo City. Preliminary data for 2005 on informal sector activities published by Mozambique's national statistical agency show that of the nonagricultural informal sector activities, 42 percent of those involved in trading and 48 percent of those involved in services (excluding transport) are located in those areas.

Figure 4.7. Mozambique: Banking Soundness, Depth, and Efficiency, 2000–06

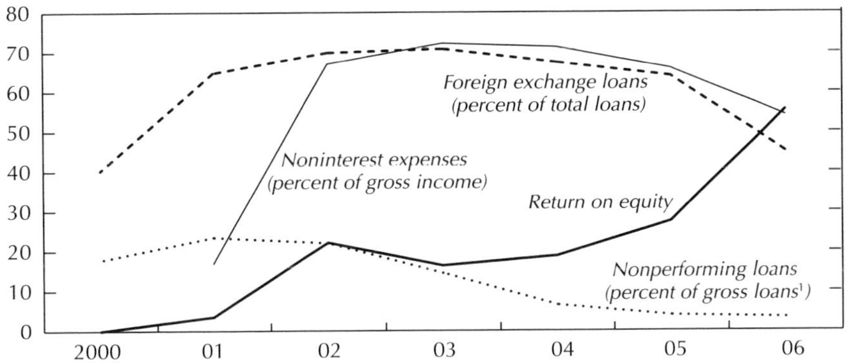

Source: Bank of Mozambique.
[1]According to Mozambican accounting standards, nonperforming loans include only part of past-due loans.

Conclusions and Lessons for Sub-Saharan Africa

A prudent macroeconomic policy mix supported by monetary and financial sector reforms is critical to reducing inflation and ensuring financial stability in the early phases of stabilization. Macroeconomic stabilization in the context of very high inflation and a debt overhang, as in Mozambique in the early 1990s, requires fiscal consolidation to anchor inflationary expectations and avoid recourse to unsustainable domestic financing (and public debt) to maintain a credible nominal anchor. In this regard, relying only on sustained sterilized intervention could backfire, since such interventions limit the growth of the money supply but raise public debt. In sum, in countries with significant debt overhangs, purely money-based stabilization is unlikely to be effective without the support of fiscal consolidation. In addition, monetary and financial sector reforms, particularly reforms that address vulnerabilities in the banking system, as well as perseverance with prudent macroeconomic policies, can help maintain single-digit inflation rates and financial stability in the face of exogenous shocks, as demonstrated by Mozambique in the past few years.

A monetary targeting framework can be employed to maintain price stability and set the stage for adopting a more formal inflation targeting regime in the post-stabilization phase. Analysis of the monetary transmission mechanism in Mozambique suggests that base money could be a suitable operational instrument in controlling inflation in a country with

Table 4.2. Mozambique: Sectoral Contribution to Credit Growth,[1] 2005–06
(In percent of total credit growth)

	December 2005	December 2006
Economic activity		
Agriculture	9.8	–0.4
Industry	2.4	42.1
of which:		
Extractive industry	–0.9	19.8
Manufacturing industry	–2.2	13.7
Construction	5.2	11.6
Commerce[2]	42.2	27.5
Transport and communications	5.1	7.4
Other	35.3	11.7
of which:		
Monetary and financial institutions	2.3	–3.6
Private[3]	14.6	15.6
Housing	–2.7	3.4
Diverse[4]	21.2	–3.6
Total	100	100
Memorandum items:		
Credit growth, Monthly Credit Survey	56.6	25.0
Credit growth, Monetary Survey	57.0	29.2

Source: Bank of Mozambique, Monthly Credit Survey.

[1]Total and sectoral growth on a 12-month basis and derived from the Bank of Mozambique's (BM's) Monthly Credit Survey. This survey covers only a sample of the universe of financial institutions covered in the BM's Monetary Survey.

[2]Includes all loans to finance domestic and foreign trade activities such as oil and food imports.

[3]Includes credit cards and consumer credit lines for vehicles and durable goods.

[4]Nonclassified activities.

shallow domestic financial markets, where interest rates may not yet have an identifiable transmission to prices, and there is a continuous need to mop up excess structural liquidity injected by a large fiscal deficit financed by buoyant aid inflows. Broader monetary aggregates could also provide a useful intermediate target but require further research, particularly regarding the stability of long-run money demand. Further research into the credit channel of monetary policy, interest rate determination, and degree of capital mobility in sub-Saharan Africa is also needed, given the difficulties of explaining real economic activity and exchange rate movements. As suggested in Chapter 5, "lite" inflation targeting that employs the instruments available to monetary policy to achieve a broad inflation objective is operationally close to the base money–targeting framework practiced in Mozambique and much of the rest of sub-Saharan Africa. It can be seen as an intermediate step toward switching to a full-fledged inflation targeting regime in which a specific level or range of expected

Figure 4.8. Mozambique: Bank Depth, 2000–06

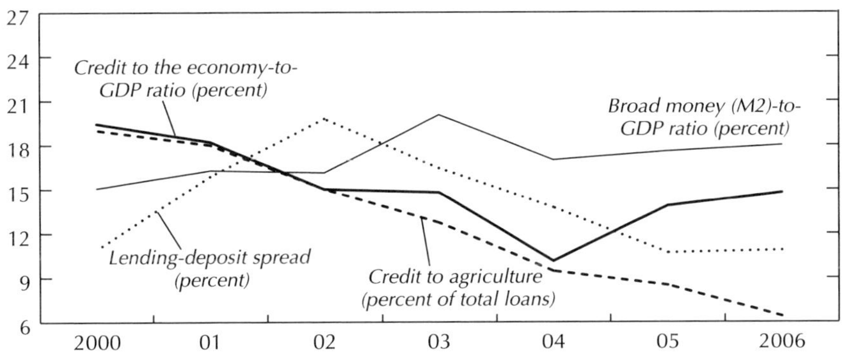

Source: Bank of Mozambique.

inflation, instead of a monetary aggregate, is the intermediate target, and where the interest rate, rather than base money, is the operational instrument. In the interim, the focus should be on strengthening the monetary policy and liquidity management framework; providing greater central bank independence; and deepening debt, money, and foreign exchange markets—in other words, continuing to build the preconditions for a full-fledged inflation targeting regime.

Improving the outreach of the financial system remains a key challenge. With the soundness of the banking system restored, reforms to improve financial sector intermediation and access to financial services are assuming center stage. Policies and reforms in this area will need to continue strengthening the lending environment and facilitating the outreach of banks and MFIs and other private sector financial services to small and medium-size enterprises and rural areas. Looking ahead, it will be important to identify new quick wins. In this regard, special attention could be given to credit registries, particularly by expanding their scope and ensuring that their coverage increases in line with outreach growth. However, to ensure the soundness of an expanding financial system, outreach reforms will need to be accompanied by improvements in supervision practices, prudential regulations, and accounting standards beyond the banking sector. In the near term, introduction of risk-based supervision and international reporting standards in the banking sector will facilitate monitoring of capital adequacy during a period of strong credit growth. Rolling out International Financial Reporting Standards to the corporate sector will

Figure 4.9. Mozambique: Growth in Microfinance Activities

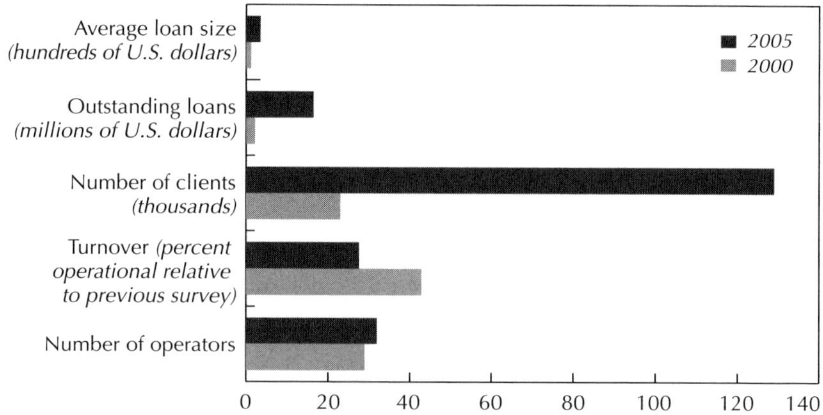

Source: Mozambique Microfinance Facility, 2006, Survey of Microfinance Operators.

further reduce credit risk by improving the ability of the financial system to evaluate the quality of loan portfolios. Increasing attention will also need to be devoted to rural financing issues.

Mozambique's relatively successful financial sector reform program has some important lessons to offer other low-income countries:

- Getting the sequencing of reforms right is crucial. Mozambique's reform experience highlighted the importance of making sure that first-generation reforms promoting financial sector liberalization and market-based banking systems are complemented at an early stage by efforts to strengthen the supervisory capacity and regulatory environment of the banking system to ensure the soundness of financial intermediation. Thus, reforms that ensure the soundness, efficiency, and stability of the banking system could be given higher priority than second-generation reforms aimed at promoting the access, outreach, and innovation of financial services.
- Successful reform often requires making good use of brief windows of opportunity when there is broad political support for implementation. This widely recognized lesson is confirmed by Mozambique's financial sector reforms as well as by business environment reforms (the latter are discussed in Chapter 9). Mozambique's reform effort—particularly in the areas of banking supervision and reporting standards—was timely in the aftermath of bank restructuring in the early 2000s.

Bibliography

Adam, C., and S. O'Connell, 2005, "Monetary Policy in Sub-Saharan Africa" (unpublished; Washington: International Monetary Fund).

Agénor, P., and P. Montiel, 1999, *Development Macroeconomics* (Princeton, New Jersey: Princeton University Press, 2d ed.).

Alesina, A., and A. Drazen, 1991, "Why Are Stabilizations Delayed?" *American Economic Review*, Vol. 81 (December), pp. 1170–88.

Aron, J., and J. Muellbauer, 2001, "Interest Rate Effects on Output: Evidence from a GDP Forecasting Model for South Africa," *Staff Papers*, International Monetary Fund, Vol. 49 (November), pp. 185–213.

Ball, L., and G. Mankiw, 1995, "Relative-Price Changes as Aggregate Supply Shocks," *Quarterly Journal of Economics*, Vol. 110 (February), pp. 161–93.

Barnichon, Régis, and S.J. Peiris, 2007, "Sources of Inflation in Sub-Saharan Africa," IMF Working Paper 07/32 (Washington: International Monetary Fund).

Barth, J.R., G. Caprio, and R. Levine, 2004, "Bank Regulation and Supervision: What Works Best?" *Journal of Financial Intermediation*, Vol. 13 (April), pp. 205–48.

Batini, Nicoletta, and Anthony Yates, 2003, "Hybrid Inflation and Price-Level Targeting," *Journal of Money, Credit and Banking*, Vol. 35 (June), pp. 283–300.

Bernanke, Ben S., and Alan S. Blinder, 1992, "The Federal Funds Rate and the Channels of Monetary Transmission," *American Economic Review*, Vol. 82 (September), pp. 901–21.

Bernanke, Ben S., and Ilian Mihov 1998, "Measuring Monetary Policy," *Quarterly Journal of Economics*, Vol. 113 (August), pp. 869–902.

Bernanke, Ben S., and others, 1999, *Inflation Targeting: Lessons from the International Experience* (Princeton, New Jersey: Princeton University Press).

Calvo, G.A., 1983, "Staggered Prices in a Utility-Maximizing Framework," *Journal of Monetary Economics*, Vol. 12 (September), pp. 383–98.

———, and C. Végh, 1999, "Inflation Stabilization and BOP Crises in Developing Countries," in *Handbook of Macroeconomics*, Vol. 1C, ed. by J. Taylor and M. Woodford (Amsterdam: North-Holland), pp. 1531–614.

Canzoneri, M., R. Cumby, and B. Diba, 2001, "Is the Price Level Determined by the Needs of Fiscal Solvency?" *American Economic Review*, Vol. 91 (December), pp. 1221–38.

Carare, Alina, Andrea Schaechter, Mark Stone, and Marc Zelmer, 2002, "Establishing Initial Conditions in Support of Inflation Targeting," IMF Working Paper 02/102 (Washington: International Monetary Fund).

Castro, R., C. De Resende, and F. Ruge-Murcia, 2003, "The Backing of Government Debt and the Price Level," Centre for Interuniversity Research in Quantitative Economics (CIREQ), Working Paper 16–2003 (Montreal: University of Montreal). Available via the Internet: http://www.cireq.umontreal.ca/publications/16-2003-cah.pdf

Catão, L., and M. Terrones, 2005, "Fiscal Deficits and Inflation," *Journal of Monetary Economics*, Vol. 52 (April), pp. 529–54.

Chopra, A., 1985, "The Speed of Adjustment of the Inflation Rate in Developing Countries: A Study of Inertia," *Staff Papers*, International Monetary Fund, Vol. 32 (December), pp. 693–733.

Christiano, L., M. Eichenbaum, and C. Evans, 2000, "Monetary Policy Shocks: What Have We Learned and to What End?" in *Handbook of Macroeconomics*, Vol. 1A, ed. by J. Taylor and M. Woodford (Amsterdam: North-Holland).

———, 2001, "Nominal Rigidities and the Dynamic Effects of a Shock to Monetary Policy," Working Paper No. 0107 (Cleveland: Federal Reserve Bank of Cleveland).

Claessens, Stijn, and Luc Laeven, 2004, "What Drives Bank Competition? Some International Evidence," *Journal of Money, Credit and Banking*, Vol. 36 (June, Part 2), pp. 563–83.

Coe, D., and C. McDermott, 1997, "Does the Gap Model Work in Asia?" *Staff Papers*, International Monetary Fund, Vol. 44 (March), pp. 59–80.

Cukierman, A., S. Edwards, and G. Tabellini, 1992, "Seigniorage and Political Instability," *American Economic Review*, Vol. 82 (June), 537–55.

Engel, Charles, Mark C. Nelson, and Kenneth D. West, 2007, "Exchange Rate Models Are Not as Bad as You Think," paper prepared for the NBER Annual Conference on Macroeconomics, Cambridge, Massachusetts, March 30–31.

Fischer, Stanley, 1993, "The Role of Macroeconomic Factors in Growth," *Journal of Monetary Economics*, Vol. 32 No. 3, pp. 45–66.

———, R. Sahay, and C. Végh, 2002, "Modern Hyper- and High Inflations," *Journal of Economic Literature*, Vol. 40 (September), pp. 837–80.

Frydl, Edward, 1999, "The Length and Cost of Banking Crises," IMF Working Paper 99/30 (Washington: International Monetary Fund).

Galí, J., and M. Gertler, 1999, "Inflation Dynamics: A Structural Econometric Analysis," *Journal of Monetary Economics*, Vol. 44 (October), pp. 195–222.

Ghosh, A., and Steven Phillips, 1998, "Warning: Inflation May Be Harmful to Your Growth," *Staff Papers*, International Monetary Fund, Vol. 45 (December), pp. 672–710.

Hakura, Dalia S., 2005, "Are Emerging Market Countries Learning to Float?" IMF Working Paper 05/98 (Washington: International Monetary Fund).

Hendry, D.F., 1995, *Dynamic Econometrics* (Oxford: Oxford University Press).

International Monetary Fund (IMF), 2003, *World Economic Outlook, April 2003*, World Economic and Financial Surveys (Washington).

———, 2004, *Republic of Mozambique: Ex Post Assessment of Mozambique's Performance Under Fund-Supported Programs*, IMF Country Report No. 04/53 (Washington). Available via the Internet: http://www.imf.org/external/pubs/ft/scr/2004/cr0453.pdf

———, 2005, *World Economic Outlook, September 2005*, World Economic and Financial Surveys (Washington).

———, 2007, *Mozambique: Selected Issues,* IMF Country Report No. 07/258 (Washington).

Kim, Soyoung, and Nouriel Roubini, 2000, "Exchange Rate Anomalies in the Industrial Countries: A Solution with a Structural VAR Approach," *Journal of Monetary Economics,* Vol. 45 (June), pp. 561–68.

Kwon, G., L. McFarlane, and W. Robinson, 2006, "Public Debt, Money Supply, and Inflation: A Cross-Country Study and Its Application to Jamaica," IMF Working Paper 06/121 (Washington: International Monetary Fund).

La Porta, R., F. Lopez-de-Silanes, and A. Shleifer, 2002, "Government Ownership of Banks," *Journal of Finance,* Vol. 57 (February), pp. 265–301.

Leeper, Eric M., and Tack Yun, 2005, "Monetary-Fiscal Policy Interactions and the Price Level: Background and Beyond," NBER Working Paper No. 11646 (Cambridge, Massachusetts: National Bureau of Economic Research).

Levine, Ross, 2005, "Finance and Growth: Theory and Evidence," in *Handbook of Economic Growth,* Vol. 1A, ed. by P. Aghion and S. Durlauf (Amsterdam: North-Holland), pp. 865–934.

Liviatan, N., and S. Piterman, 1986, "Accelerating Inflation and Balance-of-Payments Crises, 1973–84," in *The Israeli Economy: Maturing Through Crisis,* ed. by Yoram Ben-Porath (Cambridge, Massachusetts: Harvard University Press).

Loungani, P., and P. Swagel, 2001, "Sources of Inflation in Developing Countries," IMF Working Paper 01/198 (Washington: International Monetary Fund).

McKinnon, R.I., 1973, *Money and Capital in Economic Development* (Washington: Brookings Institution).

Mirakhor, Abbas, 1990, "Interest Rate Policies, Stabilization, and Bank Supervision in Developing Countries: Strategies for Financial Reforms," IMF Working Paper 90/8 (Washington: International Monetary Fund).

Noy, I., 2005, "Banking Crises in East Asia: The Price Tag of Liberalization?" Asia-Pacific Issues Analysis No. 78 (Honolulu: East-West Center).

Peersman, Gert, and Frank Smets, 2003, "The Monetary Transmission Mechanism in the Euro Area: More Evidence from VAR Analysis," in *Monetary Policy Transmission Mechanism in the Euro Area: A Study by the Eurosystem Monetary Transmission Network* (New York: Cambridge University Press).

Piñón-Farah, M., 1998, "Demand for Money in Mozambique—Was There a Structural Break?" IMF Working Paper 98/157 (Washington: International Monetary Fund).

Posen, A., 1995, "Central Bank Independence and Disinflationary Credibility: A Missing Link?" Staff Report No. 1 (New York: Federal Reserve Bank).

Sargent, T.J., and N. Wallace, 1981, "Some Unpleasant Monetarist Arithmetic," Federal Reserve Bank of Minneapolis *Quarterly Review,* Vol. 5, No. 3, pp. 1–17.

Saxegaard, Magnus, 2006, "Excess Liquidity and Effectiveness of Monetary Policy: Evidence from Sub-Saharan Africa," IMF Working Paper 06/115 (Washington: International Monetary Fund).

Shaw, E.S., 1973, *Financial Deepening in Economic Development* (New York: Oxford University Press).

Shleifer, A., and R. Vishny, 2002, *The Grabbing Hand: Government Pathologies and Their Cures* (Cambridge, Massachusetts: Harvard University Press).

Sims, Christopher, 1980, "Macroeconomics and Reality," *Econometrica*, Vol. 48 (January), pp. 1–48.

———, 1986, "Are Forecasting Models Usable for Policy Analysis?" Federal Reserve Bank of Minneapolis *Quarterly Review*, Vol. 10, No. 1, pp. 1–16.

———, and Tao Zha, 2006, "Does Monetary Policy Generate Recessions?" *Macroeconomic Dynamics*, Vol. 10, No. 2, pp. 231–72.

Stone, Mark, 2003, "Inflation Targeting Lite," IMF Working Paper 03/12 (Washington: International Monetary Fund).

Woodford, M., 2001, "Fiscal Requirements for Price Stability," *Journal of Money, Credit and Banking*, Vol. 33, No. 3, pp. 669–728.

World Bank, 2003, "Mozambique Industrial Performance and Investment Climate 2003" (Washington).

5

Monetary Policy in Sub-Saharan Africa: Lessons from a Dynamic Stochastic General Equilibrium Model Applied to Mozambique

SHANAKA J. PEIRIS AND MAGNUS SAXEGAARD

Macroeconomic conditions in a number of sub-Saharan African countries have improved markedly in the past decade (IMF, 2005a), providing greater scope for stabilization policies. Higher economic growth rates have been associated with lower inflation rates, healthier public finances, and higher international reserves in a group of countries dubbed "mature stabilizers" (Selassie and others, 2006) or post-stabilization economies. Mozambique is one of these countries.

In general, the central banks of the mature stabilizers are no longer subsumed by the fiscal authorities' financing needs, a situation sometimes referred to as "fiscal dominance" (see Chapter 4). The possibility of an activist monetary policy provides the authorities with an important mechanism that can help them in their efforts to achieve economic stability.[1] Political economy arguments provide little scope for the use of discretionary fiscal policy for stabilization in low-income countries because

[1]In the mid-1990s, almost 80 percent of non-CFA countries used some form of exchange rate peg as a nominal anchor; today, the majority rely on a monetary anchor. The decisive shift away from exchange rates and toward money as the preferred nominal anchor for inflation, along with financial liberalization, provides an added impetus to analyze monetary policy for stabilization purposes (Adam and O'Connell, 2005).

of implementation lags and its susceptibility to the political cycle (Alesina and Tabellini, 2005). This view suggests that monetary policy, rather than fiscal policy, should be considered the primary tool for stabilizing the economy in the absence of fiscal dominance.

The use of monetary policy for macroeconomic stabilization in sub-Saharan Africa poses a number of challenges that have not been fully analyzed in the literature, which focuses on the conduct of monetary policy in industrial countries. While a number of studies have analyzed the sources of inflation in sub-Saharan Africa (for example, Barnichon and Peiris, 2007), only a few papers have analyzed the trade-offs between alternative monetary policy rules in sub-Saharan African and low-income countries in general.[2] The vast literature on the science of monetary policy is focused on industrial countries and advanced emerging markets (Clarida, Galí, and Gertler, 1999; and Taylor, 1998), and provides few insights into the conduct of monetary policy in low-income countries, where the economy and monetary policy setting are quite different. Differences include the need to coordinate monetary and exchange rate policy with fiscal policy in order to manage large volatile aid inflows and government revenues from natural resource exploitation (IMF, 2005b). In particular, economic policy needs to consider the potential adverse effects of such shocks on the tradable sector—the so-called Dutch disease[3]—as well as the traditional objectives of inflation and output stabilization.[4] In addition, commercial banks in sub-Saharan Africa are at the center of a formal financial system, and, for most countries, the conduct of monetary policy focuses primarily on the supply of, and demand for, the monetary base (Adam and O'Connell, 2005). As a result, interest rates represent a reliable instrument of monetary policy only in the very few cases where interbank money markets and secondary markets for government debt are well developed, as in Mauritius and South Africa. Finally, the dominance of commercial banks and information asymmetries are likely to mean that

[2]This is due, in part, to the preoccupation with the need for fiscal control and effective nominal anchors to bring inflation down from very high levels, which has now been largely achieved in Mozambique (see Chapter 4).

[3]A key issue in sub-Saharan Africa is the impact of spending scaled-up foreign aid on the real exchange rate, exports, and competitiveness, which according to Rajan and Subramanian (2005) explains the weak link between aid inflows and growth in developing countries. Similar assertions have been made regarding the poor growth performance of natural resource rich economies (Sachs and Warner, 1995).

[4]Pallage and Robe (2003) estimate the median welfare cost of business cycles in developing countries to be between 10 and 30 times as large as in the United States.

the credit channel is a prominent part of the monetary policy transmission mechanism (Bernanke and Gertler, 1995).

This chapter attempts to analyze different monetary policy rules in sub-Saharan Africa, taking into account the sources of major exogenous shocks, transmission mechanisms, and level of financial development. We consider the best response of alternative monetary policy rules, in terms of minimizing macroeconomic volatility, to aid and numerous other exogenous shocks that are important in sub-Saharan Africa. In that sense, our focus is narrow and motivated by the interest of central bankers in sub-Saharan Africa, whose objective function is to minimize macroeconomic volatility and/or achieve a broad inflation target, given the pattern of exogenous shocks, particularly the spending of foreign aid, which is very large in many sub-Saharan African countries (IMF, 2005b). For example, aid inflows ranging between 10 and 20 percent of GDP have been mostly spent in Mozambique (see Chapter 6), requiring a monetary policy response to maintain macroeconomic stability in the face of large aid-financed liquidity injections. Although elements of these issues have been addressed, we are unaware of any study that has sought to analyze the implications of each of these factors in a unified framework applied to a country in sub-Saharan Africa. The aim of this chapter is to conduct such an analysis using a dynamic stochastic general equilibrium (DSGE) model estimated on data for Mozambique and to use such a model to evaluate the monetary policy trade-offs in the context of a full spending of scaled-up foreign aid inflows. To our knowledge, this is the first attempt to estimate a DSGE model for sub-Saharan Africa. More generally, we hope to provide a benchmark DSGE model incorporating features of sub-Saharan Africa and low-income countries that could serve as a starting point for macroeconomic policy analysis.

We will begin with a survey of the literature on the impact of macroeconomic volatility in low-income countries and go on to the role of monetary policy in sub-Saharan Africa. We will then briefly outline the DSGE model, with details in Appendix III, before outlining the estimation procedure and discussing the results of the estimation, followed by an evaluation of the response of the model to aid shocks under different assumptions about the conduct of monetary policy. The analysis will then be extended to consider the performance of different monetary policy rules—including inflation and exchange rate targeting—when the economy is subject to a larger and more realistic number of shocks. The chapter will draw insights from the experience of Mozambique and conclude by discussing the future challenges in the conduct of monetary policy for Mozambique and lessons for sub-Saharan Africa more generally.

Analytical Overiew and Literature Survey

Economic theory suggests that economic performance is related to endowments: the more endowed a country is with natural resources, labor, and human and physical capital, the greater its income and wealth.[5] Endowments are clearly an important part of the growth story, but they are not the whole story. Economies are subject to shocks of many kinds. Some of these are external: the international prices of a country's main imports/ exports or the world's generosity toward low-income countries may change dramatically over time. These terms of trade and capital account shocks may have significant impacts on domestic macro variables (Peiris, 2002). In addition, countries may be subject to internal shocks, such as changes in the policy environment owing to political upheavals and civil conflict, weather-related events, or attempts to react to changes in the external environment. When an economy suffers a shock, many things are affected. The real exchange rate, a determinant of the country's international competitiveness, may be subject to wide swings. The relative performance of different sectors—especially the export and import sectors—will be affected; once-profitable projects may go bankrupt, while other activities receive unexpected windfalls. Public budgets may be affected, causing major changes in domestic debt and interest rates, which may, in turn, result in a credit crunch, disrupting capital formation as well as leading to lower capacity utilization and, hence, reduced output and increased unemployment. In a shock-prone economy, agents must wrestle not only with the shocks that have occurred but also with those that may happen. This generates an important source of instability and uncertainty. Volatility and uncertainty negatively affect the productive capacity of the economy.

Macroeconomic stability appears to be a prerequisite for long-term economic growth. Table 5.1 shows the long-run growth rate and growth volatility for the world and major geographical regions. Low-income countries not only register, on average, lower growth rates than industrial countries, they also suffer from twice as much volatility. Sub-Saharan Africa, in particular, experiences the worst growth performance and the highest level of volatility except for the Middle East and North Africa, while Asia has the best growth performance and relatively low volatility (see also IMF, 2005c). The table is only illustrative, however: the rate of economic growth depends on many factors other than volatility, and because Table 5.1 does not account for those factors, the apparent association could be

[5]Chapter 3 provides a survey of the literature on the sources of economic growth, so this section will focus on the role of macroeconomic stability and stabilization policies.

Table 5.1 Long-Run Per Capita GDP Growth and Volatility: World and Major Regions, 1961–94

	Per capita GDP growth *(In percent)*	Per capita growth volatility *(Standard deviation)*
World	1.80	5.37
OECD	2.69	2.81
Least developed countries	1.65	5.81
Latin America	2.10	5.17
Middle East and North Africa	1.37	8.01
Asia	2.88	4.38
Sub-Saharan Africa	0.76	6.14

Source: Elbadawi and Schmidt-Hebbel (1998).

spurious. Furthermore, even if the relationship is real, the simple relationship provides no information on the mechanisms through which volatility affects growth, information that is important for the design of policy responses.

More recently, a small but growing body of rigorous empirical studies on the links between macroeconomic volatility and macroeconomic performance generally confirms a negative relation (Kose, Prasad, and Terrones, 2005). These studies have generally focused on volatility in real GDP, terms of trade, economic policy, inflation, and real exchange rates, as well as composite indices of macroeconomic volatility and their impact on GDP growth, investment, and exports.

High output volatility can adversely affect economic growth, particularly in low-income countries (IMF, 2005c). Ramey and Ramey (1995) find statistically significant evidence of a strong negative relationship between volatility in real GDP and the average rate of economic growth in a sample of 92 countries. Moreover, they show that the negative effect of volatility on growth is not transmitted through investment but is mainly a direct effect. Hausmann and Gavin (1995) also suggest that volatility in a country's terms of trade and the real exchange rate has a significant negative effect on growth. In addition, they provide evidence that monetary and fiscal policy volatility has a negative effect only when real exchange rate volatility is excluded from cross-country regressions. The negative relationship between inflation and growth at high rates of inflation is also empirically well supported (Fischer, 1993; and Ghosh and Phillips, 1998), while high inflation rates are associated with greater inflation volatility.

Solimano and Servén (1993) also find that volatility in real GDP has significant negative effects on investment. Moreover, Aizenman and Marion (1996) suggest that the finding of no statistically significant impact of GDP volatility on investment in Ramey and Ramey (1995) and many other observers was due to the measure of gross domestic investment used. Aizenman and Marion (1996) show that government spending, money growth, and real exchange rate volatility have a statistically significant negative impact on private investment in a sample of 43 countries when controlling for other potential determinants of private investment. In addition, Servén (1997) shows that inflation volatility and terms of trade volatility are significantly associated with reduced private investment in a group of predominantly African developing countries, after controlling for standard investment determinants in a panel regression approach. More recently, Servén (2002) finds that real exchange rate volatility has a negative and highly significant impact on private investment in developing countries, and the greater the volatility, the larger the impact. Bleany and Greenaway (2001) also find that real exchange rate volatility has a significant negative impact on investment in a panel of sub-Saharan African countries.

Finally, the evidence suggests that real exchange rate effects on export growth can be significant in sub-Saharan Africa (Gupta, Powell, and Yang, 2006). Balassa (1990) estimates that a 1 percent change in the level of the real exchange rate is associated with a change of 0.8 percent to 1 percent in the share of exports in GDP. In addition, Arellano and others (2005) show that manufactured exports drop by 1 percentage point of total exports in countries receiving additional aid equal to 1 percentage point of GDP, compared with the mean of a sample of 73 aid-receiving countries. Peiris (2002) also estimates that real exchange rate volatility has a significant negative impact on export performance in emerging markets, corroborating evidence from earlier work by Caballero and Corbo (1989). In this context, as in standard Dutch disease models of the kind formulated by Van Wijnbergen (1984) and Krugman (1987), the policy response becomes particularly important because the tradable sector may have a disproportionately large role to play in economic development thanks to the "learning by doing" externalities in the export sector. This line of thinking is borne out in Sekkat and Varoudakis (2000), who studied African manufacturing firms.

Consolidating macroeconomic stability in sub-Saharan Africa is likely to be a necessary condition for achieving sustained economic growth and poverty reduction—and, hence, the Millennium Development Goals (MDGs). Several studies have built on Hausmann, Pritchett, and Rodrik's (2004) analysis of jumps in countries' medium-term growth trends, which they label growth accelerations. Their study found that the onset of accelerations had a strong correlation with real exchange rate depreciation and macroeconomic stability. This finding for growth acceleration over the past decade or so in sub-Saharan Africa has been confirmed by IMF (2005c). Almost all of the sub-Saharan countries experiencing sustained growth avoided real exchange rate overvaluation during the growth period. IMF (2005c) also notes the close link between avoidance of exchange rate misalignment and achievement of macroeconomic stability, reinforcing the case for prudent macroeconomic management. Macroeconomic volatility may also directly increase poverty and worsen the distribution of income (Hausmann and Gavin, 1995), particularly if it causes an economic crisis. The welfare effects of such an impact could be very large. Overall, the literature summarized here and the available evidence suggest non-trivial gains to consolidating macroeconomic stability in sub-Saharan Africa, especially reducing variability in output, the inflation rate, and the real exchange rate. This is clearly a challenge for Mozambique, a country that not only receives large amounts of aid but that is also susceptible to terms of trade shocks and weather-related shocks to output.

Role of Monetary Policy in Sub-Saharan Africa

The monetary policy trade-offs policymakers face are determined by the structure of the shocks confronting the economy and the transmission mechanisms that link monetary policy instruments to inflation and real variables. While a vast literature on industrial countries and emerging markets focuses on the efficacy of alternative monetary policy rules,[6] the challenges in the conduct of stabilization policies in low-income countries have received less attention. We therefore extend the work of a few authors who have recently begun to analyze the monetary policy trade-offs in sub-Saharan Africa (for example, Adam and O'Connell, 2005; Buffie and others, 2004; and Mirzoev, 2007).[7] However, we will not discuss in much detail the broader impact of exchange rate regime choice in sub-Saharan Africa as in Bleaney and Fielding (2002), although their finding that the volatility of both output and inflation is higher in the CFA countries than in other developing countries with floating exchange rates provides further motivation to evaluate monetary rules in low-income countries.

[6]These include Ball (2000); Christiano, Eichenbaum, and Evans (2005); Devereux, Lane, and Xu (2004); Svensson (2000); and Taylor (1993, 1998).

[7]Prati and Tressel (2006) also analyze the role of macroeconomic polices in response to aid volatility but do not distinguish between monetary and fiscal policies.

Numerous exogenous shocks buffet sub-Saharan Africa, with foreign aid playing a dominant role in non-oil-producing countries outside the CFA zone. To characterize these sources of shocks in sub-Saharan Africa, Adam and O'Connell (2005) estimate a set of country-specific vector autoregression (VAR) models on a small panel of data spanning the period since 1970 for 11 non-CFA economies, including Mozambique. The four principal exogenous sources of volatility are export commodity prices; variations in agricultural output; intermediate input prices (specifically, oil prices); and aid flows. The estimated variance-covariance matrix suggests that the two volume and two price shocks defined by the VAR are large. The mean (conditional) standard deviation of aid is 2.07 percent of GDP a year, and that of agricultural supply 1.6 percent of GDP. The price shocks are larger, with mean standard deviations of 6.5 percent a year for oil and 4.5 percent a year for non-oil commodity prices. With commodity exports accounting for about 10 percent of total GDP in the sample countries, the income effect of commodity price shocks is only about one-fourth of the mean aid shock. Similar conclusions are obtained for Mozambique in Chapters 4 and 6, where the standard deviation of aid is about 1 percent of GDP and aid shocks dominate the impact of commodity and oil prices on the real economy. Note, however, that Raddatz (2007) finds that external shocks explain a small fraction of the output variance of a typical low-income country and that other factors, most likely internal, are the main sources of fluctuations.

Monetary operations and the transmission mechanism of monetary policies are different in sub-Saharan Africa. In industrial countries and emerging markets, short-term market interest rates are the main instrument of monetary policy. In sub-Saharan Africa, the absence of liquid interbank and other securities markets that are not dominated by the central banks' own operations makes it nearly impossible to identify a transmission mechanism from a target interest rate to the price objective so that policymakers can determine the optimal level they should seek. Instead, sub-Saharan African countries conduct monetary policy through a combination of direct instruments (for example, reserve requirements) as well as foreign exchange interventions and open market operations with the private sector that affect the monetary base.[8] Therefore, like Adam and O'Connell (2005) and Buffie and others (2004), we analyze the trade-offs of both foreign exchange sales and open market operations in the conduct

[8]Applied research on mature stabilizers like Mozambique and Uganda has shown an identifiable transmission mechanism from base money (and broader monetary aggregates) to prices but not from domestic interest rates (Mikkelsen and Peiris (2005) and Chapter 4).

of monetary policy in sub-Saharan Africa. Mirzoev (2007), on the other hand, does not include domestic bonds, so the sterilization option cannot be discussed. However, the paper does usefully provide a list of omissions in the literature, all of which are covered in this chapter, that represent an agenda for future work.

- First, we allow the stock of physical capital to be determined by monopolistic firms.
- Second, productivity is not fixed. A higher level of exports, in particular, can raise aggregate productivity through positive spillovers of know-how and through dynamic learning by doing. Similarly, more public investment could lead to greater private sector productivity.
- Third, foreign currency is used only as a medium of exchange (to purchase imports) and not as means of saving,[9] while private agents do not have access to foreign borrowing. To capture this feature, a closed capital account is assumed.[10] As a result, the exchange rate is determined mostly by external trade and central bank actions, rather than by private capital flows, and the only source of financing for the trade deficit is the sale of aid dollars by the central bank.
- Finally, the model is calibrated to a particular country (Mozambique), estimating structural parameters using Bayesian techniques where possible.

In addition, we provide a role for commercial bank credit to firms in transmitting monetary policy impulses to spending in sub-Saharan Africa. African commercial banks routinely hold nearly double the amount of legally required reserves against deposits,[11] which could imply a weak credit channel in the transmission of monetary policy. Saxegaard (2005) argues, however, that if banks maintain excess reserves on a prudential basis—for example, because of extreme volatility in the deposit base or

---

[9]Buffie and others (2004) and Adam and O'Connell (2005) examine the effects of aid inflows in a model with currency substitution, while the model presented here, like workhorse DSGE models used in the literature in industrial countries, is more explicit in accounting for the consumption-labor choice and for the effects of the profitability of domestic firms on household income.

[10]We could have assumed, however, that banks hold foreign currency sold by the central bank earning a given world interest rate, but this would not have altered the results significantly unless one assumed uncovered interest parity (UIP), which seems unlikely in the countries under discussion.

[11]The median ratios of required reserves and excess reserves to deposits at the end of 2004 were both roughly 7 percent in the 44 sub-Saharan African countries studied in Saxegaard (2005). In most sub-Saharan African countries, including Mozambique, reserves are unremunerated deposits at the central bank.

unavoidably high lending risks—then an increase in bank liquidity is likely to be allocated partly to reserves and partly to new loans. In this situation, a cost-of-capital/bank lending channel may exist even in the presence of statutory excess reserves. In any case, the recent low level of excess reserves in a number of mature stabilizers in sub-Saharan Africa, including Mozambique and Uganda, suggests that monetary innovations are likely to have an impact on bank behavior. Moreover, Mikkelsen and Peiris (2005) have shown that changes in domestic credit to the private sector have had a significant positive impact on real economic activity in Uganda, suggesting that the impact of a bank lending channel could be quite large in sub-Saharan Africa. Therefore, we incorporate credit frictions following the recent literature on "financial accelerator" effects (Bernanke, Gertler, and Gilchrist, 1999). Overall, the inclusion of a banking system in the DSGE model illuminates the potential interactions between monetary impulses and financial development as well as the crowding-out effects of domestic debt issuance.

The response to aid shocks will be used to focus the analysis of alternative monetary policy rules. The macroeconomic challenges of managing aid inflows can be subdivided to the degree of spending and absorption of foreign aid (IMF, 2005b).[12] "Spending captures the extent to which the government uses aid to finance an increase in expenditures or a reduction in taxation" (IMF, 2005b, p. 10). Even if the aid comes tied to particular expenditures, governments can choose whether or not to increase the overall fiscal deficit as aid increases. Therefore, when discussing monetary policy rules in subsequent sections, we will assume that all aid is spent and not consider alternative fiscal rules, even though the framework presented is more generally applicable.[13]

For a given fiscal policy, absorption is controlled by the central bank through its decision about how much of the foreign exchange associated with aid it should sell. The IMF has argued that "an *increase* in aid can serve some combination of three purposes: an increase in the rate of reserve accumulation, an increase in non-aid capital outflows, or an increase in the non-aid current account deficit" (IMF, 2005b, p. 9). In this

[12]This definition of aid absorption in IMF (2005b) differs from that of domestic absorption (the sum of private consumption and investment, and government expenditure).

[13]Chapter 6 discusses in more detail the fiscal response to aid shocks and concludes that a scaling up of aid should be mostly spent in normal circumstances, as has been the case in Mozambique, albeit with a few caveats. This does not mean that fiscal policy has no role to play in consolidating macroeconomic stability—quite the contrary—but it is probably ill suited for short-term demand management, the focus of this chapter.

interpretation, aid absorption is defined as the extent to which a country's non-aid current account deficit (in foreign currency terms) widens in response to an increase in aid inflows.[14] Note, therefore, that for the purpose of this paper we exclude sterilization using open market operations from the definition of absorption.

This chapter focuses on the case where aid dollars are gifted to the government, which immediately sells them to the central bank. The government decides how much to spend, while the central bank decides how much of the aid-related foreign exchange to sell on the market (absorb).[15] If the central bank chooses not to sell the aid-related foreign exchange but instead to conduct open market operations to mop up liquidity, we call this sterilization.

The structure of our model, outlined below with monetary policy rules including foreign exchange sales and domestic debt operations, allows a comprehensive analysis of the issues involved in spending and absorbing foreign aid. The spending and the degree of absorption of aid is a point of departure in the literature on sub-Saharan Africa, however, and one should also consider whether the policy rules are robust to a wider array of exogenous shocks and more general rules discussed in the literature in industrial countries and emerging markets.

DSGE Model

In this chapter, we develop a macroeconomic model for monetary policy analysis in sub-Saharan Africa using data for Mozambique. Compared with previous empirical analysis of the Mozambican economy or, for that matter, most sub-Saharan African countries, we conduct our analysis within the context of a microfounded DSGE model. DSGE models have

[14]With this definition, aid that finances capital outflows is not absorbed. However, as the capital account is closed in our model (and in much of the literature on sub-Saharan Africa), the sale of foreign exchange by the central bank is equivalent to absorption. If the capital account is open, absorption is not controlled by the central bank.

[15]If aid is received in kind, or if the government spends aid dollars directly on imports, spending and absorption are equal, and there is no impact on macroeconomic variables, such as the exchange rate, the price level, and the interest rate. Aid could also go to the private sector directly. If the private sector uses the dollars to directly finance imports, there is unlikely to be much macroeconomic impact. When the private sector sells the dollars to the central bank and uses the local currency proceeds to finance domestic expenditures, the same issues will arise as in the case of government spending (IMF, 2005b).

several benefits that make them attractive for the analysis of macroeconomic policy:

- They are structural in the sense that each equation has an economic interpretation. Policy interventions and their transmission mechanisms can therefore be clearly identified, facilitating a discussion of alternative policies.
- They are microfounded in the sense that they are explicitly derived from the optimizing behavior of households and firms in the economy. They thus describe the behavior of the agents in the economy in terms of parameters that are structural in the sense that one would not expect them to change as a result of changes in economic policy, thereby validating the analysis of alternative policies.
- They are stochastic in the sense that they explicitly discuss how random shocks, such as an aid shock or a shock to fiscal policy, affect the economy.
- They are forward-looking in the sense that agents optimize and form rational, or model-consistent, forecasts about the future evolution of the economy.

These characteristics make DSGE models particularly attractive for the purpose of analyzing the effect of alternative macroeconomic policies—for example, the appropriate policy response to an aid shock—which helps explain their widespread use by central banks and other policy institutions in countries belonging to the Organization for Economic Cooperation and Development (OECD). This chapter represents the first attempt at constructing such a model for Mozambique.

A traditional weakness of DSGE models has been the difficulty in parameterizing them using economic data. This problem is particularly severe in developing countries, such as Mozambique, where data series are short or, in many cases, lacking. To overcome this problem, research often resorts to calibrating the parameters of the model using information from previous studies or characteristics such as the volatility of the data. The difficulty of explicitly relating the model to the data can undermine its use as a tool for policy analysis.

To overcome the problem of parameterizing the data, this chapter makes use of recent advances in Bayesian econometrics. Within this framework, the Kalman filter is used to allow inferences about the unobserved variables in the model, and prior empirical or theoretical knowledge about the parameters of interest is used to increase the efficiency of the estimation, thereby overcoming the problem of short data series. These Bayesian inferences have been successfully applied to the estimation of DSGE models by, among others, Juillard and others (2006); Smets and Wouters (2003,

2005); Lubik and Schorfheide (2005); and Saxegaard (2006a). As far as we know, this chapter represents the first attempt at estimating a DSGE model using Bayesian methods on data for a country in sub-Saharan Africa other than South Africa.

The use of Bayesian inference has a number of benefits worth highlighting. First, it allows us to incorporate prior empirical or theoretical knowledge about our parameters of interest. Thus, if it is known that a parameter such as the discount rate must lie between 0 and 1, this information would be a useful addition to our estimation procedure. More generally, the incorporation of prior information allows us to formalize the use of information about parameters from prior studies.

It should be noted, however, that the impact of prior information on the estimation procedure is one of the main criticisms of Bayesian methods. However, Fernández-Villaverde and Rubio-Ramírez (2004) show that asymptotically the parameter point estimates converge to their true values and, therefore, that the importance of the prior information disappears as the sample grows. The same authors provide compelling evidence for the strong performance of Bayesian methods in small samples such as ours.

Secondly, Bayesian inference provides a natural framework for parameterizing and evaluating simple macroeconomic models such as ours, which are likely to be fundamentally misspecified. As pointed out by Fernández-Villaverde and Rubio-Ramírez (2004) and Schorfheide (2000), the inference problem is not to determine whether the model is "true" or to ascertain the "true" value of a particular parameter but, rather, to determine which parameter values maximize the ability of the model to summarize the features of the data.

Finally, Bayesian methods provide a simple framework for comparing and choosing between different misspecified models that may not be nested, based on the probability the model assigns to having observed the data (the marginal likelihood of the data, given the model). Geweke (1998) shows that this is directly related to the predictive performance of the model and is thus a natural benchmark for assessing the usefulness of economic models for policy analysis and forecasting.

Structure of the Model

The model is based on the open-economy DSGE model outlined in Kollmann (2002) and Saxegaard (2006a). The augmented model features the explicit treatment of the conduct of monetary policy in sub-Saharan Africa, as in Adam and O'Connell (2005), by assuming that the monetary authority affects the money supply through foreign exchange sales and bond issuance, although the bonds are bought by the banking sector instead of consumers, as is the case in Agénor and Montiel (2006) and Peiris (2002). The model incorporates credit frictions by assuming that firms have to borrow at a premium over deposit rates to finance some of the inputs in the production process as in Atta-Mensah and Dib (2003). The premium, in turn, is inversely related to the ratio of firms' assets (the value of their beginning-of-period physical capital stock multiplied by the price of the domestic good) to their liabilities, which consist of beginning-of-period borrowings, as in Agénor and Montiel (2006). Learning by doing is incorporated, as in Prati and Tressel (2006), by assuming that productivity is a function of the size of the tradable sector and public investment expenditure.

The basic structure of the model consists of perfectly competitive firms that produce a final nontradable good that is consumed by a representative household and the fiscal authorities, in addition to being used for investment. The inputs used in the production of the final good are either produced domestically or imported by monopolistically competitive intermediate goods firms. The domestically produced goods, which are produced using capital, labor, and credit from a financial intermediary as inputs, are either sold in the domestic market or exported overseas. For the sake of simplicity, we assume that the country has a closed capital account. The markets for capital, labor, and commercial bank loans are competitive. The model is completed with a description of the fiscal and monetary authorities.

To provide a rationale for monetary and fiscal stabilization policy, four sources of inefficiency are included in the model: (1) monopolistically competitive product markets; (2) sluggish price adjustment in the domestic economy using the specification of Rotemberg (1982); (3) capital adjustment costs and investment adjustment costs using the specification of Christiano, Eichenbaum, and Evans (2005); and (4) adjustment costs in commercial bank reserves and an interest rate spread determined by the net worth of companies as described above. This framework, which is described in detail in Appendix III, captures many of the rigidities that previous studies have found are important in describing the dynamics in the data and serves as a useful starting point for developing a DSGE model for Mozambique.

Empirical Findings

The model described above is estimated on quarterly data for Mozambique from 1996Q1 to 2005Q4 on 18 key macroeconomic variables: GDP, consumption, exports, imports, the real exchange rate, inflation, export price inflation, import price inflation, M2, currency in circulation, deposit rates, lending rates, foreign currency reserves, government bonds, commercial bank reserves, aid, government spending, and lending to the private sector. The number of variables vastly exceeds the number of observed variables in recent papers that use Bayesian techniques to estimate DSGE models, such as Juillard and others (2006) and Saxegaard (2006b). The remaining endogenous variables in the model are assumed to be unobserved.

Prior to estimation, the macroeconomic variables are transformed into real per capita measures. Following the approach in Juillard and others (2006), we remove a time trend in the data on the key macro variables using the Hodrick-Prescott filter. In addition, we remove seasonal effects in the series where these are evident using the X12arima filter and transform all variables to mean 0 variables.

Following Juillard and others (2006) and Saxegaard (2006b), our estimation strategy involves fixing the parameters that determine the steady state of the model, based either on findings from previous studies, notably Tarp and others (2002), or in order to replicate features in the data, and then estimating the parameters that determine the dynamic properties of the model. The calibrated parameter values and calibrated steady-state ratios are summarized in Appendix I.

As mentioned previously, estimation of the model by Bayesian methods allows the incorporation of prior empirical or theoretical knowledge through the specification of a prior distribution for the parameters to be estimated. Our choice of prior distributions is guided both by theoretical restrictions imposed on some of the parameters and by empirical evidence. In instances where the literature and theory provide little or no guidance, diffuse priors are chosen. The choice of priors, together with the resulting parameter estimates (posterior distribution), is summarized in Appendix II. These plots allow us to make some statements about the relative importance of the priors and the data in the construction of the posterior distribution. In other words, the plots allow us to judge whether or not the data are informative about our parameters. Overall, the Bayesian estimation methodology yields plausible parameter estimates for the model that are broadly in line with the results from previous studies. A comparison of the fitted values with the actual data reveals that the model is able to replicate the movements in the data fairly well.

Managing Aid Shocks

The discussion in the previous section suggests that the model appears to be able to deliver reasonable parameter estimates when using Bayesian estimation techniques. We now turn our attention to the use of the estimated model to analyze the appropriate monetary management of aid shocks. We analyze the effect of a persistent aid shock (autocorrelation coefficient of 0.7) that raises aid by 2 percent of steady-state GDP. With the exception of the policy rules and the assumption that all aid is spent by the government, the parameterization of the model is that resulting from the estimation discussed above.

We analyze two scenarios. In the first scenario, aid is fully spent by the government but not absorbed; in the second scenario, the aid is both fully spent and fully or partially absorbed. In the scenario in which the aid is not absorbed, we consider two cases—one in which the increase in reserves is sterilized and one in which it is not so that government bond holdings remain unchanged. Finally, we also consider a scenario in which half of the aid is absorbed and the remaining increase in reserves is sterilized. In terms of the policy rules described in Appendix III (equations (34) and (35)), these scenarios can be defined as follows:

- Spend and don't absorb ($z_2 = 0$; $b_1 = 1$)
- Spend and don't absorb, but sterilize ($z_2 = 0$; $b_1 = 1$)
- Spend and absorb ($z_2 = 1$; $b_1 = 0$)
- Spend, absorb half, and sterilize half ($z_2 = 0.5$; $b_1 = 1$)

In all cases we assume a low weight on the stabilization of government bonds and foreign exchange reserves ($z_1 = b_4 = 0.0001$). The different scenarios are presented in Figures 5.1 and 5.2 and described below.

Spend and Don't Absorb

In Figure 5.1, we consider the effects of a spend-and-don't-absorb scenario where the resulting increase in reserves matches the increase in aid. The unbroken line describes a scenario in which the increase in reserves is not sterilized, whereas the broken line assumes that the government sterilizes the increase in reserves by issuing bonds.

An increase in aid that is spent but neither absorbed nor sterilized is equivalent to a pure monetary expansion and therefore causes the depreciation of the nominal exchange rate. Inflation rises rapidly because of the instant adjustment of the nominal exchange rate and the prices of traded goods. However, because domestic prices are sticky, this adjustment is accompanied by a real depreciation of the exchange rate, as in Mirzoev (2007). This real depreciation would be even more pronounced were it not for prices rising because of the increase in government expenditure. The depreciation boosts exports, and demand for domestic goods also grows, implying an overall increase in GDP. Interestingly, unlike Mirzoev (2007),

Figure 5.1. Effects of a Spend-and-Don't-Absorb Scenario

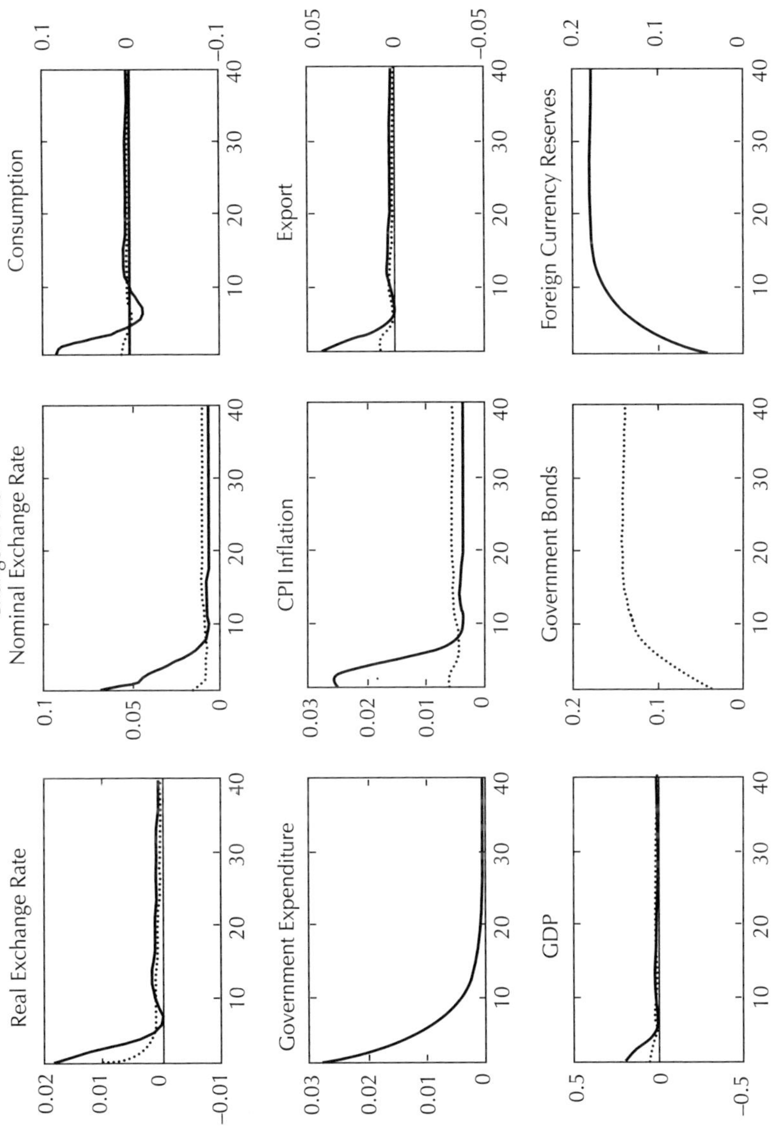

Source: Authors' calculations.

Figure 5.2. Spend and Absorb All Aid; or Absorb Half, Sterilize Half

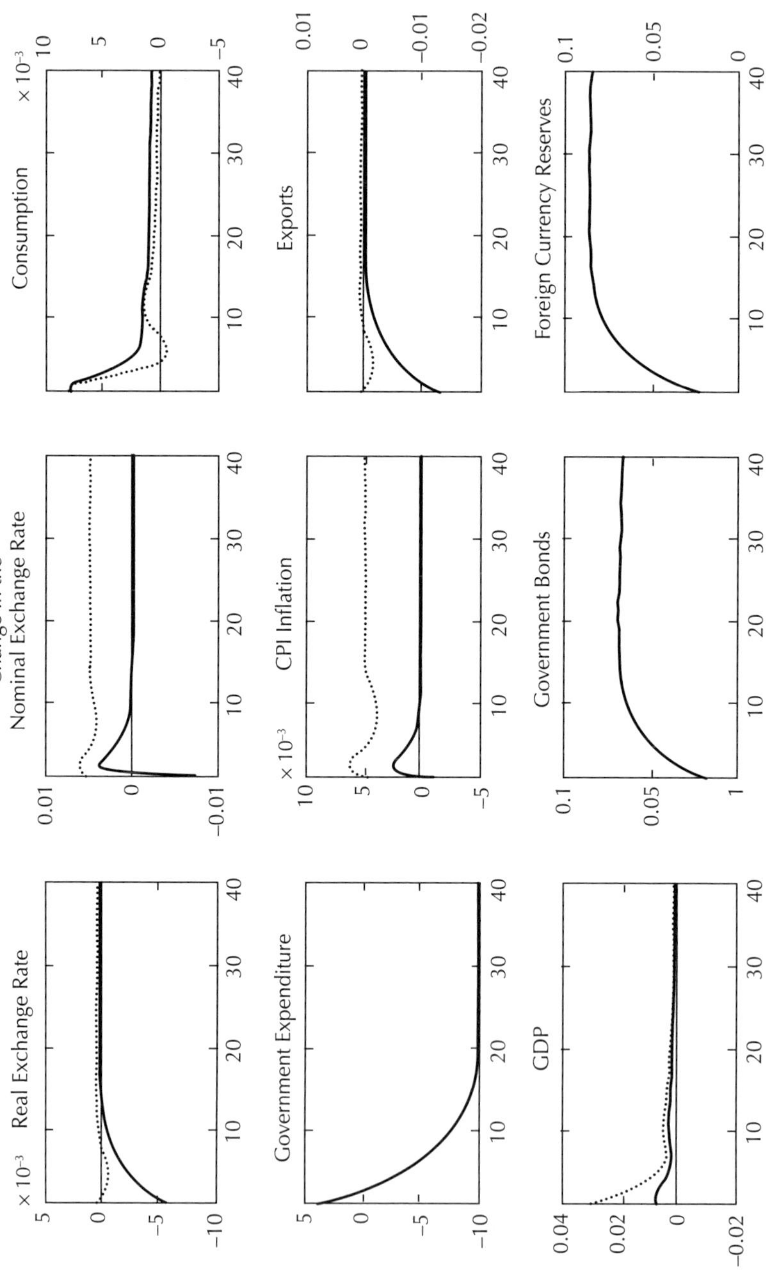

Source: Authors' calculations.

we see a temporary rise in private consumption. This is because, in our calibration, the spike in prices leads to an initial decline in real money balances, causing an increase in deposit rates and thus a wealth effect. In addition, wage income rises because price rigidity pushes up real wages and consumers try to compensate for the inflation tax by increasing labor supply. These effects offset the substitution effects of the rise in interest rates and lead to a temporary rise in consumption. As prices adjust to increased demand, the real exchange rate appreciates back to its equilibrium level and consumption falls along with household income.

Figure 5.1 also illustrates how these results change when we assume that the rise in base money is sterilized by the issuance of government bonds. The issuance of government bonds offsets the monetary expansion by driving up real interest rates. The rise in real interest rates and slowing of output expansion reduce the increase in consumption. The mopping up of liquidity reduces the initial depreciation of the nominal and real exchange rates and thus the rise in CPI inflation, dampening the impact on exports. This, together with the cost-of-capital/bank lending channel reduces the initial boost to output. Intuitively, the aid (and spending) shock has less of an impact on inflation and real variables when the monetary authority sterilizes the liquidity injected into the economy.

Spend and Absorb All of the Aid; or Absorb Half, Sterilize Half

Figure 5.2 analyzes the case where all the aid is spent and fully absorbed so that there is no change in foreign exchange reserves (unbroken line). It also shows the scenario where half of the aid is absorbed and the remaining increase in reserves is sterilized (broken line). This is equivalent to the 50-50 rule first suggested by Atingi-Ego (2005) and analyzed by Adam and O'Connell (2005). In this scenario, the performance of the recipient economy is substantially worse than it is in a spend-and-absorb scenario.

When all of the aid that is spent is absorbed, the nominal exchange rate appreciates; the real exchange rate also appreciates because of price stickiness. The real exchange rate appreciation reduces imported inflation and thus inflation. Consumers feel better off and consumption rises, whereas exports fall because of the real appreciation. This is the Dutch disease problem referred to earlier in this chapter. In spite of the drop in exports, GDP expands slightly, thanks to stronger domestic demand.

How do these results change when only half of the aid-induced spending is absorbed and the remaining increase in reserves is sterilized? Our results suggest that the partial sale of the foreign exchange dampens the appreciation of the real exchange rate. The nominal exchange rate actually depreciates in a persistent fashion, although the depreciation is offset by a persistent increase in CPI inflation. The increase in inflation reflects an increase in marginal costs caused by the higher interest rates associated with sterilization. The persistence of the rise in inflation reflects the persistent increase in the stock of government bonds. In terms of the real sector, GDP rises substantially more, largely because of the boost to exports resulting from the milder appreciation.

Optimal Response to Aid Shocks

To summarize the insights from the above discussion of alternative responses to aid shocks in Mozambique, we plot the standard deviation of output, inflation, and the real exchange rate for different assumptions regarding the degree of absorption and sterilization of aid-financed fiscal expenditures. Figure 5.3 shows that with full absorption (the spend-and-absorb scenario), output is unambiguously less volatile than in any other scenario considered. If some of the aid-financed fiscal expenditure is not absorbed, Figure 5.3 confirms our findings that output is less volatile if the resulting monetary expansion is sterilized using open market operations.

However, the conclusions are not so clear-cut for CPI inflation and the real exchange rate. In particular, the volatility of CPI inflation is largely unchanged if only part of the aid is absorbed as long as the resulting increase in liquidity is sterilized. For the real exchange rate, volatility is slightly lower if only half of the aid is absorbed than if the entire amount is absorbed, assuming the country has a closed capital account, which is probable based on the relatively limited capital mobility we have observed in the countries in question. In particular, imposing uncovered interest parity would make the real exchange rate more sensitive to domestic interest rates and thus to sterilization. To the extent this is translated into nominal exchange rate volatility, it would also affect the volatility of CPI inflation. Hence, it is likely that opening the capital account would reduce the attractiveness of sterilization in terms of inflation and real exchange rate stability.[16]

In general, the results provide support for the assertion that "to *absorb and spend* the aid would appear to be the appropriate response under 'normal' circumstances" (IMF, 2005b, p. 15; emphasis added), at least in the case of Mozambique. However, it may also answer one of the conundrums identified in IMF (2005b); most of the countries in that sample—Mozambique, Uganda, and, initially, Tanzania—resisted absorb-

[16]Extending the model to include an open capital account is a topic of future research.

Figure 5.3. Impact of Absorption and Sterilization on GDP, CPI Inflation, and the Real Exchange Rate

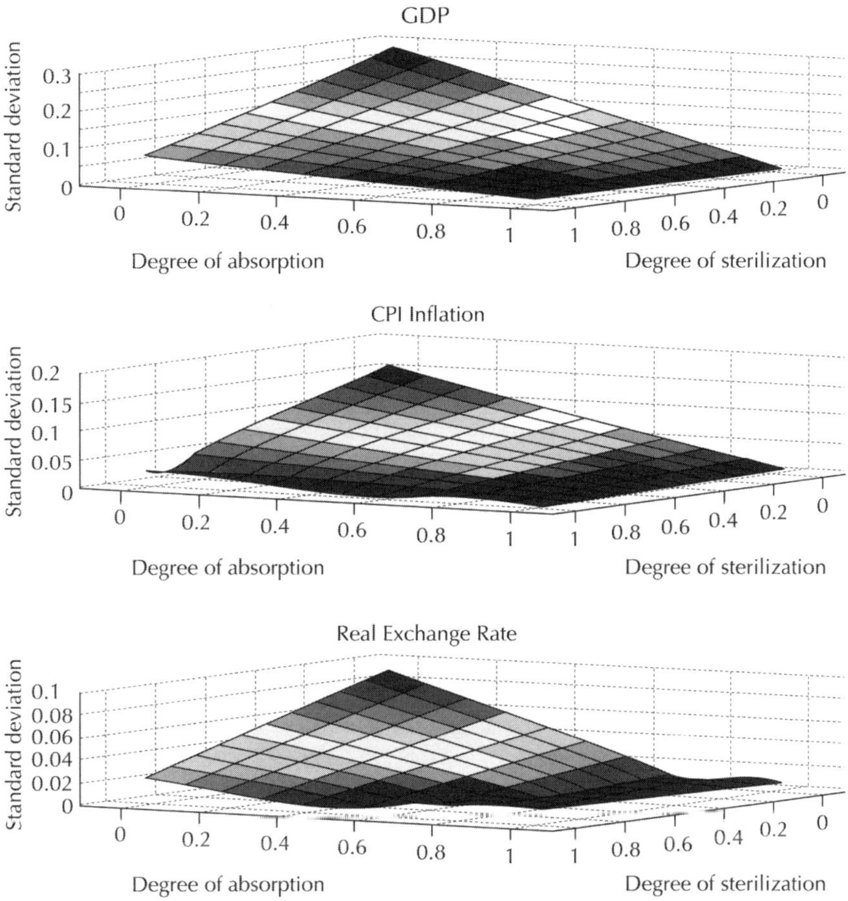

Source: Authors' calculations.

ing the aid-financed spending, partly through domestic bond issuance. These countries may have placed a greater emphasis on real exchange rate stability than on the volatility of output and inflation.

Monetary Policy Rules in a Shock-Prone Economy

Having used the estimated model to analyze the optimal response to aid shocks, we now turn to the analysis of monetary policy in a more general setting. The motivation for this analysis is the fact that while spend and absorb might provide a useful guide for macroeconomic policy in the event of an aid shock, it may not prove as useful when the economy is buffeted by a larger set of shocks. We investigate whether stabilizing CPI inflation or the nominal exchange rate in a shock-prone economy might provide a better recipe for macroeconomic policy, in terms of minimizing macroeconomic volatility, than spend and absorb.[17] While it is true that aid shocks are more clearly identifiable than other shocks, attempting to respond differently to various shocks complicates monetary policy management and could lead to greater instrument instability. Therefore, it makes sense to gauge the efficiency of a spend-and-absorb rule against more general monetary policy rules in the presence of a wider array of exogenous shocks.

Table 5.2 shows standard deviations of key macroeconomic variables for the spend-and-absorb rule, CPI inflation targeting, and the crawling exchange rate peg where the monetary policy authorities are assumed to target a rate of depreciation equal to the long-run inflation differential between Mozambique and the rest of the world.[18] The parameterization of the spend-and-absorb rule is as described above.[19] CPI inflation targeting assumes a weight ($z_4 = b_2 = 1$) on inflation stabilization in the bond and the foreign exchange reserves rules. The crawling exchange rate peg assumes a weight ($z_3 = 1$) on the exchange rate in the foreign exchange reserves rule. In all cases we use the estimated value for the share of aid that is spent and the distribution of this expenditure between the public and the private sectors.

The results suggest that a spend-and-absorb rule is significantly less successful at stabilizing the economy than inflation and exchange rate targeting. This is particularly true with respect to the volatility of the nominal exchange rate, CPI inflation, consumption, and GDP, which is greater in spend-and-absorb scenarios. As expected, inflation is significantly less volatile under the CPI-inflation-targeting rule than under either the spend-and-absorb rule or the crawling-exchange-rate-peg rule,

[17]We have not conducted a full welfare analysis of alternative policy rules at this stage because we felt that macroeconomic volatility, rather than welfare, was a more useful metric for discussing different policies with the country authorities. A full welfare analysis can easily be incorporated into the analysis, however. This may be done at a later stage.

[18]It should be recognized, however, that the crawling exchange rate peg is not operational unless the trajectory of the equilibrium real exchange rate is known (as it is in this model).

[19]In the case of shocks other than an aid shock, a shock to government bonds, and a shock to foreign exchange reserves, spend and absorb simply implies keeping the stock of government bonds and the stock of foreign exchange reserves constant.

Table 5.2. Standard Deviations of Macroeconomic Variables

	Nominal exchange rate	Real exchange rate	Consumption	CPI inflation	Exports	GDP
Spend and absorb	0.1299	0.0238	0.1183	0.1317	0.0501	0.1823
CPI inflation targeting	0.0241	0.0225	0.0960	0.0177	0.0437	0.1330
Crawling exchange rate peg	0.0193	0.0256	0.1043	0.0331	0.0365	0.1448

Source: Authors' calculations.

although the nominal exchange rate is slightly more volatile under the CPI-inflation-targeting rule than under the crawling-exchange-rate-peg rule. As a result, exports are somewhat more volatile under the inflation targeting rule, although price stability helps stabilize nontradable output to the extent that GDP and consumption are less volatile under the inflation targeting rule than under the exchange-rate-targeting rule.

Overall, these findings confirm that spend and absorb may not be an appropriate guide for the conduct of monetary policy in countries that face a larger number of shocks, whereas the choice between inflation targeting and a crawling exchange rate peg will depend on which of the following the authorities prefer to stabilize: output, inflation, exports, or the exchange rate. It should be noted that, from a practical point of view, a crawling exchange rate peg as designed in the model is unlikely to be feasible given the uncertainties surrounding the equilibrium real exchange rate in practice, making the case for an inflation targeting regime stronger.

Lessons and Challenges

This chapter has considered what would be the monetary policy rule most likely to minimize macroeconomic volatility in a country facing aid-related expenditures and numerous other exogenous shocks. To our knowledge, ours is the first attempt to estimate a DSGE model for sub-Saharan Africa and low-income countries that could serve as a starting point for macroeconomic policy analysis. While the simulations of the policy experiments largely validate the assertion "to absorb and spend the aid would appear to be the appropriate response under 'normal' circumstances" (IMF, 2005b, p. 15), we also provide insights as to why some sub-Saharan African countries, including Mozambique, have, for the most part, been reluctant to fully absorb aid shocks (IMF, 2005b). This reluctance may be related to a desire to smooth real exchange rate fluctuations—and thus the effects of Dutch disease, including its negative impact on long-term growth prospects.

It is worth reiterating the need to pay greater attention to the consistency of monetary and exchange rate policy in cases where the authorities spend but do not absorb aid—perhaps in an effort to safeguard export competitiveness. On the other hand, sub-Saharan African countries like Mozambique are prone to numerous exogenous shocks, and our simulations suggest that monetary authorities seeking to minimize overall macroeconomic volatility will be more successful if they place more weight on inflation (or exchange rate stabilization, if the authorities do not place a lot of weight on inflation stabilization) than if they apply simple rules such as spend and absorb. Monetary policy in economies subject to many exogenous shocks needs to be considered in a more general setting, and policymakers should avoid being narrowly focused on spending and absorbing foreign aid. "Lite" inflation targeting regimes, as depicted in Stone (2003), may thus be more suitable for countries in sub-Saharan Africa. Stone (2003) describes "lite" inflation targeting regimes as those that probably aim to bring inflation into the single digits and maintain financial stability, including through a relatively interventionist exchange rate policy.[20] The inflation targeting regime considered in this chapter was somewhat similar.

The model and policy rules discussed here are broadly applicable. For one thing, non-CFA sub-Saharan Africa is rich in petroleum (Angola, Nigeria, São Tóme and Príncipe, and, potentially, Uganda) and mineral resources (for example, the Democratic Republic of the Congo, Mozambique, Tanzania, and Zambia), with new producers coming on line each year. Although our model does not explicitly address oil-producing and mineral-extracting economies, the simulation evidence reported above bears directly on the monetary policy challenges facing these countries. Since most production is carried out by foreign firms, the principal linkages between volatile commodity prices and the domestic economy are fiscal (Adam and O'Connell, 2005). Variations in revenues from oil and mineral exports can therefore be treated in a manner that is directly analogous to our treatment of variations in aid, subject to the necessary

[20]Further, "lite" inflation targeting regimes employ monetary targets that are less market oriented, and the objectives of monetary policy, as well as the instruments used to conduct it, are relatively nontransparent in sub-Saharan Africa owing to shallow financial markets.

recalibration of the relevant model parameters. Many of the insights we develop in the context of managing aid flows (and a wider array of exogenous shocks) will therefore carry over to the monetary management of petroleum and mineral resource booms.

At this point, it is important to note that we have discussed the monetary policy rules that are most appropriate in response to spending aid (or revenues from natural resources) and numerous exogenous shocks mainly from the viewpoint of minimizing macroeconomic volatility,[21] which the economic literature and experience of fast-growing Asian economies have revealed to be important for growth and poverty reduction. It could, however, be the case that policymakers view the level of macroeconomic variables (for example, the inflation and real exchange rates) and the degree of volatility, even in an absorb-and-spend aid scenario or "lite" inflation targeting regime, to be too high from the point of view of consumer welfare and long-term growth. This could be relevant, particularly if the aid (or commodity price) shock is significantly larger or less persistent than the typical shock considered here. A broader look at the appropriate pattern of government spending and absorption in response to aid would need to consider (1) the beneficial effects of aid-related spending on the level of consumption or investment and (2) the costs in terms of forgone growth due to the absence of learning by doing in the export sector. To do so, one could alter the assumption in this chapter that all of the aid (or export windfall) is spent to achieve the MDGs and evaluate alternative fiscal policy rules.[22] In addition, if the possible impact of Dutch disease on macroeconomic variables, such as the real exchange rate, is of greater concern, it could be illustrative to consider the sensitivity of the impact of learning by doing in the tradable sector and of productivity spillovers from government investment expenditure. These are subjects for future research.

[21]Given the firm microfoundations of the model, we could also have easily shown the ranking of the rules in terms of maximizing a specific social-welfare function.

[22]Fiscal policy trade-offs of a longer-term nature are covered in more detail in Chapter 6.

Appendix I. Calibration

Parameter	Value	Description
ϑ	1.5	Home elasticity of substitution
η	3.5	Foreign elasticity of substitution
$\psi - 1$	1.5	Inverse of Frisch elasticity
ε	2	Inverse of elasticity of money supply
α^d	0.731	Share of nontradables in CPI
$\nu/(\nu - 1)$	1.09	Markup factor for intermediary goods
Σ	0.15	Cost share of borrowing
α	0.41	Cost share of capital
δ	0.025	Quarterly depreciation rate of capital
β	$(1.093/1.123)^{1/4}$	Quarterly subjective discount rate
u^{γ}	0.5	Steady-state learning by doing
u^{μ}	0.3	Steady-state share of government investment expenditure
π	$(1.093)^{1/4}$	Steady-state CPI inflation
π^*	$(1.059)^{1/4}$	Steady-state foreign inflation
$i + 1$	$(1.123)^{1/4}$	Steady-state domestic interest rate
$i^* + 1$	$(1.117)^{1/4}$	Steady-state foreign interest rate
$(M^c)/(M^0 + D)$	0.22	Ratio of currency to M2
$(M^0 + D)/Y$	0.7	Ratio of M2 to GDP
T/Y	0.15	Ratio of steady-state tax to GDP
A/Y	0.15	Ratio of steady-state aid to GDP
Z	4.6 months of imports	Steady-state level of foreign currency reserves
α^r	0.11	Required reserves ratio

Appendix II. Estimation Results

		Prior			Posterior		
Parameter	Description	Density	Mean	SD	Mean	90%	Interval
ϕ	Cost of nontradable goods price adjustment	normal	100.000	10.000	103.453	89.091	121.621
b	Habit persistence	beta	0.400	0.100	0.302	0.177	0.454
ϕ_1	Capital-stock adjustment costs	normal	1.000	0.100	0.996	0.850	1.180
ϕ_2	Investment-level adjustment costs	normal	80.000	10.000	81.810	64.043	98.575
ω	Share of aid spent	normal	1.000	0.100	0.844	0.687	1.036
ι	Share of aid spent by public sector	normal	1.000	0.100	0.655	0.446	0.836
ϖ_1	Commercial-bank-reserve smoothing (bonds)	gamma	0.200	0.100	0.165	0.104	0.224
ϖ_2	Commercial-bank-reserve smoothing (lending)	gamma	0.200	0.100	0.145	0.083	0.197
ϖ_3	Commercial-bank-reserve smoothing (deposits)	gamma	0.200	0.100	0.093	0.035	0.143
η	Interest-rate-spread markup factor	normal	10.000	1.000	9.924	8.237	11.461
z_1	International reserves stabilization	normal	0.001	0.100	0.067	–0.013	0.140
z_2	Exchange rate stabilization	normal	0.500	0.100	0.323	0.149	0.461
z_3	Absorption	normal	0.500	0.100	0.566	0.415	0.714
b_1	International reserves sterilization	normal	0.500	0.100	0.472	0.330	0.652
b_2	Inflation stabilization	normal	0.500	0.100	0.592	0.438	0.727

		Prior			Posterior		
Parameter	Description	Density	Mean	SD	Mean	90%	Interval
b_3	Output stabilization	normal	0.500	0.100	0.159	0.078	0.230
b_4	Bond stabilization	normal	0.001	0.100	0.075	0.008	0.133
ρ^{θ}	Technology shock persistence	beta	0.800	0.100	0.856	0.770	0.957
$\rho^{\pi*}$	Foreign inflation shock persistence	beta	0.800	0.100	0.726	0.623	0.848
ρ^{L}	Labor supply shock persistence	beta	0.800	0.100	0.760	0.589	0.912
ρ^{C}	Consumption shock persistence	beta	0.800	0.100	0.727	0.574	0.883
ρ^{A}	Aid shock persistence	beta	0.800	0.100	0.699	0.519	0.897
ρ^{i*}	Foreign interest rate shock persistence	beta	0.800	0.100	0.738	0.628	0.840
ρ^{μ}	Government investment shock persistence	beta	0.800	0.100	0.740	0.596	0.897
ρ^{γ}	Learning-by-doing shock persistence	beta	0.800	0.100	0.770	0.641	0.939
ρ^{I}	Investment shock persistence	beta	0.800	0.100	0.720	0.578	0.906
ρ^{i}	Interest rate spread shock persistence	beta	0.800	0.100	0.826	0.732	0.944
ρ^{B}	Bond shock persistence	beta	0.800	0.100	0.674	0.534	0.799
ρ^{tot}	Terms of trade shock persistence	beta	0.800	0.100	0.849	0.749	0.940
ρ^{z}	International reserves shock persistence	beta	0.800	0.100	0.753	0.592	0.899
u^{θ}	Size of technology shock	invgamma	0.002	Inf	0.009	0.005	0.015

Parameter	Description	Prior			Posterior		
		Density	Mean	SD	Mean	90%	Interval
$u^{\pi*}$	Size of foreign inflation shock	invgamma	0.002	Inf	0.014	0.008	0.018
u^{L}	Size of labor supply shock	invgamma	0.100	Inf	0.032	0.021	0.042
u^{C}	Size of consumption shock	invgamma	0.200	Inf	0.083	0.053	0.108
u^{A}	Size of aid shock	invgamma	0.100	Inf	0.015	0.012	0.017
u^{μ}	Size of government investment shock	invgamma	0.050	Inf	0.024	0.012	0.039
u^{γ}	Size of learning-by-doing shock	invgamma	0.100	Inf	0.051	0.026	0.077
u^{B}	Size of bond shock	invgamma	0.050	Inf	0.015	0.010	0.018
u^{I}	Size of investment shock	invgamma	5.000	Inf	3.200	1.321	5.421
u^{i}	Size of interest rate spread shock	invgamma	10.000	Inf	3.266	2.479	3.898
u^{tot}	Size of terms of trade shock	invgamma	0.050	Inf	0.019	0.013	0.025
u^{z}	Size of international reserves shock	invgamma	0.050	Inf	0.009	0.006	0.012
u^{i*}	Size of foreign interest rate shock	invgamma	0.050	Inf	0.021	0.016	0.026
u^{v}	Size of price markup shock	invgamma	10.000	Inf	2.286	1.652	2.860

Appendix III. Model Structure

The model used in this chapter can be described as follows.

Household Behavior

The objective of the consumer is to maximize the expected value of the discounted sum of period utility functions:

$$E_0 \sum_0^{\infty} \beta^t \left(u_t^C (1 - b) \ln(C_t - bC_{t-1}) - \frac{u_t^L}{\psi} L_t^{\psi} + \frac{\kappa}{1 - \varepsilon} \left(\frac{M_t^C}{P_t} \right)^{1-\varepsilon} \right), \qquad (1)$$

where C_t is consumption, L_t is labor supply, M_t^c/P_t is the real value of consumers' holdings of domestic currency, and P_t is the consumer price index. The consumer subjective discount factor is $\beta \in (0,1)$. Note that we assume habit formation in consumption and a closed capital account. The consumer budget constraint is therefore given by

$$\begin{aligned} & M_t^c(j) + D_t(j) + P_t(C_t(j) + I_t(j)) \\ & = M_{t-1}^C(j) + D_{t-1}(j)(1 + i_{t-1}) + \Pi_t^f \\ & + \int_0^1 \Pi_t^d(s) ds + W_t L_t(j) + R_t K_t(j) - T_t , \end{aligned} \qquad (2)$$

where Π_t^f and Π_t^d are profits from commercial banks and nontradable firms, respectively. The capital stock evolves according to the following rule:

$$K_{t+1} = (1 - \delta) K_t + \Psi_t K_t , \qquad (3)$$

where δ is the rate of depreciation and Ψ_t an adjustment cost that is a function of the ratio of investment to capital:

$$\Psi_t \equiv \frac{I_t(j)}{K_t(j)} - \frac{\phi_1}{2} \left[\frac{I_t(j)}{K_t(j)} - \delta(1 + u_t^I) \right]^2 - \frac{\phi_2}{2} \left[\frac{I_t(j)}{K_t(j)} - \frac{I_{t-1}}{K_{t-1}} \right]^2 , \qquad (4)$$

where $\phi_1, \phi_2 \geq 0$ and u_t^I is a shock to the depreciation rate as originally proposed by Ambler and Paquet (1994) as a way of accounting for the low correlation between labor productivity and hours observed in the data.

The consumer's problem can be written thus:

$$\max_{C_t, M_t^c, D_t, L_t, K_{t+1}, I_t} \sum_{t=0}^{\infty} \beta^t \left\{ \begin{array}{l} U(C_t(j), L_t(j), M_t^c(j)) \\ - \lambda_t \left[\begin{array}{l} M_t^c(j) + D_t(j) \\ + P_t(C_t(j) + I_t(j)) - M_{t-1}^c(j) \\ -D_{t-1}(j)(1 + \mathrm{i}_{t-1})\Pi_t^f \\ -\int_0^1 \Pi_t^d(s)ds - W_t L_t(j) \\ - R_t K_t(j) + T_t \end{array} \right] \\ + \omega_t[(1 - \delta)K_t + \Psi_t K_t - K_{t+1} \end{array} \right\}, \qquad (5)$$

where λ_t and ω_t are Lagrange multipliers.

The relevant first-order conditions for consumption, labor, money, and deposits are

$$\frac{u_t^C(1 - b)}{C_t(j) - bC_{t-1}} = \lambda_t P_t \qquad (6)$$

$$u_t^L L(j)_t^{\psi-1} = \lambda_t W_t \qquad (7)$$

$$\frac{\kappa}{P_t}\left(\frac{M_t^C(j)}{P_t}\right)^{-\varepsilon} = \lambda_t - \beta E_t(\lambda_{t+1}) \qquad (8)$$

$$\lambda_t = \beta Et[\lambda_{t+1}(1 + i_t)]. \qquad (9)$$

The first-order conditions for capital and investment are, respectively,

$$E_t\left\{\beta\lambda_{t+1}R_{t+1} - \omega_t + \beta\omega_{t+1}\left[(1 - \delta) + \Psi_{t+1}\frac{I_{t+1}(j)}{K_{t+1}(j)}\Psi'_{t+1}\right]\right\} = 0, \qquad (10)$$

$$P_t\lambda_t = \omega_t\Psi'_t, \qquad (11)$$

where

$$\Psi'_t = \frac{\partial\Psi_t}{\partial I_t(j)/\partial K_t(j)} = 1 - \phi_1[\frac{I_t(j)}{K_t(j)} - \delta(1 + u_t^I)] - \phi_2[\frac{I_t(j)}{K_t(j)} - \frac{I_{t-1}}{K_{t-1}}]. \qquad (12)$$

Final Goods Production

Producers of final goods produce a good Z_t by aggregating over a continuum of domestically and imported intermediate goods, indexed by $s \in [0,1]$. The aggregating technology is given by the CES aggregate:

$$Z_t = [(\alpha^d)^{1/\vartheta}(Q_t^d)^{(\vartheta-1)/\vartheta} + (1 - \alpha^d)^{1/\vartheta}(Q_t^m)^{(\vartheta-1)/\vartheta}]^{\vartheta/(\vartheta-1)} \qquad (13)$$

for some elasticity of substitution $\vartheta > 1$. The CES indices of domestic and imported intermediate goods are Q_t^d and Q_t^m:

$$Q_t^i = \left[\int_0^1 q_t^i(s)^{(\nu-1)/\nu}\right]^{\nu/(\nu-1)} \tag{14}$$

for $i = d,m$. Profit maximization implies the standard demand functions for intermediate goods,

$$Q_t^i = \alpha^i[P_t^i/P_t]^{-\vartheta} Z_t, \tag{15}$$

with an associated cost-minimizing price index and where $\alpha^d + \alpha^m = 1$.

Intermediate Goods Production

Following Prati and Tressel (2006), we incorporate learning by doing in the production function, as well as credit constraints following Atta-Mensah and Dib (2003). The credit constraints are incorporated by assuming that intermediate-goods firms use an input ϑ_t that is funded by borrowing from a financial intermediary. The production technology is Cobb-Douglas:

$$Y_t = \theta_t \vartheta_t^{\varsigma} (L_t^{\alpha} Kt^{1-\alpha})^{1-\varsigma}, \tag{16}$$

where θ_t represents productivity that we assume is affected by both the size of the tradable sector and the amount of government expenditure on capital goods:

$$\theta_t = (1 - \rho^{\theta})[h(G_t^K) + u_t^{\gamma} Q_t^x] + \rho^{\theta}\theta_{t-1} + u_t^{\theta}, \tag{17}$$

where we allow productivity to follow a stochastic autoregressive process, and where Q_t^x are exports. The function $h(.)$ embodies the technology whereby government spending on investment goods produces the productivity-enhancing public good. It satisfies $h'(.)>0$, $h''(.)<0$. u_t^{γ} captures the degree of learning by doing.

The problem facing the firm is to minimize costs subject to satisfying demand:

$$\min_{K_t, L_t, \vartheta_t^{\varsigma}} W_t L_t + R_t K_t + (1 + i_t^L) P_t \vartheta_t + P_t \lambda_t [Y_t - \theta_t \vartheta_t^{\varsigma} (L_t^{\alpha} K_t^{1-\alpha})^{1-\varsigma}], \tag{18}$$

where we assume that the firm takes prices as given. The first-order conditions for K_t, L_t and ϑ_t^{ς} are

$$R_t = (1 - \varsigma)(1 - \alpha)\lambda_t P_t \theta_t \vartheta_t^{\varsigma} (L_t^{\alpha} K_t^{1-\alpha})^{-\varsigma} K_t^{-\alpha} \tag{19}$$

$$W_t = (1 - \varsigma)\alpha\lambda_t P_t \theta_t \vartheta_t^{\varsigma} (L_t^{\alpha} K_t^{1-\alpha})^{-\varsigma} L_t^{\alpha-1} \tag{20}$$

$$(1 + i_t^L) = \lambda_t \varsigma \theta_t \vartheta_t^{\varsigma-1} (L_t^{\alpha} K_t^{1-\alpha})^{1-\varsigma}. \tag{21}$$

Nominal marginal costs can be written as the ratio of the nominal wage to the marginal product of labor:

$$MC_t = \frac{W_t}{(1-\varsigma)\alpha_t\theta_t\vartheta_t^{\varsigma}(L_t^{\alpha}K_t^{1-\alpha})^{-\varsigma}L_t^{\alpha-1}}. \tag{22}$$

We assume that each domestic firm sells its output on both the domestic and the export markets so that $Y_t = Q_t^D + Q_t^x$. For simplicity, we assume that the demand for export goods has the same structure as domestic demand:

$$Q_t^x = [P_t^x/P_t^*]^{n}, \tag{23}$$

where P_t^* is the world price index, which is considered to be exogenous.

Price-Setting by Intermediate-Goods Producers

Intermediate-goods producers face quadratic adjustment costs in setting prices measured in terms of the intermediate good and given by

$$\frac{\phi}{2}\left[\frac{P_t^d/P_{t-1}^d}{P_{t-1}^d/P_{t-2}^d}-1\right]^2 Q_t^d. \tag{24}$$

Hence, we assume that the cost of price adjustment is related to the change in inflation relative to the past observed inflation rate. Juillard and others (2006) argue that this allows for more realistic inflation dynamics in the model with a backward-looking term in the solved-out Phillips curve.

The optimal price-setting equation for the nontradable price can then be written as

$$P_t^d = \frac{\nu}{(\nu-1)}MC_t - \frac{\phi}{(\nu-1)}P_t\frac{\pi_t^d}{\pi_{t-1}^d}\left[\frac{\pi_t^d}{\pi_{t-1}^d}-1\right] + \frac{\phi}{(\nu-1)}P_tE_t\left\{\rho_{t,t+1}\frac{Q_{t+1}^d}{Q_t^d}\frac{\pi_{t+1}^d}{\pi_t^d}\left[\frac{\pi_{t+1}^d}{\pi_t^d}-1\right]\right\}, \tag{25}$$

and where $\pi_t^d = \frac{P_t^d}{P_{t-1}^d}$ reduces to the well-known result that prices, if flexible, are set as a markup over marginal cost. For simplicity, we assume that the law of one price holds in the export market, so that $P_t^x = P_t^d/e_t$. Importing firms are assumed to be owned by risk-neutral foreigners who purchase goods at the exogenous world price and resell them in the domestic market. For simplicity, we assume that changes in the exchange rate are immediately passed through to the import price, so that $P_t^m = u_t^{tot}\frac{\nu}{(\nu-1)}e_tP_t^*$, where u_t^{tot} is a shock to the terms of trade.

Financial Intermediary

The financial sector is assumed to convert deposits from households into loans to intermediate-goods firms and the public sector, and reserves, similar to Agénor and Montiel (2006):

$$D_t = B_t^P + \vartheta_t + R_t \,. \tag{26}$$

For a given level of reserves, an increase in the volume of deposits at the financial intermediary reduces the amount of money in circulation and hence the utility from liquidity services.

Deposits are assumed to earn the same interest rate as government bonds. Loans to intermediate-goods firms earn an interest rate that represents a markup over the interest rate on deposits. This markup is a function g(.) of firms' beginning-of-period net worth (the ratio of their liabilities to the value of their capital stock), as in Agénor and Montiel (2006):

$$\frac{i_t^L + u_t^i}{i_t} = g(\eta; P_t K_t / \vartheta_{t-1}), \tag{27}$$

where u_t^i is a mean 0 shock to the lending rate. Commercial banks are assumed to maintain reserves equal to required reserves in the steady state and to use reserves to smooth movements in net liabilities:

$$R_t = \alpha^r D_t + \varpi_1 \Delta B_t^P + \varpi_2 \Delta \vartheta_t - \varpi_3 \Delta D_t \tag{28}$$

The Public Sector

The central bank's balance sheet is:

$$\Delta M_t^c + \Delta R_t = e_t \Delta Z_t + \Delta B_{t+1}, \tag{29}$$

where e_t is the nominal exchange rate, Z_t are international reserves, and B_{t+1} are government securities maturing in the next period and held by the central bank. We assume for simplicity that no interest is earned on international reserves. Different assumptions about aid absorption are characterized by the response of reserves to aid inflows. Assuming that profits of the central bank are transferred to the fiscal agent, the public sector's budget constraint takes the form

$$\Delta B_{t+1} + \Delta B_{t+1}^P = P_t G_t + i_{t-1} B_t^P - T_t - e_t A_t \,, \tag{30}$$

where A_t is aid and B_t^P are bonds issued to the financial sector. We assume that these bonds earn the same rate of interest as household deposits. A share μ_t of government spending is spent on a productivity-enhancing investment good:

$$G_t = \mu_t G_t^K + (1 - \mu_t) G_t^C. \tag{31}$$

The consolidated budget constraint is then

$$M_t^0 + B_{t+1}^P - e_t Z_t = M_{t-1}^0 + (1 + i_{t-1}) B_t^P - e_t Z_{t-1} + P_t G_t - T_t - e_t A_t , \tag{32}$$

where M_t^0 is base money defined as $M_t^0 = M_t^C = R_t$.

Fiscal and Monetary Policy Rules

In our model, the fiscal and monetary authorities have access to four different instruments, of which three can be used independently. The fiscal agent controls government spending, taxation, and net domestic borrowing, whereas the monetary authority controls the level of international reserves.

Following Adam and O'Connell (2005), we can analyze fiscal policy rules of the form

$$\begin{aligned} T_t &= T - (1 - \iota)\omega(e_t A_t - eA) \\ P_t G_t &= PG + \iota\omega(e_t A_t - eA), \end{aligned} \tag{33}$$

where ω and ι determine the portion of aid used to reduce taxes and increase expenditure and thus increase the primary fiscal deficit (before grants). An ω less than 1 unambiguously lowers the primary deficit after grants. If ω equals 0, the primary deficit after grants falls by the amount of aid. If ω is between 0 and 1 so that part of the aid is spent, ι determines the allocation of that spending between the private and public sectors. If ι equals 0, the increased spending is carried out by the government, whereas if ι is 1 the increased spending is done by the private sector.

The effect of a shock to aid on international reserves and the monetary base will depend on the actions of the central bank. We follow Adam and O'Connell (2005) and Peiris (2002) in our specification of the policy rules for the central bank. Foreign exchange rate intervention is governed by

$$\begin{aligned} \Delta Z_t = {} & z_1(Z - Z_{t-1}) + (1 - z_2\omega)(A_t - A) + \\ & z_3 \log\left(\frac{e_t/e_{t-1}}{\pi/\pi^*}\right) + z_4 \log\left(\frac{\pi_t}{\pi}\right) + u_t^Z, \end{aligned} \tag{34}$$

where z_1 governs the authorities' commitment to a constant level of reserves, and z_2 determines the commitment to an absorb-as-you-spend scenario in which the sale of foreign exchange is conducted in line with government spending increases financed by aid inflows. The commitment to a crawling peg determined by the steady-state inflation differential ($\pi - \pi^*$) between at home and the rest of the world is represented by z_3. Finally, z_4 determines the extent to which the sale of foreign exchange reserves is used to achieve a given target of the inflation rate π , and u_t^Z is a shock to foreign currency reserves.

Any foreign exchange rate intervention will have an impact on the monetary base and the exchange rate, with possible implications for inflation and output volatility. The authorities have the option of conducting open market operations on a temporary basis. Thus, we have

$$\Delta B_t^P = b_1 e_t \Delta Z_t + b_2 \log(\frac{\pi_t}{\pi}) + b_3(Y_{t-1} - Y) + b_4(B^P - B_{t-1}^P) + u_t^B, \qquad (35)$$

where b_1 governs the extent to which bond operations are used to sterilize the impact of foreign exchange interventions on the monetary base; b_2 determines the commitment to the inflation target; b_3 governs the effect of output-gap considerations in the conduct of monetary policy; $b_4>0$ shows that all bond operations are unwound over time; and $u_t^{B^P}$ is a shock to domestic bonds.

Market Clearing and Aggregation

In general equilibrium, supply equals demand in the intermediate- and final-goods markets at posted prices:

$$Y_t = Q_t^d + Q_t^x$$

$$Z_t = C_t + I_t + G_t + \vartheta_t - \frac{\phi}{2}\left[\frac{P_t^D/P_{t-1}^D}{P_{t-1}^D/P_{t-2}^D} - 1\right]^2 Q_t^d. \qquad (36)$$

The model can alternatively be closed using the balance of payments identity:

$$e_t \Delta Z_t = e_t A_t + e_t P_t^x Q_t^x - P_t^m Q_t^m. \qquad (37)$$

Stochastic Shocks

A number of stochastic shocks are included in the model to ensure that the model is not stochastically singular and more capable of reproducing the dynamics in the data. In particular, the number of exogenous shocks must be at least as large as the number of observed variables to allow us to estimate the model using classical Maximum Likelihood or Bayesian methods. Our model includes 14 structural shocks: two preferences shocks to the marginal utility of consumption and labor (u_t^C, u_t^L); a shock to technology; a shock to investment; a shock to the markup (u_t^θ, u_t^I, u_t^V); four external shocks—one to aid, one to world inflation, one to world interest rates, and one to the terms of trade (u_t^A, $u_t^{\pi*}$; u_t^{i*}, u_t^{tot}); a shock to the share of capital expenditure in government expenditure (u_t^μ); a shock to learning by doing (u_t^γ); a shock to lending rates and commercial bank reserves (u_t^i); and a shock to government bonds and foreign currency reserves (u_t^B, u_t^Z). With the exception of the shock to the markup, which is assumed to be white noise, all shocks are assumed to follow a first-order process.

Bibliography

Adam, C., and D. Bevan, 2001, "Fiscal Policy Design in Low-Income Countries," WIDER Discussion Paper No. 2001/67 (Helsinki: United Nations University, World Institute for Development Economics Research).

Adam, C., and S. O'Connell, 2005, "Monetary Policy in Sub-Saharan Africa" (unpublished; Washington: International Monetary Fund).

———, E. Buffie, and C. Pattillo, 2006, "Monetary Policy Responses to Aid Surges in Africa" (unpublished).

Adolfson, M., S. Laséen, J. Lindé, and M. Villani, 2004, "Derivation and Estimation of a DSGE Open Economy Model with Incomplete Pass-Through" (unpublished; Stockholm: Swedish Central Bank).

Agénor, Pierre-Richard, and Peter J. Montiel, 2006, "Credit Market Imperfections and the Monetary Transmission Mechanism Part I: Fixed Exchange Rates," Centre for Growth and Business Cycle Research Discussion Paper No. 76 (Manchester, United Kingdom: School of Economic Studies, University of Manchester).

Aizenman, J., and N. Marion, 1996, "Volatility and the Investment Response," NBER Working Paper No. 5841 (Cambridge, Massachusetts: National Bureau for Economic Research).

Alesina, A., and G. Tabellini, 2005, "Why Is Fiscal Policy Often Procyclical?" NBER Working Paper No. 11600 (Cambridge, Massachusetts: National Bureau for Economic Research).

Ambler, S., and A. Paquet, 1994, "Stochastic Depreciation and the Business Cycle," *International Economic Review*, Vol. 44 (February), pp. 101–16.

Arellano, Christina, A. Bulíř, T. Lane, and L. Lipschitz, 2005, "The Dynamic Implications of Foreign Aid and Its Variability," IMF Working Paper 05/119 (Washington: International Monetary Fund).

Atingi-Ego, Michael, 2005, "Choice of Appropriate Monetary Policy Instrument Mix by Bank of Uganda" (unpublished; Kampala: Bank of Uganda).

Atta-Mensah, J., and A. Dib, 2003, "Bank Lending, Credit Shocks, and the Transmission of Canadian Monetary Policy," Working Paper 03-9 (Ottawa: Bank of Canada).

Balassa, B., 1990, "Incentive Policies and Export Performance in Sub-Saharan Africa" *World Development*, Vol. 18 (March), 383–91.

Ball, L., 2000, "Policy Rules and External Shocks," NBER Working Paper No. 7910 (Cambridge, Massachusetts: National Bureau for Economic Research).

Barnichon, Régis, and S.J. Peiris, 2007, "Sources of Inflation in Sub-Saharan Africa," IMF Working Paper 07/32 (Washington: International Monetary Fund).

Berg, A., and others, 2007, *The Macroeconomics of Scaling up Aid: Lessons from Recent Experience*, IMF Occasional Paper No. 253 (Washington: International Monetary Fund).

Bernanke, B., and M. Gertler, 1995, "Inside the Black Box: The Credit Channel of Monetary Policy Transmission," *Journal of Economic Perspectives*, Vol. 9 (Autumn), pp. 27–48.

———, and S. Gilchrist, 1999, "The Financial Accelerator in a Quantitative Business Cycle Framework," in *Handbook of Macroeconomics*, Vol. 1C, ed. by J. Taylor and M. Woodford (Amsterdam: North-Holland).

Bleaney, Michael, and David Fielding, 2002, "Exchange Rate Regimes, Inflation and Output Volatility in Developing Countries," *Journal of Development Economics*, Vol. 68 (June), pp. 233–45.

Bleaney, Michael, and David Greenaway, 2001, "The Impact of Terms of Trade and Real Exchange Rate Volatility on Investment and Growth in Sub-Saharan Africa," *Journal of Development Economics*, Vol. 65 (August), pp. 491–500.

Buffie, Edward, Christopher Adam, Stephen O'Connell, and Catherine Pattillo, 2004, "Exchange Rate Policy and the Management of Official and Private Capital Flows in Africa," *Staff Papers*, International Monetary Fund, Vol. 51 (June), pp. 126–60.

Caballero, R., and V. Corbo, 1989, "The Effect of Real Exchange Rate Uncertainty on Exports: Empirical Evidence," *World Bank Economic Review*, Vol. 3, No. 2, pp. 263–78.

Christiano, L., M. Eichenbaum, and C. Evans, 2005, "Nominal Rigidities and the Dynamic Effects of a Shock to Monetary Policy," *Journal of Political Economy*, Vol. 113 (February), pp. 1–45.

Clarida, R., J. Galí, and M. Gertler, 1999, "The Science of Monetary Policy: A New Keynesian Perspective," *Journal of Economic Literature*, Vol. 37 (December), pp. 1661–707.

———, 2000, "Monetary Policy Rules and Macroeconomic Stability: Evidence and Some Theory," *Quarterly Journal of Economics*, Vol. 115 (February), pp. 147–80.

Devereux, M.B., P.R. Lane, and J. Xu, 2004, "Exchange Rates and Monetary Policy in Emerging Market Economies," IIIS Discussion Paper No. 36 (Dublin: Trinity

College, Institute for International Integration Studies). Available via the Internet: http://www.tcd.ie/iiis/documents/discussion/pdfs/iiisdp36.pdf

Easterly, William, R. Islam, and Joseph E. Stiglitz, 2001, "Shaken and Stirred: Explaining Growth Volatility," in *Annual World Bank Conference on Development Economics 2000*, ed. by B. Pleskovic and N. Stern (Washington: World Bank).

Elbadawi, I., and K. Schmidt-Hebbel, 1998, "Macroeconomic Policies, Instability and Growth in the World," *Journal of African Economies*, Vol. 7, Supplement 2, pp. 116–68.

Fernández-Villaverde, J., and J.F. Rubio-Ramírez, 2004, "Comparing Dynamic Equilibrium Models to Data: A Bayesian Approach," *Journal of Econometrics*, Vol. 123 (November), pp. 153–87.

Fischer, Stanley, 1993, "The Role of Macroeconomic Factors in Growth," *Journal of Monetary Economics*, Vol. 32(3), pp. 45–66.

Geweke, J., 1998, "Using Simulation Methods for Bayesian Econometric Models: Inference, Development and Communication," Staff Report 249 (Federal Reserve Bank of Minneapolis).

Ghosh, A., and Steven Phillips, 1998, "Warning: Inflation May Be Harmful to Your Growth," *Staff Papers*, International Monetary Fund, Vol. 45 (December), pp. 672–710.

Gulde, A., C. Pattillo, J. Christensen, K. Carey, and S. Wagh, 2006, *Sub-Saharan Africa: Financial Sector Challenges* (Washington: International Monetary Fund).

Gupta, S., R. Powell, and Y. Yang, eds., 2006, *Macroeconomic Challenges of Scaling Up Aid to Africa: A Checklist for Practitioners* (Washington: International Monetary Fund).

Hausmann, R., and M. Gavin, 1995, "Overcoming Volatility in Latin America," in *Economic and Social Progress in Latin America Report* (Washington: Inter-American Development Bank).

Hausmann, Ricardo, Lant Pritchett, and Dani Rodrik, 2004, "Growth Accelerations," NBER Working Paper No. 10566 (Cambridge, Massachusetts: National Bureau of Economic Research).

International Monetary Fund (IMF), 2005a, "The Macroeconomics of Managing Increased Aid Inflows: Experiences of Low-Income Countries and Policy Implications" (Washington: Policy Development and Review Department). Available via the Internet: http://www.imf.org/external/np/pp/eng/2005/080805m.htm

———, 2005b, *Regional Economic Outlook: Sub-Saharan Africa* (Washington, May).

———, 2005c, *World Economic Outlook, April 2005*, World Economic and Financial Surveys (Washington).

Juillard, Michel, Philippe Karam, Douglas Laxton, and Paolo A. Pesenti, 2006, "Welfare-Based Monetary Policy Rules in an Estimated DSGE Model of the US Economy," ECB Working Paper No. 613 (Frankfurt: European Central Bank).

Kollmann, R., 2002, "Monetary Policy Rules in the Open Economy: Effects on Welfare and Business Cycles," *Journal of Monetary Economics*, Vol. 49 (July), pp. 989–1015.

Kose, M. Ayhan, Eswar S. Prasad, and Marco E. Terrones, 2005, "How Do Trade and Financial Integration Affect the Relationship Between Growth and Volatility?" IMF Working Paper 05/19 (Washington: International Monetary Fund).

Krugman, P., 1987, "The Narrow Moving Band, the Dutch Disease, and the Competitive Consequences of Mrs. Thatcher: Notes on Trade in the Presence of Dynamic Scale Economies," *Journal of Development Economics*, Vol. 27 (October), pp. 41–55.

Leeper, E.M., 1991, "Equilibria Under 'Active' and 'Passive' Monetary and Fiscal Policies," *Journal of Monetary Economics*, Vol. 27 (February), pp. 129–47.

Levine, R., and S. Zervos, 1998, "Stock Markets, Banks, and Economic Growth," *American Economic Review*, Vol. 88 (June), pp. 537–58.

Lubik T., and F. Schorfheide, 2005, "A Bayesian Look at New Open Economy Macroeconomics," The Johns Hopkins University Economics Working Paper Archive No. 521 (Baltimore, Maryland).

Mikkelsen, Jan, and Shanaka J. Peiris, 2005, *Uganda: Selected Issues and Statistical Appendix*, IMF Staff Country Report No. 05/172 (Washington: International Monetary Fund).

Mirzoev, T., 2007, "Modeling Aid Inflows in a Small Open Economy," in *The Macroeconomics of Scaling up Aid: Lessons from Recent Experience*, IMF Occasional Paper No. 253, ed. by A. Berg and others (Washington: International Monetary Fund).

Pallage, Stéphane, and Michel A. Robe, 2003, "On the Welfare Cost of Economic Fluctuations in Developing Countries," *International Economic Review*, Vol. 44 (May), pp. 677–98.

Peiris, S.J., 2002, "Large Capital Flows: Causes, Volatility, and Consequences" (D.Phil. dissertation; Oxford: University of Oxford).

Prati, A., and T. Tressel, 2006, "Aid Volatility and Dutch Disease: Is There a Role for Macroeconomic Policies?" IMF Working Paper 06/145 (Washington: International Monetary Fund).

Raddatz, C., 2007, "Are External Shocks Responsible for the Instability of Output in Low-Income Countries?" *Journal of Development Economics*, Vol. 84 (September), pp. 155–87.

Rajan, R., and A. Subramanian, 2005, "What Undermines Aid's Impact on Growth?" IMF Working Paper 05/126 (Washington: International Monetary Fund).

Ramey, G., and V. Ramey, 1995, "Cross-Country Evidence on the Link Between Volatility and Growth," *American Economic Review*, Vol. 85 (December), pp. 1138–51.

Rotemberg, J.J., 1982, "Sticky Prices in the United States," *Journal of Political Economy*, Vol. 90 (December), pp. 1187–1211.

Sachs, J., and A. Warner, 1995, "Natural Resource Abundance and Economic Growth," NBER Working Paper No. 5398 (Cambridge, Massachusetts: National Bureau of Economic Research).

Sargent, T.J., and N. Wallace, 1985, "Some Unpleasant Monetary Arithmetic," *Quarterly Review*, Federal Reserve Bank of Minneapolis, Vol. 9, pp. 1–17.

Saxegaard, M., 2005, "Excess Liquidity and the Effectiveness of Monetary Policy: Evidence from Sub-Saharan Africa," IMF Working Paper 06/115 (Washington: International Monetary Fund).

———, 2006a, "Fiscal and Monetary Policy in an Estimated Model of the Philippine Economy" (unpublished; Washington: International Monetary Fund).

———, 2006b, "Monetary Policy Rules in a Small Open Economy with External Liabilities" (unpublished; Washington: International Monetary Fund).

Schorfheide, F., 2000, "Bayesian Methods in Macroeconometrics." Available via the Internet: http://www.econ.upenn.edu/~schorf/papers/palgrave.pdf

Sekkat, Khalid, and Aristomene Varoudakis, 2000, "Exchange Rate Management and Manufactured Exports in Sub-Saharan Africa," *Journal of Development Economics*, Vol. 61 (February), pp. 237–53.

Selassie, Abebe Aemro, Benedict J. Clements, Shamsuddin Tareq, Jan Kees Martijn, and Gabriel Di Bella, 2006, *Designing Monetary and Fiscal Policy in Low-Income Countries*, IMF Occasional Paper No. 250 (Washington: International Monetary Fund).

Servén, L., 1997, "Irreversibility, Uncertainty and Private Investment: Analytical Issues and Some Lessons for Africa," *Journal of African Economies*, Vol. 6 (AERC Supplement), pp. 229–68.

———, 2002, "Real Exchange Rate Uncertainty and Private Investment in Developing Countries," Policy Research Working Paper No. 2823 (Washington: World Bank).

Smets, F.R., and R. Wouters, 2003, "An Estimated Dynamic Stochastic General Equilibrium Model of the Euro Area," *Journal of European Economic Association*, Vol. 1, No. 5, pp. 1123–75.

———, 2005, "Comparing Shocks and Frictions in US and Euro Area Business Cycles: A Bayesian DSGE Approach," *Journal of Applied Econometrics*, Vol. 20, No. 2, pp. 161–83.

Solimano, A., and L. Servén, eds., 1993, *Striving for Growth After Adjustment: The Role of Capital Formation* (Washington: World Bank).

Stone, Mark, 2003, "Inflation Targeting Lite," IMF Working Paper 03/12 (Washington: International Monetary Fund).

Svensson, L.E.O., 2000, "Open-Economy Inflation Targeting," *Journal of International Economics*, Vol. 50 (February), pp. 155–83.

Tarp, Finn, C. Arndt, H.T. Jensen, S. Robinson, and R. Heltberg, 2002, "Facing the Development Challenge in Mozambique: An Economywide Perspective,"

Research Report No. 126 (Washington: International Food Policy Research Institute).

Taylor, J.B., 1993, "Discretion Versus Policy Rules in Practice," *Carnegie-Rochester Conference Series on Public Policy*, Vol. 39 (December), pp. 195–214.

———, ed., 1998, *Monetary Policy Rules* (Chicago: University of Chicago Press).

Van Wijnbergen, S., 1984, "The 'Dutch Disease': A Disease After All?" *Economic Journal*, Vol. 94 (March), pp. 41–55.

6

Macroeconomic Management of Scaled-up Foreign Aid

SHANAKA J. PEIRIS

The Commission for Africa (2005) and the United Nations (UN) Millennium Project have identified a need for donors to scale up aid flows to well-governed low-income countries, including Mozambique, to enable them to meet the Millennium Development Goals (MDGs). While large aid inflows can play an important role in helping countries achieve the MDGs, they also pose a number of macroeconomic challenges. Scaling-up scenarios are intended to illustrate a potential medium- to long-term macroeconomic outcome and to identify some of the key measures and policies that would help countries absorb larger amounts of aid and use it efficiently (Gupta, Powell, and Yang, 2006). In practice, donors might be less likely to offer more aid, and recipient governments might be less likely to accept it, on a sustained basis if either party started to observe significant macroeconomic absorption problems—such as rising inflation, crowding-out of the private sector, or a serious loss of international competitiveness—and microeconomic capacity constraints, such as severe skill shortages, a deterioration in the quality of services, or other bottlenecks.[1]

There are three basic approaches to preparing scaling-up scenarios (Gupta, Powell, and Yang, 2006). The first approach assesses the mac-

[1]Mozambique's new Poverty Reduction Strategy Paper (PRSP), or *Plano de Acção para a Redução da Pobreza Absoluta II* (PARPA II), for 2006–09 considers a modest increase in external financing, including from the Multilateral Debt Relief Initiative (MDRI); more detailed scaling-up scenarios could also be prepared in annual progress reports.

roeconomic implications of a fiscal scenario based on an explicit costing of achieving the MDGs that do not focus on income levels (for example, those related to education, health care, and access to safe water). The costing exercise, which is typically carried out with assistance from development partners such as the World Bank and the United Nations, provides a judgment about the resources required in each sector. It may also illustrate trade-offs among policies, resources, and macroeconomic outcomes, and identify bottlenecks that need to be addressed. The second approach is to assess the macroeconomic impact of a significant but arbitrary increase of external finance (for example, 1–2 percent of GDP or a doubling of aid). This approach is probably more suitable for Mozambique because an explicit MDG costing is not yet available, and aid inflows continue to be large and rising (about 15 percent of GDP). The third approach is to target a specific growth rate if achieving the income poverty MDG—halving the poverty rate by 2015—is unrealistic given a country's present resources and policies, which is not the case in Mozambique.[2]

The chapter is organized as follows: first we provide an overview of the literature; then we analyze the past impact of aid in Mozambique, after which we present illustrative scaling-up scenarios geared to identifying macroeconomic policy trade-offs and improving potential outcomes; and we conclude by identifying the challenges for Mozambique and lessons for the rest of sub-Saharan Africa.

Analytical Overview and Literature Survey

Assessing the macroeconomic impact of scaling up foreign aid is important, since it may have significant effects on competitiveness, economic growth, and poverty reduction. The spending and absorption of aid-financed expenditures in the short to medium term could cause a significant appreciation of the real exchange rate, thereby discouraging the expansion of exports and hurting long-term growth.[3] This is often called the "Dutch disease" effect of aid, because the decline of the tradable goods sector relative to the nontradable sector could impair productivity growth, which is particularly strong in the export sector owing to the

---

[2]See Chapter 2 for a discussion of the likelihood that Mozambique will achieve this MDG.

[3]Chapter 5 also shows that aid shocks can be associated with greater macroeconomic instability, which the economic literature has shown to be detrimental to private investment, exports, and economic growth.

high rate of learning by doing in this sector. This has been borne out by empirical studies, including for African manufacturing firms. According to Rajan and Subramanian (2005), the potential adverse effects of aid on competitiveness and exports explain the weak link between aid inflows and growth in developing countries.

Because aid largely accrues to governments, the macroeconomic consequences are determined by what governments do with the aid (Adam, 2005). If it is entirely saved, or if the ultimate recipient of the aid, whether in the public or the private sector, spends the entire increase on imports, the real exchange rate will be unaffected, at least initially. On the other hand, it is far likelier that aid inflows will boost demand for both imports and domestically produced (nontradable) goods. If the public sector has a greater propensity to consume domestically produced goods, the demand for nontradable goods could be stronger if aid is used to finance increased public expenditure rather than direct transfers to households or tax cuts. In either case, the mechanism is the same so that differences in outcomes are a matter of degree (Adam, 2005).[4]

As noted by Heller (2005), fiscal policy can become even more complicated in a high-aid environment. If government scales up basic services—an action associated with hiring workers, delivering services to the public, and maintaining new infrastructure—it faces the challenge of what to do if and when donors do not sustain the aid. If governments find it difficult to reduce expenditures from aid-financed levels, the pressure for greater domestic financing of the deficit may increase significantly. Buffie and others (2006) argue that if the public suspects that donor financing of scaled-up and partially irreversible public spending commitments may be temporary, an aid surge may be highly inflationary in the short run. Monetary policy alone cannot handle this problem, because with thin and undeveloped bond markets, sterilization causes interest payments and future seigniorage requirements to balloon, and the resulting increase in expected future inflation creates inflation problems in the near term. Barring interventions that directly address concerns about aid volatility

[4]Unless there is considerable excess supply in an economy, higher demand for domestic goods requires their prices to rise to induce the necessary supply response. For small open economies like Mozambique, import prices are fixed in world markets while nontradables can, by definition, be supplied only by domestic producers. In other words, the real exchange rate (the price of nontradables relative to tradable goods) must appreciate to entice resources, including labor, to switch from the production of exportable and import-substituting goods to the production of nontradable goods. In the process, as the real exchange rate appreciates, the tradable goods sector shrinks relative to the nontradable sector (Adam (2005)).

(Bulíř and Hamann, 2005) or the reversibility of fiscal commitments (for example, through temporary wage contracts), some degree of near-term fiscal restraint is a necessary component of a successful strategy. According to Buffie and others (2006), the right policy package combines a critical minimum degree of fiscal restraint with either reverse sterilization (buying back some internal debt) or a reserve buffer stock scheme (allocating some of the aid inflow to reserve accumulation). It is also important to project an exit strategy—that is, the macroeconomic path the country envisages following after scaled-up aid flows fall to more normal levels or, perhaps, if aid flows have been front-loaded, to lower-than-normal levels. Given the vast socioeconomic needs and infrastructure gaps in Mozambique, as in much of sub-Saharan Africa (Ndulu, 2007), the exit strategy is best accomplished through higher domestic revenue mobilization in order to maintain long-term fiscal sustainability, particularly when countries are below their potential for raising tax revenues.[5]

The short-run impact on demand of spending aid could be mitigated—or even reversed—depending on the supply side response over the medium to long term. When learning by doing also has externalities in the nontradable sector, the long-term adverse impact of spending aid will be limited, even if the real exchange rate appreciates in the short term (Torvik, 2001). Investments in physical and human capital, both in the government and in the private sector, can increase productivity not only in the tradable sector but also in the nontradable sector, potentially offsetting the initial loss of competitiveness. If productivity gains from aid-financed public investment can be secured so that the export sector's share of total output expands in the medium to long term, the issue is simply an intertemporal one, at least in the aggregate; future growth in the export sector will compensate for the temporary growth-retarding effects of a short-run real exchange rate appreciation (Adam, 2005). Containing unproductive spending and targeting the poor, to efficiently absorb larger amounts of foreign aid and improve public service delivery, are critical, and will require a well-functioning public financial management (PFM) system, including at the subnational level.[6]

---

[5]There is also some concern that a substantial scaling up of aid flows—especially grants—could dampen a county's domestic revenue effort (Gupta and others, 2004). To the extent that a weaker tax effort reduces domestic distortions, it might help spur economic activity. However, when lower revenue collections reflect weak compliance or unnecessary tax exemptions, they are more likely to breed aid dependency.

[6]A sound PFM system also provides assurance to donors that their resources are being used for intended purposes, and helps aid-recipient countries reduce the transac-

Real exchange rate misalignment should be avoided because it may be more costly than shifts in the equilibrium real exchange rate. The interaction of the demand- and supply-side effects of aid means that the real exchange rate may "overshoot" its long-run value and may, in fact, move in the opposite direction, so that a short-run appreciation is followed by medium-term depreciation. Temporary movements of this kind can be very costly because firms face high adjustment costs and are unable to access credit from underdeveloped financial markets to finance the short-run losses caused by unfavorable temporary real exchange rate movements, even if these movements are anticipated. In such circumstances, firms may run down their capital, lay off skilled workers, or, in a worst-case scenario, close down completely, even though the long-run prospects for the tradable sector may be strongly favorable. Hence, short-run movements in real exchange rates may have permanent effects on the structure of production and growth. Bleaney and Greenaway (2001) estimate a negative effect of lagged exchange rate misalignment on growth covering 14 sub-Saharan African countries over 1980–95, while overvaluation might hurt investment even though it lowers the price of imported capital goods. If firms falsely believe temporary real exchange rate movements to be permanent, they incur costs as they first move into (what they think is) the booming sector and then out again when the temporary effects pass. It is important to distinguish here between the volatility of aid flows and the volatility of the real exchange rate itself. It is the latter that matters for intersectoral resource allocation decisions. Whether the former mitigates or exacerbates the latter depends on whether aid is pro- or countercyclical (Adam, 2005).

The dynamic macroeconomic effects of large aid flows in sub-Saharan Africa remain largely an empirical issue, but the literature has yielded somewhat inconclusive results, warranting further analysis. Econometric estimates of the impact of aid on the real exchange rate often show what Bulíř and Lane (2002) have referred to as "traces" of aid-induced real exchange rate appreciation, while evidence of aid-financed contraction of the export sector is equally mixed (Arellano and others, 2005; and Yano and Nugent, 1999). The small or insignificant Dutch disease effects may be explained by the tendency for the real exchange rate to depreciate as a result of policy reforms (for example, trade liberalization) associated with aid conditionality that are difficult to capture but that bias the effects of aid and fiscal, monetary, and exchange rate policy responses to aid down-

tion costs involved in meeting donor-specified requirements as well as in improving aid predictability.

ward.[7] Aid inflows can also play an important role in financing imported inputs, which may affect short-run supply responses as otherwise idle capacity is brought into use or leads to stronger productivity growth in the nontradable sector as noted above, potentially triggering a depreciation in the real exchange rate (Adam, 2005). As shown in Prati and Tressel (2006), sterilization may also be an effective tool for depreciating the real exchange rate in the short run, although attempts to target the real exchange rate below its equilibrium level are likely to be associated with higher inflation or real interest rates (Calvo, Reinhart, and Végh, 1995). An excessive reliance on open market operations is also likely to crowd out private sector credit (Christensen, 2004), thereby reducing private investment (Servén, 2002) and, ultimately, undermining economic growth in low-income countries (Abbas and Christensen, 2007).

Following the literature, the next section attempts to estimate the fiscal and macroeconomic effects of aid in Mozambique over the past decade or so by using quarterly data in the post-stabilization phase (1996–2006), in an attempt to overcome some of the weaknesses of previous analyses of foreign aid in low-income countries, such as small sample biases and structural breaks that make estimates sensitive to different test specifications. The insights in the section "Aid and Macroeconomic Management in Mozambique" will help guide a discussion in the following section of the potential macroeconomic implications and policy trade-offs of a further scaling up of aid to Mozambique.

Aid and Macroeconomic Management in Mozambique

Identifying the fiscal effects of aid is a prerequisite to understanding the macroeconomic effectiveness of aid (McGillivray and Morrissey, 2001). However, there has been limited analysis of the fiscal effects of aid in Mozambique.[8]

There is a growing literature on how aid affects the fiscal behavior of governments (reviewed in McGillivray and Morrissey, 2001). The most common approach is through fiscal response models (FRMs). These studies tend to find that aid ultimately leads to increased spending, and total spending often increases by more than the value of aid (McGillivray and Morrissey, 2001). There is evidence that aid has had a beneficial impact

---

[7]See Chapter 5 for a discussion of the latter.

[8]See Benito-Spinetto and Moll (2005); and Arndt, Jones, and Tarp (2007) for an overview.

on investment and recurrent spending in sub-Saharan African countries (Commission for Africa, 2005). IMF (2005) suggests that Mozambique spent most of the aid it received. The degree of spending was calculated by the widening in the government fiscal deficit, net of aid, that accompanies an increase in aid. IMF (2005) shows that public expenditures actually increased, on average, more than the increment in net aid inflows, leading to a substantial widening of the fiscal deficit net of aid during the aid surge of 2000–02. The aid surge was roughly equally distributed between current and capital expenditures. However, this study focuses on short periods when aid surged and takes a relatively simplistic approach compared with the fiscal response literature of aid. It may therefore have missed more complicated dynamic effects (Mavrotas, 2002).

The fiscal effects of aid in Mozambique are assessed by estimating an FRM within a vector autoregression (VAR) modeling framework as in Osei, Morrissey, and Lloyd (2005). The variables of the fiscal response VAR model are ordered as follows: foreign aid (*AID*), government expenditure (*Expenditures*), tax revenue (*Tax*), and the change in net credit to the government from the banking system (*NCG*). Note that since nontax components of revenue and nonbank borrowing are omitted, we are not estimating an identity. We also estimate a model in which foreign aid is divided into grants and loans as well as project aid and budget support. Total government expenditure is disaggregated into capital and current components. We use quarterly data over the period 1996Q1–2006Q3, with all the variables measured in constant 2004 prices expressed in millions of new meticais (MT). Data on domestic fiscal variables and external financing are from the IMF.

The dynamic effects of aid shocks can be evaluated using impulse response functions. An analysis of the time-series properties of the variables reveals that the variables are integrated of order one or I(1), except for *AID* and *NCG*, which are stationary I(0). However, cointegration tests did not identify a significant cointegrating vector between the variables. Therefore, the series are first differenced for estimation purposes to avoid the spurious and inconsistent regression problem (Hendry, 1995).[9] Results of Granger causality tests are somewhat mixed but clearly point to aid Granger-causing fiscal variables but not vice versa, suggesting that aid disbursements have not been influenced by the budget balance over the period. The results also suggest that shocks to foreign aid are exogenous to the system, rather than determined by it, and offer statistical support for the

[9]The VARs were also estimated using detrended data. The results were largely unchanged from that of first differencing the data and thus are not reported here.

legitimacy of the impulse response analysis of aid shocks in Mozambique below. The structural shocks are recovered from the VAR residuals using the Cholesky decomposition of the variance-covariance matrix.[10]

Plots of the impulse response functions for a one standard deviation shock in aid are shown in Figures 6.1 and 6.2. A one standard deviation shock corresponds to about MT 1,200 million (about 1 percent of GDP in 2004). Figure 6.1 shows that the impulse response to an aid shock of one standard deviation gives a full pass-through (change in spending *t* periods after the shock over an initial percent change in aid) within four quarters. In fact, as observed in IMF (2005), public expenditures actually have a tendency to increase more than the original shock to aid in Mozambique. However, in contrast with the findings in IMF (2005), the aid shock seems to result in more capital expenditures, with only about one-third of aid financing current spending within a year (Figure 6.2).[11] Not only does *AID* result in an increase in capital spending but it also seems to lead to an increase in domestic taxation. Moreover, these results are largely unaltered, whether they relate to loans or grants.[12] The picture is somewhat less clear regarding the impact of *AID* on *NCG*, possibly because of the smoothing of expenditures or issuance of domestic debt.

The spending of foreign aid could undermine competitiveness, although such effects can be mitigated, depending on the supply-side response over the long term. Given that aid inflows have been spent by the government in Mozambique, the next issue is whether these expenditures have induced a significant appreciation of the real exchange rate and thus discouraged the expansion of exports, thereby hurting long-term growth. The results presented in Chapter 10 show that government spending (both current and total expenditures) has tended to lead to the appreciation of the fundamental equilibrium real exchange rate, but some of those effects are

---

[10]The Cholesky decomposition imposes the correct number of restrictions for just identification and imposes a recursive structure on the system so that the most endogenous variable is ordered last—that is, it is affected by all contemporaneous "structural" shocks.

[11]It should be noted, however, that all donor-financed projects are classified as capital spending in the fiscal accounts even though it is likely that a significant share of such spending goes to wages and goods and services. In addition, the unavailability of expenditures on a quarterly basis according to a functional classification also limits an analysis of the impact of foreign aid on the composition of spending.

[12]The increase in government taxation allays concerns identified in Gupta and others (2004) that grants can substitute for domestic revenues and, hence, are more likely to dampen domestic efforts to collect more revenue.

Figure 6.1. Fiscal Effects of Foreign Aid (Total Expenditures)

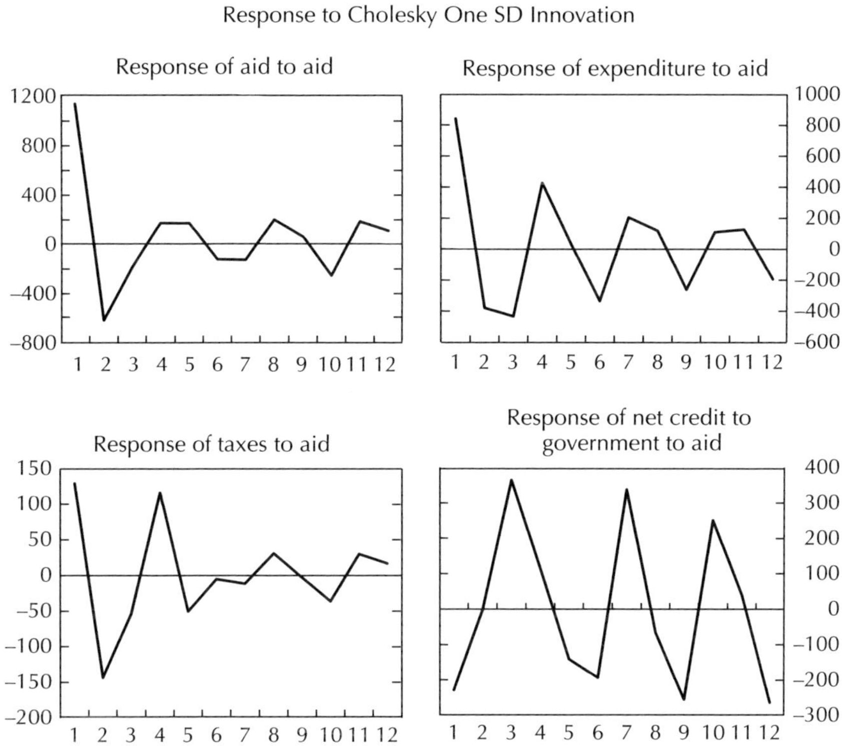

Source: Author's calculations.

mitigated by trade liberalization and negative terms of trade movements.[13] In addition, even though the share of Mozambique's total exports in world trade has increased, the strong growth of megaprojects accounts for most of this increase.[14] The share of non-megaproject exports in world trade and the ratio of non-megaproject exports to GDP have remained roughly constant. Concerns therefore remain regarding the impact of scaled-up

[13]Another issue frequently discussed in the literature is the degree of real equilibrium exchange rate (REER) misalignment. The econometric results of Chapter 10 suggest that the REER may have been overvalued during times of tight exchange rate management. As a result, export performance might have been weaker than it would have been had the REER been aligned with its underlying equilibrium rate. However, it is difficult to infer whether such deviations from equilibrium can be attributed to Mozambique's response to aid.

[14]See Chapter 10 for more detail.

Figure 6.2. Fiscal Effects of Foreign Aid (Current and Capital Expenditures)

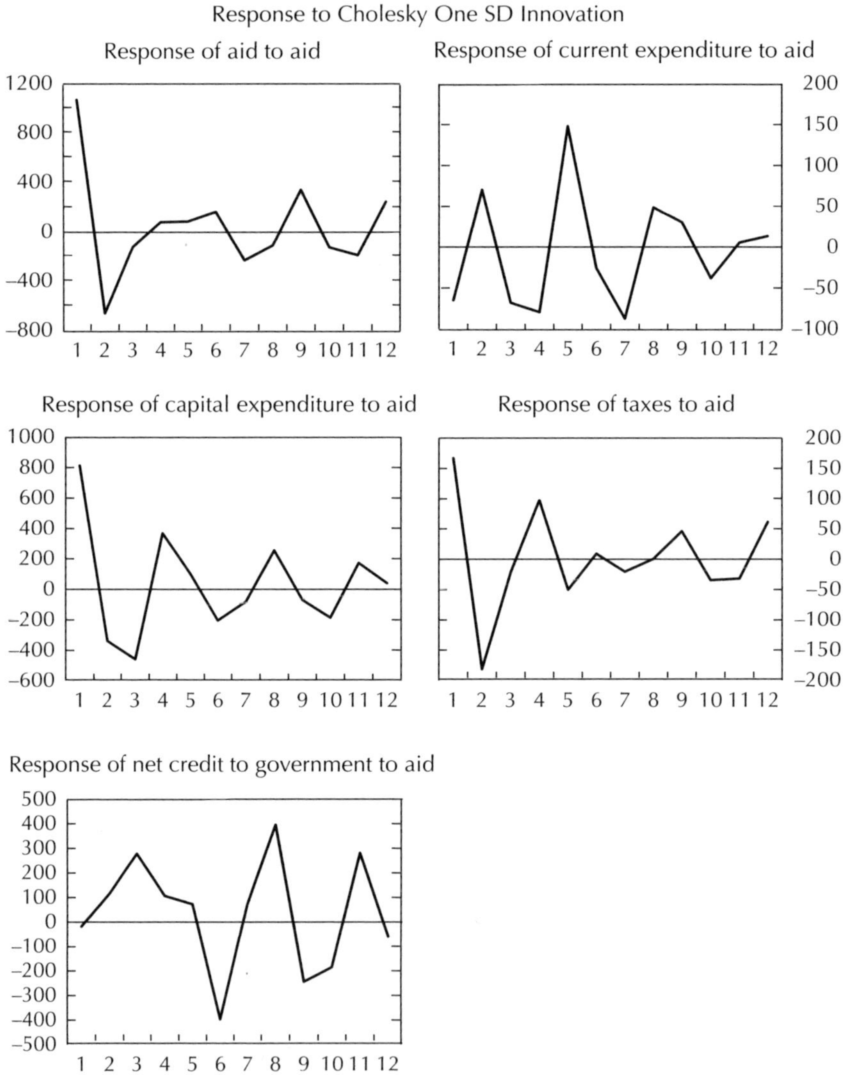

Source: Author's calculations.

aid on Mozambique's competitiveness. These results are somewhat different from those presented in Benito-Spinetto and Moll (2005), who simulate a simple 1-2-3 model in the spirit of Devarajan and others (1994) and indicate that Dutch disease appears not to be an important factor in Mozambique. They argue that the supply-side effects of aid in the form of investment in health care and infrastructure could help mitigate a real exchange rate appreciation. The lack of visible evidence that supply-side effects are strong enough to dampen appreciation pressures on the real exchange rate stemming from the demand-side impact of aid spending may, however, be explained by well-known lagged (and possibly nonlinear) effects, as well as by the rudimentary state of Mozambique's PFM systems, which, at least until recently, were weaker than those in most other sub-Saharan African countries.[15]

Even the short-run response to aid is dependent on a number of factors, including the degree of aid absorption.[16] As discussed in Chapter 5, the impulse responses of the estimated dynamic stochastic general equilibrium (DSGE) model for Mozambique show that the degree of absorption of aid-financed spending can have very different effects on the short-term dynamics of the exchange rate, output, and inflation. To see how those effects may have played out in Mozambique, we estimate an identified six-variable VAR from 1996Q1 to 2006Q3.[17] The ordering of the variables embodies two key identifying assumptions—that is, that aid shocks contemporaneously affect all variables in the system and that economic variables do not respond contemporaneously to policy variables, except for the exchange rate. As an asset price, the exchange rate is expected to respond faster to policy shocks than real economy variables. The following ordering is chosen: foreign aid, real GDP[18] (or real non-megaproject exports), inflation, reserves, domestic debt, and the nominal exchange rate. The structural shocks are recovered from the VAR residuals using the Cholesky decomposition of the variance-covariance matrix. While the ordering is certainly debatable, and a non-recursive structural VAR could have been

---

[15]See International Development Association and IMF (2005) for a comparison of PFM systems in highly indebted poor countries.

[16]IMF (2005) defines aid absorption as the extent to which a country's nonaid current account deficit (in foreign currency terms) widens in response to an increase in aid inflows. If one assumes that the capital account is closed, as in Chapter 5, full aid absorption is equivalent to an unchanged level of international reserves in response to an aid shock. This second definition is the one used in this chapter.

[17]An analysis of the time-series properties of the variables reveals that the variables are integrated of order one or I(1), except for aid, which is stationary I(0). Therefore, the series are detrended for estimation purposes to avoid the spurious and inconsistent regression problem (Hendry, 1995). Results of Granger causality tests are somewhat inconclusive, showing little evidence of Granger causality in either direction, but lend support for a transmission of aid shocks to the domestic economy.

[18]Quarterly GDP series are not yet available in Mozambique; therefore a quarterly GDP proxy was constructed statistically by estimating the correlates of real GDP annually and using predictions based on the quarterly explanatory variables.

used for identification, the estimation provides a generalized view of the impact of aid shocks in Mozambique. In addition, it is fairly well accepted that many macroeconomic variables do not respond instantaneously to policy shocks, particularly when we consider quarterly time intervals (see Christiano, Eichenbaum, and Evans (2005) for the general approach).

Aid-financed expenditures have been mostly absorbed in Mozambique, with only hints of Dutch disease affecting the export sector (Figures 6.3 and 6.4). The impulse responses suggest that aid (most of which has been spent) has, at least initially, resulted in a nominal exchange rate appreciation and, possibly, lower output. Inflation declines initially but picks up gradually. A similar picture emerges when one considers real non-megaproject exports instead of our proxy for real GDP, suggesting only modest contractions of the export sector in response to aid shocks. Interesting, most of the foreign exchange associated with aid inflows appears to have been sold by the central bank within five quarters of the initial aid shock, facilitating a textbook spend-and-absorb response to aid. The results do indicate, however, that the central bank may have somewhat smoothed sales of foreign exchange in the very short term through temporary net domestic debt issuance (that is, sterilization), possibly to avoid excessive exchange rate volatility in a thin market. Temporarily mopping up excess liquidity through sterilization but ultimately selling the foreign exchange may have helped keep a rise in prices at bay and minimized the likelihood of crowding out private sector credit at the same time. This contrasts with the response to aid shocks of most other non-CFA countries in sub-Saharan Africa, which seem to have relied more heavily on sterilization (IMF, 2005), contributing to unfavorable debt dynamics and, probably, greater crowding out of the private sector. Overall, the macroeconomic impact of aid shocks seems to go roughly in the same direction as the model simulations for Mozambique in Chapter 5, in the case where aid has been absorbed through sales of foreign exchange by the central bank.

Illustrative Scaling-up Scenarios

The purpose of illustrative scaling-up scenarios for Mozambique is to identify the potential macroeconomic implications and key measures and policies that would help the country absorb a higher level of aid and use it efficiently. A full costing of the MDGs has not been undertaken for Mozambique, but the country appears to be well placed to achieve the income poverty MDG (halving the poverty rate by 2015) with present

Figure 6.3. Mozambique: Macroeconomic Effects of Foreign Aid (Total Exports)

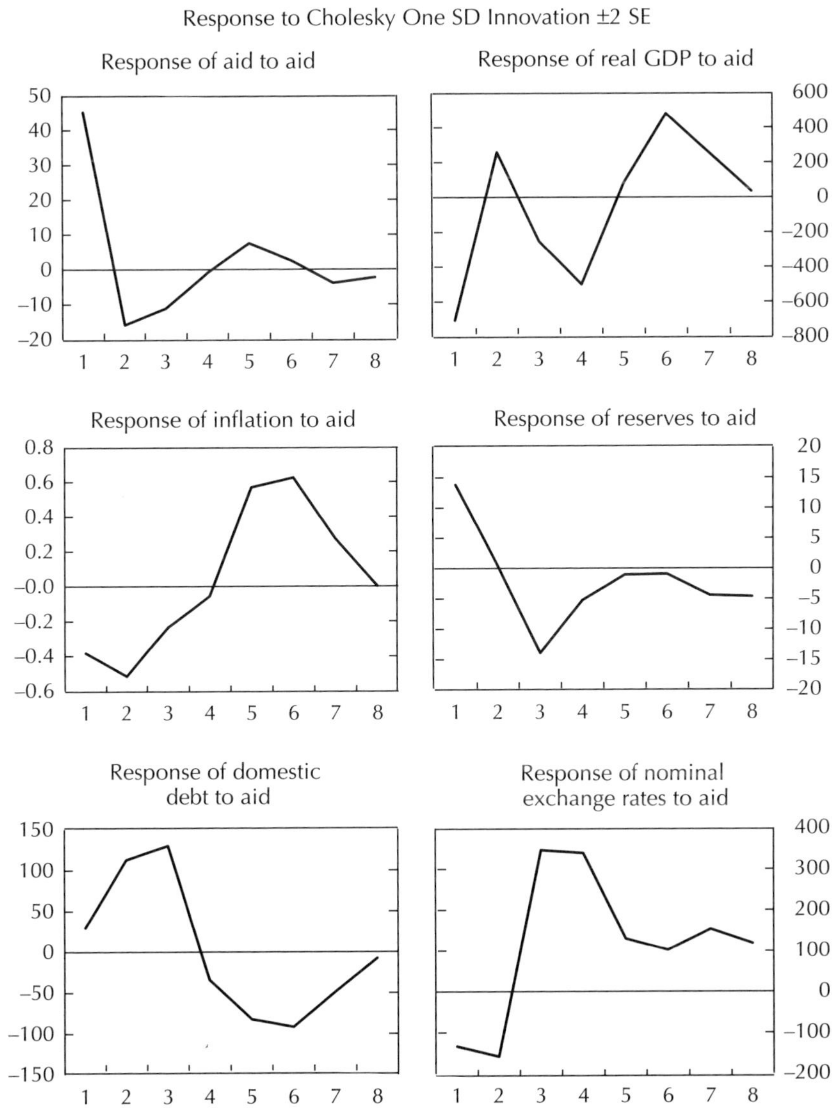

Source: Author's calculations.

Figure 6.4. Mozambique: Macroeconomic Effects of Foreign Aid (Non-Megaproject Exports)

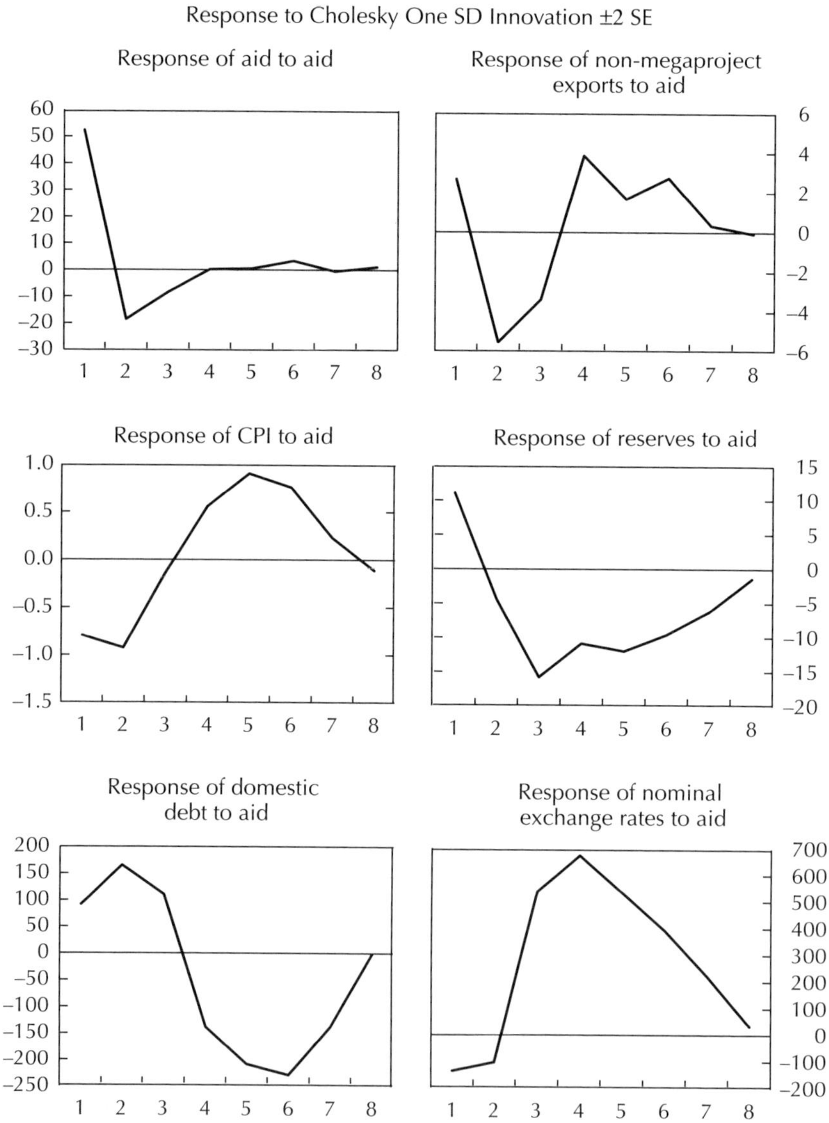

Source: Author's calculations.

resources and policies.[19] Therefore, we consider the macroeconomic consequences of an arbitrary but moderate and sustained increase of external finance for illustrative purposes.[20] This contrasts with scaling-up scenarios presented for a few other countries (for example, Mattina, 2006) based on costing the MDGs and targeting a specific growth rate to meet the income poverty MDG. The focus of this chapter is to discuss the macroeconomic implications and policy trade-offs involved in spending and absorbing a modest scaling up of foreign aid, which currently amounts to about 15 percent of Mozambique's GDP.

Macroeconomic Implications and Policy Trade-offs

The impact on medium- to long-term growth of a further scaling up of aid is difficult to gauge, but research points to areas for further analysis and prioritization of reform strategies. A number of research papers that have undertaken growth accounting exercises for Mozambique (for example, Chapter 3 of this book; Manoel and others, 2005; and World Bank, 2005) suggest that physical capital accumulation and total factor productivity have played a fundamental role in explaining the post-conflict growth acceleration supported by the first generation of structural reforms.[21] They also confirm the possibility of achieving about 7 percent annual growth in the medium term and 5–6 percent in the long term, which would be sufficient to halve the poverty rate by 2015, assuming strong productivity growth continues, given relatively low productivity in agriculture and manufacturing (Chapter 2 of this book; and Eifert, Gelb, and Ramachandran, 2005). On the specific issue of the impact of scaling up, Chapter 3 highlights the upside potential from more public investment (depending on the ratio of current expenditures to capital spending), and crowding-in private investment and spillovers from infrastructure and human capital accumulation. While the formal modeling of absorptive capacity is in its infancy (for a discussion, see Bourguignon and Sundberg, 2006), a preliminary estimation in Chapter 3 also shows the possible negative consequences of a further scaling up in Mozambique operating through private investment

[19]See Chapter 2 for a discussion of Mozambique's chances of halving the poverty rate by 2015.

[20]The macroeconomic trade-offs involved in the event of a more substantial or possibly volatile flow of foreign aid are not analyzed in detail, although the issues are outlined at the end of this section.

[21]Chapter 3 also shows that advances in education have contributed significantly to Mozambique's growth.

and the growth of the quality of human capital. The former is intended to reflect diminishing returns while the latter reflects labor market effects, including the challenge for Mozambique of maintaining educational quality in the face of rapid aid-financed expansion of the school network (see Arndt, Jones, and Tarp, 2007). Recent evidence suggests that primary education completion rates and the quality of education are relatively low, probably because of high pupil-to-teacher ratios and the growing number of untrained teachers, although innovative steps have been taken recently to address the shortage of trained teachers.[22]

The literature and evidence presented in the section "Aid and Macroeconomic Management in Mozambique" above call for paying particular attention to potential Dutch disease effects related to aid-financed scaling up of expenditures and thus ways to mitigate such effects. While it is fairly well accepted that to spend and absorb is likely to be the best response to an aid shock in normal circumstances (see Buffie and others, 2006; IMF 2005; and Chapter 5 of this book), such a response could still entail a significant loss of competitiveness and thus dampen exports and real GDP growth. Therefore, we analyze this issue further by simulating the estimated DSGE model for Mozambique in Chapter 5 in response to a persistent aid shock (autocorrelation coefficient of 0.7) that raises aid by 2 percent of steady-state GDP.[23] For illustrative purposes, we consider three scenarios (Figure 6.5). In the first scenario, we assume that there are no productivity spillovers from public investment. The second scenario assumes a modest level of spillovers (the baseline in Chapter 5). In the third scenario, we consider a high level of productivity spillovers from public investment. All scenarios assume the full spending and absorption of foreign aid, the usual assumption in scaling-up scenarios. Note that the function form, as in Prati and Tressel (2006), assumes that productivity is an increasing function of the size of public investment expenditure, so the higher levels of productivity could come from greater spillovers (for example, related to infrastructure investments) or a decrease in the ratio of current expenditures to capital spending.[24] The unbroken line describes a scenario where there are no productivity spillovers; the thick broken line assumes a modest level of spillovers; and the light broken line depicts a

[22]A similar situation prevails in the health care sector, particularly with regard to human resource constraints.

[23]See Chapter 5 for the structure of the DSGE model, estimation, and steady-state calibration.

[24]The calibration of the DSGE model uses the ratio of current expenditures to capital spending estimated for Mozambique.

higher level of productivity spillovers from public investment in response to aid shocks (Figure 6.5).

Greater productivity-enhancing public investment expenditure could ameliorate or even reverse the Dutch disease effects of additional government spending in Mozambique. The impulse responses in Figure 6.5 on a quarterly time interval clearly show the role productive government investment expenditures can play in mitigating the Dutch disease effects of aid-financed government spending by dampening appreciation pressures on the real exchange rate and thus stimulating stronger export performance. Moreover, as expected, consumption and output are unambiguously higher with greater productivity spillovers, while the pickup in inflation following an initial decline (as in the section "Aid and Macroeconomic Management in Mozambique") is milder. At this point, it is important to note that analysis of this kind comes with a number of caveats. For example, we assume for simplicity and tractability that productive government spending affects the transitional dynamics of the economy but not the steady state. Although this makes sense when considering fairly persistent but stationary aid shocks as observed in the past in Mozambique, one could also consider the impact of a permanent increase in aid on steady-state variables, an area for future research.[25] Finally, it is important to note that none of the outcomes of productivity spillovers from public investment are assured; the composition of government expenditure and efficiency of public service delivery will be critical in determining outcomes. However, the discussion emphasizes the importance of prioritizing productive government investments and accelerating the implementation of second-generation reforms in PARPA II to increase returns to investment:

- **Infrastructure and human capital accumulation.** Since 2000, about 65 percent of scaled-up spending has been allocated to the priority sectors (for example, education, health care, and infrastructure) identified in Mozambique's first Poverty Reduction Strategy Paper—*Plano de Acção para a Redução da Pobreza Absoluta I* (PARPA I)—for 2000–05. The number of children in primary school has doubled; infant and maternal mortality has been reduced; and antiretroviral (ARV) treatment has begun to be provided to Mozambicans infected with HIV. These achievements have been financed, in part, by resources made available by the Heavily Indebted Poor Countries

[25] Further analyses could also consider the impact of absorptive capacity, for example, through the World Bank's Marquette for MDG simulations as piloted on Ethiopia (see Mattina, 2006). This is particularly true for Mozambique, as it is one of the few countries identified in the literature as being in the range of saturation points for aid.

Figure 6.5. Illustrative Scaling-up Scenarios

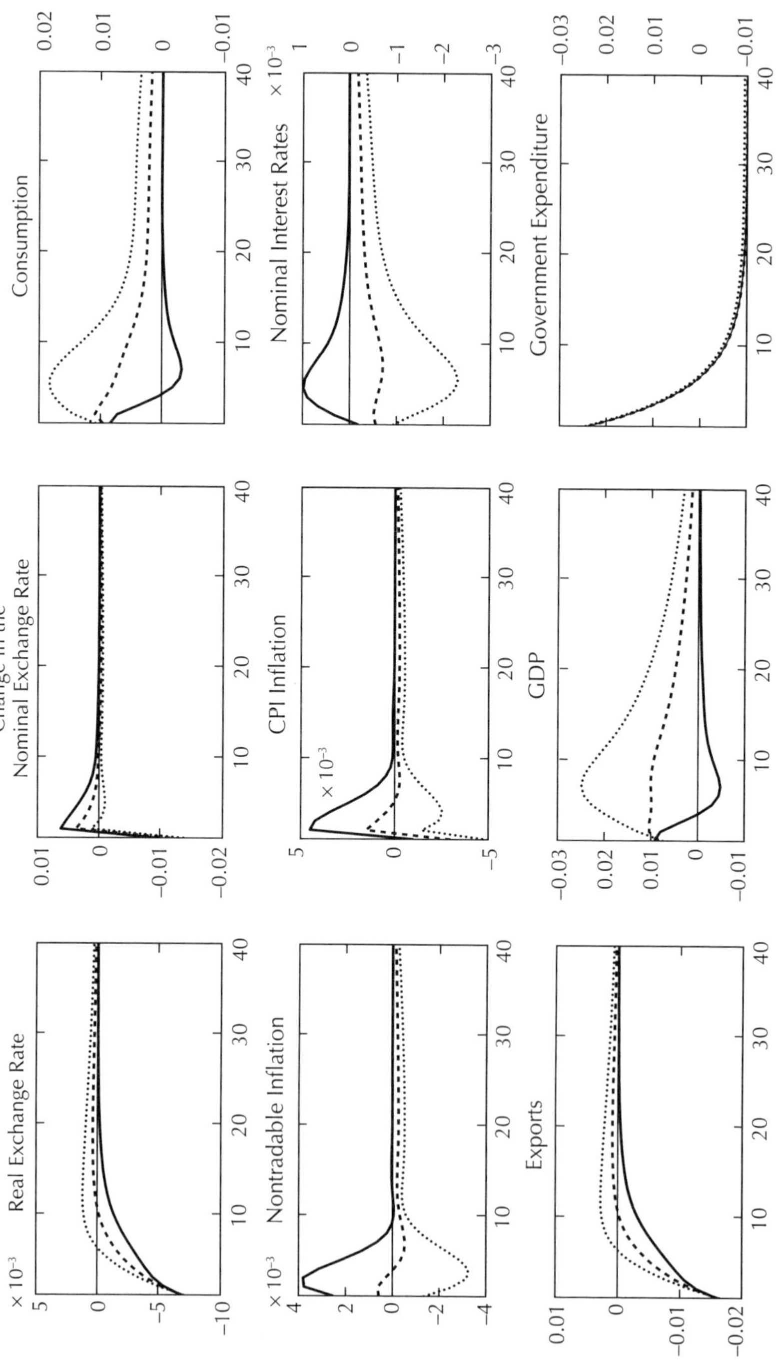

Source: Author's calculations.

Table 6.1. Increasing Returns to Public Investment: Lessons From Asia

	Human capital		Infrastructure	
	Primary education[1] (In percent)	Secondary education[1] (In percent)	Telephone mainlines (Per 1,000 people)	Total road surface area (In kilometers)
	Sub-Saharan Africa[2]			
Mozambique	86.0	8.7	4.0	38.0
SADC average	102.0	42.5	66.0	227.5
SSA average	91.4	31.8	35.6	166.4
	Selected Asian countries that have sustained growth acceleration[3]			
China	112.6	45.9	2.0	123.0
ASEAN-4 average	83.4	22.6	6.9	184.5
Indonesia	80.0	16.1	1.5	151.6
Malaysia	88.7	34.2	13.8	261.2
Thailand	81.4	17.4	5.5	140.6

Source: Johnson, Ostry, and Subramanian (2007).

Note: SADC = Southern African Development Community; SSA = Sub-Saharan Africa; ASEAN-4 = Indonesia, Malaysia, the Philippines, and Thailand.

[1]Gross enrollment ratio.

[2]Data are for the most recent period available.

[3]Data refer to year closest to growth takeoff.

(HIPC) Initiative. While substantial progress has been made, large human capital and infrastructure gaps remain. Comparisons of Mozambique with the fast-growing Asian economies indicate the importance of expanding secondary education and addressing acute infrastructure gaps, particularly in communication and transportation networks (Table 6.1).

- **Improving agricultural productivity** lies at the heart of growth prospects and poverty reduction (Chapter 2). Much of the increase in crop income has been achieved through area expansion and greater use of available labor, both family and hired. As a result, basic food crops widely grown by smallholder farmers, predominantly for subsistence, have exhibited relatively stagnant yields (output per hectare). Improving the security of land tenure and increasing the use of new technologies associated with cash crops mostly grown under contract by agroindustrial firms could help boost productivity. Smallholders could also increase land productivity and crop income by diversifying into profitable cash crops, many of which are tied to contract farming schemes. The use of productivity-enhancing inputs (particularly fertilizers, seeds, and irrigation) and development of rural credit and input markets could facilitate diversification to such crops. Further development of the agriculture sector would require the development of good roads, storage facilities, and extension services. Mozambique also has the potential to further cultivate high-value vegetables and flowers for export to Europe by improving quality and the marketing infrastructure.[26]

- **Strengthening the business environment** is key to building a manufacturing base and generating employment. Sustained growth accelerations tend to be associated with manufacturing exports, but Mozambique's manufacturing base remains underdeveloped because of a lack of competitiveness. Low factory-floor productivity levels are explained by high indirect costs and output losses, including those stemming from burdensome regulations that squeeze firms' value added and reduce total factor productivity (TFP), and the use of obsolete and ill-maintained equipment and absence of modern management techniques (see Chapter 9, Figure 9.9). The wide gap in business competitiveness between Mozambique and the fast-growing Asian economies and competitors in sub-Saharan Africa, as measured by the World Bank's Doing Business indicators, suggests that the authorities' reform strategy must center on lowering the costs of doing business by (1) streamlining burdensome regulatory practices; (2) reducing the costs of hiring and firing workers; (3) removing infrastructure bottlenecks; (4) further reducing the cost of, and expanding access to, financial services; and (5) reducing expropriation risks.
- **Strengthening public financial management systems** and undertaking wider public sector reforms will be vital to ensure that resources efficiently reach the most economically and socially productive priority sectors, including at the subnational level, where some of the scaled-up resources will ultimately be spent (Box 6.1). Enhancing administrative capacity is also essential to the effective absorption of scaled-up donor assistance. To improve the link between policy objectives, appropriations, and performance indicators, the government is embarking on a transition to program-based budgeting. The government could proceed on a pilot basis with a few line ministries in the 2008 budget. In support of this initiative, the medium-term fiscal framework (CFMP) will also require strengthening through a better costing of policies and more comprehensive sector strategies. In addition, the significant role played by state-owned or public-participating enterprises[27] in the provision of public services, and their impact on macroeconomic developments—including domestic

---

[26]See World Bank (2006) for an agricultural strategy that would build on the present approach.

[27]Public-participating institutions are enterprises with some private equity participation.

and external borrowing levels, and fiscal risks—argue for including them in the budgetary accounts or, at a minimum, enhancing the monitoring of their activities. Finally, the international community has a role to play by including donor-financed projects in the single treasury account and e-SISTAFE (see Box 6.1 for a description of e-SISTAFE) to improve timely fiscal reporting on all development expenditures and thus gauge their impact better.

An Exit Strategy and Fiscal Sustainability

Domestic revenue needs to gradually increase to enable Mozambique to end its dependence on donors in an orderly manner. Donors could decrease foreign aid from present levels after the 2015 target date for achieving the MDGs. As a result, the strategy for exiting from aid dependence should aim to raise domestic revenue during the next eight years so that Mozambique will be able finance recurrent spending, at a minimum, from its own resources, without recourse to unsustainable domestic borrowing (or a disruptive expenditure contraction) to offset declining external assistance.

To evaluate whether the authorities' long-term revenue target as described in World Bank and IMF (2007) is sufficient to maintain a scaling up of aid-financed expenditures in a sustainable manner, we assume a fiscal framework with additional expenditures of US$200 million from 2008 to 2015 compared with the baseline in IMF (2007).[28] Given the absence of a costing of the policies and sectoral interventions needed to achieve the MDGs, the increased expenditures are assumed to be divided between current and capital spending in a 1:2 ratio based on the historical distribution of aid shocks estimated above.[29] This is a simplifying assumption, and the ratio would no doubt be different for different programs, but it fulfills the requirement of planning for the recurrent expenditures and hiring of additional personnel in priority sectors targeted by the MDGs.

The authorities' ambitious revenue targets are adequate to gradually reduce Mozambique's dependence on donors without accumulating unsus-

---

[28]Note that the assumption of an additional US$200 million in foreign aid is based on an indication by donors of a likely scaling up in 2008 compared with the baseline scenario presented in IMF (2007).

[29]Note, however, that a concrete scaling-up scenario would preferably distinguish between the sectoral composition of spending and type of aid (for example, project or program), and allocate adequate current expenditures to support projected increases in investment, including increasing demands on recurrent expenditures stemming from the cumulative impact of (aid-financed) public investments, which is not captured here.

Box 6.1. Public Financial Management (PFM) Reforms in Mozambique

The public expenditure and financial accountability (PEFA) assessment of 2006 shows that PFM systems in Mozambique have undergone major improvements in recent years. The government has been implementing a nationwide PFM reform called SISTAFE, initially with substantial IMF technical assistance and more recently with financing from a multidonor common fund. Mozambique's medium-term fiscal framework (CFMP) is also closely aligned with the priorities of Mozambique's Poverty Reduction Strategy for 2006–09 (PARPA II). It was approved by the Council of Ministers for the first time in 2006 and subsequently in 2007, making it a credible tool to guide the preparation of annual budgets. A government financial management information system (e-SISTAFE) was rolled out to all ministries at the central and provincial levels in 2007, facilitating better monitoring of expenditures. It is also possible to identify programs through the budget formulation module of e-SISTAFE, and to track priority expenditures defined in PARPA II on a real-time basis.

According to the authorities' medium-term PFM action plan and budget (APB), e-SISTAFE will be progressively rolled out to districts and municipali-

Overview of 2004 PEFA Scores and Identified Potential Scores for 2006

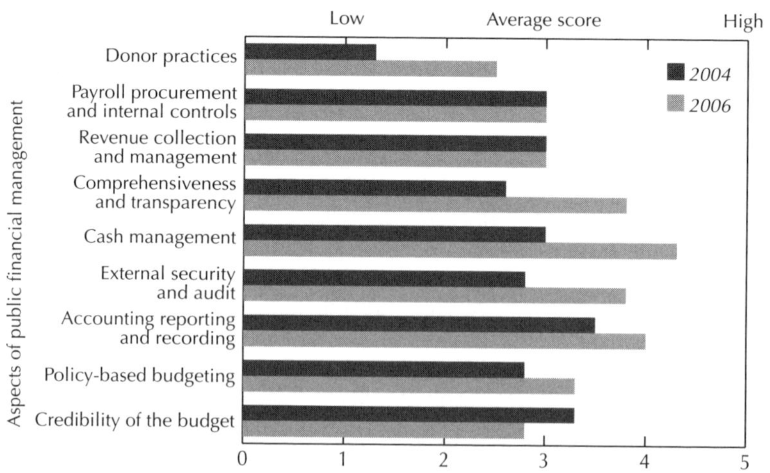

Source: PEFA (2006).

Projected SISTAFE Outputs, 2006–09

1. Financial and budget execution in operation in all ministries at the central, provincial, and district levels, and in the municipalities and public enterprises.
2. The module of payment of salaries and pensions implemented.
3. The budget-formulation module implemented (Phase II).
4. The asset-management module and procurement interface implemented.
5. The ATM revenue-management module implemented.
6. Program budgets under preparation by ministries.
7. The debt-management module implemented.
8. The internal audit-module implemented.
9. The Data Processing Center operating as an effective and sustainable unit.
10. Project Implementation Unit for SISTAFE operating as an effective and sustainable unit.

Source: UTRAFE, Action Plan and Budget Report, 2006–09. (UTRAFE, the Technical Unity of Financial Administration of the State, was created to manage the reform of SISTAFE.)

ties (initially to 37 districts in 2008), as well as to state organs at the central level in 2008. An integrated payroll database compatible with e-SISTAFE was developed following the completion of the civil services census in April 2007. The validation of the database by the Administrative Tribunal is now expected for 2008. However, the salary payments via e-SISTAFE will start in 2008 while the validation process continues to eliminate the fiduciary risk identified by the PEFA assessment.[1] A limited number of separate foreign currency accounts are now operational within the single treasury account (CUT), facilitating the inclusion of donor-financed projects on CUT. As part of Mozambique's decentralization efforts, a National Decentralization Strategy, including a review of intergovernmental fiscal relations, will be prepared by end-2008. A new wage policy to sharpen incentives and increase accountability is also being designed with the help of the World Bank. Implementation of the new procurement system up to the district level will also be continued. Finally, the capacity of internal and external audit bodies is being increased, with specific milestones set for 2007–08.

[1]Payments of salaries and pensions continue to be executed centrally by the accounting department of the Ministry of Finance.

tainable debt in the event of a moderate scaling up of expenditures. The projected revenue ratio of about 19½ percent of GDP in 2015 (increasing from 14 percent of GDP in 2006) would cover both a scaled-up level of recurrent spending and a portion of the country's public investment program.[30] In addition, even if one assumed that all of the scaled-up spending was financed through concessional external borrowing, the external debt-to-export ratio would still remain below the indicative performance-based debt-burden thresholds (the ratio of the net present value of debt to exports is 150 percent for Mozambique), which take into account the empirical finding that the debt levels that a low-income country can sustain increase with the quality of its policies and institutions. This highlights the fiscal space available to scale up concessional external borrowing focused on achieving the MDGs, partly as a result of aid delivered under the Multilateral Debt Relief Initiative (MDRI). Mozambique's prudent external debt-management strategy of avoiding recourse to nonconcessional external borrowing has also helped and is assumed to continue. In addition, the low level of domestic public debt in Mozambique (about 8½ percent of GDP), which is due partly to the willingness of the central bank to mop up excess liquidity through foreign exchange sales and thus absorb foreign aid, has also contributed to a low level of debt distress. It should be noted, however, that exports, revenues, and real GDP growth will play an important role in defining the scope for expanded real government spending in the context of fiscal sustainability and an acceptable level of aid dependency.[31] Given this, and to safeguard the exit strategy, spending plans would need to be carefully reassessed regularly in light of the growth and Dutch disease effects of the initial expansion in spending as well as realized revenue outcomes. As discussed in World Bank and IMF (2007), any nonconcessional financing of large infrastructure projects would need to be considered case by case, based on the projects' economic returns, impact on debt sustainability, and potential effects on the financing decisions of donors and concessional lenders.

[30]However, one must take this result with caution given the uncertainties regarding the propensity of current spending in aid-financed expenditures and present classification of most donor-financed spending as capital expenditure.

[31]Mozambique's sovereign Standard & Poor's credit rating (B) is expected to improve, especially as Mozambique builds institutional capacity and maintains debt levels closer to the emerging market thresholds established by World Bank–IMF debt sustainability analyses. This could allow Mozambique to access international capital markets to smooth any shortfalls in donor disbursements after 2015 or to finance large infrastructure projects to realize its full growth potential.

Mozambique would need to support this ambitious revenue increase by continuing revenue administration reforms and strengthening tax policies (particularly the fiscal regime for exploitation of mineral and petroleum resources). Varsano and others (2007) estimate the tax gap for Mozambique. Actual tax collection is considered to be a function of taxing capability—that is, the maximum collection possible given the country's economic, social, institutional, demographic, and other characteristics—and of the effort exerted to mobilize funds for public use (determined by the tax laws and how strictly they are enforced). The study concludes that Mozambique's tax effort (the ratio of actual collection to taxing capability) is about 50 percent, one of the lowest in sub-Saharan Africa, suggesting that there is significant scope for raising revenues, up to a level of nearly 22 percent of GDP. Schenone (2004) also estimates the difference between potential collection and actual collection, which is lower because of weaknesses in the tax laws (exemptions and nonassessments) and noncompliance (evasion). The study finds that noncompliance accounts for a much larger portion of the gap than the tax laws. The implication is that although there is room for increasing revenues through tax policy measures, the prospects are much greater for measures that increase the efficiency of the tax administration.[32] There is a possibility that Mozambique could achieve medium-term revenue targets by widening its tax base without resorting to tax rate increases. The next phase of revenue administration reforms (2007–10), which will be supported by a multidonor common fund, will focus on implementing the strategic plan of the central revenue authority (ATM) and will be important in this regard. The ATM will be established in three stages: a transition period to end-2007, a gradual integration of the tax and customs agencies to take place during 2008, and further strengthening and consolidation in 2009 and 2010.

Mozambique's vast natural resources and the present boom in world commodity prices are providing the country with a tremendous opportunity to attract greater foreign direct investment (FDI) in the mining and petroleum sectors. The goal should be to maximize the fiscal returns and economic linkages of FDI while minimizing environmental damage and social dislocation. Now that investor confidence in Mozambique is stronger, the authorities recognize that the fiscal contribution of new projects in these sectors could be substantially increased by reducing the generous tax exemptions put in place to attract private investment during the post–civil

[32]For example, Manoel and others (2005) estimate that nearly 8 percent of GDP of the total 12 percent of GDP of the revenue gap in 2003 was attributable to noncompliance, especially with the value-added tax.

war period.[33] As discussed in Chapter 8, Mozambique is making important strides in this regard by putting in place a new fiscal regime for the mining sector and building the capacity of personnel to negotiate effectively with multinationals through the use of financial models and model contracts.

A significant amount of FDI has also flowed to the country's petroleum sector.[34] Following agreements negotiated in 2000, the Pande-Temane gas field installations, processing facilities, and gas export pipeline to South Africa were commissioned in 2004, representing some US$1 billion in FDI. The Pande-Temane project (including the pipeline) is currently in a period of cost recovery and high debt service, so government revenues have been modest, comprising mainly petroleum production tax and a small amount of corporate income tax, but these are set to increase significantly as production ramps up and joint venture investors recover their initial development costs.[35] Further exploration is continuing and sufficient additional reserves have been identified that the joint venture partners[36] are considering a possible 50 percent expansion of the volume of annual gas sales to about 180 million gigajoules. Mozambique has also secured more than US$300 million in petroleum exploration commitments from the recent Rovuma Basin round, which may add US$200 million in planned drilling and evaluation activities to contracts awarded earlier. Mozambique has the potential to become a significant regional gas producer. Companies are exploring both for oil and for significant gas deposits that might supply liquefied natural gas (LNG) export facilities.

Even though fiscal incentives were granted for petroleum exploration and the investors benefit from stability assurances, the current combination of economic terms for exploration- and production-concession contracts (EPCCs), if properly administered, should yield returns that are competitive (for both the government and the companies) by international standards. In addition, the authorities are reviewing the fiscal regime for this sector and intend to put in place a comprehensive fiscal regime that

---

[33]The mining sector is broadly interpreted here to include Mozal, a megaproject that produces aluminum billets from imported alumina using electricity generated by the Cahora Bassa hydroelectric plant.

[34]See Daniel and others (2007).

[35]Under the Petroleum Production Agreement the joint venture partners are allowed 25 percent depreciation, resulting in reduced income tax revenues in the early years of the project in addition to numerous other tax exemptions.

[36]The joint venture partners are South Africa's gas giant, Sasol (70 percent); a Mozambican state-owned enterprise, CMH (25 percent); and the International Finance Corporation (5 percent).

would be embodied in the general tax law to avoid case-by-case negotiation of petroleum tax and production-sharing terms.

The mining and petroleum projects in the pipeline, including the multibillion dollar Moatize coal mine project now under development, could yield revenues in the range of 2–4 percent of GDP after 2010. Further oil and gas discoveries would result in significant revenue over the long term.

Policymakers need to take the budgetary importance of foreign aid and its volatility into account when designing the appropriate macroeconomic policy response to a scaling up of aid if it is much larger than the scenarios considered here. Foreign aid (both grants and loans) accounts for about 50 percent of total expenditures and about 120 percent of revenues in Mozambique. An increasing share of this net aid flow is also in the form of direct budget support, as opposed to project financing (see Chapter 7), and often explicitly or implicitly conditional on the expansion of public expenditure programs that tend to exhibit relatively high inertia, such as the expansion of health and education services. In the absence of institutional mechanisms to lock in high aid levels or guarantee rapid fiscal adjustment in the event of a decline in aid, it may be impossible to rule out the possibility that a further aid surge could be fiscally destabilizing. In this situation, a further large scaling up of foreign aid—even one that ultimately proves highly persistent—brings with it the expectation of an increase in future domestic financing requirements and seigniorage (Chapter 4). While a moderate scaling up of aid may not be a cause for concern in a country that has adequate international reserves and low public debt, which could help cushion a reversal of aid, a larger aid surge could sharply reduce money demand in the short run and lead to both high inflation and private capital outflows (Buffie and others, 2006). To avoid such a scenario, the authorities may consider smoothing the expenditure pattern and saving part of the aid surge in international reserves to be spent and absorbed at a later date.

Conclusions

Mozambique has fully spent and mostly absorbed scaled-up foreign aid (ranging between 10 percent and 20 percent of GDP) over the past decade or so. The additional expenditures have allowed Mozambique to scale up basic services, including doubling the number of children in primary school, reducing infant and maternal mortality, and beginning to provide ARV treatment for HIV infections, while sustaining economic growth of

8 percent a year on average and reducing the poverty headcount index from 69 percent in 1997 to 54 percent in 2003. The pursuit of prudent macroeconomic policies and first wave of structural reforms has helped Mozambique keep up this growth momentum by maintaining macroeconomic stability and a sustainable fiscal and external position. Looking forward, illustrative scaling-up scenarios highlight the need to carefully manage a further scaling up of foreign aid.

A modest scaling up of foreign aid inflows (about 2 percent of 2008 GDP) could continue to be spent on programs that are designed to help Mozambique achieve the MDGs and absorbed. A scaling up of spending, whether financed by donors or not, will put pressure on the real exchange rate to appreciate and thus has the potential to hurt the export sector and long-run growth. Therefore, there is a need to elicit a supply response in the most productive priority sectors (for example, agriculture, education, health care, and infrastructure as defined in PARPA II) and mitigate potential Dutch disease effects by strengthening PFM systems while embarking on a public sector reform program to improve efficiency and public service delivery. Enhancing productivity growth requires not only greater productive public investment but also complementary second-generation reforms aimed at strengthening the business environment and buttressing agricultural production. It could, however, be the case that policymakers view the level of macroeconomic variables (for example, inflation and the real exchange rate) as well as macroeconomic volatility, even in a spend-and-absorb aid scenario, to be too high from the point of view of consumer welfare and long-term growth, depending on developments in the real economy. This could be particularly relevant if the scaling up is significantly larger or less persistent than the aid shock considered here or if microeconomic capacity constraints become binding in some sectors. In such a case, the authorities may consider smoothing expenditures and saving part of the aid in international reserves to be spent and absorbed at a later date.

Debt relief and prudent macroeconomic management have provided the fiscal space for Mozambique to sustain scaled-up spending, albeit with a continued need to consolidate long-term fiscal sustainability. The HIPC Initiative and MDRI have reduced Mozambique's debt and allowed the country to maintain a relatively high level of expenditures (about 25–30 percent of GDP), which are being financed through concessional external borrowing and foreign grants. The authorities' strategy of absorbing foreign aid through sales of foreign exchange and avoiding recourse to nonconcessional external borrowing has also helped create an environment conducive to scaled-up expenditures. However, given the low tax-to-GDP ratio and the need to guard against aid volatility and gradually reduce dependence on donors, an annual average revenue increase of 0.5 percent of GDP should continue to be targeted through the CFMP by widening the tax base and improving revenue administration. Beyond the PARPA II period, strong growth and increased fiscal revenues from mega-projects will help Mozambique maintain long-term fiscal sustainability and possibly allow it to start tapping international capital markets. This approach will provide an exit strategy from aid dependence in the long run and ensure that Mozambique can finance at least recurrent spending from its own resources.

The lessons from Mozambique's experience of managing foreign aid inflows include the following:

- A full spending of scaled-up foreign aid, if carefully managed, could help a country make vast strides in human development and poverty reduction in a short time without resulting in significant macroeconomic absorption problems and microeconomic capacity constraints, although the latter may be reflected with a lag and call for a coordinated approach to capacity building, particularly training of frontline workers (for example, teachers, nurses, and agriculture extension workers).
- Prudent macroeconomic policies and well-sequenced structural reforms are key to maintaining macroeconomic stability and sustaining rapid broad-based growth.
- The willingness of a central bank to sell foreign exchange associated with aid inflows to mop up excess liquidity, and thus mostly absorb foreign aid, could avoid building up unsustainable domestic debt and crowding out the private sector without a significant loss of competitiveness.
- A prudent external borrowing strategy and encouragement of FDI, particularly in the natural resource and infrastructure sectors, can help consolidate long-term fiscal sustainability and gradually reduce dependence on donors.
- Sustained large foreign aid inflows (concessional external borrowing and grants) in the range of 10–20 percent of GDP need not result in a weaker revenue effort and fatigue with reforms, including more difficult second-generation institutional reforms such as public financial management, if the country takes a longer-term perspective and the international community continues to provide appropriate technical assistance.

Bibliography

Abbas, S.M. Ali, and Jakob E. Christensen, 2007, "The Role of Domestic Debt Markets in Economic Growth: An Empirical Investigation for Low-Income Countries and Emerging Markets," IMF Working Paper 07/127 (Washington: International Monetary Fund).

Adam, C., 2005, "Exogenous Inflows and Real Exchange Rates: Theoretical Quirk or Empirical Reality?" paper presented at the Seminar on Foreign Aid and Macroeconomic Management, Maputo, Mozambique, March 14–15.

———, Stephen O'Connell, Edward Buffie, and Catherine Pattillo, 2007, "Monetary Policy Rules for Managing Aid Surges in Africa," IMF Working Paper 07/180 (Washington: International Monetary Fund).

Arellano, Christina, A. Bulíř, T. Lane, and L. Lipschitz, 2005, "The Dynamic Implications of Foreign Aid and Its Variability," IMF Working Paper 05/119 (Washington: International Monetary Fund).

Arndt, C., S. Jones, and F. Tarp, 2007, "Aid and Development: The Mozambican Case," in *Theory and Practice of Foreign Aid, Frontiers of Economics and Globalization*, ed. by S. Lahiri (Amsterdam: Elsevier), pp. 235–88.

Benito-Spinetto, Maria Teresa, and Peter G. Moll, 2005, "Macroeconomic Developments, Economic Growth and Consequences for Poverty," background paper for the Country Economic Memorandum (World Bank, February 24).

Bleaney, Michael, and David Greenaway, 2001, "The Impact of Terms of Trade and Real Exchange Rate Volatility on Investment and Growth in Sub-Saharan Africa," *Journal of Development Economics*, Vol. 65 (August), pp. 491–500.

Bourguignon, F., and M. Sundberg, 2006, "Absorptive Capacity and Achieving the MDGs," WIDER Research Paper No. 2006/47 (Helsinki: United Nations University, World Institute for Development Economics Research).

Buffie, Edward, Christopher Adam, Stephen O'Connell, and Catherine Pattillo, 2004, "Exchange Rate Policy and the Management of Official and Private Capital Inflows in Africa," *Staff Papers*, International Monetary Fund, Vol. 51 (June), pp. 126–60.

———, 2006, "Fiscal Inertia, Donor Credibility and the Monetary Management of Aid Surges" (unpublished). Available via the Internet: http://www.swarthmore.edu/SocSci/soconnel/documents/Aidcred1.pdf

Bulíř, Aleš, and A. Javier Hamann, 2005, "Volatility of Development Aid: From the Frying Pan into the Fire?" paper presented at the Seminar on Foreign Aid and Macroeconomic Management, Maputo, Mozambique, March 14–15.

Bulíř, Aleš, and Timothy Lane, 2002, "Aid and Fiscal Management," IMF Working Paper 02/112 (Washington: International Monetary Fund).

Burnside, Craig, and David Dollar, 2000, "Aid, Policies, and Growth," *American Economic Review*, Vol. 90 (September), pp. 847–68.

Calvo, Guillermo A., Carmen Reinhart, and Carlos Végh, 1995, "Targeting the Real Exchange Rate: Theory and Evidence," *Journal of Development Economics*, Vol. 47 (June), pp. 97–133.

Christensen, J., 2004, "Domestic Debt Markets in Sub-Saharan Africa," IMF Working Paper 04/46 (Washington: International Monetary Fund).

Christiano, L., M. Eichenbaum, and C. Evans, 2005, "Nominal Rigidities and the Dynamic Effects of a Shock to Monetary Policy," *Journal of Political Economy*, Vol. 113 (February), pp. 1–45.

Commission for Africa, 2005, "Our Common Interest: Report of the Commission for Africa" (London). Available via the Internet: http://www.commissionforafrica.org/english/report/introduction.html

Daniel, Philip, Ana Paula Dourado, Diego Mesa Puyo, and Alistair Watson, 2007, "The Petroleum Sector: Fiscal and Economic Terms," Aide-Mémoire of the IMF's Fiscal Affairs Department Mission (unpublished; Washington: International Monetary Fund).

Devarajan, Shantayanan, Delfin S. Go, Jeffrey D. Lewis, Sherman Robinson, and Pekka Sinko, 1994, "Policy Lessons from a Simple Open-Economy Model," Policy Research Working Paper No. 1375 (Washington: World Bank).

Eifert, Benn, Alan Gelb, and Vijaya Ramachandran, 2005, "Business Environment and Comparative Advantage in Africa: Evidence from the Investment Climate Data," Working Paper No. 56 (Washington: Center for Global Development).

Fagernäs, Sonja, and John Roberts, 2004, "Fiscal Impact of Aid: A Survey of Issues and Synthesis of Country Studies of Malawi, Uganda and Zambia," ESAU Working Paper No. 11 (London: Economic and Statistics Analysis Unit, Overseas Development Institute). Available via the Internet: http://www.odi.org.uk/esau/publications/working_papers/esau_11_synthesis.pdf

Gupta, Sanjeev, Benedict Clements, Emanuele Baldacci, and Carlos Mulas-Granados, 2004, "Fiscal Policy, Expenditure Composition, and Growth in Low-Income Countries," in *Helping Countries Develop: The Role of Fiscal Policy*, ed. by Sanjeev Gupta, Benedict Clements, and Gabriela Inchauste (Washington: International Monetary Fund).

Gupta, S., R. Powell, and Y. Yang, eds., 2006, *Macroeconomic Challenges of Scaling Up Aid to Africa: A Checklist for Practitioners* (Washington: International Monetary Fund).

Hausmann, Ricardo, Lant Pritchett, and Dani Rodrik, 2004, "Growth Accelerations," NBER Working Paper No. 10566 (Cambridge, Massachusetts: National Bureau of Economic Research).

Heller, Peter S., 1975, "A Model of Public Fiscal Behavior in Developing Countries: Aid, Investment, and Taxation," *American Economic Review*, Vol. 65 (June), pp. 429–45.

———, 2005, "'Pity the Finance Minister': Issues in Managing a Substantial Scaling Up of Aid Flows," IMF Working Paper 05/180 (Washington: International Monetary Fund).

Hendry, D.F., 1995, *Dynamic Econometrics* (Oxford: Oxford University Press).

International Development Association and International Monetary Fund, 2005, "Update on the Assessments and Implementation of Action Plans to Strengthen

Capacity of HIPCs to Track Poverty-Reducing Public Spending" (Washington). Available via the Internet: http://www1.worldbank.org/publicsector/pe/HIPC/HIPCBoardPaperApril2005.pdf

International Monetary Fund (IMF), 2005, "The Macroeconomics of Managing Increased Aid Inflows: Experiences of Low-Income Countries and Policy Implications" (Washington: Policy Development and Review Department) Available via the Internet: http://www.imf.org/external/np/pp/eng/2005/080805a.pdf

———, 2007, *Mozambique: 2007 Article IV Consultation*, IMF Country Report No. 07/262 (Washington).

Johnson, Simon, Jonathan D. Ostry, and Arvind Subramanian, 2007, "The Prospects for Sustained Growth in Africa: Benchmarking the Constraints," IMF Working Paper 07/52 (Washington: International Monetary Fund).

Manoel, Álvaro, Teresa Dabán, Hervé Joly, and María Méndez, 2005, *Mozambique: Selected Issues and Statistical Appendix*, IMF Country Report No. 05/311 (Washington: International Monetary Fund).

Mattina, Todd D., 2006, "Money Isn't Everything: The Challenge of Scaling Up Aid to Achieve the Millennium Development Goals in Ethiopia," IMF Working Paper 06/192 (Washington: International Monetary Fund).

Mavrotas, G., 2002, "Foreign Aid and Fiscal Response: Does Aid Disaggregation Matter?" *Review of World Economics*, Vol. 138 (September), pp. 534–59.

McGillivray, M., and O. Morrissey, 2001, "Fiscal Effects of Aid," WIDER Discussion Paper No. 2001/61 (Helsinki: United Nations University, World Institute for Development Economics Research).

Ndulu, B., 2007, *Challenges of African Growth: Opportunities, Constraints, and Strategic Directions* (Washington: World Bank).

Osei, R., O. Morrissey, and T. Lloyd, 2005, "The Fiscal Effects of Aid in Ghana," WIDER Research Paper No. 2005/61 (Helsinki: United Nations University, World Institute for Development Economics Research).

Prati, A., and T. Tressel, 2006, "Aid Volatility and Dutch Disease: Is There a Role for Macroeconomic Policies?" IMF Working Paper 06/145 (Washington: International Monetary Fund).

Rajan, Raghuram, and Arvind Subramanian, 2005, "What Undermines Aid's Impact on Growth?" NBER Working Paper No. 11657 (Cambridge, Massachusetts: National Bureau of Economic Research).

Schenone, O., 2004, "Mozambique: A Methodology for Tax Revenue Estimation," Technical Assistance Report from the Fiscal Affairs Department (Washington: International Monetary Fund).

Servén, L., 2002, "Real Exchange Rate Uncertainty and Private Investment in Developing Countries," Policy Research Working Paper No. 2823 (Washington: World Bank).

Sims, C.A., 1980, "Macroeconomics and Reality," *Econometrica*, Vol. 48 (January), pp. 1–48.

Torvik, R., 2001, "Learning by Doing and the Dutch Disease," *European Economic Review*, Vol. 45 (February), pp. 285–306.

Varsano, R., Odette de Oliveira, R. M. Villela, and Irene Yackovlev, 2007, "Mozambique: Evaluation of the Post-Reforms Tax System," Technical Assistance Report from the Fiscal Affairs Department (Washington: International Monetary Fund).

World Bank, 2005, "Mozambique—Country Economic Memorandum: Sustaining Growth and Reducing Poverty," Report 32615-MZ (Washington).

———, 2006, "Mozambique Agricultural Development Strategy: Stimulating Smallholder Agricultural Growth," Report No. 32416-MZ (Washington).

———, and International Monetary Fund, 2007, "Mozambique: Joint World Bank–IMF Debt Sustainability Analysis," Staff Supplement to IMF Country Report No. 07/262 (Washington). Available via the Internet: http://www.imf.org/external/pubs/ft/scr/2007/cro7262.pdf

Yano, Makoto, and Jeffrey B. Nugent, 1999, "Aid, Nontraded Goods, and the Transfer Paradox in Small Countries," *American Economic Review*, Vol. 89 (June), pp. 431–49.

7

Government-Donor Partnerships: Mozambique as a Model of Donor Coordination

Felix Fischer, Emmy Bosten, and Victor Lledó

Mozambique's model of donor coordination has considerably improved aid effectiveness, holding lessons for sub-Saharan Africa. In 2006, the Mozambican government formulated its second poverty reduction strategy (PRS)—entitled in Portuguese the *Plano de Acção para a Redução da Pobreza Absoluta* (PARPA II)—which sets out goals and performance indicators for 2006–09.[1] Since 2000 an increasing number of donors have agreed to common financing schemes that support the government's poverty reduction strategies in an efficient, predictable, and noncumbersome way. This chapter sheds light on how this framework, referred to as the "Mozambique model," has evolved into an institutional setup that is often praised internationally as a best practice.

The next section reviews the theoretical and empirical literature on donors' role in promoting aid effectiveness through the aid modalities they choose and their ability to coordinate aid delivery among themselves and with the government. The section ends with a discussion of the Paris Declaration on Aid Effectiveness as the model to follow.[2] The section "Donor Coordination in Mozambique" measures the country's perfor-

[1]PARPA II was finalized in 2006. PARPA I, formulated in 2001, spanned 2001–05.

[2]The Paris Declaration is an international agreement endorsed by over 100 ministers and other senior officials on March 2, 2005.

mance against the indicators established under the Paris Declaration, regrouped under the criteria of "ownership," "harmonization," "alignment," and "managing for results." Where possible, we compare Mozambique's performance with that of other countries. The section is followed by a discussion of the challenges the Mozambican government and donors face in increasing aid effectiveness. The last section draws lessons for other sub-Saharan African countries.

Literature Review: Donor Coordination and Aid Effectiveness

There has been growing recognition of the role donors play in promoting aid effectiveness, based not only on their choice of modalities for aid delivery but also on their ability to coordinate delivery with other donors and with recipient governments. Well aware that such choices can affect aid outcomes, the development community has designed best principles to guide recipient governments and donors as they work together so as to maximize aid effectiveness. This section reviews the theoretical and empirical literature on this subject and provides background on the relevance of donor practices in promoting or deterring aid effectiveness.[3] It also introduces the major yardsticks against which the Mozambique model, described in the following section, will be assessed.

The Current Debate

An influential view in academic and policy circles is that the effectiveness of foreign aid in promoting development is highly conditional on country-specific factors and the circumstances surrounding aid delivery. The effectiveness of foreign aid in promoting development, while always a contentious topic in academic and policy circles, has become particularly polarized, with aid enthusiasts on one side, arguing that aid has worked and should be scaled up (Sachs, 2005; and UN Millennium Project, 2005), and aid skeptics on the other side, saying that the role of aid in fostering development should be downplayed, given all that has gone wrong (Easterly, 2006). Controversies aside, following the influential work of Burnside and

[3]There is a vast literature on the determinants of aid effectiveness. This chapter will touch on a smaller but fast-growing subset of the literature that looks at the role played by government and donor interactions in enhancing aid effectiveness. Clemens, Radelet, and Bhavnani (2004) and Tarp (2008) provide comprehensive updated surveys of the empirical literature. A more theoretical survey can be found in Drazen (2000).

Dollar (2000)—who contend that aid effectiveness should be conditioned on "good policies"—most of the academic and policy discussions have centered on identifying the necessary and sufficient conditions for aid to have a positive effect on development. As reviewed in Clemens, Radelet, and Bhavnani (2004), this strand of the literature can be split into two subcategories: (1) studies arguing that aid effectiveness is conditioned on recipient country characteristics and (2) studies arguing that donor practices and procedures are the relevant conditioning factors.

Most of the attention has gone to *recipient country characteristics*. Country characteristics shown to affect aid include the degree of vulnerability to terms of trade shocks (Collier and Dehn, 2001); post-conflict economics (Clément, 2004); institutional quality (Burnside and Dollar, 2004); policy and warfare (Collier and Hoeffler, 2002); and geographical location (Dalgaard, Hansen, and Tarp, 2004).[4] Aid effectiveness has also been shown to depend on the type and duration of the foreign aid intervention (Clemens, Radelet, and Bhavnani, 2004).[5]

Donor Practices and Aid Effectiveness

More attention has recently been devoted to the role of *donor practices* in promoting aid effectiveness. The literature has focused, in particular, on three issues: (1) the criteria used to allocate foreign aid; (2) the commitment to timely, predictable, and stable aid disbursements; and (3) the modalities of aid delivery.

Donor Motives

Aid ineffectiveness in achieving growth and development objectives may be simply the result of strategic and political considerations among donors that did not allocate aid based on effectiveness considerations in the first place. There is ample statistical and anecdotal evidence that aid is not always delivered for purely developmental reasons. Humanitarian, military, and commercial interests have also come into play,[6] as confirmed

---

[4]However, most of these studies were not resilient to modest robustness checks, as shown by Roodman (2004).

[5]Aid effectiveness is divided into three groups: "no impact" (humanitarian aid); "early impact aid" (transport, communications, business services, construction); and "late impact aid" (for example, health care and education).

[6]The pattern of aid flows to developing countries during the cold war was based largely on such countries' alignment with then Communist countries. Other examples are the

by cross-country empirical work attempting to uncover specific country characteristics that help explain the allocation of bilateral and multilateral aid flows. Studies have shown that most donors give more aid to poorer countries, but that the underlying motives behind such aid vary considerably. For example, former colonial ties have been an important determinant of bilateral aid patterns, and voting behavior at the United Nations can affect allocation both bilaterally (Alesina and Dollar, 2000) and through the multilateral system (Andersen, Harr, and Tarp, 2006). Commercial and other strategic interests have also been shown to affect aid allocation (Berthélemy, 2006). However, this trend may have changed somewhat in countries where aid is allocated on the basis of a well-defined and homegrown poverty reduction strategy guided by the Millennium Development Goals (MDGs) and supported by the Heavily Indebted Poor Countries (HIPC) Initiative and the Multilateral Debt Relief Initiative (MDRI).[7]

Timing, Predictability, and Stability of Aid Disbursements

A nascent literature shows that donors' inability to commit to timely, predictable, and stable aid disbursements hampers aid effectiveness. Aid-dependent countries are particularly prone to large external shocks, yet they face inherent liquidity constraints and lack the countercyclical policy tools needed to weather such shocks. Foreign aid has been shown to be highly volatile, unpredictable, and procyclical (Bulíř and Hamann, 2003) and to have a sizable impact on aggregate growth and consumption (Lensink and Morrisey, 2000; Pallage and Robe, 2003; and Arellano and others, 2005).[8] Bulíř and Hamann (2006), updating earlier work, find that aid disbursement practices remain erratic and procyclical, despite various initiatives to improve country ownership and aid coordination.

Aid Modalities: Conditionality and Financing Channels

A number of studies have also looked at the links between aid effectiveness and different aid modalities. Aid can be channeled to specific proj-

substantial aid flows directed by the United States for political reasons to Israel and Egypt and, more recently, to the Islamic Republic of Afghanistan and Iraq.

[7]See IMF (2005a).

[8]Aid volatility refers to the variance of aid disbursements in different years, while aid unpredictability refers to unanticipated deviations within a given year in aid commitments and disbursements.

ects, sectoral programs, or general budget support. Aid modalities can also differ according to the conditions that apply to the disbursement of aid.

Most of the initial theoretical and empirical research on aid modalities has focused on the *conditionality of aid disbursements,* a common feature of most aid agreements. The literature, however, has focused mostly on loans granted by international financial institutions such as the World Bank and the IMF for macroeconomic policy reforms and structural adjustment. While policy conditionality in this case has usually been associated with improved macroeconomic stability, the literature has been somewhat mixed on the role conditionality plays in promoting structural reforms (Dollar and Svensson, 1998; World Bank, 1998; and IMF, 2001). Conditionality has been said to undermine aid effectiveness by (1) not encouraging structural reforms because of distortions resulting from its enforcement and the implied lack of country ownership (Svensson, 2000); (2) focusing on inputs rather than outcomes (Killick, 1997) or on measurable but less relevant outcomes (Azam and Laffont, 2003); and (3) demanding excessive administrative resources to monitor compliance (Berg, 1997). The streamlining of structural conditionality at the IMF was a response to such findings; by focusing related actions on a small number of growth-critical reforms, it has helped build greater country ownership. Initial evidence points to observed improvements in structural reform implementation, particularly in low-income countries.[9]

Recent research has started to look at the impact of different *financing channels for aid delivery,* particularly the role of project versus general budget support (Box 7.1). Theoretical, empirical, and case study research has in general favored general budget support over project support as the financing channel most conducive to aid effectiveness. In spite of delivering faster, more visible, and easily monitorable results and ensuring lower fiduciary risk, donor-financed projects have been shown to compromise recipients' control of expenditure programs and tax efforts, weakening accountability channels and leading to spending allocations and domestic revenue mobilization levels incompatible with recipient countries' poverty reduction strategies (Devarajan and Swaroop, 1998; and World Bank, 2003). These problems tend to increase, as shown below, with the number of donors working in individual and isolated projects in the recipient country. By relying on recipient countries' own public finance institutions, aid channeled directly to the budget avoids these problems, thus enhancing country ownership, facilitating donor coordination, and improving aid

[9]IMF (2002) summarizes the new guidelines, while IMF (2005b) reviews the implementation record following the enactment of such guidelines.

Box 7.1. Why Many Aid Agencies Prefer Giving Project, Rather Than General Budget, Support

Aid agencies have usually granted more project financing than general budget support for several reasons:

1. Aid agencies often want to be able to identify their own contributions, often through distinct projects, to increase the visibility of their efforts and sustain political support for aid flows. A new hospital, for example, is easier to showcase than the outcome of policy reform or budget support.
2. Aid agencies facing disbursement pressures need to show taxpayers and other stakeholders quick results. This is easier when donors are in charge of interventions.
3. Spending preferences of donors and recipients differ. For instance, taxpayers in donor countries may prefer social sector projects or humanitarian aid over capacity building or infrastructure projects. A donor's geographical allocation of aid within the recipient country might not fit with the recipient country's priorities.
4. Fiduciary concerns often cause donors to monitor inputs and processes. Monitoring is easier with project aid because the donor controls the design and implementation of each intervention.

effectiveness. However, budget support is no panacea, and its appropriateness has been shown to be conditional on, among other things, previous agreement among donors and recipient governments on development objectives and budget allocations, and a reasonably sound policy and institutional framework, including transparent and adequate budget planning mechanisms and public financial management arrangements (Cordella and Dell'Ariccia, 2003). Recent evidence of the greater effectiveness of general budget support comes mostly from case studies stressing that the quality of countries' public financial management systems is critical for its success (World Bank, 2006a).[10]

Donor Coordination and Donor Practices

A growing literature has looked at *donor coordination failures*. The common conclusion is that lack of coordination compromises aid effective-

[10]A number of case studies evaluate the effectiveness of general budget support without comparing it explicitly with the effectiveness of other modalities (Batley, Bjørnestad, and Cumbi, 2006; and OECD 2005b).

ness by inducing the choice, and amplifying the effects, of weak donor practices. Donors' inability to coordinate has led them to concentrate on projects and less-concerted financing schemes to finance government activities (World Bank, 2003), increasing transaction costs for recipient countries (OECD, 2003) and leading to declines in the administrative quality (Knack and Rahman, 2004) and planning capacity of their governments. Ultimately, donor coordination failures have been shown to weaken the accountability of both public officials (Devarajan and Swaroop, 1998) and donors (Easterly, 2003, 2006) in ensuring the effectiveness of donor interventions (Box 7.2).[11] History provides some counterfactual support to the donor-proliferation hypothesis—examples of aid success (Marshall Plan, Taiwan Province of China, Botswana, and Korea) have usually been marked by the presence of a single dominant donor (Brautigam, 2000; and Azam and Laffont, 2003).[12]

The implications of donor coordination for aid effectiveness have been formalized using a common-agency framework. Dixit (2003) and Murshed (2002, 2006) have looked at the implications of donor coordination for aid effectiveness by extending the multitask agent model developed in Holmström and Milgrom (1991) to a common-agency framework.[13] They demonstrate that, in the absence of coordination, the presence of multiple principals and multiple tasks leads to suboptimal efforts, compounding the moral hazard distortions already imposed given the unobservability of effort. Failure to coordinate weakens incentives to perform any one task when the various activities of the agents do not reflect the principals' real interests. Weak incentives, in turn, lead to suboptimal effort levels and, ultimately, to suboptimal project outcomes. The appendix contains the model in more detail. This model has two clear policy implications for donor practices to improve aid effectiveness. The first is that it is in donors' own interests to coordinate more with one another regardless of their preferences, particularly as the number of donors increases. The second is that

[11]Fischer (2006) also shows that lack of donor coordination, as well as the loss of institutional knowledge in donor agencies because of the high turnover of expatriates, has played into the hands of rent-seekers in Tanzania.

[12]Studies looking at the origins of the donor coordination problem have argued that the lack of coordination lies in the origins of aid agencies (Martens, 2005; and Kanbur and Sandler, 1999). Coordination of agencies accountable to different constituencies and created with different development strategies is inherently difficult.

[13]They consider a situation where the aid recipient government is an agent receiving several conflicting tasks commissioned by different principals or donors. Conflicting tasks may be seen as donor-financed projects with different objectives and conditionalities, as a result of donors' different preferences.

Box 7.2. Donor Coordination Failures: Implications for Aid Effectiveness

1. **Donor-financed projects proliferate.** Divergence of objectives increases and the visibility of efforts is blurred in countries with multiple donors, leading to growing reliance on projects in the absence of coordination mechanisms.
2. **Transaction costs are compounded.** Different donors adopt different management practices, such as numerous and diverse donor rules and procedures for evaluating aid projects and programs; different fiscal calendars and disbursement schedules, and financial accounting requirements; multiple missions, reports, and country-specific analytical work (for example, poverty assessments, public expenditure reviews, fiduciary analysis).
3. **Bureaucratic quality is further compromised.** Donor competition for scarce human resources halts and even reverses the development of public sector capacity as donor hiring practices increasingly (1) rely on expatriates instead of promoting on-the-job training or capacity building for local officials, and (2) poach qualified government officials.
4. **Planning and absorptive capacity is reduced.** Lack of donor coordination in aid delivery further compromises the control of recipients' policymakers over expenditure programs, leading to spending allocations and service provision incompatible with poverty reduction strategies and absorptive capacity. The latter is a consequence of uncoordinated actions resulting, for instance, in (1) excessive spending in social sectors (health care, education) to the detriment of infrastructure; and (2) prioritization of investment projects that, in the aggregate, imply unrealistically high recurrent expenditures or are not in line with absorptive capacity in future years (for example, roads that will be too costly to maintain, value-added-tax provisions that require excessive counterpart funding on the part of the government, schools or hospitals without enough personnel to run at full capacity).
5. **Government and donor accountability for aid effectiveness weakens.** In a country in which the bulk of public expenditure allocation, finance, and management reflects primarily donor preferences for individual projects, local citizens cannot hold elected officials directly responsible for the individual or overall outcome of such projects. Nor can they hold donors responsible, if aid delivery is provided by multiple donors and is fragmented. In such cases, each donor will be responsible for only a small part of development assistance; responsibility for success or failure is diffused; and any single donor will likely not have much stake in the country's economic and social development.

in order to promote country ownership of development projects, donors should try to allocate aid to projects (programs) that are more complementary with other donors' projects and, above all, with the preferred projects of the recipient governments. Donors can improve complementarities or synergies, for instance, by financing projects that the government is willing to pursue in the first place and, as such, that complement rather than compete with already existing government projects.

Best Donor Practices to Improve Aid Effectiveness

The development community's answer to improving donor practices so as to promote country ownership and donor coordination illustrated in the previous section came in the form of the "development partnership model" implemented through the Harmonization and Alignment (H&A) operational guidelines and monitored through indicators agreed under the Paris Declaration of Aid Effectiveness in 2005.

The development partnership model

The development partnership conceptual framework can be graphically summarized in the following pyramid structure (Figure 7.1).[14] At the top of the pyramid is the principle of *country ownership and partnership*, which states that recipient governments should take the lead in setting the development agenda with the support of donors, civil society, and other partners. The principles of *harmonization* and *alignment* form the base of the pyramid and are meant to provide support for the principles of *country ownership and partnership*. The principle of harmonization advocates increasing coordination and streamlining activities among different aid agencies. It comprises three main best-practice guidelines: (1) the development of a common arrangement for planning, funding, disbursing, monitoring, evaluating, and reporting on aid delivery (for example, increased use of common fund–based modalities); (2) the gradual simplification of procedures and specific requirements to reduce the burden these place on recipient governments (for example, by reducing the number of missions and reviews); and (3) the sharing of information among development part-

[14]The original concept of development partnership dates back to Lester (1969). It was relaunched in the late 1990s by the Development Assistance Committee (DAC) at the Organization for Economic Cooperation and Development (OECD, 1996), the government of the United Kingdom (U.K. Secretary of State for International Development, 1997), and the World Bank (World Bank, 1999). De Renzio and Mulley (2006) provide a detailed historical background.

Figure 7.1. Partnership for Greater Aid Effectiveness

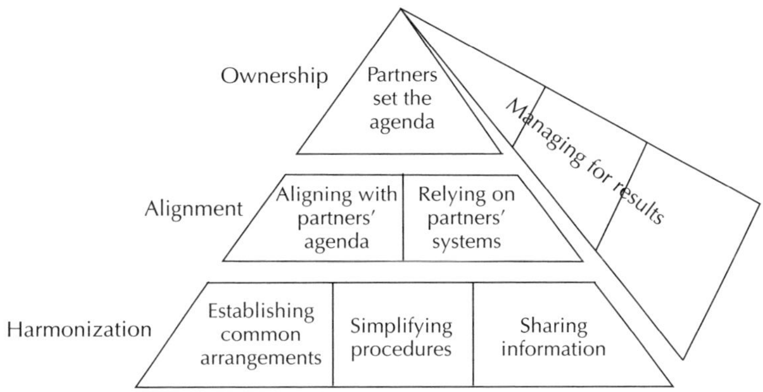

Source: OECD (2005b).

ners to promote transparency and improve coordination. The principle of alignment is twofold, comprising guidelines to increase (1) donors' reliance on recipient countries' systems (for example, public financial management, accounting, auditing, and procurement systems); and (2) donors' attention to recipient countries' development strategies (for example, donors' financial and analytical support could be linked to recipient countries' strategies). Both sets of guidelines expand the reach of harmonization best practices while providing more direct support to the improvement of country ownership. For instance, donors' increased alignment with the recipient countries' systems and strategies should stimulate the use of common-fund arrangements that would improve donor coordination and promote country ownership. The principle of *managing for results* reflects the cultural shift in the aid system from an emphasis on input delivery and compliance with individual institutional requirements to a focus on the performance and management strategies in place for the achievement of outputs, outcomes, and impacts.

Implementing the development partnership model

The development partnership model came into being with the PRS required of governments seeking debt relief under the HIPC Initiative of the World Bank and the IMF (IMF, 2007). To be eligible for debt relief, governments need to draft Poverty Reduction Strategy Papers (PRSPs) with input from civil society in their own countries, enhancing country ownership of the PRS, and the coordinated participation of active donors.

The principles of harmonization and alignment were operationalized into the H&A guidelines and monitored against indicators agreed under the Paris Declaration of Aid Effectiveness. The H&A operational guidelines were led by OECD's DAC and formalized in general best practice commitments set in 2003 by the Rome Declaration on Harmonization. They contain a set of best practices on how donors can best deliver program support as the preferred aid modality and guiding principles and strategic frameworks, while stressing the need for effective and accountable public financial management (PFM) systems (OECD, 2006).[15] H&A guidelines also recognize that donors often work with a mix of various other aid modalities and that circumstances determine which modalities and instruments are chosen. H&A guidelines were further refined in a number of monitorable indicators under the Paris Declaration on Aid Effectiveness in 2005 (OECD, 2005a, 2005b, and 2006) (Table 7.1).

In the remainder of this chapter, we assess the Mozambican donor coordination framework against the partnership model and the H&A operational guidelines. Where possible, we refer to available quantitative results to measure any impact of improved donor coordination on aid effectiveness.

Donor Coordination in Mozambique

Mozambique's approach to the coordinated donor provision of direct budget support, referred to here as the Mozambique model, is often praised, both nationally and internationally, as a model for donor coordination. To provide insight into its strong points as well as the challenges it faces in the short and medium terms, we compare it in this section with the model that the OECD-DAC proposes for donor coordination, by assessing the degree to which the Mozambique model observes the main elements (ownership, harmonization, and alignment) and overarching goal of the OECD-DAC model, namely managing for results. The Mozambique model encompasses 19 bilateral and multilateral donors, organized in Mozambique in a group referred to as the G19,[16] providing general budget support, which at year-

[15]While the preferred aid modality of the G19 (see definition in footnote 16) for Mozambique is general budget support (GBS), the OECD-DAC prefers program aid, comprising both GBS and sector-wide approaches (SWAPs).

[16]Austria, Belgium, Canada, Denmark, Finland, France, Germany, Ireland, Italy, the Netherlands, Norway, Portugal, Spain, Sweden, Switzerland, the United Kingdom, the

end 2006 accounted for 86 percent of aid in Mozambique registered in the database Official Development Aid Mozambique, or ODAMOZ (95 percent, if observers USAID and Japan are included).[17] This section first lays out the history and institutional setup of the donors providing direct budget support, which is an essential background for understanding the Mozambique model. The section then focuses on some key OECD-DAC success indicators in more detail to illustrate donor coordination.[18]

At the outset it is important to highlight some of the caveats of this analysis. As shown below, at times it is not possible to measure improvements in compliance with the DAC model. This is due to the lack of consistent time series, the ever-changing definitions of concepts, and the inconsistent application of these concepts, resulting in some contradictory empirical results. Evaluating the donors providing budget support, Castel-Branco (2007) notes the lack of clarity and precision of definitions as an impediment to a thorough analysis.

Furthermore, even if improvements are demonstrated, there are no counterfactual studies that would show improvements in compliance with the DAC model if a different donor coordination model was used. Therefore, many of the conclusions remain intuitive and have to be taken with caution. Caveats aside, this analysis provides an important contribution to understanding how ideal donor practices derived from the development partnership model and operationalized through the Paris Declaration are taking shape in the field and to what extent they may be improving aid effectiveness.

The Mozambique Model

History and main principles

In the late 1990s many of Mozambique's donors began to provide some of their assistance in the form of program support in order to overcome

---

African Development Bank, the European Commission, and the World Bank are members of the G19. Japan, the IMF, the United Nations Development Program, and USAID are observers.

[17]Source: ODAMOZ as of June 2007. Total aid excludes donors such as the Millennium Challenge Corporation, the Islamic Development Bank, and the Arabic Development Bank, as well as donors such as China, Iceland, India, and South Africa. There are few data on aid outside those provided by the program aid partners that would enable us to assess the success (or failure) of the Mozambique model from the perspective of its impact on the other donors.

[18]For a more exhaustive analysis of Mozambique donors' compliance with the Paris Declaration, see OECD-DAC (2007a, 2007b) and World Bank (2006b).

Table 7.1. Paris Declaration of Aid Effectiveness: Commitments and Indicators

	Ownership	Target for 2010	
1	*Partners have operational development strategies*—Number of countries with national development strategies, including poverty reduction strategies (PRSs), that have clear strategic priorities linked to a medium-term expenditure framework and are reflected in annual budgets.	At least 75 percent of partner countries have operational development strategies.	
	Alignment	**Targets for 2010**	
2	*Reliable country systems*—Number of partner countries that have procurement and public financial management (PFM) systems that either (a) adhere to broadly accepted good practices or (b) have a reform program in place to achieve these.	(a) Public financial management—Half of partner countries move up at least one measure (i.e., 0.5 points) on the PFM/CPIA (Public Financial Management/Country Policy and Institutional Assessment) scale of performance. (b) Procurement—One-third of partner countries move up at least one measure (i.e., from D to C, C to B, or B to A) on the four-point scale used to assess performance for this indicator.	
3	*Aid flows are aligned with national priorities*—Percent of aid flows to the government sector that is reported on partners' national budgets.	Halve the gap—Halve the proportion of aid flows to government sector not reported on government budget(s) (with at least 85 percent reported on budget).	
4	*Strengthen capacity by coordinated support*—Percent of donor capacity-development support provided through coordinated programs, consistent with partners' national development strategies.	50 percent of technical cooperation flows are implemented through coordinated programs consistent with national development strategies.	
5a	*Use of country PFM systems*—Percent of donor and aid flows that use PFM systems in partner countries that either (a) adhere to broadly accepted good practices or (b) have a reform program in place to achieve these.	Score[1]	Target
			Percent of donors
		5+	All donors use partner countries' PFM systems.
		3.5 to 4.5	90 percent of donors use partner countries' PFM systems.
			Percent of aid flows
		5+	A two-thirds reduction in the percentage of aid to the public sector not using partner countries' PFM systems.
		3.5 to 4.5	A one-third reduction in the percentage of aid to the public sector not using partner countries' PFM systems.

5b	*Use of country procurement systems*—Percent of donors and of aid flows that use partner country procurement systems that either (a) adhere to broadly accepted good practices or (b) have a reform program in place to achieve these.	Percent of donors	
		A	All donors use partner countries' procurement systems.
		B	90 percent of donors use partner countries' procurement systems.
		Percent of aid flows	
		A	A two-thirds reduction in the percentage of aid to the public sector not using partner countries' procurement systems.
		B	A one-third reduction in the percentage of aid to the public sector not using partner countries' procurement systems.
6	*Strengthen capacity by avoiding parallel implementation structures*—Number of parallel project implementation units (PIUs) per country.	Reduce by two-thirds the stock of parallel PIUs.	
7	*Aid is more predictable*—Percent of aid disbursements rebased according to agreed schedules in annual or multiyear frameworks.	Halve the gap—Halve the proportion of aid not disbursed within the fiscal year for which it was scheduled.	
8	*Aid is untied*—Percent of bilateral aid that is untied.	Continued progress over time.	
	Harmonization	Targets for 2010	
9	*Use of common arrangements or procedures*—Percent of aid provided as program-based approaches.	66 percent of aid flows are provided in the context of program-based approaches.	
10	*Encourage shared analysis*—Percent of (a) field missions and/or (b) country analytic work, including diagnostic reviews, that are joint.	(a) 40 percent of donor missions to the field are joint. (b) 66 percent of country analytic work is joint.	
	Managing for results	Target for 2010	
11	*Results-oriented frameworks*—Number of countries with transparent and monitorable performance assessment frameworks to assess progress against (a) the national development strategies and (b) sector programs.	Reduce the gap by one-third—Reduce the proportion of countries without transparent and monitored performance assessment frameworks by one-third.	
	Mutual accountability	Target for 2010	
12	*Mutual accountability*—Number of partner countries that undertake mutual assessments of progress in implementing agreed commitments on aid effectiveness including those in this Declaration.	All partner countries have mutual assessment reviews in place.	

Source: OECD (2005a, 2005b, and 2006).

[1]Scores for Indicator 5 are determined by the methodology used to measure quality of procurement and PFM systems under Indicator 2 above.

the disadvantages of traditional project assistance. This program support was initially in the form of untied common funds within individual line ministries, and the funds were linked to sectoral strategy plans. In view of the Rome and Paris Declarations on aid effectiveness, aid was increasingly being channeled in the form of general budget support (GBS). While the use of sectoral common funds reduced the fragmentation caused by project financing in line ministries, the non-earmarked GBS was channeled directly to the government of Mozambique using the government's own allocation, procurement, and auditing systems.

In this context, donors started to harmonize their actions and agreed on a coordinated approach for budget support in 1999, which was formalized in 2000 with a Common Framework Agreement for a Joint Donor Program for Macro-Financial Support between the government and bilateral donors. This agreement was updated and replaced in 2004 by a memorandum of understanding (MOU) between the government of Mozambique and the subscribing donors, referred to as Program Aid Partners (PAPs), for the provision of direct budget and balance of payment support. The MOU lays out the mutual responsibilities of the donors and the government as well as their corresponding monitoring mechanisms. The original PAP group consisted of four bilateral donors (G4),[19] but it expanded rapidly to 19 in 2007, including the World Bank and the African Development Bank. While the MOU covered GBS, in practice, the G19 used its platform to align and harmonize other aid modalities, including sector-wide approaches (often via common funds), sector development programs, and projects.[20]

In the joint MOU, the government and the PAPs commit to improving the quality of development cooperation and provision of aid through alignment with the government's instruments, processes, and systems of financial management:

---

[19]Denmark, Ireland, Norway, and Switzerland.

[20]General budget support (in this chapter also referred to as program aid) is defined by OECD-DAC as "a method of financing a partner country's budget through a transfer of resources from a donor to the partner government's national treasury. The funds thus transferred are managed in accordance with the recipient's budgetary procedures. Funds transferred to the national treasury for financing programs or projects managed according to different budgetary procedures from those of the partner country, with the intention of earmarking the resources for specific uses, are therefore excluded from this definition of budget support" (OECD, 2006, p. 26). In the context of the G19, general budget support under this definition includes non-earmarked budget support provided to the government but excludes SWAPs, common funds, and sector budget support, since these do not (fully) follow the recipient's budgetary procedures.

> Government and PAPs declare their commitment to the modality of Program Aid, given the potential to improve aid effectiveness and country ownership of the development process through increased donor harmonization, increasing recipients' institutional capacities in planning, implementing, monitoring, and evaluating their programs; strengthening domestic accountability; reducing transaction costs; allowing allocative efficiency in public spending, and increasing predictability of aid flows (Government of Mozambique and Program Aid Partners, 2004b, p. 3).

The government further commits itself to the reduction of absolute poverty, as spelled out in the PRS, while the donors engage for greater transparency, predictability, and harmonization, as well as for a reduction of the administrative burden for the government.[21]

Monitoring arrangements

Dialogue and monitoring under the Mozambique model is conducted on the basis of the government's planning and fiscal institutions (Box 7.3). Consistent with the MOU, progress in poverty reduction in the PARPA priority sectors[22] is assessed twice a year—during the joint review of the government and development partners in April/May, following the drafting by the government of the annual PRS progress report *(Balanço do PES)*, and a lighter midyear review in September prior to submission of the annual Economic and Social Program (PES, or annual PRS) and the budget to parliament (Box 7.3). In the joint review, the government and PAPs come to a joint view on the government's performance in the previous year, measured against the indicators and targets to which the government committed itself in a performance matrix. The midyear review has an important forward-looking component in which the donors analyze plans for the following year, and the government and PAPs agree on the performance matrix for that same year. Since 2005 civil society representatives have also participated in these assessments.

The joint steering committee of the government and the donors has become the main mechanism for policy dialogue and donor harmonization, using as a reference the government's Performance Assessment Framework (PAF). The PAF is a multiannual matrix of priority targets and

---

[21]See http://www.pap.org.mz

[22]PARPA I priority sectors included health care, education, roads, agriculture and rural development, basic infrastructure, good governance, and macroeconomic and financial management. PARPA II priority pillars are poverty and macroeconomic management, governance, economic development, human capital, and cross-cutting issues.

Box 7.3. Planning and Fiscal Accountability Systems Under the Mozambique Model

The government and PAPs rely on a number of planning and fiscal institutions or systems to ensure accountability under the Mozambique model. They include (1) the PARPA; (2) the medium-term fiscal framework (*Cenário Fiscal de Médio Prazo*—CFMP); (3) the Economic and Social Plan (*Plano Económico e Social*—PES, or annual PRS) and its progress report (*Balanço do PES*); (4) the annual state budget (*Orçamento do Estado*—OE) and its quarterly execution reports; and (5) the final state accounts (*Conta Geral do Estado*—CGE) and the report of the Controller and Auditor General (*Tribunal Administrativo*). The PARPA is developed through interactive and consultative processes with Mozambican political and economic stakeholders, including the private sector and civil society. The annual PRS (PES) operationalizes the PARPA annually by listing the activities that the government intends to undertake in a given year and its targets. The OE is approved by parliament as a law.

indicators based on the PARPA, updated annually following the publication of the annual PRS (PES) and negotiations between the donors and the government. The PAF now contains 40 indicators out of the more than 200 indicators of the annual PRS. The PARPA matrix, including the 40 PAF indicators, is annexed to the annual PRS (PES) and submitted to parliament to keep it informed about the government's performance. The subset of 40 PAF indicators is the centerpiece of the donors' assessment of the government's performance. Unlike PARPA I, PARPA II includes a strategic performance framework as a tool for tracking poverty reduction in the four priority pillars.

Donors disburse aid if the government has successfully complied with the performance matrix and if the underlying principles are not violated. For the former, donors' disbursements in year $n + 1$ depend on the assessment made in year n of the performance criteria set in year $n - 1$. Hence, in the event of unsatisfactory performance, GBS would be affected only in year $n + 1$, allowing the government to implement corrective measures between year n and $n + 1$. Nonetheless, aid disbursements can be interrupted at any time if the government violates the following governance principles:

> (1) peace; (2) promoting free, credible, and democratic political processes; (3) independence of the judiciary; (4) rule of law; (5) human rights; (6) probity in public life, including the fight against cor-

Figure 7.2. Donors' Alignment and Harmonization with Government Planning Cycles

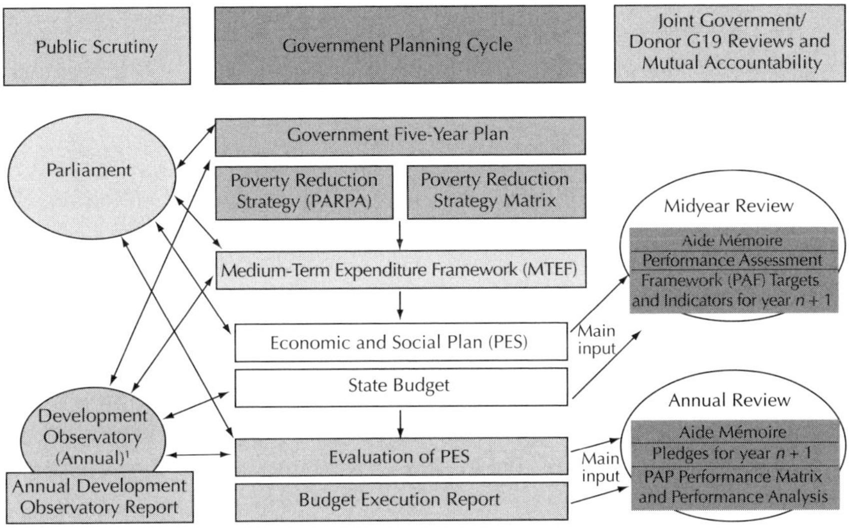

Source: IMF staff.
Note: PAP = Program Aid Partners.
[1]Previously called the Poverty Observatory, for which an Annual Poverty Observatory Report was produced.

ruption; (7) Millennium Development Goals, including through a pattern of public expenditure consistent with PARPA priorities; and (8) sound macroeconomic policies (Government of Mozambique and Program Aid Partners, 2004b, p. 5).

The performance of donors is also assessed annually on the basis of harmonization and alignment with national instruments, processes, and systems, as well as in terms of donors living up to their commitments. Figure 7.2 illustrates the G19's alignment and harmonization with the government's planning cycles.

Alignment and harmonization by the IMF

The IMF-supported programs and policy recommendations are fully aligned with the government's PARPA and medium-term expenditure framework (MTEF). Given its track record of macroeconomic stability, policy performance, and comfortable level of international reserves, Mozambique was able in June 2007 to graduate from a program supported by the IMF's Poverty Reduction and Growth Facility to a program supported by the IMF's Policy Support Instrument. Only a few good performers in sub-Saharan Africa are benefiting from the Policy Support Instrument, which demonstrates increased ownership. Under this facility, the country does not draw any resources from the IMF.

The IMF has joined the 19-member GBS donor group as an observer and participates in macroeconomic-relevant coordination meetings at all levels. The IMF has been synchronizing the timing of its missions with the timing of the semiannual joint donor-government reviews. This has allowed donors to increasingly rely on the IMF's analysis for their macroeconomic assessment during the semiannual reviews and reduce the number of missions and meetings with the government. In 2006 and 2007, for example, donors refrained from an analysis of the draft budget and relied on the findings of the IMF budget-preparation mission instead. Recognizing its role, it is customary for the IMF to have its missions meet with the donor community three times during IMF review missions. Through these meetings, development partners become, among other things, involved in specific policy discussions on the structural reforms that they are supporting. The IMF is also teaming up with the World Bank for its review missions and missions of joint interest—for example missions providing technical assistance to the government for a new fiscal code covering mineral resources. More generally, the over 1,000 staff hours of technical assistance provided by the IMF per year are coordinated with the government and donors providing technical assistance in the same area.

Benchmarking the Mozambique Model

In this section we assess the Mozambique model against the indicators and criteria mentioned in Table 7.1 (see previous section) and which are sub-grouped into ownership, alignment, harmonization, and managing for results. Selected related PAP indicators are also discussed. As the analysis shows, Mozambique scores well on most counts and has been improving steadily without significant setbacks.

Ownership

OECD-DAC defines ownership as respecting the right—and responsibility—of the partner country to establish its development agenda and set out its own strategies for poverty reduction and growth (Indicator 1, OECD, 2005b).

The literature on four years of donor coordination experience in Mozambique supports the view that the government is increasingly owning the development process (OECD, 2004a, 2004b; Batley, Bjørnestad, and Cumbi, 2006; and de Renzio and Sulemane, 2006). For example, while the influence of donors was rather prominent when PARPA I was drafted, the government's leadership strengthened significantly in the formulation and approval of PARPA II. The formulation of the two Poverty Reduction Strategy Papers is perceived to have helped the authorities set policy priorities for growth and poverty reduction and has strengthened the strategic budgeting process, with a strong focus on the improvement of public financial management systems.

This improvement also holds true from an international perspective. A survey by the Strategic Partnership with Africa (SPA) reveals that only in five other African countries are the annual PRS and the annual PRS implementation report sent to parliament for discussion (SPA, 2007). The World Bank highlights Mozambique as an example of a country that developed a PRS through which the government has taken a more assertive role in leading the process of deriving priority measures from PRS policy matrices resulting "in a much more prioritized set of actions directly linked to the PRS, which all budget support donors use as a joint framework to draw disbursement triggers and to assess performance" (World Bank, 2005, p. 52). The World Bank also praises Mozambique for its "long-term holistic vision," given that it has developed action plans that are tied to the MDGs. Out of a sample of 20 countries in the World Bank study, 8 countries—4 of which are in Africa (Mauritania, Mozambique, Tanzania, and Uganda)—have taken such an approach. Mozambique is also among the 15 percent of 59 countries where long-term vision has produced a set of well-developed targets.[23] The strong evidence of leadership and progress has put Mozambique, together with Tanzania and Uganda, in the "best performers group" (World Bank, 2005).

Mozambique also scores well in the implementation of the PRS process. The World Bank assessed the progress achieved in 20 categories underpinning the implementation of the PRS in 20 countries that have had a PRS process for more than two years (World Bank, 2005). The 20 categories can be divided into four main groups: holistic vision, country ownership, country-led partnership, and results focus. Mozambique has largely developed processes in 8 of the 20 categories and has taken, or is taking, action in the remaining 12. This puts Mozambique in fifth place, after Uganda, Vietnam, Tanzania, and Rwanda (Table 7.2).

Mozambique is mentioned as an example of good practice with regard to country ownership and country-led partnership. Of the sample of

[23]The other countries are Cambodia, Kenya, Mauritania, Pakistan, Tanzania, Uganda, Vietnam, and the Republic of Yemen.

Table 7.2. Progress in 20 Categories Underpinning the Poverty Reduction Strategy Process[1]

	Number of categories per level of progress					
Country	Substantially in place	Largely developed	Action has been or is being taken	Elements exist or are being considered	Little or no action	Rank
Uganda	4	13	3	0	0	1
Vietnam	3	7	10	0	0	2
Tanzania	0	13	7	0	0	3
Rwanda	0	11	9	0	0	4
Mozambique	**0**	**8**	**12**	**0**	**0**	**5**
Ethiopia	0	7	13	0	0	6
Mauritania	0	6	12	2	0	7
Burkina Faso	0	5	14	1	0	8
Mali	0	2	12	6	0	9
Yemen	0	2	10	8	0	10
Malawi	0	1	15	4	0	11
Zambia	0	1	14	5	0	12
Honduras	0	0	20	0	0	13
Bolivia	0	0	17	3	0	14
Senegal	0	0	16	4	0	15
Nicaragua	0	0	13	7	0	16
Albania	0	0	12	8	0	17
Benin	0	0	12	7	0	18
Guyana	0	0	7	13	0	19
Sri Lanka	0	0	0	19	1	20

Source: World Bank (2005).

[1]The 20 categories underpinning the implementation of the PRS process are (I) holistic vision: coherent long-term vision (1); medium-term strategy derived from vision (2); country-specific development targets (3); holistic, balanced, and well-sequenced strategy (4); capacity and resources for implementation (5); (II) country ownership: government initiative (6); institutional mechanism for stakeholder involvement (7); civil society involvement (8); private sector involvement (9); parliamentary involvement (10); capacity to formulate strategy (11); (III) country-led partnership: government leadership of coordination (12); partner's assistance strategy alignment (13); financial and analytical partnership (14); coherent and coordinated capacity support (15); harmonization with country systems (16); partnership organization (17); and (IV) results focus: quality of development information (18); stakeholder access to development information (19); coordinated country-level monitoring and evaluation (20).

59 countries, only Cameroon, Ethiopia, Rwanda, Timor-Leste, Uganda, and Vietnam also have policy-level interministerial coordination mechanisms that help enhance the role of line ministries in strategy development. Mozambique, along with Pakistan and Uganda, is also mentioned as having made some progress in synchronizing local development-planning processes with national poverty reduction strategy processes, facilitating both local input nationally and national influence locally. In terms of country-led partnership, the governments of Ethiopia, Ghana, Rwanda, Tanzania, Uganda, and Vietnam take a correspondingly strong lead in

development assistance around a policy framework like Mozambique's. In this sample of 59 countries worldwide, Mozambique is one of seven countries (the others are Ethiopia, Mauritania, Rwanda, Timor-Leste, Uganda, and Vietnam) deemed to have considered all development elements within a vision with appropriate prioritization and sequencing over the medium term (World Bank, 2005).

In addition, the most recent cross-country OECD-DAC survey on monitoring the Paris Declaration for 2005 (OECD, 2007a, 2007b), in which the achievements of 34 countries worldwide are analyzed, recognizes that Mozambique's long-term strategy is largely set, that the country has made clear progress toward the achievement of the MDGs related to poverty reduction, and that the development strategy and the budget are increasingly connected.

The prevalence of budget support in Mozambique has contributed to stronger government ownership. Aid in the form of general budget support is perceived to have been influential in the improvement of the dialogue between the Ministries of Finance (MF) and Planning and Development (MPD) and the sectors on the national and sector budgets. The MF and MPD are increasingly playing a leading role vis-à-vis the line ministries through coordination and directives, and more and more funds are being channeled through the treasury as opposed to separate project bank accounts, which are often managed by temporary nongovernmental project staff. The improved planning and financial management capacity in the MF and MPD now needs to follow suit in the line ministries, where such capacity is still weak (de Renzio and Sulemane, 2006). Consequently, the latest OECD-DAC assessment for Mozambique rates government ownership as moderate, pending improvements in Mozambique's medium-term strategies across all sectors and levels of the government (OECD, 2007a, 2007b).

Some recent structural reforms have fundamentally strengthened the government's role in planning and budgeting public finance. The SISTAFE Law—a law governing public financial management—has institutionalized the medium-term fiscal framework (CFMP) as a fundamental planning instrument in budget formulation, setting out the main macroeconomic forecasts and defining the overall resource envelope and sectoral budget ceilings. In 2006, the CFMP 2007–09 was, for the first time, presented to and approved by the Council of Ministers, a significant step forward in the dialogue with the sectors and ministries and in garnering political support for the overall fiscal policy and strategy. The involvement of sector ministries in the negotiation on the budget is also being strengthened. For the CFMP 2008–10, the MF and MPD have, for the first time, requested the sectors to prepare their own sectoral CFMPs, which should form the basis for the formulation of the annual sector budgets and facilitate the budget preparation process.

Alignment: General principle

The OECD-DAC donor coordination model foresees donors aligning their development assistance with both the development priorities and the results-oriented strategies set out by the partner country. In delivering this assistance, donors would progressively depend on partner countries' own state-of-the-art (or soon to be state-of-the-art) systems, providing capacity-building support to improve these systems, rather than establishing parallel systems of their own. Partner countries would undertake the necessary reforms that would enable donors to rely on their country systems (OECD, 2005b). Seven of the twelve OECD-DAC indicators relate to alignment (see Table 7.1).

Overall, PAPs in Mozambique have fully aligned GBS and program aid with the government's annual planning processes—the budget law, the PES, and the PAF targets, which are reported with the annual PRS (PES) to parliament. For aid modalities other than GBS and program aid, alignment with government planning processes still needs strengthening. As a result, the OECD-DAC (OECD, 2007b) considered alignment in Mozambique to be moderate.

Alignment: Reliability of country systems

The first OECD-DAC indicator on alignment (Indicator 2) relates to the government's current public financial management and procurement systems. The quality of these systems has to be judged sufficient, or, at a minimum, the systems must be undergoing reforms to address deficiencies before donors can be asked to align their aid to them.[24] In Mozambique, although fiduciary risk is considered to be still relatively high under PEFA criteria,[25] the government is seen as committed to reforms to fur-

---

[24]See, in particular, World Bank (2006b), Chapter 10, "Reconciling Alignment and Performance in Budget Support Programs: What Next?"

[25]PEFA: Public Expenditure and Financial Accountability. The goals of the PEFA Program are to strengthen recipient and donor ability to (1) assess the condition of country public expenditure, procurement, and financial accountability systems; and (2) develop a practical sequence of reform and capacity-building actions in a manner that encourages country ownership, reduces the transaction costs to countries, enhances donor harmonization, allows monitoring of progress of country PFM performance over time, better addresses developmental and fiduciary concerns, and leads to improved impact of reforms.

ther reduce the level of fiduciary risk and strengthen PFM (Hodges and Tibana, 2004).

Arndt, Jones, and Tarp (2006) mention that, with the introduction of an integrated budget, treasury management, accounting, and internal control system (e-SISTAFE), Mozambique is addressing many of its initial systemic weaknesses, including (1) input-based budgets that are hard to relate to plans and programs; (2) a state budget that covers mostly recurrent costs, while investments are largely directly funded by donors operating at sector and provincial levels; and (3) weak linkages between approved budgets and actual expenditures. The new, modern public financial management information system has improved the quality of bank reconciliation and financial reporting, introduced a modern functional budget classification, established a disciplined budget preparation calendar, and provided budget controls. The successful rollout of e-SISTAFE to all sectors at national and provincial levels has made it possible for GBS and common funds to be directly executed through the single treasury account (CUT, for *Conta Única do Tesouro*), thus increasing transparency. In 2008, e-SISTAFE was rolled out to 37 of Mozambique's 128 districts, facilitating the gradual decentralization of resources. From an international perspective, the successful rollout of e-SISTAFE is particularly remarkable since such reforms have been politically difficult to implement and prone to setbacks in most sub-Saharan African countries (World Bank, 2006b).

With regard to the quality of the procurement system, the OECD-DAC 2007 report (OECD, 2007a, 2007b) mentions that in 2005 fewer than 50 percent of contracts above the national threshold for small transactions were awarded through an open and competitive process, and describes the procurement complaint mechanism as relatively ineffective. Hence, the OECD has not rated Mozambique's compliance with the alignment criteria for procurement. At the end of 2005, however, a new procurement code was approved; since then follow-up plans and guidelines, such as a procedures manual, standard bidding documents, and formal institutional procurement units, have been approved and implemented. A comprehensive monitoring and evaluation system is yet to be put in place. The PAPs report that the portion of official development aid using public procurement systems increased from about 42 percent in 2005 to about 52 percent in 2006.

Alignment: Reliance on country systems

For the remainder of the alignment criteria, we focus on aid flows reflected in the national budget (Indicator 3); aid disbursed through the government's budget execution, financial reporting, and auditing systems (Indicator 5a); and more predictable aid (Indicator 7).[26]

The bulk of foreign aid received by the government is currently reflected in the state budget (Indicator 3). Until recently, the high levels of off-budget spending, financed by departmental revenues (*receitas próprias*) and, more particularly, by external projects, have seriously limited the coverage of the budget and the effectiveness of treasury management systems, undermining the ability of the government to plan strategically and to assess recurrent and investment costs effectively. Joint efforts of both the government and the PAPs to strengthen the capability of the MF and the MPD for financial management have resulted in the inclusion of substantial aid funds in the budget. According to the 2007 OECD-DAC report, about 84 percent of government aid has been on-budget in 2005, against a target of 92 percent for 2010. The on-budget number for 2005 reported by OECD-DAC seems too high, considering that the common funds (SWAPs) and a large number of projects were brought on-budget only in fiscal years 2006 and 2007. The SWAPs alone represent some 20 percent of government aid in fiscal year 2006. Compared with the OECD-DAC, the PAPs report a considerably more moderate level of aid being on budget in 2005—59 percent of their development aid—with a subsequent increase to about 67 percent in 2006. Notwithstanding the discrepancies between the different databases, it is safe to conclude that the proportion of expenditures that are on budget has increased substantially in recent years and that systematic checks have been put in place to complete this process. Two recent initiatives are helping to increase the coverage of donor aid in the budget:

- *Alignment of aid commitments with the budget cycle.* According to the new practice, PAPs present their indicative commitments to the

[26]For the indicators not discussed in detail, the OECD-DAC (OECD, 2007a) reports the following results, measured against the 2010 targets. Indicator 4: 38 percent of technical assistance is delivered through coordinated programs, against a target of 50 percent. Indicator 5b: 22 of the 24 donor agencies, which provide 38 percent of the aid, (partially) use the country's procurement system. The target for this indicator is a reduction in the amount of aid not yet going through the procurement system. The PAPs report an increase in the use of the government's procurement system from 41.9 percent in 2005 to 52.2 percent in 2006. Indicator 6: by end-2005 there were 40 parallel project implementation units (PIUs) in Mozambique, placing it among the top third of the 34-country sample (OECD, 2007a). The target is to reduce this number by two-thirds. No data are available on previous stocks. Indicator 8: 89 percent of aid to Mozambique is untied, placing the country eighth in the sample of 34 countries (OECD, 2007a, 2007b). The target is "continued progress over time."

authorities and to the public for the next budget year in the first quarter of the current year, which is well in time for the government at national and sector levels to prepare the annual budget. The indicative donor commitments become firm four weeks after the joint review (second half of May)—or well before the budget is submitted to parliament at the end of September. The firm commitments include general budget support and a growing number of sector support funds. Commitments on the project portfolio are less firm.

- *Improved data collection and evaluation.* The ODAMOZ database provides an overview of the financial support from donors, including for projects, common funds, and GBS.[27] However, the database still contains inconsistencies, and data for the medium term are incomplete and less reliable. In an effort to make ODAMOZ a planning instrument for the government, a multiministerial task force has been created to lead improvements, following recommendations from this task force. The January 2007 ODAMOZ data collection round for the first time included budget reference numbers for all government aid. These reference numbers will help identify aid that is still off-budget and allow for consistency checks with government budget data.

Mozambique's improvement in alignment has also been highlighted in cross-country analysis. A report by the SPA shows that Mozambique is one of the three countries out of a sample of 15 countries where the PRS review is fully aligned with the budget cycle, in terms of both indicative MTEF preparations and the annual budget. This is the case not only for GBS but also for sector budget support and project support. Referring to the donors' annual reviews of budget support as well as to the timing of IMF and World Bank missions, the report considers Mozambique a country with an ideal calendar to facilitate harmonization and alignment (SPA, 2007).

The OECD concludes that progress in African countries has been uneven, and that less advanced countries can learn much from countries such as Mozambique, which is "more advanced in harmonization, alignment and managing for development results" (OECD, 2005b, p. 68). The World Bank refers to Mozambique as a country where significant progress is being made with donor coordination and harmonization (World Bank, 2005).

---

[27]The ODAMOZ database, created with help from the European Commission, gives a full listing of all aid that G19 donors and most observers are providing. The database was handed over to the government by end-2006. It is currently being extended to cover all donors and is updated on a quarterly basis. To increase accountability and the quality of data, heads of corporations are asked to sign the quarterly data submissions.

Some increase has been recorded in the use of country financial systems (Indicator 5a), although the current level of budget execution through the single treasury account remains low. Thanks to the joint efforts of the government and the donors, as well as the successive introduction of e-SISTAFE and the increasing share of GBS, notable increases were recorded in reported investment budget execution rates, albeit from low levels. The overall reported execution rate of the investment budget increased from 57 percent in 2002 to 86 percent in 2006 (Table 7.3). In addition, all of the local currency operations of the central level common funds were incorporated in the single treasury account on September 1, 2005, when the single treasury account was established.[28] The number and financial volume of these common funds have increased considerably over the years (Table 7.3). The use of the single treasury account for project implementation has remained modest owing partly to the late issuance by the government in June 2007 of the necessary guidelines on how to include external project funds in the single treasury account and e-SISTAFE. In September 2007, the government opened a multicurrency single treasury account to allow the use of country financial systems—initially for domestic payments in foreign currency—by those donors that are legally prohibited from converting their funds into local currency.[29]

The OECD-DAC survey (OECD, 2007b) ranks Mozambique exactly in the middle of the 34 participating countries in 2005. As the study indicates, "the use of national systems is limited largely to budget support, whereas the large proportion of aid delivered through projects remains untouched by this process" (OECD, 2007b, p. 1).

Alignment: Aid predictability

The OECD-DAC survey (OECD, 2007a) recognizes that donors' alignment with Mozambique's PRS advanced significantly in 2005, which has contributed to the comprehensiveness and realism of the government's estimates of donor contributions. Of the 34 countries in the survey, Mozambique ranked fifth, with 83 percent of the government's estimates accurately predicting actual donor disbursements.

OECD-DAC Indicator 7 aims at halving by 2010 the proportion of aid not disbursed within the fiscal year for which it is scheduled. The PAPs have

[28]The following central level common funds were incorporated in the CUT: ProAgri (agriculture), FASE (education), ASAS (water), and ProSaúde (health). Provincial common funds are not yet incorporated.

[29]Before the foreign-currency single account was available, foreign exchange transactions had to be handled outside the single treasury account.

Table 7.3. Investment Budget Execution Rates, 2000–06
(In millions of meticais unless otherwise specified)

	2002	2003	2004	2005	2006
Total investment budget					
Budgeted	14,136	14,783	14,332	19,001	21,791
Executed	8,067	9,763	10,293	12,594	18,635
Executed as percentage of budgeted	57	66	72	66	86
Internal component					
Budgeted	4,129	4,129	4,126	5,763	6,566
Executed	2,899	3,307	4,074	4,335	6,552
Executed as percentage of budgeted	70	80	99	75	100
External component					
Budgeted	10,007	10,655	10,206	13,239	15,224
Executed	5,168	6,457	6,218	8,259	12,084
Executed as percentage of budgeted	52	61	61	62	79
of which donations					
Budgeted	7,217	6,814	7,116	7,576	10,434
Executed	2,737	3,833	3,592	5,333	7,888
Executed as percentage of budgeted	38	56	50	70	76
of which credit					
Budgeted	2,790	3,840	3,090	5,662	4,790
Executed	2,431	2,623	2,626	2,926	4,195
Executed as percentage of budgeted	87	68	85	52	88

Source: Ministry of Finance, Budget Execution Reports, 2003, 2004, 2005, 2006.

made improved predictability probably the single most important objective; a third of the PAPs' indicators relate to predictability (see Table 7.4). After some initial difficulties, especially for in-year disbursements, donors are disbursing budget aid according to their annual pledges and the agreed treasury plan (Ernst & Young, 2006). Short-term predictability of foreign aid from the donors providing GBS improved substantially between 2003 and 2005, while medium-term predictability needs substantial improvement, as in other countries. A major strength of short-term aid predictability in the PAF MOU is the lagged response mechanism under which an ex post assessment in year n of the government's performance in year $n - 1$ forms the basis for disbursements in year $n + 1$. For the 2007 budget, the PAPs' commitments covered, for the first time, not only GBS but also common funds. Since 2006, the PAPs have publicly announced their budget contribution forecasts for the next calendar year early in the government's budget preparation cycle. For 2008, the PAPs have also committed to improving the coverage of project aid pledges through ODAMOZ.

Mozambique has the lowest aid volatility of eight African countries covered in a World Bank study.[30] Disbursements to Mozambique had the

[30]Benin, Burkina Faso, Ghana, Mali, Mozambique, Senegal, Tanzania, and Uganda.

Table 7.4. Mozambique: PAP Performance Indicators Related to Predictability of Aid

Activities	Indicators	2003 actual	2004 targeted	2004 actual	2005 targeted	2005 actual	2006 targeted	2006 actual
Donors agree with government on disbursement schedules for *n* + 1 by December 31 of year *n*.	Percentage of donors disbursing according to agreed schedule of disbursements and commitments (subject to no breach of underlying principles).	40	>60	80	>80	100	100	94 and 78[1]
	Same as above, but in terms of the percentage of total budget/balance of payments support.		>60	89	>80	94	100	—
Donors inform government of commitments within four weeks of the annual review and do not change the size of commitments afterward. Donors confirm commitments for year *n* + 1 by August 31 (exceptions exist in MOU, Annex 10).	Number of instances of agencies not meeting these commitments as stated in the MOU (taking account of MOU exceptions).	n.a.	0	1	0	0	0	1
Donors commit funds on a multiyear basis.	Percentage of donors with a multiyear indicative commitment.[2]	60	>70	80	>80	100	100	72[3]
Donors harmonize response mechanism.	Number of donors not using the core MOU response mechanism (disbursement in year *n* + 1 based on performance in year *n* – 1).	n.a.	3	3	3	3	0	2
Based on performance in year *n* – 1, donors commit funds for year *n* + 1 at the start of the government's budget preparation cycle.	Percentage of total budget/balance of payments support committed for year *n* + 1 within four weeks of the year *n* joint review and for which disbursement in year *n* + 1 is guaranteed unless there is a breach of underlying principles.[4]	n.a.	55 (estimate)	62	tbm	100 69 guaran-teed	tbm	[5]

Sector aid is made more harmonized, aligned, and predictable.	Number of sectors with an MOU containing donor commitments comparable to the PAPs' MOU.	0	tbm	0	tbm	3	tbm	[6]

Sources: Killick, Castel-Branco, and Gerstner (2005); Ernst & Young (2006); and Castel-Branco (2007).

Note: PAP = program aid partners; MOU = memorandum of understanding; tbm = to be monitored.

[1]Indicator split in two. (1a) Two agencies did not disburse within the fiscal year to which they had committed: Denmark argued a breach of the underlying principles by the Mozambican government, and Italy disbursed ahead of schedule. (1b) Within the budget year, five agencies did not disburse according to schedule because of bureaucratic delays (Spain), delays in signing the new indicative cooperation program (Belgium), lack of response by government on one agreed trigger indicator (Sweden), and other reasons (Denmark and Italy, see 1a).

[2]In addition to the agreed disbursements (100 percent performance), three donors made disbursements without pre-agreed schedules.

[3]Indicator was tightened to multiyear agreements of not less than three years. Five donors have programs of less than three years: Finland, France, Germany, Sweden, and the African Development Bank.

[4]Taken to be total budget/balance of payments support minus the variable tranches and World Bank balance of payments support.

[5]One agency did not meet the criteria.

[6]Agriculture and education have a new MOU. Health is finalizing its MOU. All are now more harmonized and aligned with the PAPs' MOU.

lowest standard deviation from projections (0.58 against 1.25 for the whole sample), and the standard deviation was smaller than for tax revenues (0.63). Moreover, the standard deviation for Mozambique improved substantially from 1993 to 1999 (0.58 versus 3.60), and the improvement was more substantial for Mozambique than for any other country in a sample of eight African countries (World Bank, 2006a). Budget aid projections for 2000–04 were consistently below actual disbursements, an error that is less disruptive than overestimates for public finance. For 2005/06, out of a sample of 15 countries, only Mozambique's quarterly disbursements for budget support were made as planned (SPA, 2007).

This positive assessment is consistent with the PAPs' performance review for 2004 and 2005, a period in which their performance improved considerably. While in 2004, 80 percent of the donors disbursed budget aid according to the agreed schedule, or 89 percent in terms of the volume of budget support, in 2005 all donors disbursed according to the agreed schedule, or 94 percent in terms of the volume of budget support (Ernst & Young, 2006).[31] With the exception of one indicator in 2004, the PAPs consistently exceeded their objectives in improving budget aid predictability between 2003 and 2005 (Table 7.4). In 2005, all PAPs pledged, committed, and disbursed budget aid fully in accordance with the agreed schedule, while all PAPs had multiyear indicative commitments. However, the result for 2006 (Castel-Branco, 2007) shows a decline in predictability (two PAPs failed to disburse in the fiscal year committed to, and five PAPs did not disburse according to the schedule within the fiscal year). The report attributed this deterioration to the revision by most PAPs of their aid strategies, which led to delays in the approval of new strategies or agreements and, ultimately, to delays in disbursements. However, the report argues that the full benefit of these revised and more aligned strategies should be realized by 2008.

The OECD-DAC assessment of 24 bilateral and multilateral donors in Mozambique reports that for 2005, 70 percent of overall aid committed was recorded as disbursed by the government, which put the country tenth in the 34-country sample; Ghana, which saw 92 percent of its aid disbursed, was first (OECD, 2007a).

[31]This percentage is not 100 because three PAPs disbursed budget support without a pre-agreed schedule. Two of them were not PAP members at the time the schedule was agreed, and one did not have a bilateral agreement with the government in place on time (Ernst & Young, 2006).

Harmonization

The harmonization component of the OECD-DAC model for donor coordination entails good-practice principles in development assistance delivery; streamlining and harmonization of donor policies, procedures, and practices; intensified delegated cooperation; increased flexibility of country-based staff to manage country programs and projects more effectively; and the development of incentives within the donor agencies to foster management and staff recognition of the benefits of harmonization (OECD, 2005b). There are two OECD-DAC indicators measuring harmonization. Indicator 9 calls for the use of common arrangements or procedures by providing at least 66 percent of aid by 2010 using program-based approaches. Indicator 10 calls for joint missions and country analytical work by development partners to be done jointly (at least 40 percent of all missions and at least 66 percent of country analytical work). The PAPs, in addition to the percentage of program-based approaches (72 percent by 2007), called for increasing GBS to 40 percent of total aid to the government in 2006 and limiting joint donor missions related to GBS to two a year—the annual and midyear reviews.

Program-based approaches are estimated to have accounted for about half of total aid delivery in Mozambique since 2005.[32] It is worth noting that most of the sector common-fund arrangements have some sort of MOU—or are developing one—and efforts are being undertaken to move these MOUs closer to the terms of the MOU for GBS. The road sector is witnessing a shift from dispersed project support to sector budget support.

The SPA report (SPA, 2007) indicates that Mozambique, after Tanzania, Uganda, and Ghana, receives the highest levels of GBS; the remaining 11 countries in the sample have a much lower GBS component. Over the past three years, Mozambique has experienced a consistent but slow upward trend in GBS, from 31 percent to 34 percent, although the level has remained below the PAPs' target of 40 percent.

Two indicators, while not formally part of the OECD-DAC performance assessment, are good proxies for harmonization, the first being the number of donors that pool budget support and the second the government's satisfaction with donors. Mozambique excels by both indicators.

---

[32]According to the 2007 OECD-DAC report, 46 percent of the total aid of 34 donors was provided using program-based approaches in 2005, albeit with project aid increasing more rapidly than direct budget support (OECD, 2007a). From an international perspective, this puts Mozambique in the top third of the 34 countries ranked. According to the PAPs' review, program aid for 2006 was about 55 percent of total aid delivery, against 53 percent in 2005 (Castel-Branco, 2007).

- In the sample of 15 countries (SPA, 2007), Mozambique has the highest number of donors—19—coordinating their general budget support in one pool (with 13 donors, Tanzania has the second-highest number). The 19 donors as well as, increasingly, the countries with observer status, have streamlined their procedures (OECD, 2005a, 2005b; Batley, Bjørnestad, and Cumbi, 2006; Ernst & Young, 2006). Since the formalization of the government-PAP partnership for general budget support, common procedures have progressively been put in place for joint analysis and policy dialogue, as well as for streamlined conditionality, joint and harmonized assistance strategies, harmonized operational approaches, joint financing arrangements, enhanced focus on delivery of development results, and common procurement procedures. Mozambique is one of the five countries that have only one shared analysis mechanism. This means that Mozambique has only one joint review, in which the government, donors, and civil society participate, and no individual donor reviews, in contrast with 10 other countries in the SPA survey (SPA, 2007). A World Bank report highlights Mozambique as a good example of a country where alignment with national systems has been achieved and an annual report to parliament is the main instrument for assessing PRS implementation and also serves as the basis for an annual joint donor-government assessment of budget support (World Bank, 2006b).
- Mozambique has the highest level of average satisfaction with the group of donors with which satisfaction increased between 2005 and 2006. Out of the total sample of 15 countries in the SPA study, Mozambique scored third, after Tanzania and Benin. Moreover, Mozambique is the only country in the sample whose satisfaction has increased in each of the past three years. The main factors for government satisfaction in the survey are (1) coordinated selection of donor conditionalities, (2) joint donor missions or reviews, (3) minimized and coordinated donor reporting requirements, (4) coordinated support on public financial management reforms, (5) strengthened statistical systems, (6) minimized overall number of donor conditions, and (7) usefulness of donor conditionalities in implementing the government's PRS (SPA, 2007). On the last two criteria, it is worth noting that the total number of PAF targets has been reduced to a more manageable 40 and that there is no conditionality outside the common performance framework. Furthermore, in 2006 for the first time, all PAF indicators were a subset of existing monitoring indicators defined by the government for the implementation of the PARPA. Finally, there is no duplication of reporting requirements;

the annual PRS (PES), the evaluation of the annual PRS (BdPES), the budget, the budget execution report, the General State Account, and the annual audit reports are the sole documents used for the joint reviews. After Burkina Faso, Mozambique relies the most on the annual progress reports produced by the government as information for donors (SPA, 2007).

Initial progress was achieved in 2003–04 in encouraging shared analysis (Indicator 10). During that period, joint missions (excluding the World Bank) increased from 17 to 37 percent of total missions (Killick, Castel-Branco, and Gerstner, 2005). By 2005, the OECD-DAC (2007a, 2007b) ranked Mozambique as the best performer out of a sample of 34 countries, with 46 percent of its missions coordinated. Mozambique ranked second in the same group of countries in terms of coordinated country analysis (OECD, 2007a, 2007b). For 2006, the PAP evaluation counted 10 general budget support missions, 3 more than targeted (Castel-Branco, 2007). The report also identified 203 non-GBS missions, of which 10 percent were joint efforts. To facilitate government and donor planning, the IMF timed its mission around the government budget cycle and the donor-government joint review, facilitating the decision of the government and the PAPs' decision to rely since September 2006 entirely on the IMF's assessment of the draft budget for their midyear review rather than duplicating this analysis, as had been done in the past.

Managing for results

The OECD-DAC model envisages partner countries embracing the principles of managing for results at all stages of the development cycle—from planning through implementation to evaluation. Donors should rely on and support partner countries' own priorities and objectives, and work in coordination with other donors to strengthen partner-country institutions, systems, and capabilities to plan and implement projects and programs, report on results, and evaluate development processes and outcomes.

In Mozambique, the use of the PAF framework has meant a shift from a focus on inputs and outputs to a focus on results, outcomes, and impacts; highest-priority policies and actions; and monitoring of outcome indicators. By also using a framework that is a subset of the performance indicator framework of the country's poverty reduction strategy and that is linked to the yearly PRS (PES) and the budget, the PAF framework is a good example of integrated results management. According to SPA (2007), the perceived usefulness of donor conditionality among recipient governments decreased in a number of countries in 2006. In Mozambique, unlike in many other countries, donors choose indicators from the government-developed PARPA strategic matrix; thus, by definition, the indicators are considered important and useful.

Mozambique is cited for its well-developed national monitoring and evaluation systems, which not only are linked to the line ministries but also produce reports for domestic and external stakeholders (World Bank, 2005). Its intermediate indicators are considered manageable in number and relatively easy to monitor, although there is room for improvement of data reliability. The World Bank report reflects on the type of goals that countries have been developing (World Bank, 2005). Among the countries with more experience in PRS implementation, Uganda and Vietnam stand out; each has largely completed putting a set of goals in place. The Ugandan government has refined the indicators and linked them to the MDGs; it has also developed a detailed policy matrix linking the indicators to specific policy actions. The evaluation study states that similar efforts are under way in Mozambique and Tanzania. Also, the OECD-DAC survey for 2005 (OECD, 2007a, 2007b) concluded that the quality of development information had improved owing to regular household surveys and a national statistical development strategy. Nonetheless, the report mentions that more effort has to go toward disseminating development information, such as strategies, budgets, and policies; as a result, it ranked Mozambique as average in the sample of 34 countries.

In order to improve mutual accountability (Indicator 12), the PAPs contract external consultants to evaluate the PAPs' compliance with PAP targets. Such a review has been undertaken every year since 2005. In addition, starting in 2004, the OECD-DAC has analyzed on a yearly basis donors' compliance with the Paris Declaration. The 2006 OECD-DAC survey recognizes the well-developed mutual accountability framework for donors providing budget support and provides evidence of its positive effect on donor performance. It is worth mentioning that the PAPs have in their performance assessment indicators that relate to overall aid and that thus include aid modalities other than GBS, such as the percentages of program aid, aid on-budget, aid using the single treasury account, and aid using the government procurement system, and other items such as the number of non-GBS missions.

Furthermore, since 2006 the donors have been carrying out a joint analysis of their individual multiannual country strategies to improve consistency with the PARPA and the Paris Declaration, reduce transaction costs, and increase aid effectiveness. All these strategies have been mapped and analyzed in terms of complementarities, proposed modalities, and relationship to the government's priorities, with the ultimate aim of producing a road map for increased aid effectiveness (SIDA, 2006). This is the first comprehensive review in which the PAPs are sharing their strategies with the government and other donors.

Challenges Ahead

In the previous section we measured Mozambique's record against the OECD-DAC indicators for 2010. As shown, Mozambique scored well on most counts. Using data from the OECD-DAC cross-country analysis, out of a sample of 26 countries Mozambique ranks second on an aggregate level.[33] Table 7.5 gives the sample averages and Mozambique's score and rank for each individual indicator. As the table shows, there is room for improvement by both the Mozambican government and the donor community.

As noted in the previous section, Mozambique has been improving steadily in terms of ownership, alignment, harmonization, and managing for results. In this section, we focus on the challenges ahead and the continued improvements needed to make aid more effective. In most areas, projects have already been initiated toward this end. We use the same thematic sequencing as in the previous section.

Ownership

Looking ahead, ownership needs to be enhanced by increasing the involvement of line ministries, local governments, and civil society in the planning process.

Ownership in the Mozambique model can be enhanced by building capacity at the sectoral level and by increasing the involvement of line ministries in the elaboration of the MTEF. There is the frequent perception by line ministries that the elaboration of the MTEF is an exercise internal to the MF and MPD, and not a policy instrument for constructive dialogue with line ministries and other agencies (Arndt, Jones, and Tarp, 2006). Until sectors have built up the capacity to formulate output-oriented and well-costed multiyear spending plans that are reflected in the national MTEF, the elaboration process of a coherent MTEF with adequate sectoral

[33]Scores for Indicators 1, 2, 6, and 12 were converted into percentages, and all percentages of Indicators 1–12 were added up. The aggregate analysis excludes eight countries for which not all indicators were available. One of the countries excluded is Tanzania, which is among the best performers for many indicators. The rank for Mozambique does not change when rescaling the results by giving 0 percent to the worst observed and 100 percent to the best observed result in the sample.

Table 7.5. Mozambique's Performance in 2005 According to the OECD-DAC Criteria on Harmonization and Alignment

	Score	Unweighted average	Rank
Mozambique's overall rank for indicators 1–12 *(26 countries)*			2
Total aid reported in the 2006 survey *(in millions of US$)*	1,267	487	6
Indicator 1:			
Do countries have operational development strategies? *(29 countries)*[1]	C	C	6
Indicator 2:			
How reliable are country public financial management systems? *(29 countries)*[2]	3.5	3.4	10
Indicator 3:			
Are government budget estimates comprehensive and realistic? *(percent)*	83	65	8
Indicator 4:			
How much technical assistance is coordinated with country programs? *(percent)*	38	39	15
Indicator 5-1:			
How much aid for the government sectors uses country public financial management systems? *(percent)*	36	34	17
Indicator 5-2:			
How much aid for the government sectors uses country procurement systems? *(percent)*	38	34	17
Indicator 6:			
How many PIUs are parallel to country structures? *(number)*	40	55	12
Indicator 7:			
Are disbursements on schedule and recorded by governments? *(percent)*	70	63	13
Indicator 8:			
How much aid is untied? *(percent)*	89	76	11
Indicator 9:			
How much aid was program-based? *(percent)*	46	39	14
Indicator 10-1:			
How many donor missions were coordinated? *(percent)*	46	18	1
Indicator 10-2:			
How much country analysis was coordinated? *(percent)*	63	43	2
Indicator 11:			
Do countries have monitorable performance assessment frameworks? *(28 countries)*[3]	C	C–	3
Indicator 12:			
Do countries have reviews of mutual accountability?[4]	Yes		1

Source: OECD (2007b).

Note: Size of sample in parentheses if different from 34.

[1]No country has A (best); 5 countries have B; 18 countries have C and 6 countries have D; no country has E (worst).

[2]No country has 5 (best); 1 country has 4.5; 8 countries have 4; 11 countries have 3.5; 5 countries have 3; 3 countries have 2.5; one country has 2. No country is below 2.

[3]No country has A; 2 have B; 17 have C; and 9 have D. Six countries have no score.

[4]Yes, 15 countries; no, 19 countries.

input can be expected to be rather weak. However, the donor community can play an essential role in accelerating this process. Sectors will need technical assistance in drafting coherent multiyear strategies, making adequate financial plans, and lobbying for their sectoral budget allocations in the centralized planning process. As mentioned earlier, in 2007 sectors developed for the first time their sectoral MTEFs for 2008–10, which will in time become a core input for strategic planning by the MF and MPD.

The government should exercise stronger leadership in defining priorities and performance indicators. Ulens (2006) and de Renzio and Sulemane (2006) argue that the setting of priorities and performance indicators at central, sectoral, and provincial levels are still driven largely by donors, both individually and collectively. Many donors prefer to finance projects according to their own priorities, as long as the planning process of the MTEF is relatively weak. Furthermore, most of the recent donor-country strategies were formulated with little government input. To support the government in its efforts to strengthen its planning expertise, donors should use the sectoral and central planning mechanism in the selection of their aid portfolio. This would be easier to accomplish if the government developed an aid policy as well as an institutional setup for aggregate guidelines and responsibilities for aid management (SIDA, 2006).

Civil society participation could also be strengthened further. Civil society has been more engaged in formulating PARPA II than PARPA I, but there is room to further strengthen its role. While the government has formalized its relationship with the PAPs, it is fundamental that accountability and transparency vis-à-vis the Mozambican public are also strengthened and deepened.

Alignment: Reliance on country systems

In the years ahead, donors will need to align financial support at the provincial level (SIDA, 2006). The government's decentralization strategy, which will include policies on decentralized planning and financing, should become instrumental in this regard. The e-SISTAFE rollout to the districts should facilitate the process, since it allows districts to request the required funds via the e-SISTAFE system.

A growing number of projects will need to be disbursed through the single treasury account to allow for more accurate and transparent monitoring. This will also help strengthen data collection and improve clarity and consistency in the use of definitions. Projects are still covering a large amount of external funds; nearly all of these are financially managed outside the government's financial system. While foreign-financed projects are considered part of the investment budget, most projects also include recurrent costs such as salaries.[34] Several initiatives are being implemented to increase the level of funds being disbursed directly to contractors through e-SISTAFE:

- The government has finalized guidelines for donors on how to execute projects using the single treasury account. These guidelines will be instrumental in substantially increasing the current low level of development aid being executed through the single treasury account, considering that 45 percent of PAPs' development assistance to the government is in the form of project aid.
- An improvement to the aid database ODAMOZ being discussed is to include information about the financial execution of aid—that is, whether or not it is disbursed using the single treasury account, which would allow donors and the Ministry of Finance to reconcile their data. It would also make it possible to monitor progress in putting donor projects on the single treasury account.
- The introduction in September 2007 of e-SISTAFE's direct budget execution functionality in foreign currency is making it possible to record and analyze almost all donor funds.

Alignment: Aid predictability

To improve the government's planning capability, donors will need to make multiyear commitments. Although many of the donors have a two- to five-year country strategy, the medium-term predictability of available financial information is weak. At present, only one donor has committed to a five-year rolling budget, and 28 percent of donors have a commitment horizon of less than three years. Only 37 percent of the overall pledges for 2006–09 have a clear disbursement schedule (SIDA, 2006). Not surprisingly, however, the further one looks into the future, the weaker the predictability. Of the different aid modalities, budget aid is the most predictable, and project aid the least (Figure 7.3). This result makes sense, considering that budget support tends to be a more political commitment, whereas project support requires more detailed planning (for example, identification of project, costing of project components). Overall aid predictability could thus be most easily increased by upping the share of budget support in the overall aid envelope. In addition, a full costing of the PARPA and

[34]With the introduction of program budgeting, the monitoring and evaluation capability will further improve.

the MDGs would likely increase the predictability of project aid as well, because it would facilitate project planning and commitments.

Although GBS has been increasing steadily in Mozambique with continued satisfactory government performance, there is considerable scope for raising the GBS share of total aid. According to a benchmarking exercise comparing the evolution of budget support and project aid in 2000–06, Burkina Faso, Tanzania, and Uganda have improved their portfolio composition more rapidly than Mozambique (Figure 7.4).

While the alignment of donor conditionality has improved the short-term predictability of aid, the criteria of nonviolation of the underlying principles for the purpose of aid disbursements referred to in the MOU can potentially lead to a sudden and massive aid reversal, with strong adverse macroeconomic consequences. Recognizing this risk, development partners are currently proactively discussing a response mechanism and early indicators that could lead to such an event.[35]

Harmonization

To improve shared analysis, there would need to be better monitoring of aid disbursements, more pooled missions for project aid, and more precise definitions of assessment criteria. The monitoring of progress in the context of increased program-based aid remains difficult; the weak data collection of projects and programs outside the single treasury account and the lack of clarity and consistency in the use of definitions make monitoring outcomes difficult. The OECD-DAC assessment for Mozambique argues that, while budget-support-related missions are coordinated more often, they alone will not get Mozambique to the harmonization target because the number of nonbudget support missions remains high (OECD, 2007b). In addition, challenges in alignment are particularly daunting for some institutions. For example, under some of its programs (such as the Poverty Reduction Support Credit), the World Bank requires a specific assessment of government performance over the past year before making a disbursement. Strict adherence to the MOU would entail using the joint reviews for analyzing the government's performance, conducting the World Bank board discussion within four weeks after the joint review of program aid, and subsequent pledging for the next year in accordance with the gov-

[35]Measures to address the inherent political risk of GBS are being formulated by the European Commission, which proposes increases over and above a stable foundation tranche as an incentive for good governance, as opposed to total withdrawal as a punishment for poor governance or condition performance (Oxfam International, 2007).

Figure 7.3. PAP Aid Commitments, 2006–11
(In millions of U.S. dollars)

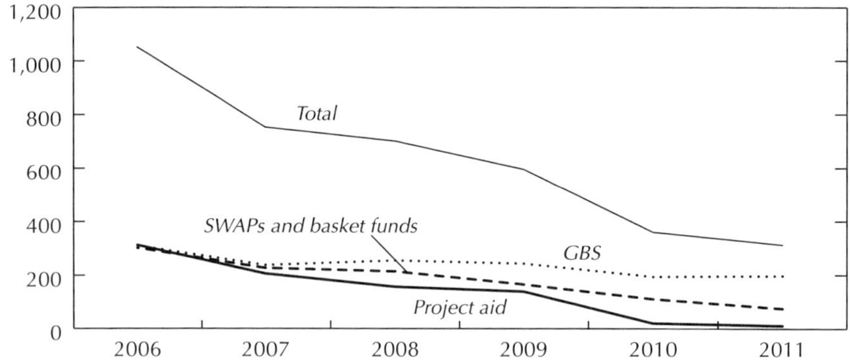

Source: KPMG (2007, draft).

ernment's budgeting cycle. Booth, Christiansen, and de Renzio (2006) go even further and see the G19 reviews themselves as a violation of the principle of alignment, since they constitute parallel exercises to existing government performance reviews, such as the implementation report of the annual PRS, which is submitted to parliament.

Other exceptional treatments donors require include the supremacy of the Cotonou Agreement, compliance with the donor agency's financial rules for budget support (African Development Bank), or bilateral exceptions to the MOU allowing for an interruption of disbursements on the basis of additional rules besides the ones agreed in the MOU. In 2006, 7 of the then 18 donors had such exceptions, though with a view to eliminating them. Nonetheless, the government must make an extra effort to satisfy individual PAP requirements or additional rules of the game. To improve efficiency and harmonization, the United Nations Development Program (UNDP) recently decided to streamline UN work in Mozambique, to reach out to the G19 platform, and, increasingly, to harmonize UN activities with the PAP approach.

Managing for results

Improvements in results-based reporting are key to monitoring results. In the 2007 joint review, the PAPs (Government of Mozambique and Program Aid Partners, 2007) noted that the annual PRS (PES) and the annual PRS implementation report (BdPES) should be improved by aligning the PARPA implementation report with execution reports, by analytically link-

Figure 7.4. Mozambique and Comparators: Evolution in Budget Support, 2000–06
(Percent change in total aid)

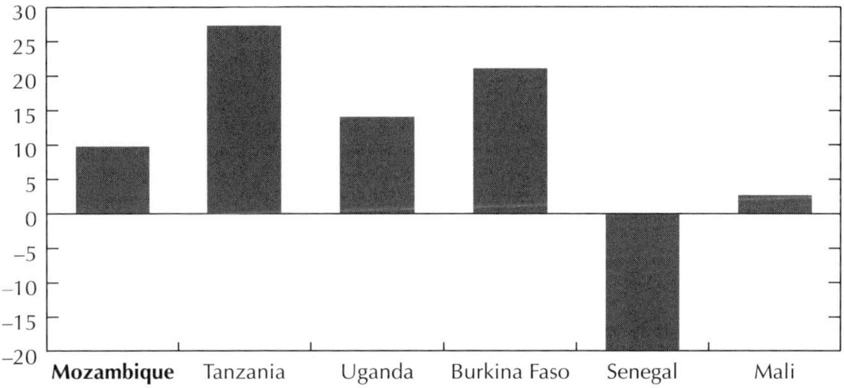

Source: IMF staff estimates.

ing the program (PES) with the results (BdPES), and by reorienting and better organizing data collection and data analysis from the district up to the central level. Furthermore, the performance matrix for PARPA II needs to be translated into sectoral performance matrices as well as into the local governments' performance matrices. It is worth noting that the country's statistical capacity has been strengthened to enable the government to measure results against baseline data. While the existing budget classification system is mainly input-oriented and thus does not allow for inferences on expenditures and outputs/outcomes, a shift to the program-budgeting approach will allow for cost-benefit analysis of development programs. Program budgeting has been piloted in some sectors for the first time under the 2008 budget thanks to ongoing developments in e-SISTAFE, such as the introduction of sector-specific budget classifiers, which will allow for customized reporting and statistics. It is also worth noting that a second household survey was recently conducted; this survey tracks progress in social indicators since the first survey was conducted five years ago.

Conclusions and Lessons for Sub-Saharan Africa

The literature on aid effectiveness makes a strong case in favor of aid coordination and harmonization. The donor community has taken this forward with the Paris Declaration on Aid Effectiveness, which defines 12 indicators relating to ownership, harmonization, alignment, and managing for results. On many of these indicators, Mozambique ranks in the top 20 percent despite a number of factors that have made it difficult to harmonize and align aid in Mozambique (for example, the large amount of aid flowing in from a large number of donor agencies). Tanzania and Uganda have almost consistently exceeded Mozambique's scores, and the OECD-DAC has deemed Mozambique's compliance with the Paris Declaration as moderate. Nonetheless, there are a number of important lessons to be drawn for sub-Saharan Africa.

- First, Mozambique can be considered a model for other sub-Saharan African countries in terms of donor coordination and processes that lead to continuously improved aid effectiveness. Mozambique is the only country in which government satisfaction with donors has increased year after year, resulting in the substantial reduction of aid volatility in a short period of time and one of the lowest levels of aid volatility in sub-Saharan Africa.
- Second, Mozambique's experience confirms that budget support produces better outcomes than project aid. PAP donors—which deliver general budget support—have scored much better than the donor community as a whole on measures of aid predictability; strengthened budget planning, execution, and control capacity; and other indicators of aid effectiveness. Looking forward, PAP donor coordination could be the platform for donors not yet providing budget support (for example, China, India, and the United States), thereby improving Mozambique's overall efficiency in using aid. Mozambique's donors should set and implement more ambitious targets for budget support, which would improve the scores on a number of indicators simultaneously.
- Third, donors' increased reliance on government systems increases the government's responsibility for—and the urgency of—following through on needed reforms. Such reforms in Mozambique include improvements in good governance and the rule of law, public sector reform, and the rollout of integrated financial management information systems. Regarding the last, remarkable progress has already been achieved in Mozambique over the past few years with the rollout of e-SISTAFE to all line ministries at the central and provincial levels.
- Fourth, it is important that the national authorities lead efforts to get donors to comply with the Paris Declaration. The authorities should also avoid accepting the creation of parallel structures and instead require donors to use existing systems.

- Fifth, the IMF can play a catalytic role in facilitating compliance with the Paris Declaration. Its involvement in public financial management reforms, for example, lays the foundation on which donors can align their aid with government mechanisms; the timing of IMF missions also reduces duplication of policy analysis.

Appendix. Common-Agency Models of Donor Coordination and Aid Effectiveness

Consider the model developed in Dixit (2003) and Murshed (2002, 2006) of an aid-recipient government undertaking two projects referred to as x_1 and x_2 and financed by donors 1 and 2, respectively. Each project entails unobserved symmetric effort levels, which are also equal to its output. Donor 1 derives a benefit equal to B from project x_1, but none from project x_2; the reverse applies to donor 2. The cost to the recipient government of exerting efforts x_1 and x_2 for the two tasks is given by

$$C(x_1, x_2) = \varepsilon x_1^2 + \varepsilon x_2^2 + 2kx_1x_2, \qquad (1)$$

where the parameter k determines the degree of substitutability of the two tasks. If $k > 0$, the tasks are substitutes because greater effort in one task increases the marginal cost of effort on the other. As such, achieving a greater marginal reward in one would require the recipient government to withdraw effort from the other. If $k < 0$, the two are complements.

A payment is made to compensate the recipient government for managing the project. The incentive payment made to the recipient government is w, and the payment schedule is linear on observed outputs x. Both principals will need to meet the participation constraint of the agent. Therefore, each principal's profit function will take the following form:

$$P_i = Bx_i - w[x_i + \varepsilon x_1^2 + \varepsilon x_2^2 + 2kx_1x_2] \text{ with } i = 1, 2. \qquad (2)$$

In the absence of coordination, each donor would optimize its desired project level, taking the other donor project as given by maximizing equation (2) with respect to x_i. The optimal payment schedule in this case would equal

$$w^{nc} = \frac{B}{1 + 2x(\varepsilon + k)}, \qquad (3)$$

where nc stands for noncooperative and $x = x_1 = x_2$ by the symmetry of the model.

If both donors decide to coordinate their actions, a solution could be derived by maximizing the donors' profit functions jointly (by summing equation (2) over i) with respect to x. The optimal payment schedule in this case would equal

$$w^c = \frac{B}{1 + x(\varepsilon + k)} . \tag{4}$$

Therefore, the model delivers three important results:

1. Coordination improves the recipient government's accountability (commitment) to project outcomes. A cooperative or coordinated equilibrium, by allowing donors to provide a better payment schedule for any given level of output, would increase the incentives of donors and recipients to exert optimal effort and deliver a corresponding optimal output.
2. Benefits from coordination increase with the number of donors, given that coordination failures increase with donor proliferation. Assuming a one-to-one relationship between donors and projects, equation (3) states that payments to recipient governments decline as the number of donors increases, given that the magnitude of the term 2 in the denominator rises with the number of projects.
3. The commitment of the recipient government to individual projects increases the more execution projects complement each other. A low degree of substitutability (lower k) delivers higher payment schedules, both in the cooperative and the noncooperative equilibria.

Bibliography

Alesina, Alberto, and David Dollar, 2000, "Who Gives Foreign Aid to Whom and Why?" *Journal of Economic Growth*, Vol. 5 (March), pp. 33–63.

Andersen, T.B., T. Harr, and F. Tarp, 2006, "On U.S. Politics and IMF Lending," *European Economic Review*, Vol. 50 (October), pp. 1843–62.

Arellano, C., A. Bulíř, T. Lane, and L. Lipschitz, 2005, "The Dynamic Implications of Foreign Aid and Its Variability," IMF Working Paper 05/119 (Washington: International Monetary Fund).

Arndt, Channing, Sam Jones, and Finn Tarp, 2006, "Aid and Development: The Mozambican Case," Discussion Paper No. 27E (Maputo, Mozambique: National Directorate of Studies and Policy Analysis, Ministry of Planning and Development). Available via the Internet: http://www.mpd.gov.mz/gest/documents/27E_Aid_and_Development.pdf

Azam, J.P., and J.J. Laffont, 2003, "Contracting for Aid," *Journal of Development Economics*, Vol. 70 (February), pp. 25–58.

Batley, Richard, Liv Bjørnestad, and Amélia Cumbi, 2006, *Evaluation of General Budget Support—Mozambique Country Report: A Joint Evaluation of General Budget Support 1994–2004* (Birmingham, United Kingdom: IDD and Associates).

Berg, E., 1997, "Dilemmas in Donor Aid Strategy," in *Perspectives on Aid and Development*, ed. by C. Gwin and J.M. Nelson (Washington: Overseas Development Council).

Berthélemy, J.C., 2006, "Bilateral Donors' Interest vs. Recipients' Development Motives in Aid Allocation: Do All Donors Behave the Same?" *Review of Development Economics*, Vol. 10 (May), pp. 179–94.

Booth, David, Karin Christiansen, and Paolo de Renzio, 2006, "Reconciling Alignment and Performance in Budget Support Programs: What Next?" in *Budget Support as More Effective Aid? Recent Experiences and Emerging Lessons*, ed. by S. Koeberle, Z. Stavreski, and J. Walliser (Washington: World Bank).

Brautigam, Deborah, 2000, *Aid Dependence and Governance* (Stockholm: Almqvist and Wiksell International).

Bulíř, Aleš, and A. Javier Hamann, 2003, "Aid Volatility: An Empirical Assessment," *IMF Staff Papers*, Vol. 50 (March), pp. 64–89.

———, 2006, "Volatility of Development Aid: Unpleasant Bean Counting," in *The Macroeconomic Management of Foreign Aid: Opportunities and Pitfalls*, ed. by Peter Isard, Leslie Lipschitz, Alexandros Mourmouras, and Boriana Yontcheva (Washington: International Monetary Fund), pp. 197–215.

Burnside, C., and D. Dollar, 2000, "Aid, Policies, and Growth," *American Economic Review*, Vol. 90 (September), pp. 847–68.

———, 2004, "Aid, Policies and Growth: Reply," *American Economic Review*, Vol. 94 (June), pp. 781–84.

Castel-Branco, Carlos Nuno, 2007, "Mozambique Programme Aid Partners Performance Review 2006" (Maputo, Mozambique).

Clemens, M., S. Radelet, and R. Bhavnani, 2004, "Counting Chickens When They Hatch: The Short-Term Effect of Aid on Growth," CGD Working Paper No. 44 (Washington: Center for Global Development).

Clément, Jean A.P., ed., 2004, *Postconflict Economics in Sub-Saharan Africa: Lessons from the Democratic Republic of the Congo* (Washington: International Monetary Fund).

Collier, P., and J. Dehn, 2001, "Aid, Policy, and Shocks," Policy Research Working Paper No. 2688 (Washington: World Bank).

Collier, Paul, and Anke Hoeffler, 2002, "Aid, Policy, and Growth in Post-Conflict Societies," Policy Research Working Paper No. 2902 (Washington: World Bank).

Cordella, T., and G. Dell'Ariccia, 2003, "Budget Support Versus Project Aid," IMF Working Paper 03/88 (Washington: International Monetary Fund).

Dalgaard, Carl-Johan, Henrik Hansen, and Finn Tarp, 2004, "On the Empirics of Foreign Aid and Growth," *Economic Journal*, Vol. 114 (June), pp. F191–216.

de Renzio, Paolo, and Sarah Mulley, 2006, "Donor Coordination and Good Governance: Donor-Led and Recipient-Led Approaches," Working Paper No. 2006/21 (Oxford: Global Economic Governance Program, University College).

de Renzio, Paolo, and José Sulemane, 2006, "Integrating Reporting of PRS and Budget Implementation: The Mozambican Case" (unpublished; London: Overseas Development Institute).

Devarajan, Shantayanan, and Vinaya Swaroop, 1998, "The Implications of Foreign Aid Fungibility for Development Assistance," Policy Research Working Paper No. 2022 (Washington: World Bank).

Dixit, Avinash K., 2003, "Some Lessons from Transaction-Cost Politics for Less-Developed Countries," *Economics and Politics*, Vol. 15 (June), pp. 107–33.

Dollar, D., and J. Svensson, 1998, "What Explains the Success and Failure of Structural Adjustment Programs?" Policy Research Working Paper No. 1938 (Washington: World Bank).

Drazen, Allan, 2000, *Political Economy in Macroeconomics* (Princeton, New Jersey: Princeton University Press).

Easterly, William, 2003, "The Cartel of Good Intentions: The Problem of Bureaucracy in Foreign Aid," *Journal of Policy Reform*, Vol. 5 (December), pp. 223–50.

———, 2006, *The White Man's Burden: Why the West's Efforts to Aid the Rest Have Done So Much Ill and So Little Good* (New York: Penguin Press).

Ernst & Young, 2006, *Review of the PAPs' Performance in 2005 and PAPs' PAF Matrix Targets for 2006*. Available via the Internet: http://www.open.ac.uk/technology/mozambique/pics/d60872.pdf

Fischer, P.V., 2006, *Rent-Seeking, Institutions and Reforms in Africa: Theory and Empirical Evidence for Tanzania* (New York: Springer).

Hodges, Tony, and Roberto Tibana, 2004, *Political Economy of the Budget in Mozambique* (London: U.K. Department for International Development). Available via the Internet: http://www.dfid.gov.uk/pubs/files/political-economy-mozambique.pdf

Holmström, Bengt, and Paul Milgrom, 1991, "Multitask Principal Agent Analysis: Incentive Contracts, Asset Ownership, and Job Design," *Journal of Law, Economics and Organization*, Vol. 7 (January), pp. 24–51.

International Monetary Fund, 2001, "Structural Conditionality in Fund-Supported Programs" (Washington: Policy Development and Review Department). Available via the Internet: http://www.imf.org/external/np/pdr/cond/2001/eng/struct/index.htm

———, 2002, "Guidelines on Conditionality" (Washington: Legal Department and Policy Development and Review Department). Available via the Internet: http://www.imf.org/External/np/pdr/cond/2002/eng/guid/092302.htm

———, 2005a, "Review of the 2002 Conditionality Guidelines—Selected Issues" (Washington: Policy Development and Review Department). Available via the Internet: http://www.imf.org/external/np/pp/eng/2005/030405.htm

———, 2005b, "Strengthening the IMF's Support for Low-Income Countries" (Washington). Available via the Internet: http://www.imf.org/external/np/exr/ib/2005/092105.htm

———, 2007, *Debt Relief Under the Heavily Indebted Poor Countries (HIPC) Initiative: A Factsheet*. Available via the Internet: http://www.imf.org/external/np/exr/facts/hipc.htm

Kanbur, Ravi, and Todd Sandler, 1999, "The Future of Development Assistance: Common Pools and International Public Goods," ODC Policy Essay No. 25 (Washington: Overseas Development Council).

Killick, T., 1997, "Principals, Agents and the Failings of Conditionality," *Journal of International Development*, Vol. 9 (December), pp. 483–95.

———, Carlos N. Castel-Branco, and Richard Gerstner, 2005, *Perfect Partners? The Performance of Programme Aid Partners in Mozambique, 2004* (London: U.K. Department for International Development).

Knack, S., and A. Rahman, 2004, "Donor Fragmentation and Bureaucratic Quality in Aid Recipients," Policy Research Working Paper No. 3186 (Washington: World Bank).

Lensink, Robert, and Oliver Morrisey, 2000, "Aid Instability as a Measure of Uncertainty and the Positive Impact of Aid on Growth," *Journal of Development Studies*, Vol. 36 (February), pp. 31–49.

Lester, Pearson, 1969, *Partners in Development: Report of the Commission on International Development* (New York: Praeger).

Martens, B., 2005, "Why Do Aid Agencies Exist?" *Development Policy Review*, Vol. 23 (November), pp. 643–63.

Mozambique, Government of, and Program Aid Partners, 2004, "Joint Review, Agreed Between the Government of Mozambique and the Program Aid Partners" (Maputo).

———, 2004b, "Memorandum of Understanding between the Government of Mozambique and Program Aid Partners for the Provision of Direct Budget and Balance of Payments Support" (Maputo).

———, 2004c, "Mid-Year Review, Agreed Between the Government of Mozambique and the Program Aid Partners" (Maputo).

———, 2005a, "Joint Review, Agreed Between the Government of Mozambique and the Program Aid Partners" (Maputo).

———, 2005b, "Mid-Year Review, Agreed Between the Government of Mozambique and the Program Aid Partners" (Maputo).

———, 2006a, "Joint Review, Agreed Between the Government of Mozambique and the Program Aid Partners" (Maputo).

———, 2006b, "Mid-Year Review, Agreed Between the Government of Mozambique and the Program Aid Partners" (Maputo).

———, 2007, "Joint Review, Agreed Between the Government of Mozambique and the Program Aid Partners" (Maputo).

Mozambique Ministry of Finance, 2000, "Relatório de Execução do Orçamento do Estado" (Maputo).

———, 2001, "Relatório de Execução do Orçamento do Estado" (Maputo).

———, 2002, "Relatório de Execução do Orçamento do Estado" (Maputo).

———, 2003, "Relatório de Execução do Orçamento do Estado" (Maputo).

———, 2004, "Relatório de Execução do Orçamento do Estado" (Maputo).

———, 2005, "Relatório de Execução do Orçamento do Estado" (Maputo).

———, 2006, "Relatório de Execução do Orçamento do Estado" (Maputo).

———, 2007, "Relatório de Execução do Orçamento do Estado" (Maputo).

Murshed, S. Mansoob, 2002, "Strategic Interaction and Donor Policy Determination in a Domestic Setting," WIDER Discussion Paper No. 2002/107 (Helsinki: United Nations University, World Institute for Development Economics Research).

———, 2006, "On the Nature of Third-Party Interaction with Recipients in Post-Conflict Mediation and Reform" (unpublished; Birmingham, United Kingdom: University of Birmingham).

Organization for Economic Cooperation and Development (OECD), 1996, *Shaping the 21st Century: The Contribution of Development Co-operation* (Paris: Development Assistance Committee). Available via the Internet: http://www.oecd.org/dataoecd/23/35/2508761.pdf

———, 2003, *Harmonising Donor Practices for Effective Aid Delivery*, DAC Guidelines and Reference Series (Paris: Development Assistance Committee). Available via the Internet: http://www.oecd.org/dataoecd/0/48/20896122.pdf

———, 2004a, "Survey on Harmonisation and Alignment" (Paris: Development Assistance Committee). Available via the Internet: http://www.oecd.org/document/61/0,2340,en_2649_201185_31659517_1_1_1_1,00.html

———, 2004b, "Survey on Harmonisation and Alignment: Mozambique" (Paris: Development Assistance Committee). Available via the Internet: http://www.oecd.org/dataoecd/53/46/34060251.pdf

———, 2005a, "Harmonisation, Alignment, Results: Report on Progress, Challenges and Opportunities" (Paris: Development Assistance Committee).

———, 2005b, *Paris Declaration on Aid Effectiveness* (Paris: Development Assistance Committee). Available via the Internet: http://www.oecd.org/dataoecd/11/41/34428351.pdf

———, 2006, *Harmonising Donor Practices for Effective Aid Delivery*, DAC Guidelines and Reference Series, Vol. 2, Budget Support, Sector Wide Approaches and Capacity Development in Public Financial Management (Paris: Development Assistance Committee). Available via the Internet: http://www.oecd.org/dataoecd/53/7/34583142.pdf

———, 2007a, *The 2006 Survey on Monitoring the Paris Declaration*, Vol. 1, Overview of the Results (Paris: Development Assistance Committee). Available via the Internet: http://www.oecd.org/document/52/0,2340,en_2649_15577209_36162932_1_1_1_1,00.html

———, 2007b, *The 2006 Survey on Monitoring the Paris Declaration*, Vol. 2, Country Chapters (Paris: Development Assistance Committee). Available via the Internet: http://www.oecd.org/document/52/0,3343,en_2649_3236398_38542068_1_1_1_1,00.html

Oxfam International, 2007, *Paying for People. Financing the Skilled Workers Needed to Deliver Health and Education Services for All*, Oxfam International Briefing Paper No. 98 (Oxford). Available via the Internet: http://www.oxfam.org/en/files/bp98_paying_for_people.pdf/download

Pallage, Stéphane, and Michel A. Robe, 2003, "On the Welfare Cost of Economic Fluctuations in Developing Countries," *International Economic Review*, Vol. 44 (May), pp. 677–98.

Roodman, D., 2004, "The Anarchy of Numbers: Aid, Development, and Cross-Country Empirics," CGD Working Paper No. 32 (Washington: Center for Global Development).

Sachs, J., 2005, *The End of Poverty: Economic Possibilities for Our Time* (New York: Penguin Press).

Strategic Partnership with Africa (SPA), 2005, "Survey of the Alignment of Budget Support and Balance of Payments Support with National PRS Processes," Vols. I and II (final draft) (Washington).

———, 2007, "Budget Support Survey, 2006" (Washington).

Svensson, J., 2000, "Foreign Aid and Rent-Seeking," *Journal of International Economics*, Vol. 51 (August), pp. 437–61.

Swedish International Development and Cooperation Agency (SIDA), 2006, "Supporting Team to Government and Donor Committee Review. Donor Cooperation Strategy with Mozambique" (unpublished; Stockholm).

Tarp, F., 2008, "Foreign Aid," in *The New Palgrave Dictionary of Economics*, ed. by S. Durlauf and L. Blume (Houndsmills, United Kingdom: Palgrave Macmillan, 2nd ed.).

U.K. Secretary of State for International Development, 1997, *Eliminating World Poverty: A Challenge for the 21st Century*, White Paper on International Development (London: The Stationery Office Ltd).

Ulens, Wim, 2006, "Harmonising Donor Practices for Effective Aid Delivery. Case of PFM Capacity Building in Mozambique" (unpublished; Brussels: Belgium Technical Cooperation).

UN Millennium Project, 2005, *Investing in Development: A Practical Plan to Achieve the Millennium Development Goals* (New York: United Nations Development Program).

World Bank, 1998, *Assessing Aid: What Works, What Doesn't and Why* (New York: Oxford University Press).

———, 1999, *A Proposal for a Comprehensive Development Framework* (Washington).

———, 2003, *World Development Report 2004: Making Services Work for Poor People* (New York: Oxford University Press).

———, 2005, *2005 CDF Progress Report: Enabling Country Capacity to Achieve Results* (Washington).

———, 2006a, *Budget Support as More Effective Aid? Recent Experiences and Emerging Lessons* (Washington: World Bank).

———, 2006b, *Donor Harmonization in Mozambique* (unpublished; Washington). Available via the Internet: http://siteresources.worldbank.org/MOZAMBIQUEEXTN/Resources/MozambiqueFINALDecember112006.pdf

8

Managing Mineral Resources: From Curse to Blessing

JULIEN HARTLEY AND JAMES OTTO

Attempts to explain the relationship between a country's natural resource endowments and its economic performance have generated a significant body of literature highlighting the risk that resource abundance may not only have an adverse impact on growth but may also, in many cases, contribute to corruption and social unrest. The so-called resource curse is not inevitable, however. While there are many examples of poor management of resource wealth, a range of countries (including Botswana, Canada, Chile, Malaysia, and Norway) appear to have avoided the resource curse through prudent and transparent resource management practices. Thus, the key question for a large number of countries is how they can turn their abundant resources into a blessing, rather than a curse, using them to set off a virtuous cycle of economic growth, development, and poverty reduction.

The extraction of mineral resources in large international projects—megaprojects—plays a dominant role in the economies of many developing countries, as a source both of export earnings and, to a lesser extent, of infrastructure development. But the most important impact of mineral extraction may be fiscal, the taxation of mining projects being a major source of government revenue. To ensure that the state receives an appropriate share of the economic rent from these projects, fiscal regimes must be well designed, with special care given to balancing the desire to maximize short-term revenue against any deterrent effects this may have on investment.

Mozambique is a resource-rich country that has so far avoided the resource curse, but significant resource-related fiscal revenues have yet to be generated. The country changed its economic regime in the 1990s, shifting from socialism to market-oriented policies. Accordingly, it has revised its fiscal regime from one that was inward-looking to one designed to attract foreign direct investment. In this regard, Mozambique can be seen as a success story. However, the future of its extractive industries' contribution to growth and poverty alleviation will crucially depend on the adoption of a comprehensive, uniform fiscal regime and a transparent policy framework that will allow Mozambique to avoid the curse and reap the benefits of its resource wealth. Recently adopted tax legislation and steps to improve revenue transparency seem to indicate that the country is moving in the right direction.

In the next section we review the literature on the resource curse, after which we analyze the main fiscal policy elements needed to turn the curse into a blessing. We then look at Mozambique's progress through different phases, including the reforms in 2007, in creating a virtuous cycle, and in the last section we draw lessons for other developing countries.

Literature Survey

Common sense would indicate that large revenues from mineral resources should, in principle, be an engine of growth, generate wealth, and, ultimately, alleviate poverty. We would expect this to be particularly true for developing countries rich in mineral resources. Yet much of the economic literature has focused on the possibility that these resources might be the cause of the developing countries' poor macroeconomic performance and are thus a curse, not a blessing. Some authors have even suggested that countries would be better off avoiding export-oriented extractive industries altogether (Ross, 2001). Moreover, empirical studies have shown that resource-rich countries have performed worse in terms of growth and poverty reduction than countries without these endowments. While most of this strand of literature has focused on the negative impacts of mineral resources, some work has been done on what a country needs to do to get things right (Gocht, Zantop, and Eggert, 1988; Gelb and Associates, 1988; and Tilton, 1992).

The theory that the production and export of minerals could hobble growth originated in the field of development economics in the early 1950s, in studies focused on the deterioration of the terms of trade (Prebisch, 1950). The literature from this period predicted that declining revenues would result in declining imports of capital goods, thus constraining investment. In addition, there would be fewer backward and forward linkages between primary exports and the rest of the economy (a concept developed by Hirschman, 1958) than between exports of manufactured goods and the economy.

With the first oil shock of the 1970s, attention shifted to oil-exporting countries, generating a body of literature concerned with the "Dutch disease" effect of oil, gas, and mineral resources. The term "Dutch disease" was coined in the 1960s in connection with the harmful impact on the Dutch economy of the huge increase in the Netherlands' wealth after the discovery of large natural gas deposits in the North Sea. As the Dutch guilder became stronger in real terms, the country's non-oil exports became less competitive, and the non-mineral tradable manufactures sector contracted. The ultimate result was deindustrialization.

Over time, the use of the term has broadened to encompass all poor macroeconomic performance related to the resource curse. Much of the empirical work in this area has found evidence of a negative relationship between growth rates and natural resource abundance. A much-quoted empirical study by Sachs and Warner (1997) found that over a 20-year period (1970–90) a sample of 95 resource-abundant developing countries had slower growth than resource-scarce developing countries. The authors did not offer any single explanation for this phenomenon, nor did they suggest any specific policies that countries could follow to avoid the resource curse. In general, much of the criticism of this empirical work has focused on the methodological approach or the period chosen rather than on the authors' conclusions.

Some studies have focused on the definition of natural resource abundance. For instance, Stijns (2005) found that the Sachs-Warner result is not robust "to changes in the measure of natural-resource abundance from trade-flows to reserves or production" and that natural resource abundance has not been a significant structural determinant of economic growth.

Some of the empirical work has focused on mineral-exporting countries. For instance, Auty and Mikesell (1998) compared the economic performances of mineral-exporting countries with those of other developing countries with different natural resource endowments and found that the first group underperformed, compared with the second, especially the resource-scarce developing countries. However, they also noted that underperformance was not inevitable but could be avoided if countries implemented the right macroeconomic policies.

One of the macroeconomic explanations for the resource curse has focused on revenue volatility. For instance, Auty and Mikesell (1998) noted that minerals are "more subject to world price fluctuations than are manufactures or services." The volatility is greater in "mineral-led economies" where the largest share of government revenues is derived from mineral taxation. This volatility, in turn, makes it difficult for governments to pursue a prudent fiscal policy. Too often, windfalls are consumed rather than invested during export booms and, because of political pressure, governments maintain expenditures at the same level during downturns, resulting in deficit spending and increased indebtedness.

The nature of the mining sector has also been analyzed. Often it has been argued that large-scale mining is an enclave activity, where the extraction of minerals requires large, durable, location-specific investments. For megaprojects, inputs are usually imported, very little value added is produced domestically, and much of the ore or concentrate is exported. In addition, modern large-scale mining operations have a high capital-to-labor ratio and, initially, even the few skilled workers employed come from abroad. Further, there are very few positive externalities to forward and backward industries (Hirschman, 1958; and United Nations Economic and Social Council, 1998), and learning by doing is not as important as in manufacturing. The main benefits the country gets from megaprojects usually come through the fiscal linkage and the emplacement of infrastructure. In contrast to megaprojects, smaller-scale mining, such as in the quarry sector, can have substantial linkages to the economy but limited impact on macroeconomic indicators.

Large revenue inflows from extractive industries may encourage rent-seeking and corruption in the ruling elite. Considerable resources may be devoted to obtaining control of these rents, which, in the end, will lower income and welfare while leading to distortionary economic policies (Torvik, 2002). Sala-i-Martin and Subramanian (2003) found that "oil and mineral resources in particular exert a negative and nonlinear impact on growth via their deleterious impact on institutional quality." The policy implication is that revenues should be distributed directly to citizens. More recently, Hodler (2006) found that the positive income aspect of natural resource endowment holds only in homogeneous countries, not in fractionalized ones.

In general, much of the resource-curse literature has focused on problems rather than on solutions and does not explain differences in outcomes between countries that have suffered from the resource curse and ones that have not. Apart from some extreme views (Ross, 2001), it has been recognized that some developing countries have benefited from their mineral endowment while others have not. As a result, as noted by Davis and Tilton (2005), "one uniform policy toward all mining in the developing world is not desirable." For them the right public policy question is "not should we or should we not promote mining in the developing countries, but rather where should we encourage it and how can we ensure that it contributes as much as possible to economic development and poverty alleviation" (see also International Council on Mining and Metals (ICMM), 2006). Stijns (2005) also noted that "the story behind the effect of natural resources on economic growth is a complex one that typical growth regressions do not capture well." Finally, it appears that there is no single reason certain countries manage to turn their endowment into a blessing instead of a curse.

Although there is no consensus on the reasons behind the few successes, agreement has emerged on the importance of transparent and prudent management of tax revenues from mining projects and of public understanding of the policies and framework adopted by the government. Recently, a case study of some success stories (Botswana, Chile) confirmed that mining may affect national poverty levels primarily through fiscal and consumption linkages (ICMM, 2006), especially in developing countries where economic linkages and the impact on employment may be limited both because of capacity constraints and because of the capital-intensive nature of mining projects. A few governments have prudently saved and invested surplus revenues during booms, setting up stabilization funds that allow them to smooth spending and continue funding social programs and investment needs during downturns.

From Curse to Virtuous Cycle

At the national level, mining can contribute to poverty reduction indirectly, by providing the government with revenue, provided that government policies ensure the sound use of revenues for poverty alleviation programs and that these programs are efficient. The design of a comprehensive fiscal regime for the mining sector is crucial so that the state, which is usually the resource owner, can receive the appropriate share of the economic rents generated by the sector. In addition, prudent and transparent management of resource revenues is needed to ensure fiscal sustainability.

General Principles for a Mineral Sector Fiscal Regime

Mining is a global activity, and international investors have many countries to choose from. As a result, a country's fiscal regime for minerals

Table 8.1. Ranking of Investment Criteria at the Exploration/Mining Investment Stage

Ranking		
Exploration stage	Mining stage	Decision criteria
1	n.a.	Geological potential for target mineral
2	3	**Measure of profitability**
3	1	Security of tenure
4	2	Ability to repatriate profits
5	9	Consistency and constancy of mineral policies
6	7	Company has management control
7	11	Mineral ownership
8	6	Realistic foreign exchange regulations
9	4	Stability of exploration/mining terms
10	5	**Ability to predetermine tax liability**
11	8	Ability to predetermine environmental obligations
12	10	**Stability of fiscal regime**
13	12	Ability to raise external financing
14	16	Long-term national stability
15	17	Established mineral titles system
16	n.a.	Ability to apply geological assessment techniques
17	13	**Method and level of tax levies**
18	15	Import-export policies
19	18	Majority equity ownership held by company
20	21	Right to transfer ownership
21	20	Internal (armed) conflicts
22	14	Permitted external accounts
23	19	Modern mineral legislation

Source: Otto (1992).

cannot be too far out of line with the regimes of countries with competing deposits. Generally, nations with prospective geology, reasonable and stable tax terms, acceptable legislation, and political stability have brighter prospects for long-term mineral sector development than those that fail to meet one or more of these criteria, each of which will be considered by companies analyzing long-term investment decisions (see Table 8.1). If political risk is high, a country can make itself more attractive to investors by strengthening macroeconomic and fiscal stability. Governments can take actions to minimize risk, which, in turn will reduce the supply price of investment and increase the amount of economic rent that can be taxed without discouraging investment.

As shown in Table 8.1, in a survey undertaken by the United Nations the fiscal regime is one key criterion that investors take into account. Of investors' top 10 criteria, all but one—geological potential—are in some way related to, or affected by, the regulatory system. Of the top 20, four are related to taxation: measure of profitability, ability to predetermine tax liability, stability of the fiscal regime, and method and level of tax levies.

International best practice has tended to favor comprehensive fiscal regimes that are largely embodied in general tax laws, that take features specific to mining into account, and that are comprehensively set out in government policy statements. In principle, policies underlying such regimes should be stated openly to the public, and the tax treatment of the mining industry should be subject to normal budgetary and public scrutiny. The overriding transparency objective should be to move toward a clear definition of the fiscal regime and reduce discretionary options.

In practice, a wide spectrum of regimes are in place because the mining sector is considered unique as a high-risk and, depending on commodity price cycles, occasionally a high- or no-return sector, and special tax treatments are often devised. The result is frequently a complex fiscal regime and—especially in Africa—great scope for discretionary arrangements set up on a case-by-case basis. The farther the tax system governing the mining sector is from the general tax laws, the greater the degree of discrimination. Such discrimination can be (1) by sector—for example, all mines being subject to a tax not imposed on other types of activities; (2) by subsector—for example, a special incentive for gravel mines producing less than 1 million tons a year; or (3) project-based, such as an individual mine operating under a negotiated tax agreement. The extent to which mines are taxed specially will depend on the government's desire to provide tax uniformity or to take into account special attributes.

Uniqueness of the Mining Sector

The justification often given for setting up a different fiscal regime for the mining sector is the special role played by economic rent—the difference between the existing market price for a commodity and the opportunity cost of engaging in supply—in this sector. Economic rent appears as a surplus that is not required to motivate desired economic behavior and that could therefore be taxed without altering resource allocation, while the opportunity cost consists of all necessary costs of production, including an ex ante minimum return to capital required to induce investment. The return on investment should cover the cost of exploration, development, and production; the cost of capital; and a risk premium for both sovereign and project risks.

In theory, a fiscal system with rent as the tax base will come closest to tax neutrality. Because a resource rent tax appropriates only returns in excess of the producer's opportunity cost of capital, it does not distort investment and can be considered superior to other fiscal instruments, such as royalties. In principle, governments can tax rent without affecting the input of effort and sacrifice. In practice, however, no nation taxes mineral producers based solely on rent, whose value is difficult to determine. Most governments lack the ability to measure and audit it. The trade-off for governments is to establish a fiscal regime that captures a fair share of resource rent through traditional types of taxes and methods without driving away potential investors. At present, countries vary widely in the degree to which they utilize taxes to appropriate rent. In a number of countries, the taxation of petroleum is more oriented toward capturing rents than is the taxation of mines. This is particularly true of many production-sharing agreements in which the concept of "cost oil" and "profit oil" help identify and distribute rent to stakeholders.

What distinguishes mineral extraction projects from other types of projects is the high degree of uncertainty regarding investment outcomes, particularly in view of the large amount of capital involved (see Box 8.1).

Specificities of Mineral Fiscal Regimes

Maximizing short-term versus long-term fiscal revenues

A fundamental fiscal policy question for governments is whether the primary tax objective is to maximize the fiscal take in the short term or to grow the tax base through increased investment in the long term (see Box 8.2). If the goal is short-term maximization, the system needs a high effective tax rate (EFT)—the share of the present value of all taxes and fees paid by the mine divided by the present value of pretax net cash flow. If the EFT is high, individual mines pay more, but in the long run there will be fewer mines, thus fewer taxpayers, a smaller tax base, and a smaller contribution to the treasury. If a nation has untapped and largely unexplored minerals potential, a policy that emphasizes attracting new investors that will discover and build more taxpaying mines is clearly a better strategic choice. This concept is illustrated in Figure 8.1. If the EFT is too low, the government will needlessly forgo fiscal revenues. If it is too high, the tax base will not grow over time and revenues will be forgone (companies will not come, explore, and discover more mines). Good tax policy will strive to set the effective tax rate at T^*, where an optimal balance is found. For most nations, the optimal EFT for mines is usually between 40 and 50 percent. The EFT for petroleum projects ranges widely but is often much higher than for mining.

Recent experience suggests that the effective tax rate—the combined impact of taxes and fees—in the mining sector (other than diamonds) is unlikely to go above 50–60 percent, and that the EFT is 40–50 percent in countries actively seeking exploration and development.

Box 8.1. Characteristics Unique to the Mining Sector

The following attributes distinguish mining enterprises from other types of projects:

- There is a lengthy period of exploration during which there is high risk and no revenue.
- The amount of capital required during the development and construction phase is lumpy and proportionately larger than in most other businesses.
- Once the mine is built, the capital is captive and not transportable.
- Equipment tends to be specialized and available from only a few manufacturers worldwide, and must be imported.
- Mines may have long lives and be subject to regime changes and policy instability.
- Revenues are cyclical as commodity prices, determined by global markets, move up and down, more so than is experienced by most other businesses.
- The scale of operations can be very small or very large.
- Large costs are incurred at the time the project closes and reclamation is completed.
- Substantial costs unrelated to production may be incurred, such as investment in community infrastructure or programs.

State equity participation

Today, most governments do not take an equity interest in mining projects. Such an interest is viewed very negatively by almost all mineral sector investors. And, from a purely financial perspective, taking a stake in mining projects is risky, since governments cannot know if they are making a good investment. Taxation is more likely to maximize government revenue flows than an equity interest, given that future dividends may never be paid. In addition, potential governance issues could arise when the government is acting both as a shareholder and as a regulator. As a result, improvements in mining tax systems have prompted governments to focus on risk-free tax measures rather than on risk-prone equity as the primary means of reaping financial benefits.

There are many different ways governments can take an equity stake in mining projects, but the three that have dominated over the past two decades are paid (working) interest; free interest equity; and, more rarely, carried interest equity (government free equity requirements are very rare today). Of the three, a free equity share more closely resembles a tax than

Box 8.2. Mineral Fiscal Regimes—Common Features

Optimal fiscal regimes can be achieved through different tax combinations. The specific design of a regime has an impact on project profitability and risk sharing and, therefore, the impact on the government and investors must be carefully assessed. Mineral fiscal regimes vary greatly across countries but they do share common features.

Direct taxes

- Normal corporate income tax (25–35 percent), but with the valuation basis calculated taking into account special features of the mineral sector, such as its capital intensity. Most nations allow capital assets to be depreciated on an accelerated basis. Thin capitalization rules are often imposed to cap debt interest deductions. Tax holidays, a feature of mineral sector fiscal systems several decades ago, have fallen into disfavor and are now rare.
- Moderate withholding taxes on dividends and interest payments (10–20 percent). For a foreign-owned profitable mine, withholding tax will be one of the three largest taxes paid, along with income tax and royalty. Withholding tax, when required to be paid by the mineral project, is deductible in many mineral-producing nations.
- Tax accounts are usually not ring-fenced project by project, unless a project is subject to a negotiated agreement that includes fiscal terms.

Indirect taxes

- Royalties of about 2 to 3 percent for metals, imposed on the sales value. While some nations use a netback value as the royalty basis, this introduces administrative challenges because verification and auditing of deductible costs is beyond the capacity of tax authorities in most developing nations. Likewise, care is taken to avoid transfer-pricing situations where less than the full value of the product sold is reported for royalty and tax purposes. This is particularly relevant where sales are to affiliates, or to processors in duty-free zones.
- Mineral projects are usually exempted from paying import and export duties on goods, or such duties are zero-rated or low.
- Value-added taxes on inputs and sales are often not imposed or benefit from crediting or refund schemes that negate their impact.

a return on government capital. If a government takes an equity stake and pays for it through a working interest, the opportunity cost can be substantial. State revenues invested in the mine will be diverted from other

Figure 8.1. Optimal Effective Tax Rate
(In percent)

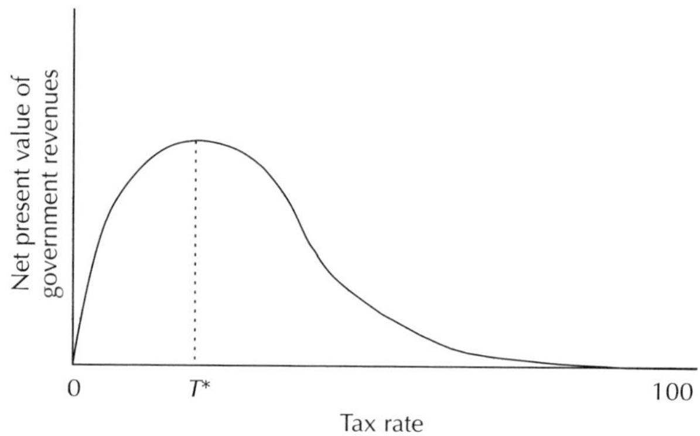

Source: Otto and others (2006).

possible uses and put at risk. Not all mines are successful; some fail or do not generate sufficient profits to justify a distribution to shareholders. The primary motivation for state participation is often a government's desire to demonstrate ownership and control rather than to maximize revenues. Ideally, government involvement in the sector through equity participation should be fully disclosed to the public and the implications clearly stated. In practice, particularly in Africa, many agreements that establish state participation in mining projects are confidential.

Nontax fiscal benefits of mineral projects

It is important to recognize that mineral titleholders contribute more to the economy than just tax revenues: nonfiscal economic linkages can confer greater benefits on host countries than taxes. While some, perhaps most, of the sums spent on megaproject capital and operating costs may go to foreign entities, governments can greatly influence the amount spent inside the country. Because of an economic multiplier effect, this, in turn, can have an even larger impact than the actual revenues received and spent by the government. Statutory law or mining agreements may require that foreign companies invest in local communities, develop infrastructure (or pay user fees), hire a certain percentage of their workers locally, or buy power from a local company at a given rate. Distribution of revenues to local governments can also be embodied in law to avoid fractional conflict. In addition, companies can have separate contracts with the communities affected by their projects or be required to set up programs with local suppliers for value addition.

At the local level, forward and backward linkages as well as job creation can contribute to economic development and poverty alleviation. Mining and processing companies can be encouraged or required to use local suppliers as well as public-private partnerships for the provision of infrastructure and inputs such as power and water. To maintain competitiveness, such programs need to be based on the ability of local enterprises to provide goods and services under competitive conditions. It is increasingly common for countries to require, either by law or by agreement, a local sourcing effort. Even though such linkages are encouraged, in many countries linkage requirements have been difficult to implement.

For instance, a cornerstone of Botswana's mineral policy and a key element in the country's economic development has been to avoid an enclave situation and to plan infrastructure that promotes regional linkages and broader development. The development of mine-related infrastructure has provided the country not only with the capacity to accommodate other industries but has also been a source of revenue for the water and power companies, as is illustrated by the Selbi-Pikwe nickel-copper mine project. The mine turned out to be subeconomic and rarely paid any tax, including royalties (royalties were assessed on operating profits rather than on sales). However, even though the mine added little to the national treasury, it has been a substantial springboard for development, paying for critical parts of the national infrastructure through user fees, which often exceeded the income from royalties and fees. Chile has also developed strong linkages between the copper mining industry and the local economy.

Model mining agreements and stability clauses

Investors in megaprojects want assurances that they will not be subject to changes in the fiscal regime that could be detrimental to them, in particular when taking into account the sunk costs of their up-front investment. They may therefore seek an agreement with stability clauses that freeze the tax system as of the date the agreement is signed. However, mining agreements between the state and the mineral companies are not always needed when a complete and historically stable mineral sector statutory system is in place. While some nations negotiate each megaproject agreement on an ad hoc basis, other nations negotiate based on a model agreement. Model agreements do not have to supersede statutory law but, rather, can complement and supplement it. Many developing countries provide a form of stabilization, and a model agreement can be a useful way in which to document the fiscal system being stabilized. Care should be taken in such an agreement to avoid stabilization of the entire fiscal system and to stabilize only discrete taxes and rates. In any case, stability clauses should be disclosed to the public along with their potential implications. As a country's legal and fiscal systems develop and stabilize, the need for special agreements lessens.

Institutional strengthening

Large mining companies generally have experts on staff with specialized knowledge of the industry as well as training or experience in negotiation strategies, techniques, and approaches. In contrast, many developing nations do not have officers trained and skilled in megaproject negotiations and may lack the resources or the political will to bring in outside experts. Government negotiators who are well trained or assisted by experts would be better able to maximize nontax benefits, minimize tax losses, and understand which terms should be negotiated and which should be rigidly defined in a model agreement or left to statutory law. Project financial (fiscal) analysis is a key part of project negotiations unless tax terms are not open to negotiation. Without a financial (fiscal) model for understanding the magnitude of the taxes forgone or secured, policymakers may make mistakes. A financial model typically comprises spreadsheets that estimate all cash flows for the project, including revenues and all costs. It incorporates the principal taxes, fees, and other payments to government as well as tax deductions, credits, and other incentives. Such models can be used to understand the implications of each tax type and incentive individually for both government and investor cash flows as well as determine whether the overall tax take is reasonable. Fiscal models are also useful for revenue forecasting. For example, in Botswana:

> the negotiation of agreements by the government has been done after a major discovery is known and after the government has been able to build a financial model of the planned mining development. Government analysis includes an estimation of the internal rate of return to the investor in both current and constant terms and also estimates the government's net present value of revenues for different fiscal regimes. The government places considerable importance on having effective representation on the board of directors of major mining companies and has generally placed professionals, not figureheads, on the boards to represent its interests. Representatives appointed by the government are senior civil servants. Financial, legal, and technical experts are included on the team that advises government directors prior to, and where necessary, during each mining company board meeting. Government officials have not played a "rubber stamp" role on important issues and

have thus succeeded in influencing board decisions on issues that are important to the government.[1]

By the same token, Chile put a strong institutional framework in place to prevent capture of economic policy by special interest groups and to strengthen the governance and transparency of the mining sector.

Revenue transparency and management

It has been mentioned above that revenue and expenditure transparency can play a role in avoiding the resource curse. Some resource-rich nations have chosen not to negotiate fiscal terms but instead to rely on general laws; others make negotiated terms open to public scrutiny. However, some nations still keep negotiated terms secret, and most governments do not provide a direct link between revenues derived from megaprojects and expenditure. This may change in the near future. The Extractive Industries Transparency Initiative (EITI) is aimed directly at defeating the resource curse by improving transparency and accountability in resource-rich countries through the full publication and verification of company payments and government revenues from the oil, gas, and mining sectors. Implementing EITI as part of a program of improved governance can help ensure that revenues from extractive industries contribute to sustainable development and poverty reduction by holding decision makers accountable for the use of those revenues.

The following principles guarantee the transparency of revenue flows to the government and can contribute to improved governance in public financial management:

- Regular reporting, in an agreed format, of all payments by companies (including state-owned enterprises) to all levels of government and of all revenues received at all levels of government;
- Independent audits, applying international auditing standards, of payments and revenues; reconciliation of any discrepancies by an independent administrator; and public dissemination of this information on a regular and consistent basis;
- Engagement of civil society in monitoring the process and ex post independent external validation to enhance credibility.

However, the mining sector's contribution to sustainable development is an even bigger issue than revenue transparency. The advantage of the EITI is the simplicity of its approach. It can be a good starting point for a country seeking to improve the transparency of revenue flows from the

[1]Johnson (1981, p. 353).

sector, increase the potential to defeat the curse, and make sustainable development a priority. In that regard, revenue transparency should also be linked to how and where revenues are used. If the issue of revenue transparency is not linked to the broader objective of using the funds derived from mining to promote sustainable development in a particular area or country, then transparency is not particularly useful to the mining industry. Consequently, priority should also be given to establishing clear policies for the use of resource revenues. Many nations now dedicate a portion of mineral revenues to special uses (for example, the development funds established by Ghana and Namibia), or for distribution to local governments or communities affected by the projects (for example, Brazil, Indonesia, Mozambique, Papua New Guinea, Peru, and the Philippines). The disbursement of earmarked mineral revenues can be a challenge for governments. While it works well in some countries, such as Brazil, other countries, such as Peru and Indonesia, have encountered operational difficulties. Clear fiscal rules associated with revenue stabilization and expenditure based on mining revenues, and transparency in the use of mineral rents—in particular, disclosure to the public—have helped Chile avoid governance issues.

Mineral Resource Development and Megaprojects in Mozambique

Most of Mozambique's abundant natural resources are untapped, and the country has a favorable geology for exploration and mining activities. It has world-class deposits of minerals, sands, and coal as well as other identified resources, including bauxite, bentonite, beryl, brick clay, diatomite, gold, granite, graphite, kaolin, limestone, marble, nickel, semiprecious stones (amethyst, aquamarine, emerald, garnet, rose quartz, tourmaline), tantalite, tin, uranium, natural gas, and oil. There is substantial undeveloped hydropower potential in addition to the existing Cahora Bassa Dam, which produces most of Mozambique's electricity. Moreover, the country benefits from a good geographical location and is well served by major rivers and several deep sea ports.

Since independence, Mozambique has gone through two phases, and is about to enter a third phase, with respect to its strategy for investment in the mineral sector. The first phase, from 1979 to 1985, focused on state ownership of mines in line with the socialist political regime at the time, resulting in declining production and low investment. The second phase, from 1986 to 2006, aimed at private ownership with generous fiscal exemptions. After years of isolation from the rest of the world, Mozambique's main goal during this phase was to attract foreign investment through case-by-case negotiation of fiscal terms. Initially, this led to a complex and opaque fiscal regime with considerable discretion. In 2002, Mozambique enacted a series of new laws aimed at simplifying and rationalizing the tax code. Mozambique was indeed successful, judging by the volume of foreign investment it was able to attract in a relatively short time. The trade-off, however, has been negligible or low tax revenue generation. This situation will change during the third phase, following the enactment of the new mining fiscal regime in 2007 and the development of a new model mining agreement, as the country adopts a comprehensive fiscal regime similar to that of other mineral-producing countries and encourages private ownership of mines.

Aside from the extraction of gas and the processing of imported alumina, mineral production is presently at a low level but is expected to increase rapidly as projects in the feasibility and development phase commence production. These projects will exploit deposits that have been known for decades, but the high level of current exploration bodes well for the discovery of new resources.

State Ownership and the Socialist Experience, 1979–85

After independence Mozambique had a government with Marxist leanings, which nationalized most of the privately held mines. Between 1979 and 1985, the production of most minerals declined (see Table 8.2). This was attributable to the deterioration of both the security situation and other operating conditions.

The state enterprises attempted to operate but faced increasingly difficult structural issues, including a highly regulated, centrally planned economy with little scope for planning at the enterprise level, little or no reward for entrepreneurship, and a low priority on profitability; an overvalued currency that discouraged exports and reduced export earnings; foreign exchange reserves that were insufficient for purchasing the equipment and spares necessary not only for expansion and modernization but even for maintenance of capacity; and an inflexible labor and wage system that set wages and levels of employment and did not reward efficiency.

From independence to 1983, two-thirds of the country was systematically investigated and geological, geophysical, and geochemical maps became available. During the mid-1980s the ministry responsible for mines, which was cut off from most field operations by the country's civil war, began targeted marketing and published and distributed a number of specialized reports with the intention of attracting investors from specific countries, such as Japan and the United States. Given the security situation at the time, the marketing effort was unsuccessful. The devastating

Table 8.2. Production of Mineral Commodities, 1973–85
(Metric tons unless otherwise specified)

	1973	1975	1977	1979	1981	1983	1985
Asbestos	150	191	0	789	1,424	0	55
Bentonite	2,990	1,400	2,643	1,657	716	1,455	361
Coal	394,000	575,000	288,000	320,000	535,000	59,000	20,000
Coking	216,000	316,000	178,000	105,000	167,000	30,000	n.a.
Steam	178,000	259,000	147,000	95,000	163,000	28,000	n.a.
Copper[1]	3,175	3,224	0	1,125	880	1,189	590
Feldspar	830	0	815	585	775	696	67
Garnets							
Gem	4	2	2	1	2	1	1
Waste	7	7	6	8	11	10	7
Kaolin	100	119	201	139	297	292	152
Marble (m^3)	368	0	0	304	167	406	714
Mica, waste	280	900	432	101	300	309	n.a.
Microlite	54	51	41	35	49	23	6
Stone (m^3)	200	197	200	192	579	417	n.a.
Tantalite[2]	30	51	38	24	34	22	4
Ta^2O^5	33	40	32	29	46	21	n.a.

Source: Jordan (1986).
[1]Concentrate, 20 percent Cu.
[2]Concentrate.

civil war that began in earnest in 1981 resulted in a collapse of production and the destruction of physical infrastructure.

Attracting Foreign Direct Investment and Shifting to Private Ownership, 1986–2006

After the civil war, Mozambique attempted to attract investment by granting generous tax benefits to compensate investors on an ad hoc basis for the risks arising from the high degree of uncertainty resulting from years of central planning, state ownership, and civil war. Then, as Mozambique became a new player in southern Africa, the country progressively improved its fiscal regime in line with that of countries with competing mineral and gas deposits. Significant progress was achieved in simplifying and modernizing the tax system. In particular, investment tax incentives, which were previously provided through a plethora of different laws and regulations and other means, were rationalized in 2002 with the adoption of a comprehensive Code of Tax Benefits for Investment and the Corporate Income Tax code (IRPC).[2]

[2]Decree 16/2002. For a comprehensive description of the changes in the fiscal regime, see International Monetary Fund, "Tax and Customs Reforms in Mozambique: An Overview,"

In 1987 the government embarked on a comprehensive and well-sequenced set of reforms to create a socioeconomic environment that would open the country to foreign direct investment (FDI) and promote the development of the private sector. A strong motivation in attracting FDI was to put Mozambique back on the map and showcase the country to other potential investors in the hope of significantly accelerating economic growth. Of critical importance to potential investors was the decision by the ruling party, Front for the Liberation of Mozambique (FRELIMO), to formally abandon Marxism in 1989 and embrace the role of the private sector. The new constitution adopted in 1990 provided for multiparty elections and a free market economy.[3]

In line with this strategy, the government considered that foreign investors would bring not only capital but also knowledge and would contribute to learning by doing as the country recovered from the civil war, which had isolated it from the rest of the world. In addition, the government believed that megaprojects would develop backward and forward linkages as well as positive labor externalities, creating jobs for the local labor force. However, until the civil war ended in 1989, the mineral sector remained unattractive to investors.

The government adopted its first mining law in 1986.[4] The licensing authority was granted the power to enter into exploration and mining agreements that could supplement, but not conflict with, the mining law. The mining law was mainly a framework that provided basic licensing rights and assorted fiscal incentives; the intent was that details would be negotiated case by case. The law provided the state with the option of reserving areas for operation only by state enterprises or ventures with state participation.

In 1993 a new Investment Act was passed, and in 1997 the Investment Promotion Center (CPI) was created with the mandate of promoting and facilitating national and foreign investment in Mozambique. With the assistance of the Commonwealth Secretariat during 1992–94, a model contract and general fiscal system for mining were proposed but never implemented. In 1999 legislation on industrial free zones (IFZs) was adopted. A tax benefit code was approved that remained in effect with few changes until 2002.

---

in *Mozambique: Selected Issues and Statistical Appendix,* IMF Country Report No. 05/311. Available via the Internet: www.imf.org/external/pubs/cat/longres.cfm?sk=18529.0

[3]United States Department of State, *Background Note: Mozambique,* https://www.state.gov/r/pa/ei/bgn/7035.htm, accessed May 14, 2007.

[4]Mining Law No. 2/86 of April 16, 1986.

The ministry responsible for mining commissioned a detailed mineral sector fiscal study (Otto, 2002), which provided the basis for detailed draft mineral sector tax regulations. The draft regulations were completed in 2002 and revised in 2004, but they were not promulgated. This created a challenge for Mozambique's government, as each major new investor sought to negotiate an agreement advantageous to its project with terms that were at least as favorable as those granted to prior investors. As a result, during this period fiscal systems were negotiated case by case within the context of mining agreements subject to general tax law and special incentives. These laws provided incentives unlike those in other mining nations and, lacking sufficient detail and protective provisions, led to some agreements that were arguably unbalanced in favor of investors—for example, agreements that allowed mining companies to sell mine output to affiliated processing companies located in free trade zones not subject to income tax. Under such agreements, sales between affiliates were specifically allowed to be valued at transfer prices resulting in low or no profits subject to income tax. Unfortunately, fiscal models were not available to guide policymakers in these negotiations.

Two major pieces of legislation were adopted in 2002: a new mining law[5] and a new tax benefit code designed to attract foreign investment and which provided tax incentives to qualifying investors.[6] Subsequently, in 2003 mining licensing regulations were promulgated.

The new mining law was well timed—it took effect just as a worldwide boom in mineral exploration was beginning. The law considerably improved governance in the sector with a nondiscretionary and transparent system for managing mining licenses and created the Mining Cadastre based on a "first come, first served" basis (see Table 8.3). As a result, it considerably reduced the discretionary power of the government and, by increasing transparency, improved security for potential investors. By 2006, Mozambique's known world-class deposits of mineral sands and coal were under license for mining development, and almost all geologically attractive ground was licensed for exploration (see Table 8.4).

Mozambique's main policy following its socialist phase was to establish an attractive socioeconomic environment favorable to the development of the domestic private sector and to foreign direct investment. One of the main vehicles for implementing this policy was the use of negotiated agreements and fiscal incentives. In contrast to some other mining

[5]Mining Law No. 14/2002 of 26 June 2002; and Mining Law Regulations, Decree No. 28/2003 of 17 June 2003.

[6]Fiscal Benefits Code, Decree No. 16/2002 of 27 June 2002.

Table 8.3. Number of Mining Titles by Type, 2002–07

	2002/03	2003/04	2004/05	2005/06	2006/07
Reconnaissance license	0	3	5	43	38
Exploration license	69	127	172	362	312
Mining license	25	19	30	22	18
Mining certificate	4	42	24	27	20

Source: Mozambique, Ministry of Mineral Resources.

countries—such as Indonesia, Papua New Guinea, and the Philippines—there was no application before 2007 of a uniform model mining agreement. An important purpose of a model agreement is to reduce, to the greatest extent possible, the number of clauses subject to negotiation so as to avoid case-by-case negotiations and derogations to the common law. Although such a model agreement was drafted by the government in 2000, individual agreements did not conform to it.

Special exemptions and tax reductions were negotiated for each project, and, as a result, the government will receive less in fiscal revenues from these projects than is typical in most other countries. Negotiations were hampered by the government's lack of capacity to use financial models to measure and understand the implications of fiscal incentives. The 2000 model mining agreement was originally envisaged as a means to supplement, not supersede, existing laws, including the mining law, but the final version of the 2002 mining law that emerged from parliament removed restrictions on subject matter, thus opening the way for the minister responsible for mines to exercise a great deal of control over the fiscal content of the agreements. Additionally, Mozambique's Council of Ministers had wide latitude with regard to mineral sector tax matters. All investors in large-scale mineral projects before 2007 (Mozal, Corridor Sands, Moma) negotiated agreements containing substantial fiscal incentives.

The 2002 tax benefit code consolidated in a single piece of legislation the rules on tax incentives that had been enacted by several different decrees as well as generic tax benefits and special regimes (see Box 8.3).[7] The code was drafted when there was little or no foreign investment in Mozambique's mineral resources sector and risks were perceived by potential investors to be high. In addition, there was an expectation that fiscal regulations under the mining law, which were not yet promulgated, would

[7]Tax Benefits Code, Decree No. 16/2002.

Table 8.4. Production of Mineral Commodities, 2001–05
(Metric tons unless otherwise specified)

	2001	2002	2003	2004	2005
Aluminum:					
Bauxite	8,592	9,119	11,793	6,723	9,518
Aluminum, refined	266,000	273,000	407,000	549,000	555,000
Coal, bituminous	27,600	43,512	36,742	16,525	3,417
Columbium (niobium) and tantalum, columbite-tantalite, ore and concentrate:					
Gross weight *(kilograms)*	27,000	46,900	188,695	712,095	281,212
Nb content[1] *(kilograms)*	3,300	5,500	23,000	87,000	34,000
Ta content[1] *(kilograms)*	7,700	13,000	54,000	205,000	81,000
Gold[2] *(kilograms)*	22	17	63	56	63
Natural gas *(million cubic meters)*	1	2	1	1,295	2,316
Quartz *(kilograms)*	24,765	31,363	30,985	173,478	n.a.

Source: U.S. Geological Survey.
[1]Estimated; estimated data are rounded to no more than three significant digits.
[2]Does not include unreported production; total output of gold was estimated to be roughly 600 to 900 kilograms per year.

act as a stand-alone fiscal system for the mineral sector. Therefore, the tax benefit code did not cover mining fiscal issues comprehensively.

Under the tax benefits code, investment tax incentives could be granted, at the government's discretion, for specific schemes for large-scale projects, rapid development zones, mining projects, petroleum projects, and industrial free zones (IFZs). Investors could apply to the Minister of Planning and Finance for exceptional incentives, which could be granted under a contractual (mining agreement) regime by the Council of Ministers. Incentives are wide-ranging and include exemptions or reductions from most taxes on inputs (value-added tax (VAT), import duties, excise taxes); accelerated capital recovery; reduced income tax rates for defined periods; investment tax credits; special treatment for withholding taxes; and so forth.

To understand the current fiscal system with regard to megaprojects for which agreements were negotiated before 2007, it is critically important to consider the special fiscal treatment of projects that have IFZ status. These projects can be exempted from the VAT, excise duties, customs duties on capital goods, and real property transfer tax and benefit from a reduced corporate income tax rate (12.8 percent). In most countries, free trade zones are set up for a specific activity: the transformation of imported raw materials or intermediate goods into intermediate goods or finished products for export—for example, a garment factory in the tropics importing nylon cloth for the production of ski clothing for export. Countries see these zones, often mistakenly, as a means to foster employment or attract seed investment. They are not typically intended or used to transform locally produced raw materials, such as output from direct mineral extraction, for domestic use or export.

There are three IFZs in Mozambique linked to megaprojects: Mozal, Moma, and Limpopo Corridor Sands. Mozal, like projects in free trade zones elsewhere in the world, imports raw material for transformation into a product that will be exported (imported alumina is transformed into exported aluminum). Moma and Corridor Sands are different. Both transform locally sourced raw materials for export, and it is likely that IFZ status for this use was not originally intended at the time the IFZ legislation was drafted. Beyond the IFZ exemptions listed above, for Mozal, a 1 percent substitute corporate income tax has been levied on net turnover. Deductions have also been granted for expenses related to staff training and improvement of infrastructure in the free zone.

In addition, taxation in these IFZs leaves open the possibility of abusive transfer pricing between the two stages of production—mining and processing. For example, in some of Mozambique's mineral sands agreements, mine output can be sold to the processing affiliate that enjoys IFZ status. Oddly, the negotiated agreements do not bar transfer pricing as is common in most such agreements in other nations but instead embrace and specifically allow it. The expected outcome is that the profits of the mining affiliate may be minimal because it will sell its output at an artificially low price to its processing affiliate, and the latter will enjoy higher profits and a much lighter fiscal burden. Accordingly, with these incentives, net tax payments from the megaprojects are extremely low and are likely to remain so, since these zones were created for periods of between 20 and 50 years. Hence, the Mozambican authorities should not grant IFZ status to any mineral project in the future.

These agreements highlight the need for fiscal models to be used in mineral projects whenever discretionary fiscal incentives are being negotiated. Such models would have identified the magnitude of forgone fiscal revenues from the mineral sands projects. The development of large-scale extractive industries has been fairly recent in Mozambique and capacity building at the governmental level has been progressing slowly. In particular, in regard to negotiating the megaproject agreements, government officials had very little training and knowledge of the industry. This shortcoming impeded the ability of official negotiators to maximize nontax benefits, such as local community development obligations and forward and backward input and output linkages; minimize tax losses that could result from transfer pricing; and fully understand which terms should be negotiated and which ones should be rigidly defined in law or in a model

Box 8.3. Tax Benefits Code, Decree No. 16/2002

Type of tax benefit	Tax rate	Ceiling
Exemptions		
1. ***Import duties*** on Class K equipment goods.	0%	Up to 100% of the tax base
2. ***Value-added tax (VAT)*** on imports of Class K equipment goods.	0%	Up to 100% of the tax base
3. ***Stamp tax*** on formal acts related to the establishment of the mining company and to changes in its capital and Articles of Association during the first five years after investment or the start of operations.	0%	Up to 100% of the tax base
Reductions		
SISA tax on purchase of real estate for industrial, agroindustrial, or hotel use, provided real estate is acquired within three years of the date the investment is authorized or operations begin.	50%	
Deductions from income tax		
1. ***Investment tax credit (CFI)*** on total investment during the first five fiscal years.	5%	Up to 100% of the tax base
2. In Gaza, Sofala, Tete, and Zambézia provinces, a ***special CFI rate*** applies to the total investment made during the first five fiscal years.	10%	Up to 100% of the tax base
3. In Cabo Delgado, Inhambane, and Niassa provinces, a ***special CFI rate*** applies to the total investment made during the first five fiscal years.	15%	Up to 100% of the tax base
4. ***Deduction on sums invested in specialized equipment*** intended for modernization and introduction of new technologies during the first five years after the start of the investment or operations.	100%	Up to 15% of the tax base

5. ***Deduction on sums spent on vocational training*** for Mozambican workers during the first five years after investment or the start of operations.	100%	Up to 5% of the tax base
6. ***Deduction on the sums spent on vocational training in the use of*** equipment considered high-tech by Mozambican workers during the first five years after investment or the start of operations.	100%	Up to 10% of the tax base
Accelerated amortization and reinvestment in fixed assets		
Deduction of up to double the normal tax rate legally stipulated for calculation of the ***amortization of, and reinvestment in,*** new buildings used in authorized undertakings.		Up to 100% of the tax base
Fiscal costs		
1. Expenses related to the construction of works of public utility in Maputo during the first 10 years.	120%	Up to 100% of the tax base
2. Expenses related to the construction of works of public utility in other provinces during the first 10 years.	150%	Up to 100% of the tax base
3. Purchases of Mozambican art works.	50%	Up to 100% of the tax base

Source: Mozambican authorities.

Figure 8.2. Mozambique: FDI Flows, 1990–2007
(In millions of U.S. dollars)

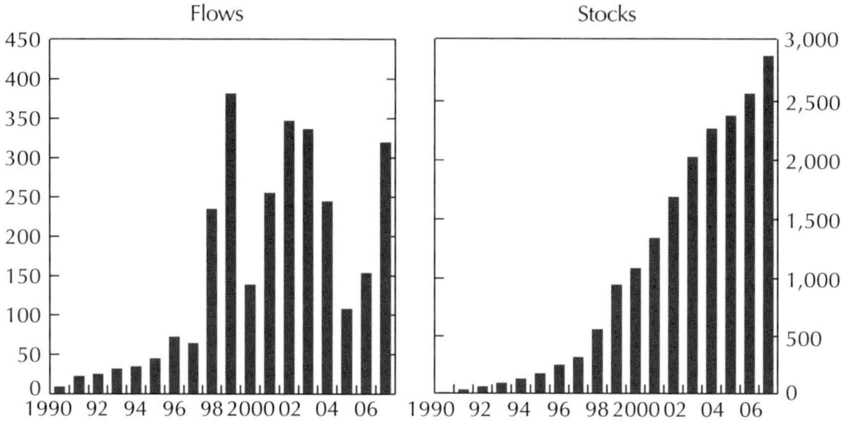

Source: UNCTAD, FDI/TNC database, Banco de Moçambique.

agreement. In addition, the capacity to undertake fiscal modeling in order to examine the fiscal impact of incentives on revenue generation has been lacking. The ministry responsible for mining did not employ a mineral economist during the period when the existing megaproject agreements were negotiated. The World Bank provided support under its Mineral Resources Management Capacity Building Project, and many of the technical departments, such as the Cadastre, have benefited greatly from this project, but capacity shortfalls remain a challenge.

The second-phase strategy certainly attracted foreign direct investment, which has been growing since 1998 (Figure 8.2). One of the early successes of Mozambique in attracting FDI was the development of the two main capital-intensive export-oriented megaprojects, Mozal and Sasol. Although other mineral megaprojects have since come into existence, Mozal and Sasol still dominate the sector.

Mozal. The first megaproject was the Mozal aluminum project, a joint venture led by the Australian–South African firm BHP Billiton, the sixth largest producer of primary aluminum.[8] The project consists of a

[8]BHP-Billiton holds 48 percent of Mozal's equity; Mitsubishi of Japan, 24 percent; South Africa's Industrial Development Corporation, 24 percent; and the government of Mozambique, 4 percent.

smelter using alumina imported from western Australia as raw material. Construction started in 1998, was completed in 2000, and was followed by an expansion completed in 2002 that doubled its capacity. Total FDI comes to about US$2 billion. The expansion raised Mozal's capacity to 549,000 tons, making it one of the largest aluminum plants in the world. BHP Billiton recently completed feasibility studies for the expansion of the Mozal smelter, which would increase its rated capacity by an additional 250,000 tons a year by 2009. However, final approval of the expansion project depends on the outcome of negotiations on long-term power supply contracts.

The impact of Mozal on the Mozambican economy cannot be understated. It positioned Mozambique as one of the top aluminum producers in the world. Mozal remains the most important megaproject in Mozambique by far, and it continues to dominate the country's macroeconomic statistics as the most important investment to date and the largest industrial concern. In 2004, aluminum represented 64 percent of Mozambique's total exports of goods, and aluminum accounted for 75 percent of total growth in the country's exports from 2000 to 2004.

Mozal has benefited from its preferential industrial free zone status. At the time it was conceived and built, after the end of the civil war, Mozal faced a high degree of uncertainty and sovereign (political) and project (commercial) risks. No project of that magnitude had been attracted to Mozambique for some time, and FDI was still very limited. Eager to establish a track record of FDI, the government offered generous fiscal benefits. In addition to extremely generous tax incentives, a key component of the project was the provision of cheap electricity by the Cahora Bassa Dam (via South Africa's Eskom, because national transmission lines between the two sites were not operational). Prices charged for electricity to Mozal under its long-term contracts have become controversial because they may be below the market price. If this is the case, the government may in fact be subsidizing the project with few offsetting benefits, either fiscal or economic. This raises a number of issues regarding the sourcing and cost of power for Mozal's planned expansion.

Pande-Temane. A significant amount of FDI has also flowed to the country's petroleum sector: after agreements negotiated in 2000, the Pande-Temane gas field installations, processing facilities, and gas export pipeline to South Africa were commissioned in 2004, with further investment due to complete the initial project (some US$1 billion in all). Natural gas from the Pande and Temane fields in Mozambique's Inhambane province is exported through the 865-kilometer gas pipeline to South Africa. Construction by Sasol, the giant South African fuel company, was completed in 2004 at a cost of US$600 million. The project is a joint venture in which the Mozambican state has an equity participation; it is also entitled to royalty payments, either in cash or in kind.[9] Government revenues have thus far been modest, consisting mainly of petroleum production taxes and a small amount of corporate income tax, since the project (including the pipeline) is currently recovering its costs and making high debt-service payments. However, revenues are set to increase significantly as production ramps up and the investors recover their initial development costs. The infrastructure built for the project will probably also generate additional revenues from other users.

Moma Titanium Minerals Project. The mine is being developed by an Anglo-Irish company, Kenmare Resources PLC, and production started in mid-2007. It contains considerable reserves of the titanium minerals ilmenite and rutile. The Moma mine also has large quantities of zircon, a high-value coproduct of titanium minerals mining. In December 2000, the Mozambican government granted the project industrial free zone tax status. The mine should account for about 8 percent of the world supply of titanium. The Mineral License Agreement signed in 2001 covers an initial period of 25 years of mining, is renewable, and allows for significant future expansion. The project has been granted generous tax incentives.

Moatize coal project. The project is located in the western Tete province and is being developed by the world's largest iron-ore miner, the Brazilian Companhia do Vale do Rio Doce (CVRD). In November 2004, CVRD won the bid, for US$123 million, for rights to explore and develop the coal deposit; undertake feasibility studies for developing a 1,500-megawatt coal-fired power plant, port facilities, and a rail link to the port; and assess other domestic industrial projects linked to the mine. In 2007 the government gave authorization to proceed with the project. The feasibility study that was submitted to the government in November 2006 indicates that, by 2010, the project will mine about 15 million tons of coal a year, of which about 6 million tons will be marketed for export and 9 million tons made available to a planned domestic power plant. The area around Moatize is considered by some to be the largest unexplored coal province in the world; reserves are estimated at 2.4 billion tons, allowing the extraction of metallurgical and thermal coals. Total investment is estimated at US$2 billion.

[9]The joint venture partners are South Africa's gas giant, Sasol (70 percent); a Mozambican state-owned enterprise, CMH (25 percent); and the International Finance Corporation (5 percent).

Although Mozambique has been successful in attracting investment to its mineral sector, the question arises whether this investment has benefited the country. As noted previously, in many countries, the main benefit to development is through taxation, user fees, and improved infrastructure.

The macroeconomic impact of megaprojects and mineral resources extraction on the economy has been impressive. The megaprojects' contribution to GDP increased from 0 percent in 1998 to 8 percent in 2002 and 10 percent in 2006, and it should stabilize at about 8 percent as construction is completed and projects—Mozal, especially—begin to operate at full capacity.[10] The megaprojects' contribution to real GDP growth in Mozambique reached a peak of 23 percent annually, on average, for 2001–03, in large part because of the construction of Mozal II and the gas pipeline. Contribution to GDP will increase substantially again with the Moma and Moatize projects.

Mozambique's balance of payments has also been considerably affected by the megaprojects, starting in 2000 with Mozal's entry into operation. Subsequently, with the completion of Mozal II and the gas pipeline, merchandise exports went from 0 in 1998 to over US$1 billion in 2004 and are projected to be over US$2 billion by 2010. The megaprojects also had a substantial impact on merchandise imports, especially during the construction phases of Mozal I and II and the Sasol pipeline. Capital and financial accounts have been affected as well, because financing has been in the form of foreign borrowing and direct investment. The overall impact will be more modest in the future after taking into account interest and dividends paid to foreign shareholders. Profits and dividends are expected to rise to over US$500 million starting in 2006. Finally, megaprojects are projected to account for more than 70 percent of exports annually, on average, for 2006–10.

In contrast to these impressive macroeconomic statistics, the megaprojects' impact on central government revenues has been minimal—less than 3 percent—as shown in Table 8.5, and indirect contributions through labor and local businesses are limited as well. About half of total government expenditure is foreign-financed. In contrast, current fiscal contributions of megaprojects to the central budget are very low by any standard, compared with what might be expected from projects of this type. In 2005 Mozal, with a turnover over US$1 billion, contributed less than 1.3 percent of Mozambique's total tax revenues. If profits repatriation, dividends,

---

[10]A doubling of Mozal's capacity has been envisaged but remains on hold because of power generation constraints.

Table 8.5. Mozambique: Taxes Deposited by the Megaprojects, 2003–05
(In millions of old meticais)

	Mozal			Sasol		
	2003	2004	2005	2003	2004	2005
Total	54,144	107,829	239,452	0.682	5.654	64.395
IRPC[1]	31,874	64,941	96,768	0.682	0.851	3.053
Final tax rate[2]	22,270	42,888	142,684	0	0	0
Royalties[3]	0	0	0	0	4.803	61.342

Source: Mozambique, Ministry of Finance.
[1]IRPC denotes *Imposto de Rendas Colectivas* (corporate income tax).
[2]Final tax rate is 1 percent of gross income.
[3]Royalties are 5 percent of gross income from production of gas.

interest, and amortization on foreign borrowing are taken into account, the direct and indirect contributions to revenue remain limited.

The impact on local employment has varied greatly, especially during construction, but remains small. It is projected that total employment in 2010 by Mozal, Sasol, and the Cahora Bassa Dam, including indirect employment and excluding construction work, will be about 9,000 full-time positions, or under 2 percent of urban private sector employment.[11]

Going Forward

During the past two decades, Mozambique has been put back on the investment map, mainly through its demonstrated willingness to honor its natural resources sector agreements. However, the country has forgone substantial revenue because mining projects are the beneficiaries of large fiscal benefits that are not in line with best international practices. Given the increased confidence of investors in the economic and political stability of the country, the authorities have recognized that there is a need to reduce fiscal incentives and standardize the fiscal terms of all new mining and petroleum projects. The fiscal regime has been progressively modernized. In addition, Mozambique took a major step forward in 2007 when parliament adopted new legislative frameworks that are in line with best international practices for the mining and petroleum fiscal regimes.

Under the new legislation, fiscal incentives will be reduced and fiscal terms standardized for all new mining projects. The new fiscal regime is

[11]Benito-Spinetto and Moll (2005). This is a rough estimate—the authors admitted making "heroic assumptions."

more balanced so as to enable Mozambique to continue attracting foreign investors while providing the country with a fair share of economic rent, taking into account the features specific to mining as described above. Indeed, now that the country is back on the investment map there is a need to maximize revenues from the mineral industries while increasing the tax base. One challenge for the government is the administrative complexity that will result from the existence of both old and new project agreements whose fiscal approaches differ substantially.

In addition to introducing a more balanced approach to taxation, Mozambique recently finalized a new model mining agreement that seeks, among other things, to enhance linkages at the local, provincial, and national levels and to require formal arrangements between mining companies and affected communities. The agreement is intended to supplement the existing statutory law and not supersede it. A model agreement for oil and gas exploration and development based on international best practices has also been prepared. Efforts are under way to enhance the government's ability to better understand and negotiate user fee agreements relating to the provision of water and power to megaprojects.

The Mozambican authorities now recognize that transparency and good governance in the mining sector are necessary to ensure that revenues derived from mineral projects will contribute to sustainable development and poverty reduction beyond the contribution they can make to the government's budget. As described above in connection with avoiding the resource curse, Mozambique has decided to manage its asset wealth and revenues in a prudent and transparent manner while pursuing economic diversification strategies and developing physical infrastructure and human capital.

Currently, mineral resource projects' net contribution to the central government budget is still not known in great detail not only because of low administrative capacity but also because of contracts negotiated on favorable and confidential terms case by case when the country first opened up to foreign investment. In addition, contrary to most resource-rich countries, whose revenues tend to come from only one or two main primary materials (oil, gas, copper, diamonds), Mozambique's potential natural endowment covers a wider range of resources (including natural gas, titanium, and coal). As a result, when all projects under consideration are in operation it will be challenging to determine the share of each project's net contribution to the budget.

The Mozambican government recognizes that improving governance remains a priority and decided to become a member of the EITI in 2008. All new mineral investments—in particular, the exploitation of coal, oil, and natural gas—as well as any expansion of related megaprojects would follow the EITI principles.

In addition, the IMF's *Guide on Resource Revenue Transparency* (2007)[12] provides an overview of generally recognized good or best practices for transparent management of resource revenues, and government implementation of these guidelines would complement the EITI principles. These good practices of fiscal transparency are based on four pillars: (1) clarification of the division of roles and responsibilities among the government, national resource companies, and international companies; (2) application of open and transparent budget processes, similar to those recommended for other parts of the government budget, to the planning, allocation, spending, and reporting of resource revenues; (3) public availability of information on all resource-related transactions central to fiscal transparency; and (4) effective mechanisms for providing assurances of integrity.

Finally, transparency and fiscal stability are likely to be easier to achieve under a generally applicable fiscal regime than with case-by-case negotiations. In this regard, the new model mining and oil and gas agreements are intended to attract new investment into the sector by reducing investor risk in a transparent manner. The terms of the model agreements do not supersede statutory law but, rather, complement and supplement it by not allowing substantial negotiation of the fiscal system. With the recent adoption of fiscal regimes into law there is little justification for negotiating special tax incentives in such agreements, which can now simply refer to the relevant fiscal legislation, while terms in the agreements focus on other matters. As noted above, the standardized agreements improve the government's ability to maximize national benefits when dealing with sophisticated foreign investors and avoid costly, protracted, and legally questionable negotiations.

Mozambique has made a good start with the development and introduction of model agreements and standardized mineral sector fiscal regulations, but further work remains to be done. A macroeconomic fiscal model for the extractive sector could be developed as a tool to help authorities formulate policies. A variety of taxes and fees are currently levied on the industry and it is not always clear how they relate both in amounts and temporally. The ability to forecast revenues and understand how ongoing reforms will affect them can aid policymakers. Given the volatility

---

[12]The guide is available via the Internet at http://www.imf.org/external/np/pp/2007/eng/051507g.pdf

of revenue flows from the sector, it is important to forecast realistic fiscal revenues to ensure good budgeting practices.[13]

Monitoring compliance with tax regimes granted on a case-by-case basis is feasible as long as there are only a few big projects, but it may become a challenging task as expansion of the sector accelerates. Simplification and uniformity of the tax regime under a general law will undoubtedly ease the government's task.

Conclusion: Lessons for Other Developing Countries

As Mozambique enters a new phase of its mineral and oil investment strategy, it is moving away from the provision of ad hoc tax incentives to attract foreign investment toward a fair, transparent, and stable fiscal system supported by model agreements that enhance economic linkages. This new approach, which is in line with best international practices, should help Mozambique create a virtuous cycle in the management of its natural resources for the benefit of its population and the reduction of its still widespread poverty. To succeed, Mozambique will need to enforce related regulations and to adhere fully to the EITI principles.

The Mozambique experience holds several important lessons for other developing countries, including the following:

- Establishing an investment track record can assist in attracting future investment, and fiscal incentives are one way to encourage early investors.
- Honoring existing investment agreements is one means of encouraging new investors even though such agreements may look overly generous in changed circumstances.
- Previously negotiated agreements should not be used as precedents, and new agreements should reflect changes in risk perception, markets, financing, and other circumstances.
- Countries with a limited capacity to negotiate agreements are at a disadvantage when negotiating with sophisticated foreign investors, so it is to the advantage of governments to set out in law the principal taxes and incentives and to avoid deviating from these.

[13]See for instance Sohn (2005). The Ministry of Finance does not yet make tax projections for mineral resource projects. As the sector is expected to grow rapidly, with several new megaprojects beginning production, there is a need for the ministry that closely monitors these projects to do so.

- When devising mineral sector taxation policy, whether it be through legal reform or in negotiated agreements, the use of financial (fiscal) models is essential.
- Without a financial (fiscal) model to aid them in understanding the tax consequences of agreements, policymakers may make mistakes with negative implications for the country's future.
- Fiscal models are also useful for revenue forecasting and setting appropriate budgetary policy.
- National benefits from the mineral sector are not limited to fiscal revenues, and mineral sector policy and the regulatory system, which would ideally include a uniform model mining agreement, should strive to maximize economic linkages such as the provision of goods and services to the sector, and the integration of infrastructure with both project needs and broader development.
- Capacity building and institutional strengthening are important even when the sector is small because, as it develops, benefits may be needlessly forgone.
- Well-trained or expert-supported government negotiators are better able to maximize nontax benefits, minimize tax losses, and understand which terms should be negotiated.
- There is a need for sound and transparent management of government revenues, including predictability of taxation and application of the common law.
- A national mineral policy that is reviewed on a periodic basis can be a valuable aid in ensuring that a country's approach to regulating and taxing the mineral sector is kept up to date with changing investment perceptions and needs and with national expectations and aspirations.
- The potential for a developing economy dependent on mineral exports to suffer the resource curse is great but not inevitable—informed policymakers can look to the examples set by countries such as Mozambique, Botswana, and Chile, which have used the mineral sector as a springboard for development.

Bibliography

Auty, R., and R. Mikesell, 1998, *Sustainable Development in Mineral Economies* (Oxford: Clarendon Press).

Baunsgaard, T., 2001, "A Primer on Mineral Taxation," IMF Working Paper 01/139 (Washington: International Monetary Fund).

Benito-Spinetto, M., and P. Moll, 2005, "Mozambique. Background Paper: Macroeconomic developments, economic growth, and consequences for poverty (Washington: World Bank).

Davis, G., and J. Tilton, 2005, "The Resource Curse," *Natural Resources Forum*, Vol. 29 (August), pp. 233–42.

Gelb, A., and Associates, 1988, *Oil Windfalls: Blessing or Curse?* (New York: Oxford University Press, for the World Bank).

Gocht, W., H. Zantop, and R. Eggert, 1988, *International Mineral Economics: Mineral Exploration, Mine Valuation, Mineral Markets, and International Mineral Policies* (Berlin: Springer-Verlag).

Hirschman, A.O., 1958, *The Strategy of Economic Development* (New Haven, Connecticut: Yale University Press).

Hodler, R., 2006, "The Curse of Natural Resources in Fractionalized Countries," *European Economic Review*, Vol. 50 (August), pp. 1367–86.

International Council on Mining and Metals (ICMM), 2006, *The Challenge of Mineral Wealth: Using Resource Endowment to Foster Sustainable Development, Synthesis of Four Country Case Studies* (London). Available via the Internet: http://www.icmm.com/publications/1117Synthesis.pdf

International Monetary Fund, 2007, *Guide on Resource Revenue Transparency* (Washington). Available via the Intenet: http://www.imf.org/external/pp/longres.aspx?id=4176

Johnson, C., 1981, "Minerals Objectives, Policies and Strategies in Botswana—Analysis and Lessons," *Natural Resources Forum*, Vol. 5, pp. 347–67.

Jordan, P., 1986, "The mineral industry of Mozambique," *Raw Materials Report*, Vol. 4(4), pp. 31–45.

Magong, D., 1994, "Botswana: A Prospect for Mineral Investment," statement delivered at the SADC Mining Investment Forum, Lusaka, Zambia, December 7–9.

Matshediso, I.B., 2005, "A Review of Mineral Development and Investment Policies in Botswana," *Resources Policy*, Vol. 30 (September), pp. 203–07.

Mozambique Ministry of Mineral Resources, http://www.mirem.gov.mz

Mozambique Petroleum Institute, http://www.inp.gov.mz

Otto, J.M., 1992, "A Global Survey of Mineral Company Investment Preferences," in *Mineral Investment Conditions in Selected Countries of the Asia-Pacific Region*, United Nations ST/ESCAP/1197 (New York), pp. 330-342.

———, 2002, "Mozambique Mining Taxation System: Competitive Position and Recommendations for Reform" (Maputo: Mozambique Ministry of Minerals Resources and Energy).

Otto, James, Craig Andrews, Fred Cawood, Michael Doggett, Pietro Guj, Frank Stermole, John Stermole, and John Tilton, 2006, *Mining Royalties: A Global Study on Their Impact on Investors, Government, and Civil Society* (Washington: World Bank).

Prebisch, R., 1950, "The Economic Development of Latin America and Its Principal Problems" (New York: United Nations).

Ross, M., 2001, "Extractive Sectors and the Poor" (Boston: Oxfam America).

Sachs, J., and A. Warner, 1997, "Natural Resource Abundance and Economic Growth," NBER Working Paper No. 5398 (Cambridge, Massachusetts: National Bureau of Economic Research).

Sala-i-Martin, X., and A. Subramanian, 2003, "Addressing the Natural Resource Curse: An Illustration from Nigeria," NBER Working Paper No. 9804 (Cambridge, Massachusetts: National Bureau of Economic Research).

Sohn, I., 2005, "Long-Term Projections of Non-Fuel Minerals: We Were Wrong, But Why?" *Resources Policy*, Vol. 30 (December), pp. 259–84.

Stijns, J.-P. C., 2005, "Natural Resource Abundance and Economic Growth Revisited," *Resources Policy*, Vol. 30 (June), pp. 107–30.

Tilton, J., ed., 1992, *Mineral Wealth and Economic Development* (Washington: Resources for the Future).

Torvik, R., 2002, "Natural Resources, Rent Seeking and Welfare," *Journal of Development Economics*, Vol. 67 (April), pp. 455–70.

United Nations Economic and Social Council, 1998, "Basic Problem of Improving the Capacity of Developing Countries and Economies in Transition to Capture the Maximum Economic and Social Benefits of Their Potential for Mineral Production," Report of the Secretary General to the Committee on Natural Resources, fourth session, 10–19 March (document E/C.7/1998/4). Available via the Internet: http://www.un.org/esa/documents/ec7.htm

9

Strengthening Mozambique's Business Environment: Diagnostics, Strategies, and Outcomes

VICTOR LLEDÓ

Strengthening the business environment has been increasingly recognized as central to accelerating and sustaining broad-based and propoor growth in low-income countries. It involves policy and institutional changes in a wide range of areas, from property rights and business regulation to infrastructure and labor markets, as well as deeper institutional reforms to enhance governance and combat corruption.

Recent experience shows, however, that countries do not need to embark on simultaneous and comprehensive reforms but can reap significant benefits from gradual, sequenced reforms.[1] Policymakers need to identify and address the most binding constraints first, so as to give firms the confidence and will to address other constraints as they become more binding. Careful diagnosis and the development of an appropriately sequenced, well-coordinated action plan owned by the government and supported technically and financially by the donor community are essential.

This chapter will attempt to provide further support for this view using Mozambique as an example. Several studies have already been conducted for the purpose of identifying the main obstacles to private sector development in Mozambique. Periodic assessments of the cost of doing business

[1]See World Bank (2005a).

in Mozambique have attempted to quantify and benchmark the country's progress in addressing these obstacles.[2]

Building on this previous work, this chapter

- Introduces some basic tools and best practices that have been shown to foster business environment reforms;
- Benchmarks Mozambique's business environment against that of other countries in sub-Saharan Africa and emerging markets worldwide, with the aim of identifying reform priorities;
- Assesses Mozambique's new strategy, particularly the extent to which the reforms address the most binding constraints, have a noticeable impact, and are implemented in ways that foster ownership and coordination; and
- Drawing on the experience of other low-income countries, summarizes lessons on how to design, implement, and coordinate a reform strategy that promotes private sector development.

Fostering Business Environment Reforms

According to recent studies, there are three main challenges to fostering business environment reforms (Kikeri, Kenyon, and Palmade, 2006). First, the list of potential reforms needed, particularly in low-income countries, is long, and determining the right mix of reforms and sequencing them in a way that enhances welfare is a complex task. Second, because such reforms often have distributional consequences, they can be politically contentious. To overcome political resistance, reform proponents must be aware of the preferences and political clout of various groups and institutions. Third, sustaining reform, even in a supportive political environment, involves strengthening public officials' incentives and their capacity to implement reform and introducing institutional mechanisms for coordinating and monitoring the reform process.

Against this background, this section introduces basic tools and reform strategies that can be used to design, implement, and sustain business environment reforms. It establishes an analytical framework by which to evaluate the design, implementation, and sustainability of Mozambique's reforms to improve its business environment.

[2]See IMF and World Bank (2003); World Bank (2005a); and USAID (2004).

Getting the Priorities Right

Some sequencing of reforms is inevitable, especially in a realm as far-reaching as the business environment. Improving the business environment, particularly in low-income countries, requires governments to tackle a broad reform agenda, ranging from refining macroeconomic policies and pursuing deeper institutional changes to enhancing property rights and combating corruption. Simultaneous and comprehensive reforms, even if technically and politically feasible, could generate so much uncertainty that they might deter rather than encourage investment, at least temporarily. Deep and rapid institutional change can also impose large costs on influential segments of society, undermining public support and jeopardizing reform momentum.

The advantages of a more gradual, sequenced approach to private sector development reforms have been corroborated by several countries' recent experiences. Private sector–led growth has successfully taken off in countries that identified and addressed important constraints, giving firms the confidence to invest, while sustaining the reform process so that other constraints could be addressed as they became more binding (World Bank, 2005b; and Hausmann, Rodrik, and Velasco, 2005). Getting the priorities right is, therefore, essential for a successful reform strategy.

A growing body of new diagnostic tools and information is available to help reformers identify priorities. These tools include business surveys, benchmarking techniques, and growth-enhancing decision-based trees.

Business surveys

The most direct way of identifying business environment constraints is to survey firms. The World Bank's Investment Climate Assessments (ICAs), for example, are comprehensive, subjective reports on the business environments in different countries. ICAs draw on the results of surveys of firms and other diagnostic tools. Business surveys have proved useful in enhancing a government's credibility with firms and helping to identify possible implementation issues. However, such assessments are less effective in identifying policy barriers to competition (entry and exit) since they do not cover firms that have not yet entered the market. Business surveys also tend to overestimate the negative impact of factors such as taxes, whose costs are borne privately but which may yield positive benefits for the business environment, such as the public provision of infrastructure and the consolidation of macroeconomic stability. Reformers must take these factors into consideration when setting priorities.

Benchmarking

Benchmarking the investment climate involves comparing a country with its competitors on various factors that affect investment decisions. For example, the World Bank's Doing Business database ranks countries according to the cost and quality of their business regulations in such areas as business registration, contract enforcement, labor regulations, and access to credit.[3] The World Bank's Governance Indicators also make it possible to benchmark countries in other areas relevant to investment decisions, such as government effectiveness, corruption, and political stability.[4] Low rankings in a particular area relative to potential competitors can thus help identify what a country's reform priorities should be.

However, it is not enough to know a country's ranking. The next step is to understand the reasons for the ranking and how it can be improved. Identifying policy changes, perhaps in line with the policies of the best-performing countries, is the ultimate purpose of benchmarking the investment climate. The growth diagnostic framework provides an alternative and somewhat complementary approach.

Growth Diagnostic Framework

The Growth Diagnostic Framework developed by Hausmann, Rodrik, and Velasco (2005) identifies reform priorities on the basis of the impact of different reforms on output growth. The point of departure is the standard steady-state equilibrium for sustainable private sector growth summarized in equation (1) below. In the steady state, output, consumption, and capital grow at an identical rate γ, which equals the difference between private returns to capital accumulation ($r(1-\tau)$) and its respective cost of financing (ρ), discounted by individual preferences for immediate consumption (σ). In this context, proximate determinants of sustainable growth can be classified broadly in two categories: (1) private returns to the accumulation of production factors, namely human and physical capital; and (2) the corresponding costs required to finance their accumulation (for example, the costs of investment and education). Private returns can be modeled as a function of social return (r) and its corresponding *degree of private appropriability* ($1-\tau$). Social returns, in turn, are determined by *total factor productivity* (a), the availability of complementary factors of production, such as *infrastructure* or *human capital* (x), along with external economies (θ).

---

[3]Doing Business indicators are available via the Internet: http://www.doingbusiness.org.

[4]Governance indicators are available via the Internet: http://info.worldbank.org/governance/kkz2005.

$$\gamma = \sigma\{[r(a,x,\theta)(1-\tau)]\rho\}. \tag{1}$$

Therefore, under this proposed framework, the most binding constraints to sustainable growth can be diagnosed in two stages. In the first stage, the goal is to identify which of the proximate growth determinants is subject to the greatest economic distortions. Once the most highly distorted proximate growth determinants are identified, the diagnosis moves to a deeper level with an attempt to identify which particular policies or institutional reforms are required to remove these distortions. An appropriate reform sequence requires continuously replicating this diagnostic exercise under the assumption that the initial constraints are removed when the corresponding reform is implemented.

The tree-shaped diagram in Figure 9.1 illustrates this diagnostic process. For instance, if the problem seems to be the high cost of finance rather than insufficient returns, is that cost due to lack of access to external savings or to scarce local finance? If scarce local finance is to blame, does that reflect low domestic savings or poor financial intermediation?

The methodology for performing growth diagnostic exercises is still evolving. Initial growth exercises, including those performed by the original proponents, were conducted mostly through historical analyses of recent growth episodes in individual countries.[5] Such an analysis would basically entail defending the prevalence of a given binding constraint against the alternative, on the basis of direct or indirect measures of prices (or shadow prices) for production factor returns and the cost of financing. The exercise would then move to the second stage, where specific policies or institutional reforms would be selected on the basis of their impact on growth and political feasibility without being guided by any clear methodology.

To overcome that limitation, Johnson, Ostry, and Subramanian (2007) have proposed a simple benchmark approach that identifies constraints to sustainable growth. Their approach compares the quality of policies and institutions widely regarded as essential to sustainable growth in a given country with that observed in countries that have sustained growth at the time growth first took off. In this context, their methodology also includes assumptions to determine where and when growth became sustainable.

[5]Hausmann, Rodrik, and Velasco (2005) have attempted to identify reform priorities for Brazil and El Salvador on the basis of a historical analysis of impediments to growth acceleration.

Figure 9.1. Growth Diagnostics

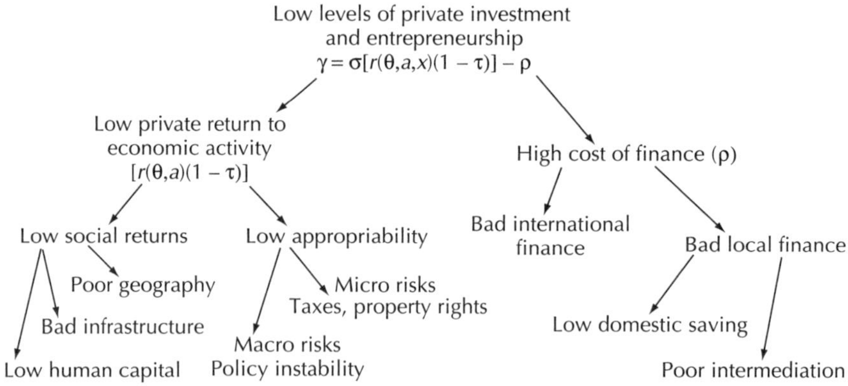

Source: Hausmann, Rodrik, and Velasco (2005).

Making Reforms Work: Implementation and Sustainability

Correctly identifying the most welfare-enhancing or growth-enhancing priorities is just the first step in the design and implementation of a successful reform strategy. Equally important are (1) packaging and building a consensus for reforms, to ensure their implementation; (2) strengthening public officials' incentives and ability to enforce such reforms; and, (3) introducing institutional mechanisms for coordinating and monitoring the reform process so it can be sustained.

Therefore, from a purely welfare-enhancing perspective, getting reforms implemented often implies that adjustments must be made to the optimal reform sequence so as to overcome political and administrative constraints. Recent experience has revealed the following successful strategies for implementing and sustaining business environment reforms:

- **Build coalitions that can support reform.** Growth-critical reforms of the business environment usually benefit a wider but less influential segment of the population, while the costs are borne mostly by smaller but more politically powerful groups. In such cases, support can be mobilized by empowering pro-reform leaders and organizations and by conducting public campaigns to disseminate information about the benefits of reform. In addition, policymakers can defuse opposition by establishing a process of consultation with reform opponents and, in cases where losses are easily measured, not substantial, and concentrated in a small identifiable group, through compensatory schemes.

- **Act swiftly.** Political resistance to highly contentious reforms usually softens during economic crises, periods of growth, post-conflict situations, and immediately after a legitimate change in political leadership. Seizing these windows of opportunity can ensure that reforms are implemented.
- **Start with reforms that are credible and feasible.** In cases where reformers lack political support and administrative capacity, pilots or other less complex, quick-win measures might reinforce a government's reform commitment, encourage the development of pro-reform constituencies, and jump-start the reform process. Pilot programs can be important catalysts for nationwide reforms through learning and demonstration effects. Identifying and implementing quick-win measures can help build constituencies that will support more contentious measures.
- **Reforms that expose the economy to international competition are a good starting point.** By increasing competition, trade and financial liberalization give domestic constituencies reasons to tackle other important business environment reforms, such as land, labor, and financial measures.
- **Monitoring should be a central part of the reform process.** This function involves several tasks: evaluating the potential costs and benefits of reforms, translating reform objectives into measurable performance targets or indicators, and reviewing compliance and outcomes once implementation begins. Monitoring is critical, as it allows citizens to hold reformers accountable.
- **Sustained reforms require strong oversight and coordination mechanisms.** Business environment reforms touch on cross-cutting issues (for example, anticorruption laws, vocational training schemes, and the provision of basic infrastructure) and therefore involve various departments and levels of governments. In low-income countries, where the bulk of reforms are externally financed, they also require donor coordination. Thus, reformers must create an oversight mechanism in the form of independent coordinating committees comprising donors as well as high-ranking representatives of different government agencies to foster policy coordination and compliance, supply technical support to local levels, and monitor results.

Diagnosing Mozambique's Business Environment

Private sector development has been considered one of the main development objectives under Mozambique's new poverty reduction strategy

(*Plana de Acção para a Redução da Pobreza Absoluta II*, or PARPA II). There has been growing recognition that private firms of all types are key actors in growth and poverty reduction; they create more than 90 percent of jobs, provide most goods and services, and pay most of the taxes needed to fund health care, education, and other services (World Bank, 2005a). A good business environment has been deemed essential in this regard, as it enhances external competitiveness and firm-level productivity, and promotes and attracts domestic and foreign investment, including from labor-intensive small and medium-size enterprises (SMEs). Moreover, as discussed in Chapter 3, Mozambique's main sources of long-term growth are investment and productivity improvements. Thus, reforms to strengthen the business environment will be important if Mozambique is to sustain its remarkable pro-poor growth record once its post-conflict catch-up recovery runs its course (World Bank, 2005a).

Promoting private sector development will require further improvements in Mozambique's business environment. Despite significant progress, Mozambique's overall business environment still has a relatively low ranking on different indices, both international and, to a lesser extent, regional (Table 9.1).[6] It is clear that there is work to be done in several areas to bring Mozambique's business environment in line with its competitors' (and similar developing countries'). However, the fact that Mozambique's ranking is not that much lower than the rankings of China, India, and some of the members of the Association of Southeast Asian Nations (ASEAN)—a particularly successful group in promoting sustainable export-led growth—seems to indicate that an attractive business environment may require only a handful of carefully selected reforms. The relevant question is, therefore, which reforms to start with.

It is useful to begin by classifying the main obstacles to a competitive business environment according to the following broad categories: (1) governance (for example, property rights, government corruption, political

---

[6]The indices presented in the table are widely used in cross-country comparisons and benchmarking analyses of a country's business environment. Throughout the analysis, Mozambique's reference groups are defined as those countries belonging to the Southern African Development Community (SADC)—namely, Angola, Botswana, the Democratic Republic of the Congo, Lesotho, Madagascar, Malawi, Mauritius, Namibia, Seychelles, South Africa, Swaziland, Tanzania, Zambia, and Zimbabwe. Comparisons will also be drawn to India, China, and the members of the Association of Southeast Asian Nations known as the ASEAN-4 (Indonesia, Malaysia, the Philippines, and Thailand), a well-known reference group with successful private sector–led growth strategies that in some cases yielded sustainable growth. For a discussion of sustainable growth episodes and potential correlates, see Johnson, Ostry, and Subramanian (2007).

Table 9.1. Ranking Mozambique: Alternative Business Environment Indicators

	Rank[1]		
	Ease of doing business 2007–08	GCI 2006–07	IEF 2007
Mozambique	**134**	**121**	**101**
Lowest sub-Saharan Africa	178	125	151
Lowest SADC[2]	178	125	118
Lowest ASEAN-4	133	77	110
Highest sub-Saharan Africa	27	45	35
Highest SADC[2]	27	45	35
Highest ASEAN-4	74	26	48
India	120	43	104
China	83	54	119
Total ranked	178	125	157

Sources: World Bank (2007); World Economic Forum (2006); Heritage Foundation (2007).

Note: GCI denotes the World Economic Forum's Global Competitiveness Index; IEF denotes the Heritage Foundation's Index of Economic Freedom.

[1]Most recent available rankings.

[2]SADC = Southern African Development Community.

stability, and security); (2) infrastructure (for example, roads, electricity, and telecommunications); (3) macroeconomic stability; (4) human capital (for example, worker skills and education); (5) regulatory practices (for example, labor regulations, tax administration, customs procedures, and business licensing and registration); and (6) finance (for example, access and cost).[7] The rest of the section will attempt to identify reform priorities among these broad categories on the basis of the tools covered in the previous section.

Business Surveys

The opinions voiced by manufacturing firms participating in ICA surveys provide us with one means of identifying reform priorities. Mozambique's last comprehensive ICA was conducted in 2002 (Nasir and others, 2003), and was recently replicated in a 2006 business survey jointly conducted by the Confederation of Mozambican Business Associations (CTA) and

[7]We use here a slightly narrower definition of governance than that adopted by Kaufmann, Kraay, and Mastruzzi (2007). The set of traditions and institutions by which authority in a country is exercised, governance encompasses the dimensions of voice and government accountability; political stability and absence of violence; the rule of law, including perceptions on crime and enforceability of contracts; control of corruption; and government effectiveness. We deal with issues related to regulatory quality separately, under category (5), as presented above.

Table 9.2. Mozambique: Developments in Perceived Constraints

	2002 survey			2006 survey			Changes	
	Mean	Major/severe obstacle *(Percent of firms)*	Rank	Mean	Major/severe obstacle *(Percent of firms)*	Rank	Mean	Rank
Cost of credit	3.28	84	1	3.00	72	1	–0.28	0
Access to domestic credit	3.08	75	2	2.42	58	3	–0.66	1
Access to foreign credit	2.93	73	3	1.55	38	9	–1.38	6
Electricity	2.65	64	4	2.06	46	6	–0.59	2
General corruption	2.76	64	5	2.11	46	7	–0.65	2
Macroeconomic instability	2.75	63	6	2.65	63	2	–0.1	–4
Anticompetitive practices	2.59	60	7	1.45	32	14	–1.14	7
Unpredictability of policies	2.58	58	8	2.03	44	8	–0.55	0
Tax rates	2.45	55	9	2.15	50	4	–0.3	–5
Crime, theft, and disorder	2.47	54	10	1.79	35	11	–0.68	1
Customs	2.11	49	11	1.70	38	10	–0.41	–1
Tax administration	2.19	48	12	1.74	35	12	–0.45	0
Labor regulations	1.80	38	13	2.07	48	5	0.27	–8
Skills/education of workers	1.79	34	14	1.68	35	13	–0.11	–1
Business registration	1.44	28	15	0.86	10	18	–0.58	3
Transportation	1.43	27	16	1.44	26	15	0.01	–1
Access to land	1.24	27	17	0.82	18	16	–0.42	–1
Telecommunications	1.28	20	18	0.76	14	17	–0.52	–1

Source: Mozambique Ministry of Planning and Development (2006).
Note: Average across firms of judgments on how much the listed factors constrain the operation and growth of their business, where 0 = no obstacle, 1 = slight, 2 = moderate, 3 = major, and 4 = serious obstacle.

the Ministry of Planning and Development (Mozambique Ministry of Planning and Development, 2006).[8]

Firms identified the same constraints in both surveys (Table 9.2):

- Respondents in both surveys named the high cost of credit as the most binding constraint on finance.

[8]The 2002 World Bank survey was preceded by a joint CTA–World Bank survey in 1998 that covered 153 manufacturing firms. However, because of data quality issues, the earlier survey cannot be properly compared with the two latest surveys. In the 2006 MPD-CTA survey, 137 out of 192 firms that had participated in the 2002 World Bank ICA plus an additional 21 replacement firms using a similar questionnaire were successfully interviewed. Of the 55 firms not interviewed, 30 have closed down; the rest refused to participate. While the two surveys could be considered a panel, no claim is made, especially in the 2006 survey, that the sample is representative, and no attempt has been made to correct for survey bias.

- Macroeconomic instability was a source of concern in 2006 because of a temporary bout of exchange rate volatility that subsided later that year.
- Obstacles posed by governance, infrastructure, and regulatory practices appear to be concentrated in specific areas.
    - ◊ In terms of infrastructure, electricity seems to be the biggest issue, but transportation and telecommunications also get low rankings in both surveys.
    - ◊ Governance-related issues represent an obstacle because of perceived levels of corruption, not because of property rights issues (access to land) or security perceptions (crime). Perceptions of other governance-related obstacles (such as anticompetitive and informal practices, on the one hand, and crime, theft, and disorder, on the other hand) have improved.
    - ◊ Apart from labor regulations and taxes, which have recently become a main source of concern for the business community, regulatory practices do not stand out as a major obstacle. Interestingly, regulatory and administrative barriers—namely, business registration, customs, and tax administration procedures—which are commonly identified in the economic literature as important deterrents to business growth in Africa, do not rank high.
- Human capital—in particular the availability of skilled workers—does not appear to be a severe obstacle according to any of the business surveys, even though a majority of workers in both survey samples had only very basic schooling.

Such initial rankings should be considered with caution given the subjective nature of the assessments. In addition, aggregate results may mask variations in perceptions of the business environment depending on the size, age, or sector of the firm surveyed. Labor regulations, for instance, are more binding for large firms, which are subject to greater government scrutiny, than for SMEs.[9] Therefore, the rest of this section uses a combination of benchmarking and growth diagnostic techniques to refine the rankings.

Benchmarking

The most recent World Bank Doing Business report (World Bank, 2007) presents a slightly different picture of the main obstacles in Mozambique's business environment. Regulatory practices in the areas of labor, licens-

[9]This survey was undertaken before the enactment of the new labor law in 2007.

ing, and trade facilitation, followed by governance issues related to the security of property rights, stand out as the most important constraints on private sector development in Mozambique, compared with the country's competitors in the Southern African Development Community (SADC) and some of the fastest-growing countries in Asia (Table 9.3). These constraints are very similar regardless of whether Mozambique is benchmarked against SADC or Asian and Pacific countries.

By increasing employment costs, labor regulations stood out as the most costly obstacle to business growth in Mozambique; the country's employment-related costs were among the highest in the SADC. Labor regulations were particularly rigid with respect to working hours (overtime, night, and weekend work and paid leave) and hiring practices, and costly with respect to firing procedures (Figure 9.2). However, this assessment did not take into account the new labor law that came into effect in 2007, which significantly increased labor market flexibility by relaxing restrictions on the use of fixed-term contracts, reducing the cost of severance pay and leave benefits, and streamlining the conflict-resolution system of labor relations (see Box 9.1).

Other regulatory practices remain burdensome. Business licensing, trading requirements, and business closure procedures are more cumbersome, costly, and time consuming in Mozambique than in other SADC countries or in Asian and Pacific countries (Table 9.3, Figure 9.3). The cost of either importing or exporting a container, though below the SADC average, is about three times as expensive as in China (Figure 9.3). On the positive side, Mozambique's business registration procedures have recently improved significantly.

Governance obstacles related directly to the security of property rights are particularly striking. Contract enforcement stands out as an important constraint, using both SADC and, particularly, Asian and Pacific countries as benchmarks. Despite the relatively small number of legal procedures required in Mozambique (Figure 9.4), it still ranks relatively low, both regionally and internationally, on contract enforcement, in terms of both the time and the cost involved in enforcing commercial contracts. A less binding but still relevant governance-related obstacle relates to the costs involved in the regulation of property transfers and registration (Figure 9.4). Simpler and less costly procedures to register property minimize corruption and, by promoting formal titling, strengthen businesses' property rights as well as financial access by increasing the availability of collateral.

If assessed only on the basis of the Doing Business report's "getting credit" indicator, finance is less of an obstacle for Mozambican businesses. This indicator is dominated by the availability of information on a

Table 9.3. Mozambique: Cost of Doing Business, 2007/08 Rankings[1]

	Ease of doing business	Employing workers	Dealing with licenses	Trading across borders	Enforcing contracts	Closing a business	Registering property	Starting a business	Getting credit	Paying taxes	Protecting investors
Mozambique	**134**	**162**	**147**	**140**	**138**	**134**	**126**	**125**	**97**	**72**	**33**
South Africa	35	91	45	134	85	68	76	53	26	61	9
Tanzania	130	151	170	100	35	109	160	95	115	104	83
Uganda	118	11	81	141	119	48	163	114	158	55	122
India	120	85	134	79	177	137	112	111	36	165	33
China	83	86	175	42	20	57	29	135	84	168	83
Indonesia	123	153	99	41	141	136	121	168	68	110	51
Malaysia	24	43	105	21	63	54	67	74	3	56	4
Philippines	133	122	77	57	113	147	86	144	97	126	141
Thailand	15	49	12	50	26	44	20	36	36	89	33
Distance to SADC[2]	107	151	128	123	105	108	90	117	71	61	24
Distance to Asia and Pacific[2]	119	119	135	119	118	90	97	89	94	16	29
Change to 2006/07 rankings[3]	–6	5	44	–1	–30	8	21	–28	14	–8	–50

Source: World Bank (2007).

[1]Out of 178 countries.

[2]Difference in rank between Mozambique and highest ranked country in the Southern African Development Community, and Asia and the Pacific (ASEAN-4, India, China); + = worse ranked.

[3]Change in rank observed in Mozambique relative to previous year; + = worsening rank.

Figure 9.2. Benchmarking Mozambique's Labor Regulations

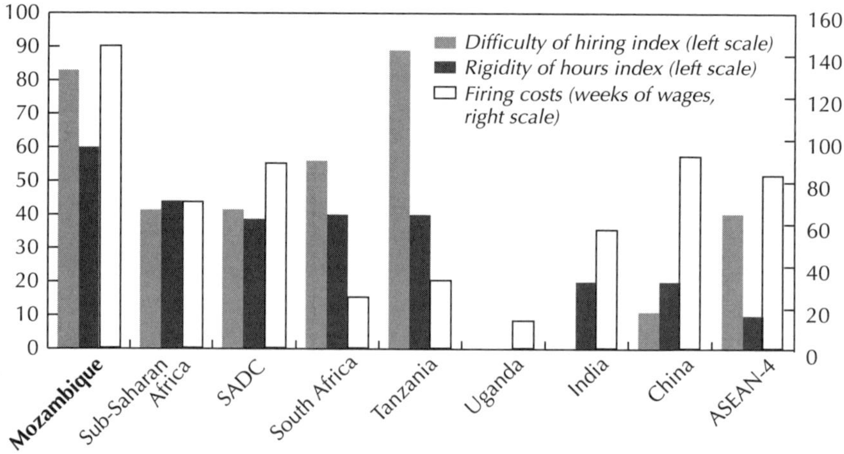

Source: World Bank (2007).
Note: SADC denotes Southern African Development Community; ASEAN-4 denotes Indonesia, Malaysia, the Philippines, and Thailand.

borrower's credit history. Access to affordable credit usually increases when lenders can count on credit registries with wide coverage and strong legal rights. Taking both these aspects into account, Mozambique's financial sector ranks better than those of other countries (Table 9.4). However, financial obstacles should not be downplayed. The availability of credit information still needs to be improved, to bring it in line with best practices in South Africa and the ASEAN-4 countries, and the ranking for this indicator seems to be slipping, implying that the availability of credit information may not be expanding fast enough (Table 9.3). Moreover, access to affordable credit is hampered when loan recovery is delayed by weak contract enforcement or constrained by unreliable collateral systems resulting from inefficient property registries—two important shortcomings that have been identified in Mozambique—as is confirmed by the relatively low ranking of Mozambique's legal rights index.

Benchmarking on the basis of the Doing Business report is not without limitations. The report does not attempt to measure the cost of doing business resulting from poor infrastructure, macroeconomic conditions, human capital, or governance in important areas such as the security of property from theft and looting. In addition, to make data comparable across countries, Doing Business indicators refer to a specific type of business—generally a limited-liability company operating in the largest business city. This last point has

Box 9.1. Strengthening Mozambique's Regulatory Practices

Protecting investors

Mozambique was the second fastest reformer overall in the category "Protecting Investors," according to the rankings in the World Bank's report "Doing Business in 2008." It jumped 63 places in the rankings, from 96th place to 33rd place. A new commercial code enacted in 2006 replaced legislation dating from 1888, introduced stricter corporate governance rules, and strengthened the rights of minority shareholders.

Business registration

Progress in reforming business registration has been remarkable. New regulations simplifying the start-up of commercial and industrial activities were issued in 2004. Since then, one-stop shops have been created in all of Mozambique's provinces to facilitate business registration. Business registration was further simplified in 2006 with the enactment of the new commercial code and a code of registry, the computerization of the company registry, and the elimination of the requirement to publish the company's by-laws in Mozambique's Official Gazette. As a result, the start-up time for new firms in Mozambique decreased by almost three months, from, on average, 113 days to 29 days, and Mozambique moved up 32 places in the rankings for the category "Starting a Business."

Progress in Business Licensing and Registration

Year	Number of days	Number of procedures
2004	540	18
2005	153	14
2006	113	13
2007	29	10

Source: World Bank (2007).

Labor regulations

Mozambique has also made considerable progress in reforming labor legislation. A decree facilitating the hiring of skilled expatriates was issued in 2004, but a tripartite commission to review the labor legislation was not set up until 2005. A new labor law was approved by the Mozambican Assembly in 2007. The new law (1) relaxes restrictions on the use of fixed-term contracts; (2) significantly reduces the cost of severance pay and other benefits; (3) creates extra-judicial conflict-resolution bodies to reverse the backlog of labor dispute cases in the ordinary law courts; and (4) simplifies the process of hiring expatriates while maintaining a quota system.

Figure 9.3. Benchmarking Mozambique's Administrative Barriers to Business

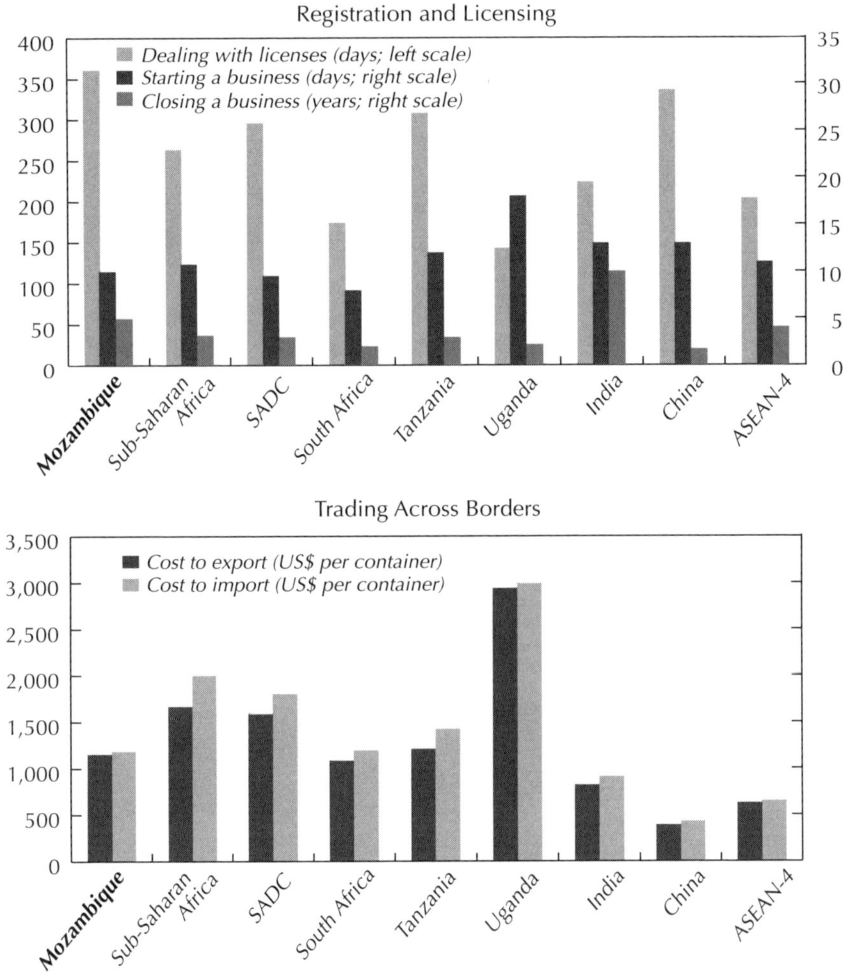

Source: World Bank (2007).
Note: SADC = Southern African Development Community. ASEAN-4 = Indonesia, Malaysia, the Philippines, and Thailand.

been mentioned as one of the reasons business registration is not consistently cited in business surveys as an important obstacle, unlike in the Doing Business report.[10] We thus perform two additional benchmarking exercises below.

[10]Business surveys conducted in Mozambique have found a positive correlation between firm size and business registration costs, which may explain the discrepancy, given that the

Figure 9.4. Benchmarking Mozambique's Property Rights, Implied Costs

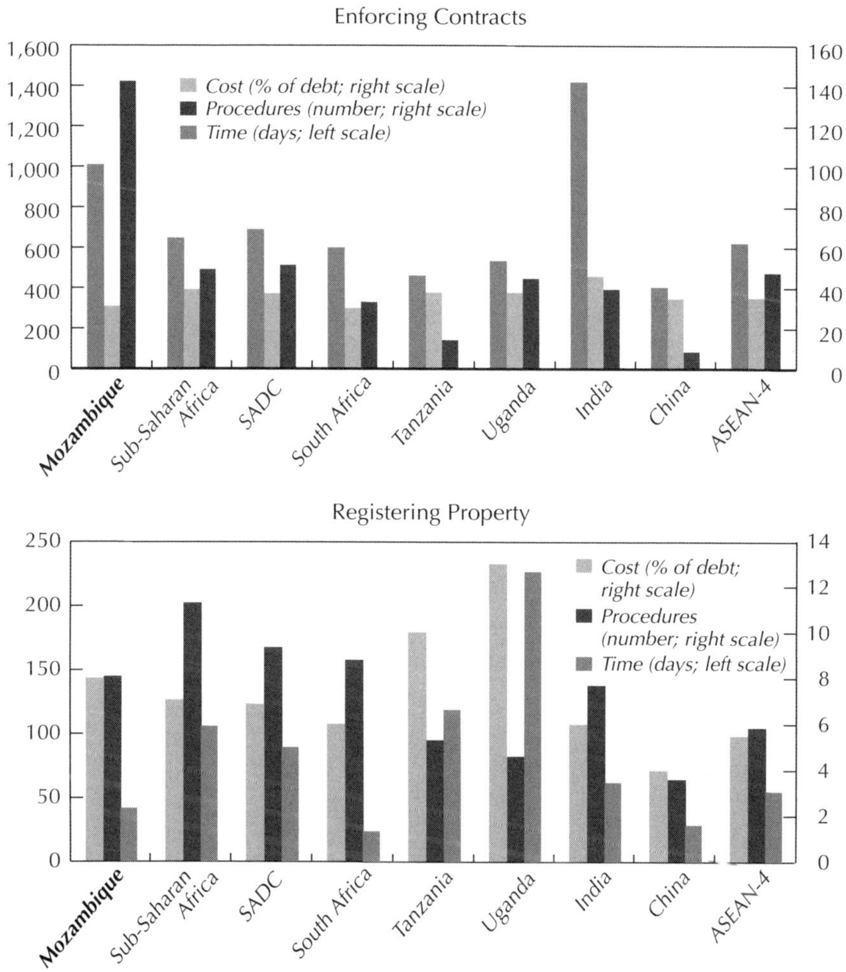

Source: World Bank (2007).

Note: SADC = Southern African Development Community. ASEAN-4 = Indonesia, Malaysia, the Philippines, and Thailand.

representative firm used for the purpose of the Doing Business report may be larger than the median size of the firms in the sample. Differences may also reflect the fact that business registration costs reported in business surveys corresponded to the "most important operating license," whereas the Doing Business report considered the cost and time of acquiring each single license.

Table 9.4. Mozambique: Benchmarking Regulatory Financial Obstacles

	Legal rights index[1]	Credit information index[2]	Public registry coverage *(Percent of adults)*	Private bureau coverage *(Percent of adults)*
Mozambique	**3**	**3**	**1**	**0**
Sub-Saharan Africa	4	1	2	5
SADC	5	2	3	14
South Africa	5	6	0	52
Tanzania	5	0	0	0
Uganda	3	0	0	0
India	6	4	0	11
China	3	4	49	0
ASEAN-4	5	4	16	11

Source: World Bank (2007).

Note: SADC = Southern African Development Community. ASEAN-4 = Indonesia, Malaysia, the Philippines, and Thailand.

[1]Increases with the reliability of loan and collateral recovery procedures.

[2]Increases with the quality and coverage of credit information.

Given its focus on external competitiveness, the World Economic Forum's Global Competitiveness Index (GCI) provides a more comprehensive overview of factors affecting the business environment. The GCI is broken down into nine subindices; the first six closely coincide with the broad categories of business environment constraints described earlier.[11] On the basis of the distances between Mozambique's rankings and those of potential competitors, obstacles related to market efficiency—broadly defined as distortions, such as regulations imposed on goods, labor, and financial markets—are the most prominent, followed by obstacles related to macroeconomic conditions, human capital, institutions, and infrastructure (Table 9.5). As such, these results seem to support the need to prioritize microeconomic reforms to address regulatory obstacles, as indicated by the World Bank's Doing Business report. However, regulatory obstacles should be broadly defined to include those related to financial markets. At the same time, the GCI benchmarking, in line with recent business surveys, finds that macroeconomic conditions, infrastructure, and institutions play a secondary, but still relevant, role in constraining the business environment in Mozambique.

---

[11]The nine subindices are institutions, infrastructure, macroeconomy, health care and primary education, higher education and training, market efficiency, technological readiness, business sophistication, and innovation. The last three were set aside given the private sector's very low comparative advantage on high-tech activities at this stage. See World Economic Forum (2006) for a detailed description.

Table 9.5. Mozambique: GCI, 2006/07 Rankings[1]

	Market efficiency	Macroeconomy	Health care and education	Institutions	Higher education and training	Infrastructure
Mozambique	**122**	**112**	**117**	**107**	**122**	**99**
South Africa	33	46	103	36	56	49
Tanzania	75	100	118	56	112	93
Uganda	84	66	123	100	107	118
India	21	88	93	34	49	62
China	56	6	55	80	77	60
Indonesia	27	57	72	52	53	89
Malaysia	9	31	42	18	32	23
Philippines	57	62	82	88	63	88
Thailand	31	28	84	40	42	38
Memorandum items:						
Distance to SADC[2]	89	73	73	71	66	57
Distance to Asia and Pacific[2]	113	106	75	89	90	76

Source: World Economic Forum (2006). GCI denotes the World Economic Forum's Global Competitiveness Index.

[1]Out of 125 countries.

[2]Difference in rank between Mozambique and the highest-ranked country in the Southern African Development Community, and Asia and the Pacific (ASEAN-4, India, China); + = worse ranked.

The quality and enforcement of regulatory practices also stand out as important constraints, based on the World Bank's governance indicators (Kaufmann, Kraay, and Mastruzzi, 2007). With respect to governance, as illustrated in Chapter 1, Mozambique ranks above not only the average sub-Saharan African country but also some high-performing ASEAN countries in such areas as political stability and voice and accountability. (See Chapter 1, Figure 1.8.) It has also consistently ranked above the median for the SADC countries in most indicators.[12] However, when it comes to the quality and enforcement of legal rules, the picture is not as good. (See Chapter 1, Figure 1.8.) Mozambique ranks below all ASEAN-4 countries and is among the three weakest performers in the SADC (Macamo, 2006).[13] Previous findings regarding deeper governance constraints related to the effectiveness of courts and the enforceability of

[12]See Macamo (2006) for an overview of Mozambique's governance rankings relative to those of the other SADC countries over the past 10 years.

[13]Regulatory quality reflects government policies affecting the business environment, including measures of market-unfriendly policies, and perceptions of the burden imposed by excessive regulation in areas such as foreign trade and business development.

contracts are also echoed in the poor ranking Mozambique received under the rule-of-law indicator, which is designed to capture such issues.

A similar picture emerges from the Country Policy and Institutional Assessment (CPIA) ratings compiled by the International Development Association (IDA), the part of the World Bank that helps the world's poorest countries.[14] Mozambique's macroeconomic policies fare well in the CPIA's Economic Management ratings in relation to average IDA borrowers and some eligible IDA borrowers in the reference group. On the other hand, Mozambique's ratings do not compare as favorably with respect to the business regulatory environment, property rights enforcement, and perceived levels of corruption (Table 9.6). As will be discussed below, weaknesses on the regulatory and governance fronts are currently being addressed as part of the government's new strategy to reduce the cost of doing business and measures to strengthen the monitoring and implementation of the government's anticorruption strategy.

Growth Diagnostics

As revealed by previous benchmarking exercises, which measure the distances between Mozambique's rankings and those of the best-performing Southeast Asian and SADC countries, the quality and enforcement of regulations appear to be the predominant constraints on Mozambique's business activity. Using growth diagnostic tools, the rest of this section identifies reform priorities through a different and, perhaps, more economically sound metric—namely their growth impact. In the case of Mozambique, this means identifying the institutional measures needed to sustain strong capital inflows and improvements in the quality of the labor force, and to accelerate total factor productivity growth, conditions identified in Chapter 3 as critical in maintaining Mozambique's post-conflict takeoff.[15] As discussed above, the methodology for linking proximate to deep determinants of growth is still evolving. As such, the analysis here should be seen as preliminary and, given its reliance on manufacturing data, particularly relevant to the development of Mozambique's manufacturing sector.

---

[14]The CPIA rates countries against 16 criteria grouped in four clusters: (1) economic management; (2) structural policies; (3) policies for social inclusion and equity; and (4) public sector management and institutions. Such ratings serve as the basis for allocating IDA resources among eligible countries.

[15]See Tahari and others (2004); IMF (2005); and World Bank (2005a) for descriptions of earlier growth accounting exercises designed to identify the proximate determinants of growth in Mozambique.

Table 9.6. Mozambique: Benchmarking CPIA, 2006 Ratings, Selected Clusters and IDA Countries[1]

Cluster	**Mozambique**	India	Indonesia	Vietnam	Tanzania	Uganda	Average IDA borrowers[2]
Economic management							
Macroeconomic management	**4.0**	4.5	4.5	5.5	5.0	4.5	3.8
Fiscal policy	**4.0**	3.5	4.0	4.5	4.5	4.5	3.4
Debt policy	**4.5**	4.5	4.5	4.0	4.0	4.5	3.4
Average	**4.2**	4.2	4.3	4.7	4.5	4.5	3.5
Structural policies							
Trade	**4.5**	3.5	4.5	3.5	4.0	4.0	3.8
Financial sector	**3.0**	4.0	3.5	3.0	3.5	3.5	3.1
Business regulatory environment	**3.0**	3.5	3.0	3.5	3.5	4.0	3.2
Average	**3.5**	3.7	3.7	3.3	3.7	3.8	3.4
Public sector management and institutions							
Property rights and rules-based government	**3.0**	3.5	2.5	3.5	3.5	3.5	2.9
Quality of budget and financial management	**3.5**	4.0	3.5	4.0	4.5	4.0	3.2
Efficiency of revenue mobilization	**3.5**	4.0	3.5	3.5	4.0	3.0	3.4
Quality of public administration	**2.5**	3.5	3.5	3.5	3.5	3.0	3.0
Transparency, accountability, and corruption	**3.0**	3.5	3.0	3.0	3.5	3.0	2.9
Average	**3.1**	3.7	3.2	3.5	3.8	3.3	3.1

Note: CPIA denotes the Country Policy and Institutional Assessment ratings compiled by the International Development Association (IDA), the part of the World Bank Group that helps the world's poorest countries.

[1]Scale 1 = lowest, 6 = highest.

[2]Current historical ceiling for IDA eligibility is US$1,735 per capita income, 2006 prices.

Figure 9.5. Mozambique and Comparators: Median Return on Capital and Profit Margins

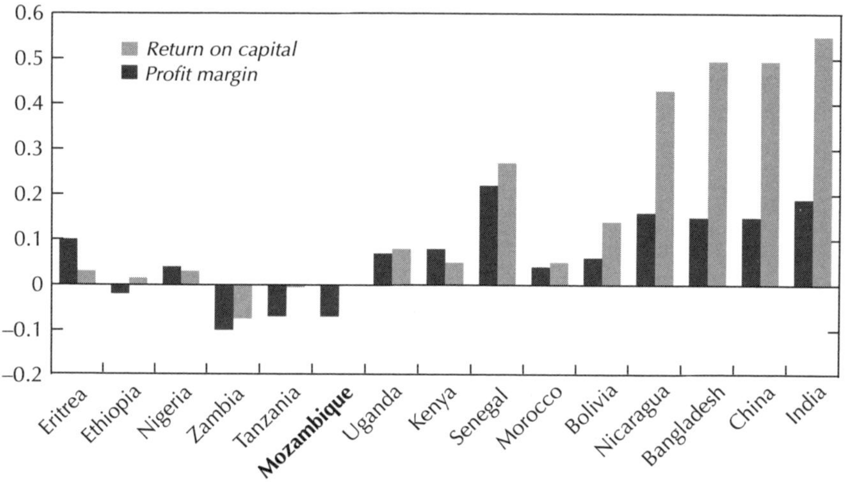

Source: Eifert, Gelb, and Ramachandran (2005).

Private returns on capital are reportedly low in Mozambique's manufacturing sector, albeit in line with those in important African competitors.[16] Manufacturing firms in Mozambique register much lower median returns on capital (the ratio of profits to capital stock) and profitability (the ratio of total sales to total costs) than firms in better-performing comparator countries, such as China and India. Median returns are near zero in Mozambique—above those in Zambia and Tanzania but below those in Uganda, Kenya, and Senegal (Figure 9.5).

Low private returns appear to be determined by the combined impact of low social returns and limited private appropriability. The scarcity of skilled workers reflected in Mozambique's elevated educational premium explains both the relatively high contribution of labor to total costs and low factory-floor productivity (Figure 9.6).[17] Private returns are further

[16]Comparable data for the ASEAN-4 and most SADC countries are not available. Asian comparators in the description of firm-level measures of profitability and productivity are limited to China and India.

[17]See Chapter 3 and Fox, Bardasi, and Van den Broeck (2005). According to these studies, returns to education are very high (5 percent per year of schooling in urban areas),

Figure 9.6. Mozambique and Comparators: Manufacturing Firms' Cost Structures
(Percentage of total costs)

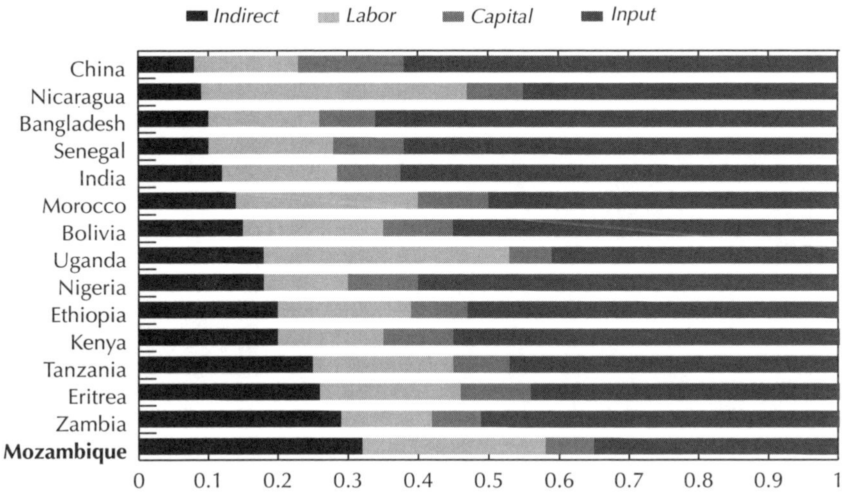

Source: Eifert, Gelb, and Ramachandran (2005).

depressed by Mozambique's considerably higher indirect costs and output losses, including costs and losses stemming from the country's inadequate infrastructure and burdensome regulations, which squeeze firms' value added and reduce total factor productivity (Figure 9.7).[18]

When benchmarked against Asian countries experiencing sustainable growth, prospects for sustainable growth in Mozambique seem to indicate the need to prioritize reforms in infrastructure, regulatory practices, and secondary education to improve private returns to capital.[19] Primary education, on the other hand, does not seem to be as binding. On the basis of the benchmarking approach in Johnson, Ostry, and Subramanian (2007), Indonesia and Thailand were capable of initiating sustainable takeoffs with low levels of primary education similar to Mozambique's (Table 9.7).

increasing sharply at higher levels of education, and have been stable since 1996.

[18]Other factors worth mentioning include the use of obsolete and ill-maintained equipment, and the absence of modern management techniques.

[19]This result corroborates findings in Chapter 3 that further improvements in secondary education are key to delivering the improvements in human capital needed to sustain growth.

Figure 9.7. Mozambique and Comparators: TFP Decomposition
(China = 1)

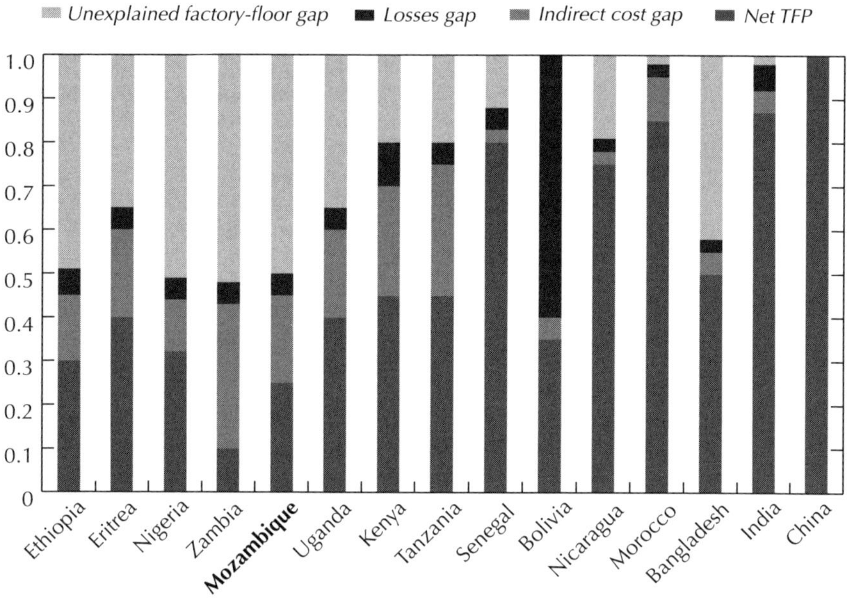

Source: Eifert, Gelb, and Ramachandran (2005).
Note: TFP = total factor productivity.

The gap in infrastructure is more accentuated, suggesting that there is a need to step up efforts in the area. In the same vein, low expected private appropriability, driven by a relatively high risk of expropriation, seems to be an important obstacle to sustained growth. According to widely accepted indicators, recent levels of economic risk and corruption in Mozambique are significantly higher than those observed in most ASEAN countries at earlier stages of their takeoffs. Once again, this calls for institutional changes that will ensure stronger and more consistent enforcement of laws and regulations, including those designed to curb corruption.

The growth of Mozambique's manufacturing sector is also constrained by the high cost of financial services. Real interest rates and lending-deposit spreads, while below the regional average, are still above those in the best SADC and East Asian performers (Figure 9.8). Lending rates for smaller Mozambican firms are more than double those for larger firms. Lack of access to finance is another major constraint on firm growth in Mozambique: more than 70 percent of Mozambican firms do not have

Table 9.7. Increasing Private Returns: Lessons from Asia

	Human capital		Infrastructure		Private appropriability	
	Primary education[1]	Secondary education[1]	Telephone mainlines *(Per 1,000 people)*	Total road surface area *(In kilometers)*	Economic risk[2]	Control of corruption[3]
			Sub-Saharan countries with growth >=2%[4]			
Mozambique	**86.0**	**8.7**	**4.0**	**38.0**	**25.5**	**1.5**
SADC average	102.0	42.6	66.0	227.5	33.3	2.9
Sub-Saharan Africa average	91.4	31.8	35.6	166.4	31.7	2.5
		Selected Asian countries under sustained growth accelerations (SGs)[5]				
China	112.6	45.9	2.0	123.0	35.5	2.0
ASEAN-4 average	83.4	22.6	6.9	184.5	34.3	3.3
Indonesia	80.0	16.1	1.5	151.6	30.1	3.0
Malaysia	88.7	34.2	13.8	261.2	37.5	4.0
Thailand	81.4	17.4	5.5	140.6	35.2	3.0

Source: Johnson, Ostry, and Subramanian (2007).
[1]Gross enrollment ratio.
[2]Scores range from 1 to 50. The higher the score, the lower the risk. Data for SGs are from 1984, for sub-Saharan Africa from 2004 and 2005.
[3]Scores range from 1 to 6. The higher the score, the less corruption there is. Data for SGs are from 1996, for sub-Saharan Africa from 2004 and 2005.
[4]Data are for the most recent period available. Refer to source for list of countries and periods.
[5]Data refer to year close to growth takeoff. Refer to source for takeoff dates and list of countries.

Figure 9.8. Mozambique and Comparators: Cost of Finance

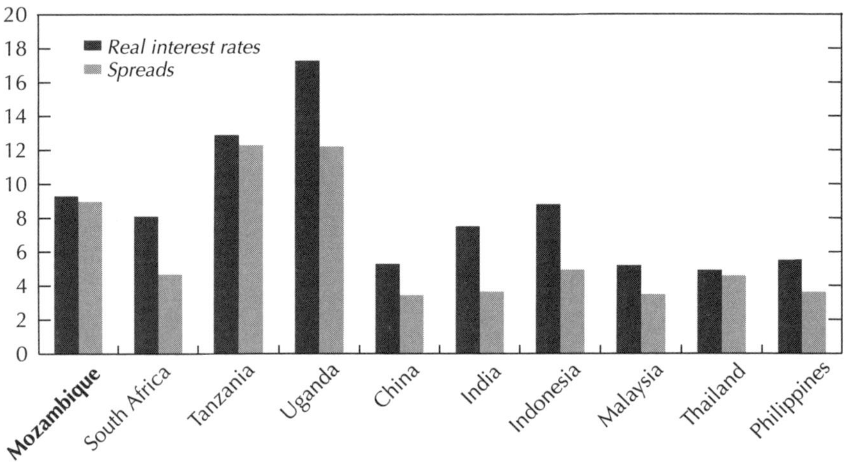

Source: IMF, International Financial Statistics.

access to bank loans or overdraft facilities (that number is even higher for smaller firms) according to the 2003 ICA and 2006 MPD-CTA survey (Mozambique Ministry of Planning and Development, 2006).

The relatively high cost of finance appears to be the result of insufficient domestic savings. Hausmann, Rodrik, and Velasco (2005) theorize that a country with scarce domestic savings but high foreign debt or a large external current account deficit is probably using its access to foreign savings to the limit. This hypothesis could in principle apply to Mozambique, which has high investment rates, a large external current account deficit, and a low domestic saving rate compared with those of comparator countries (Table 9.8).

However, while high interest rates owing to low domestic savings are an important factor, access to affordable finance is also constrained by Mozambique's poor financial intermediation and weak lending environment, as discussed in Chapter 4. The mobilization of savings is constrained not only by Mozambique's low income levels but also by a thin branch network of banks, particularly in rural areas (Figure 9.9). However, poor access to savings accounts may be only part of the story. Mozambique's low loan-to-deposit rates seem to indicate that, while scarce, domestic savings are not being used to their full potential, given the underdevelopment of the country's credit markets. Tanzania, which also has a thin branch network but higher loan-to-deposit rates, is particularly illustrative in this

Table 9.8. Mozambique: Credit Constraints
(Average for 2000–05, percent of GDP)

	Current account	Total investment	Domestic savings	Private credit
Mozambique	**–21.2**	**26.6**	**10.4**	**14.8**
SADC[1]	–2.3	16.5	17.2	46.2
Sub-Saharan Africa	–2.6	18.3	19.5	30.8
ASEAN-4[2]	4.6	21.3	26.9	71.0

Source: IMF, World Economic Outlook database.
Note: Current account figures exclude grants.
[1]SADC = Southern African Development Community.
[2]ASEAN-4 = Indonesia, Malaysia, the Philippines, and Thailand.

regard. Business surveys seem to corroborate this view by showing that more than half of the Mozambican firms that did not apply for bank loans cited stringent collateral requirements and cumbersome loan application procedures rather than high interest rates as the reason (IMF and World Bank, 2003; and Mozambique Ministry of Planning and Development, 2006). As a result, very few firms rely on bank credit; an overwhelming majority use retained earnings to finance capital accumulation.

Against this background, reforms to improve access to financial services have become a top priority on Mozambique's business environment reform agenda.[20] Several empirical studies have shown that financial sector development is a strong determinant of aggregate productivity growth.[21] Asia's sustainable growth has been particularly illustrative in this regard. Financial development, which took place at an early stage of the economic takeoff of the successful Asian countries, has sustained growth in the latter mostly by allowing capital to be allocated to the most productive manufacturing activities (IMF, 2006).

Summing Up

Alternative diagnostic tools reveal a number of areas in which Mozambique's business environment lags that of potential regional competitors and of countries that have experienced export-led growth. The analysis conducted above identifies priority areas in Mozambique that have received low ratings in business surveys and widely used business environment indices. The robustness of these results was checked against

[20]See Chapter 4 and IMF (2007) for a detailed account of reforms undertaken to improve access to financial services.

[21]See Levine (2005) for a survey of the empirical literature.

Figure 9.9. Mozambique and Comparators: Financial Intermediation

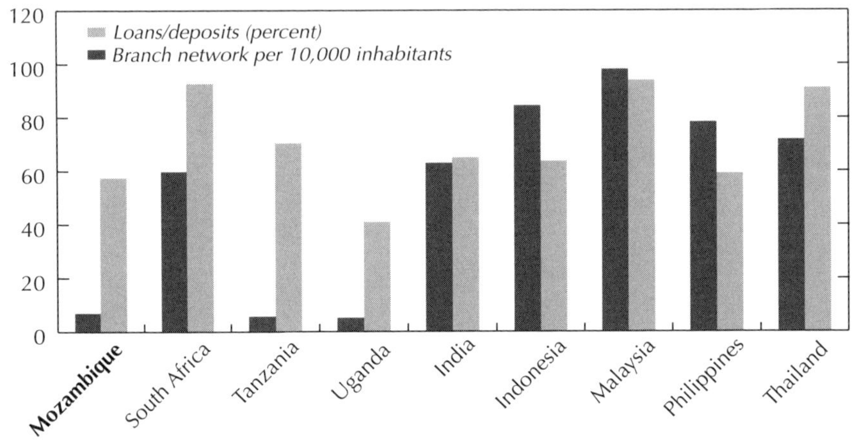

Sources: Beck, Demirguc-Kunt, and Peria (2005); IMF, International Financial Statistics.
Note: 2005 data.

the relative impact of alternative areas on overall growth, as well as on the growth of the manufacturing sector. Our main findings are as follows:

- *Governance, financial, and regulatory issues top the list of needed reforms.* More specifically, governance issues that affect financial access—namely, contract enforcement and property rights—along with regulatory obstacles to employment, business licensing, and foreign trade, are among the main constraints on private sector development. These factors appear to hurt (1) capital accumulation (and hence growth acceleration) by depressing private returns and increasing financing costs and (2) total factor productivity growth (and hence growth sustainability) by increasing transaction costs and output losses.[22] The remarkable growth performances of a number of Asian countries corroborate this finding. The relative security of property rights, streamlined regulatory practices, and a well-developed

[22]Reforms related to business start-up costs and registration are also important in making it easier for firms to enter the formal sector. This is particularly relevant in the case of Mozambique, where about 76 percent of urban employment is estimated to be in the informal sector.

financial sector have been consistently identified as important factors behind sustained productivity growth in these countries.

- *Infrastructure deficiencies deserve special attention.* When benchmarked against some Asian countries that have experienced sustained growth, Mozambique stands out for its inadequate infrastructure.[23] While the energy sector has been a major source of complaint in the business community, the telecommunications and transportation sectors are far less developed in Mozambique than in Asia and other SADC countries.
- *One of the central government's objectives should be sustaining macro-economic stability.*

The next section looks at the government's reform agenda with a view to assessing to what extent the priorities identified have been incorporated in a coherent reform strategy. The focus will be mostly on reforms that reduce the risks and costs of doing business in Mozambique in the priority areas of governance, regulatory practices, and access to finance.

The Government's Strategy and Progress

Strategy

With the help of the World Bank, the Mozambican authorities have developed a comprehensive, time-bound, and well-targeted new strategy to make Mozambique's business environment the most competitive in the SADC by 2015. This strategy consists of a number of action plans to operationalize the PARPA II objectives of (1) reducing the cost of doing business; (2) expanding access to financial services; and (3) accelerating reforms in the judiciary sector, particularly in the area of contract enforcement. (See Table 9.9.)

The plan spearheaded by the Ministry of Industry and Commerce (MIC) covers business licensing, closure, and inspection procedures; labor costs; access to credit; energy costs; and property registration. An inter-ministerial committee has been set up to coordinate and monitor the plan's implementation as many ministries are involved.

[23]Given the significant differences in infrastructure provision between Maputo province and the rest of the country, recent benchmarks and, to some extent, business surveys may underestimate the gaps in infrastructure because they tend to be focused on firms located in Maputo province.

Table 9.9. Mozambique: Action Plan to Reduce the Costs of Doing Business

	2006	2007	2010	2012	2015
Ease of doing business (overall rank)	153	110	60	45	26
Starting a business	139	70	45	35	25
Dealing with licenses	103	70	45	28	15
Hiring and firing workers	157	70	60	47	40
Registering property	105	95	65	40	23
Paying taxes	80	70	55	36	14
Trading across borders	141	90	72	46	32
Closing businesses	126	110	60	50	35
Enforcing contracts	168	130	70	45	28
Cost and quality of electricity					
Cost in kWh (US cents)	n.a.	4	3	2	2
Number of power outages/month	60	50	40	28	12
Transportation cost (US$)					
Beira/Maputo 20-foot container (by land)	770	700	450	425	400
Value-added per worker (US$)	1,000	1,500	2,000	2,500	3,000

Source: World Bank staff estimates.

A number of essential initiatives to reduce the cost of, and expand access to, financial services are also envisaged as part of Mozambique's financial sector reform strategy. The Mozambican authorities, led by the Ministry of Finance and the Bank of Mozambique, have developed a comprehensive reform strategy framed on the recommendations of the 2003 Financial Sector Assessment Program (FSAP)[24] and financed by the World Bank and other donors under the Financial Sector Technical Assistance Project (FSTAP) in 2005.[25] This strategy includes measures to improve the institutional lending environment with respect to secured transactions and credit information and to increase the outreach of banks and microfinance institutions to rural households and SMEs.[26] The gov-

[24]The FSAP is a joint IMF and World Bank initiative introduced in 1999 under which the two institutions seek to identify the strengths and vulnerabilities of a country's financial system, in order to determine how key sources of risk are being managed, ascertain the sector's developmental and technical assistance needs, and help country authorities prioritize policy responses.

[25]Under the FSTAP, the IMF plays the important role of delivering technical assistance in the areas of banking supervision and monetary policy operations and formulation.

[26]The government recently launched a package of initiatives to enhance the physical presence of banks in rural districts. Proposed measures are aimed mostly at reducing the operational costs of providing banking services in rural areas through fiscal incentives, infrastructure improvements, and the relaxation of legal reserve requirements in rural branches so as to include cash in vault. Transport costs related to the constitution of legal reserves and cash in vault for immediate withdrawal are being further minimized as the Bank of Mozambique opens branches in selected districts.

ernment is developing multiyear action plans that extend beyond the FSTAP's five-year duration and that have more precise outcomes.

Public sector reforms are also being accelerated to address governance concerns in a more timely fashion. Mozambique is increasing public sector accountability by reinforcing the capacity of the country's main public sector audit institutions—namely, the Administrative Tribunal and the Inspectorate General of Finances. The government is also committed to strengthening the monitoring and implementation of its anticorruption strategy. To this effect, a committee working with the World Bank is refining governance indicators so that they can be used as measurable and easily monitorable targets.

Mozambique has taken important steps to improve the ownership, coordination, and monitoring of its reform strategy. As previously mentioned, the government has set up an interministerial committee to oversee the reform process. This committee will play an important role in promoting intragovernmental coordination, given the cross-cutting nature of business environment reforms, and, to the extent that the committee comprises high-ranking officials, will raise the political clout of reformers. The strategy will also benefit from mechanisms put in place to increase reform monitoring.[27] As part of a number of initiatives designed to improve donor coordination and align priorities with recipient governments' objectives, since 2004 monitoring of reforms has been done jointly by donors and government representatives through the previously agreed Performance Assessment Framework (PAF).[28] The PAF collects actions and the corresponding set of performance indicators for each sector strategy and reform program outlined in PARPA II. Aid disbursements are conditional only on actions and measurable performance indicators in the PAF, which, in turn, reinforces government ownership of the reform program. To further strengthen the monitoring of business environment reforms, it will be important to ensure that some of the key measures are included in the PAF on a systematic basis.

[27]In addition, Mozambique's FSTAP has set in place novel implementation arrangements to facilitate coordination and monitoring (for example, implementation is monitored by a single agency, which is accountable to the Ministry of Finance), and minimize transaction costs. Progress is assessed each quarter on the basis of a matrix that specifies objectives and corresponding performance indicators.

[28]Mechanisms for coordination and dialogue between government representatives and donors are described in more detail in Chapter 7.

Taking Stock of Mozambique's Reform Effort

Mozambique is starting to emerge as a reform champion by regional standards. This is clearly reflected in the World Bank's most recent Doing Business report (World Bank, 2007): Mozambique moved up three notches to rank 134th out of 178 economies surveyed, from 137th in the previous report. Mozambique was among the top four reforming countries in sub-Saharan Africa, the others being Ghana, Kenya (which were among the top 10 reformers worldwide), and Madagascar (Table 9.10). Progress was particularly impressive in regulations designed to protect investors and accelerate business registration (Box 9.1). Recent changes to labor regulations are expected to further improve Mozambique's ranking.

With the steadfast and timely implementation of its far-reaching reform agenda, Mozambique is well placed to become the best country in which to do business in the SADC.

Lessons Learned

Mozambique provides a good example of how low-income countries should get their business environment reforms right. The country has, for the most part, correctly identified its reform priorities, developed mechanisms to promote reform ownership, and started to refine its reform strategy to improve the targeting, effectiveness, and sustainability of its reform interventions. Results are starting to show, with Mozambique emerging as a top African reformer. Some of the useful lessons learned follow:

- *Reformers should make good use of brief windows of opportunity, implementing reforms when there is broad political support for them.* This widely recognized lesson is confirmed in the case of Mozambique. Elected governments in Mozambique's post-conflict years drew on their high stock of political capital to implement first-generation reforms, reestablishing the basis for private sector development. Important financial sector reforms were implemented in the aftermath of the 2000 banking crisis; the restructuring process that followed was an important catalyst for reform of banking supervision and reporting standards.
- *Quick-win reforms must take priority.* Mozambique's recent experience in reforming business registration procedures is particularly illustrative. Its successful implementation—measured and widely publicized in the World Bank's Doing Business report—aroused media awareness of the need for business environment reforms and raised the

Table 9.10. Gauging Mozambique's Reform Impact
(Change in rank for ease of doing business, 2007–08)

Egypt	–26
Ghana	–22
Georgia	–17
India	–12
Madagascar	–11
Indonesia	–10
Kenya	–10
China	–9
Mozambique	**–6**
Mauritius	–3
Thailand	–2
South Africa	–2
Tanzania	1
Uganda	2
Malaysia	3
Philippines	3

Source: World Bank (2007).
Note: Positive value denotes worsening in rank.

political capital of pro-business advocates inside the government and in the donor community.

- *The creation of coordination mechanisms among government agencies and between governments and donors are important preconditions for successful reform in low-income countries.* The cross-cutting nature of business environment reforms requires several ministries and government agencies to be involved in the reform process. This problem is compounded in low-income countries, given their dependency on aid from multiple donors to finance reforms. Donors are important agents for reform in that they directly finance reform programs or tie aid disbursements to reform progress. However, the heavy presence of donors in many low-income countries today introduces conflicting priorities and monitoring standards, thereby undermining government ownership of reform. Therefore, mechanisms capable of generating a reform plan with consensual support inside the government and agreed to by donors and the government must be in place before an implementation plan can be designed to ensure that reform leaders inside the government will own the strategy and effectively allocate donor support. Mozambique's donor coordination model, discussed in Chapter 7, is an important example in this regard.
- *Getting the reform impact right is also important.* Significant improvements in the business environment may require reformers to address the right priorities and to identify measures capable of reducing the

cost of doing business. For instance, reform strategies need to identify not only which regulations should be implemented but also how these regulations should be changed to decrease costs of compliance. This point also highlights the need to select appropriate indicators to monitor reform progress. Mozambique's proposed action plan, which set yearly targets on the basis of the World Bank's Doing Business report, is an example.

- *Identifying the right priorities in low-income countries requires the comprehensive use of all available diagnostic tools and databases.*[29] Getting priorities right is not an easy task in low-income countries, given the wide range of factors constraining the business environment. Identifying the most binding constraints usually requires a careful analysis of business surveys and benchmarking on the basis of alternative business environment indices. Rather than being used as an alternative, growth diagnostics should be used to reconcile the sometimes conflicting results of business surveys and benchmarking exercises.
- *Priorities may shift over time, so reformers should constantly update their diagnostic exercises as reforms progress in order to gauge the appropriateness of their reform strategy.* For example, business surveys only recently identified labor regulations in Mozambique as one of the most severe constraints. With the enactment of a new labor law, the business environment in Mozambique is likely to improve further, and this improvement should be reflected in upcoming business surveys.
- *Reform strategies should also be reassessed if obstacles persist.* Reform strategies aimed at certain obstacles should be revisited if business environment surveys show that these obstacles persist, or if benchmarking exercises continue to give low rankings to a country on certain issues. In the case of Mozambique, the persistence of the high cost of, and limited access to, finance as a major constraint on business growth even after substantial improvements in the banking system suggests that there is a need to further prioritize deeper institutional reforms, with the aim of improving the governance and legal framework that shapes Mozambique's lending environment. Mozambique is rightly addressing these challenges, with the help of the World Bank, by strengthening the monitoring and implementation of its anticorruption strategy and focusing on delivering measurable improvements in governance.

---

[29]Ideally, these tools should also ensure coverage of both rural areas and the informal sector—two key and often overlooked segments.

Bibliography

Beck, Thorsten, Asli Demirguc-Kunt, and Maria Soledad M. Peria, 2005, "Reaching Out: Access to and Use of Banking Services Across Countries," Policy Research Working Paper No. 3754 (Washington: World Bank).

Eifert, Benn, Alan Gelb, and Vijaya Ramachandran, 2005, "Business Environment and Comparative Advantage in Africa: Evidence from the Investment Climate Data," Working Paper No. 56 (Washington: Center for Global Development).

Fox, Louise, Elena Bardasi, and Katleen Van den Broeck, 2005, "Poverty in Mozambique: Unraveling Changes and Determinants," Africa Region Working Paper No. 87 (Washington: World Bank).

Hausmann, Ricardo, Dani Rodrik, and Andrés Velasco, 2005, "Growth Diagnostics" (Cambridge, Massachusetts: Harvard University). Available via the Internet: http://ksghome.harvard.edu/~drodrik/barcelonafinalmarch2005.pdf

Heritage Foundation, 2007, "2007 Index of Economic Freedom" (Washington). Available via the Internet: http://www.heritage.org/index/

International Monetary Fund, 2005, *Republic of Mozambique: Selected Issues and Statistical Appendix,* IMF Country Report No. 05/311 (Washington).

———, 2006, *World Economic Outlook, September 2006,* World Economic and Financial Surveys (Washington).

———, 2007, *Republic of Mozambique: Selected Issues and Statistical Appendix,* IMF Country Report No 07/258 (Washington).

———, and World Bank, 2003, "Mozambique: Financial Sector Assessment Program" (Washington).

Johnson, Simon, Jonathan D. Ostry, and Arvind Subramanian, 2007, "The Prospects for Sustained Growth in Africa: Benchmarking the Constraints," IMF Working Paper 07/52 (Washington: International Monetary Fund).

Kaufmann, Daniel, Aart Kraay, and Massimo Mastruzzi, 2007, "Governance Matters VI: Aggregate and Individual Governance Indicators for 1996–2006," Policy Research Working Paper No. 4280 (Washington: World Bank).

Kikeri, Sunita, Thomas Kenyon, and Vincent Palmade, 2006, *Reforming the Investment Climate: Lessons for Practitioners* (Washington: World Bank).

Levine, Ross, 2005, "Finance and Growth: Theory and Evidence," in *Handbook of Economic Growth,* Vol. 1A, ed. by P. Aghion and S. Durlauf (Amsterdam: North-Holland).

Macamo, José Luís, 2006, "Mozambique Governance Indicators: Trends and Comparisons, 1995–2005" (unpublished; Washington: World Bank).

Mozambique Ministry of Planning and Development (MPD), 2006, "Enterprise Development in Mozambique: Results Based on Manufacturing Surveys Conducted in 2002 and 2006," Discussion Paper No. 33E (Maputo: National Directorate of Studies and Policy Analysis). Available via the Internet: http://www.mpd.gov.mz/gest/documents/33E_Enterprise_Developing.pdf

Nasir, John, Gilberto de Barros, Dileep Wagle, Manjukedia Shah, Chad Leechor, Pradeep Srivastava, Alan Harding, and Vijaya Ramachandran, 2003, *Mozambique Industrial Performance and Investment Climate 2003* (Washington: World Bank).

Tahari, Amor, Dhaneshwar Ghura, Bernardin Akitoby, and Emmanuel Brou Aka, 2004, "Sources of Growth in Sub-Saharan Africa," IMF Working Paper 04/176 (Washington: International Monetary Fund).

United States Agency for International Development (USAID), 2004, *Removing Obstacles to Economic Growth in Mozambique: A Diagnostic Trade Integration Study* (Washington).

World Bank, 2005a, "Mozambique: Country Economic Memorandum: Sustaining Growth and Reducing Poverty," Report No. 32615-MZ (Washington).

———, 2005b, *World Development Report 2005: A Better Investment Climate for Everyone* (Washington).

———, 2007, "Doing Business in 2008" (Washington).

World Economic Forum, 2006, "Global Competitiveness Report 2006–2007" (London: Palgrave Macmillan).

10

Export Performance and Competitiveness in Mozambique

MAGNUS SAXEGAARD

Mozambique has experienced impressive economic growth over the past decade. GDP growth has averaged about 8 percent a year, which compares favorably with the growth takeoffs of Indonesia, Malaysia, the Philippines, and Thailand (the four members of the Association of Southeast Asian Nations referred to in this book as the ASEAN-4) and other Asian countries in the mid-1970s (see Chapter 1).

The literature seeking to explain the rapid economic growth of several Asian countries since the 1970s has emphasized the important role played by their export sectors. This is especially true of the ASEAN-4 countries. The contribution of these countries' export sectors to economic growth has increased dramatically in the three and a half decades since their growth takeoffs, as evidenced by the spectacular rise in the ratio of exports to GDP during this period. In addition, as Bigsten and Söderbom (2006) note, there is some evidence that firms become more productive when they export. Thus, an upturn in exports could lay the foundation for sustained growth. (See Table 10.1.)

Mozambique has experienced a similar improvement in its export performance since 2001. Although impressive, this rise is due almost exclusively to exports produced by the megaprojects exploiting the country's vast mineral resources, most notably aluminum. Excluding megaproject exports, the contribution of the export sector to the Mozambican economy has remained relatively stable.

Table 10.1. Selected Indicators for Mozambique and Other Countries

	Average real GDP growth (In percent)				Average export growth (In percent)				Average export-to-GDP ratio (In percent)			
	1971–80	1981–90	1991–2000	2001–06	1971–80	1981–90	1991–2000	2001–06	1971–80	1981–90	1991–2000	2001–06
Mozambique	**3.9**	**0.5**	**5.4**	**8.8**	**–3.1**	**–0.7**	**15.0**	**7.0**	**9.5**	**7.2**	**15.3**	**31.1**
ASEAN-4	7.1	5.1	4.4	4.8	12.9	6.8	11.3	4.2	22.3	28.2	47.7	60.8
Vietnam	3.9	5.9	7.6	7.6	–4.5	16.4	25.2	5.2	2.5	7.6	39.7	63.1
India	3.0	5.8	5.6	7.0	6.3	6.0	11.2	14.0	5.3	6.2	10.5	17.1
Tanzania	3.8	3.3	2.9	6.4	7.2	16.5	4.8	18.5	16.7	12.1	18.4	18.9
Sub-Saharan Africa	3.3	2.2	2.2	5.0	n.a.	2.8	5.8	4.7	25.8	24.6	27.6	34.8

Source: IMF, World Economic Outlook database.

The increasing number of megaprojects has had a clear positive effect on the economy—for example, by putting Mozambique on the map for foreign direct investment (FDI) and through knowledge spillovers. However, their importance should not be overstated. Megaprojects are typically neutral in terms of a country's balance of payments, contribute little to overall employment, and have not—at least until recently—had a significant impact on fiscal revenues.[1] As a result, it is clear that for Mozambique's impressive growth to translate into employment generation and a reduction in poverty, the source of export growth must be diversified. This requires understanding the causes underlying the comparatively lackluster performance of Mozambique's traditional export sector, which is the aim of this chapter.

Based on our analysis, efforts to enhance the performance of Mozambique's export sector should focus on (1) maintaining a flexible exchange rate system; (2) implementing structural reforms, notably through improvements in the business environment aimed at improving competitiveness and diversifying the export base, as discussed in Chapter 9; and (3) supporting broad-based multilateral trade liberalization initiatives.

The remainder of this chapter is organized as follows: the next section documents the performance of the export sector in Mozambique and compares it with that of other countries that have experienced a growth takeoff similar to Mozambique's. Then we discuss possible reasons underlying the relatively lackluster performance of Mozambique's traditional export sector, including the competitiveness of the Mozambican economy—as measured by the real effective exchange rate (REER)—and

[1]See Chapter 8 for a comprehensive survey of megaprojects in Mozambique.

the demand for Mozambique's exports in the world market. This is followed by a section in which we estimate Mozambique's equilibrium real effective exchange rate (EREER) in an effort to determine whether corrective macroeconomic policies to remove disequilibria in the economy are required to improve the country's competitiveness or whether this can best be achieved through structural reforms aimed at influencing the underlying EREER. After discussing the effect of limiting exchange rate flexibility, we briefly discuss structural policies aimed at improving the business climate in Mozambique as well as Mozambique's trade policy environment, both of which are key determinants of economic competitiveness and the underlying EREER. The chapter concludes with a summary of the main findings and policy recommendations.

Background

The ratio of exports to GDP in Mozambique rose from approximately 15 percent in 1999 to more than 35 percent in 2006, while Mozambique's share of world exports rose from approximately 0.009 percent to about 0.019 percent during the same period (Figure 10.1). However, as mentioned in the introduction, this rise is due almost exclusively to megaproject-related exports; other exports have remained more or less flat since 1991 as a share of both GDP and world trade.

The importance of megaproject exports for the recent increase in Mozambique's share of world exports can also be seen in Table 10.2, which shows that, with the exception of aluminum, the market share of Mozambique's main exports has remained relatively stable.

Confirming these findings, Figure 10.2 shows that although the contribution of megaproject exports to overall GDP growth has been increasing, the contribution of non-megaproject exports has remained relatively stable since 1994. Since 1994, real annual GDP growth in Mozambique has averaged 7.8 percent, with investment accounting for 3.8 percent and consumption for 2.8 percent. Since 1999, when megaprojects started to make a contribution to GDP growth, the main drivers of economic growth have been investment (4.3 percent), followed closely by megaproject exports (3.2 percent). Since the first megaprojects were launched in 1999, non-megaproject exports have contributed only 0.8 percent, on average, to real GDP growth.

Figure 10.3 shows that movements in the price of Mozambique's exports have been an important component of the recent increase in Mozambique's share of world exports. The price of Mozambique's exports remained relatively stable until 2002 but has since then increased dramatically in line

Figure 10.1. Exports of Goods and Services, 1983–2006
(In percent)

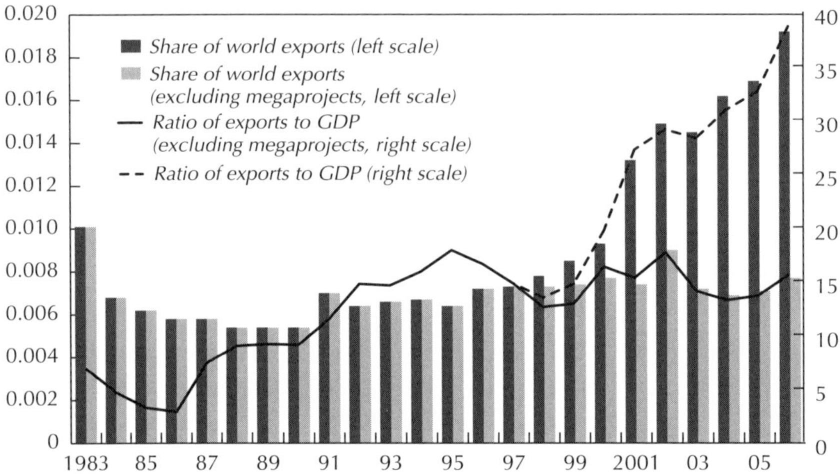

Sources: IMF, World Economic Outlook database; and IMF staff estimates.

with the increase in the world price of aluminum.[2] This implies that the increase in Mozambique's share of world exports from 1999 to 2002—when the export deflator was relatively stable—was due to an increase in the volume of Mozambique's exports. Since then, however, Mozambique's share of world exports in volume terms has actually decreased by more than 50 percent, although this has been more than offset by an increase in the export deflator of 260 percent. These developments illustrate the sensitivity of Mozambique's exports—in particular megaproject exports such as aluminum—to changes in commodity prices.

Another potential source of concern is the declining importance of non-megaproject manufacturing exports in Mozambique. Although a variety of export patterns can lead to income growth, as noted in IMF (2007), manufacturing exports are often considered to have been the drivers of export-led growth in the Southeast Asian countries during the past three decades.[3] In Mozambique, the share of non-megaproject manufacturing exports in total exports declined from 6.3 percent in 1995 to approxi-

[2]The world price of aluminum at the end of 2006 was more than double its level at the end of 2002.

[3]See, for example, Johnson, Ostry, and Subramanian (2007).

Table 10.2. Mozambique: Market Share of World Exports
(In percent)

	1995	2000	2001	2002	2003	2004	2005
Aluminum	0.1	0.0	0.8	0.7	1.0	1.2	1.3
Electric current	n.a.	0.6	0.4	0.9	0.7	0.5	0.6
Natural gas	n.a.	n.a.	n.a.	n.a.	0.0	0.0	0.1
Crustaceans, mollusks, etc.	0.6	0.5	0.6	0.7	0.4	0.6	0.5
Tobacco, raw and waste	0.2	0.0	0.1	0.4	0.4	0.6	0.6
Heavy petrol/bitum oils	0.0	0.0	0.0	0.0	0.0	0.0	0.0
Sugar/molasses/honey	0.0	0.1	0.1	0.1	0.1	0.2	0.0
Fruit/nuts, fresh/dried	0.1	0.1	0.1	0.1	0.0	0.1	0.1
Cotton	0.3	0.3	0.1	0.3	0.4	0.3	0.4

Source: United Nations Comtrade database.

mately 1.5 percent in 2005. Taken together, these trends pose a series of challenges and opportunities for increasing the contribution of the export sector to the Mozambican economy.

Explaining the Performance of Mozambique's Traditional Export Sector

The lack of dynamism in Mozambique's non-megaproject export sector could be attributable to Mozambique's lack of competitiveness or to developments in Mozambique's export markets. A deterioration in competitiveness represents an increase in the price of domestic tradable goods relative to foreign tradable goods.[4] However, because this is not directly observable we rely on movements in the REER to draw inferences about competitiveness. The analysis of Mozambique's export markets is based on a comparison between the growth of export volumes and prices for the products that Mozambique exports, and total exports.

The REER warrants careful monitoring because of the inflow of large amounts of aid to Mozambique, as well as the growth of revenues from megaprojects. It is now accepted that large capital inflows—arising, for example, from a scaling up of aid—can lead to real exchange rate appreciation (a deterioration in competitiveness) and Dutch disease,[5] in much the same way that Dutch disease can result from an increase in natural

[4]See Agénor (2004). Note that the real exchange rate as defined here does not correspond to the relative price of tradable and nontradable goods inside the country (sometimes called the internal real exchange rate).

[5]See Chapter 8 for a discussion of Dutch disease.

Figure 10.2. Contributions to Economic Growth, 1994–2005
(3-year moving average, in percent)

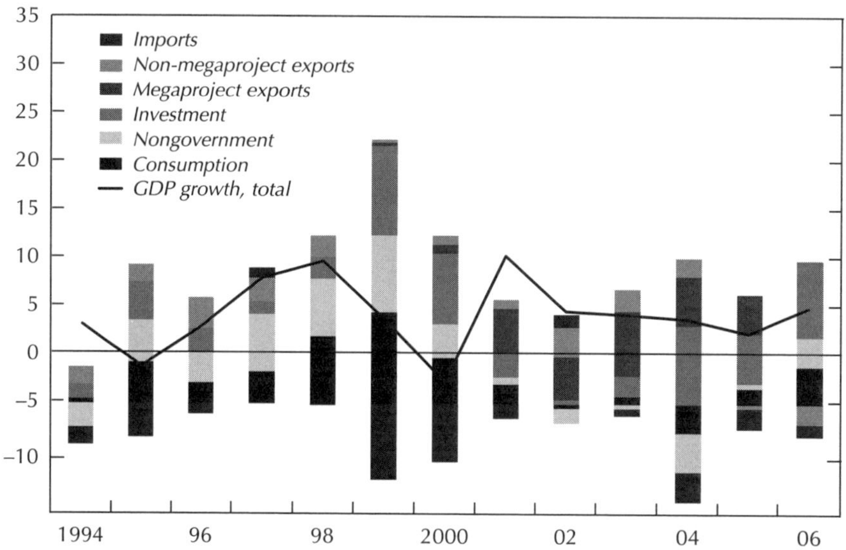

Source: IMF staff estimates.

resource prices or the discovery of new natural resources.[6] This argument, which is based on what Corden and Neary (1982) call the "spending effect" of Dutch disease, assumes that aid is spent, in part, on nontradables, implying an increase in their prices. While the demand for tradables may also increase—for example, if part of the aid is spent on imported goods—this does not affect the prices of tradable goods to the extent that these prices are determined in international markets. The result is an increase in the prices of nontradables relative to tradables, implying real exchange rate appreciation. As a result, the export sector—in particular, the traditional export sector—may suffer.

Exchange Rate Developments[7]

As Figure 10.4 shows, the Mozambican REER has remained relatively stable over the past 10 years, which suggests that there has not been a

[6]See, for example, Younger (1992); Bulíř and Lane (2002); Adam and Bevan (2003); Nkusu (2004); and Rajan and Subramanian (2005).

[7]This section draws heavily on material in Oomes (2006).

Figure 10.3. Mozambique's Share of World Exports, 1983–2006
(In percent)

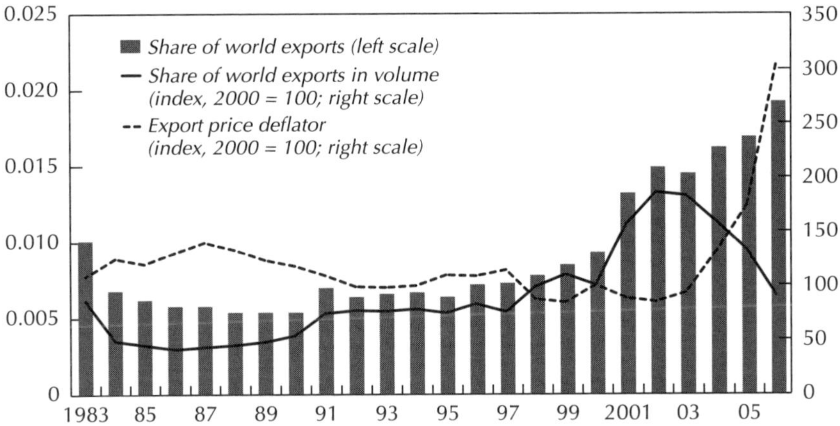

Sources: IMF, World Economic Outlook database; and IMF staff estimates.

substantial change in competitiveness.[8] While the nominal exchange rate has depreciated gradually since 2001, this has been offset by an increase in relative prices. Broadly speaking, the REER appreciated between 1994 and 1998, was roughly stable during 1998–2000, depreciated during 2001, and was roughly stable again during 2002–03. The past three years have been characterized by high volatility, with a significant real and nominal appreciation in late 2004 that was largely undone in early 2005, largely because of the introduction of a foreign exchange auction system in January 2005.

The period 1990–2006 can be divided into six subperiods with distinct de facto exchange rate regimes. These six periods are summarized in Table 10.3 and are indicated in Figure 10.5, on the basis of the de facto regime classification constructed by the IMF for all of its member countries. The de facto exchange rate regime is the regime that appears to have been actually followed, based on a close analysis of the data, and may be different from the de jure exchange rate regime announced by the authorities.[9]

The exchange rate regime in the first period, which began just prior to January 1990 and lasted until March 1992, is best characterized as a

[8]Figure 10.4 shows the consumer price index–based REER for Maputo.

[9]In comments on an earlier draft of this chapter, the Bank of Mozambique expressed some misgivings about this classification. These misgivings are reflected in the discussion of each time period.

Figure 10.4. Exchange Rate Developments, 1996–2006
(In percent)

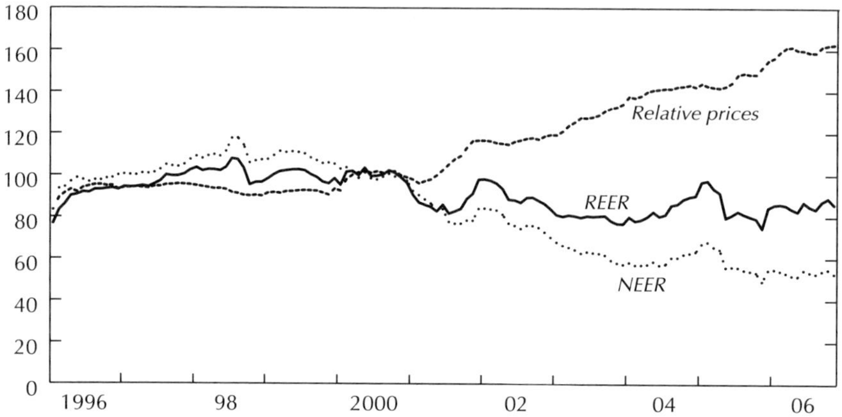

Source: IMF staff estimates.
Note: REER = real effective exchange rate. NEER = nominal effective exchange rate.

backward-looking crawling peg. Under this regime, the metical gradually depreciated vis-à-vis a basket of 18 major currencies, with the weights of these currencies determined by the relative importance of each trading partner in Mozambique's overall trade. In October 1990, a more depreciated market-determined secondary market was initiated, and the objective of exchange rate policy was to gradually reduce the gap with the secondary market rate.

The regime in the second period, which lasted from April 1992 to May 1993, can be described as a managed floating exchange rate, with no preannounced exchange rate path. In April 1992, most transactions were transferred to the secondary market, which was still heavily controlled and different from the parallel market rate.[10] The nominal effective exchange rate continued depreciating until August 1992 but began to appreciate in the fall of 1992, possibly because of the resumption of aid following the end of the Mozambican civil war with the signing of the cease-fire agreement between Frelimo and Renamo on October 15, 1992.[11]

[10]The de facto exchange rate regime classification is based on the secondary market exchange rate from this period on.

[11]According to the World Bank's World Development Indicators, aid nearly doubled as a percentage of gross national income in 1992, while aid per capita in current U.S. dollars rose by one-third between 1991 and 1992.

Table 10.3. Mozambique: De Facto Exchange Rate Regimes, 1990–2006

Regime	Period	Classification
I	Jan. 1990–Mar. 1992	Backward-looking crawling peg
II	Apr. 1992–May 1993	Managed floating with no predetermined path
III	Jun. 1993–Dec. 2001	Independently floating
IV	Jan. 2002–Sep. 2002	Managed floating with no predetermined path
V	Oct. 2002–Apr. 2004	Forward-looking crawling peg
VI	May 2004–Present	Managed floating with no predetermined path

Source: IMF staff estimates.

The IMF classification suggests that the regime in the third period—which was a long one, from June 1993 through December 2001—was a de facto independent floating exchange rate, although, as the Bank of Mozambique points out, several significant changes to the institutional setup of the exchange rate market were made during this time.[12] The exchange rate system was unified in June 1993, and the exchange rate became market-determined. While interventions continued, it appears that these were aimed largely at achieving reserves targets, not at influencing the exchange rate. Although the exchange rate was surprisingly stable from November 1995 on, there is no evidence of a de facto pegged regime, given that the spread with the parallel market rate continued to narrow.[13]

During January 2002–April 2004 (the fourth and fifth periods), the exchange rate was more strongly managed. From January to September 2002 (the fourth period), the de facto regime was again best described as a managed floating exchange rate, while from October 2002 to April 2004 (the fifth period) there appeared to be a clear forward-looking crawling peg against the U.S. dollar. From an operational point of view, however, the Bank of Mozambique suggests that these two periods were similar insofar as no significant changes were made to the exchange rate regime.

From May 2004 onward, the exchange rate became more flexible but was still tightly managed. While the de jure regime during this period was a nominally floating exchange rate, the de facto regime was a tightly managed exchange rate subject to various exchange controls. The Bank of Mozambique continued to be a major player in the foreign exchange market and initially would set the price at which the sales and purchases of foreign currency were to be transacted.

[12]This includes the creation of an exchange rate interbank market (MCI) in 1996.

[13]Other countries that had a de facto fixed exchange rate or an exchange rate anchor typically had a much more depreciated parallel market rate.

Figure 10.5. De Facto Exchange Rate Regimes, 1996–2006
(In percent)

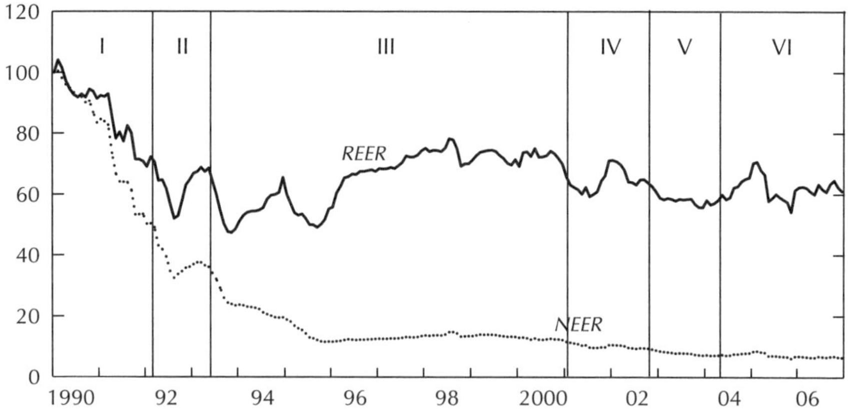

Source: IMF staff estimates.
Note: REER = real effective exchange rate. NEER = nominal effective exchange rate.

Although it is not classified as a new regime, major changes were introduced in January 2005 when the Bank of Mozambique moved to a more flexible exchange rate regime with the introduction of foreign exchange auctions. Following the introduction of this auction mechanism, Mozambique experienced bouts of rapid exchange rate depreciation, which appear to have stemmed partly from a correction of a somewhat overvalued exchange rate at end-2004, lumpy oil import transactions, and portfolio shifts in the shallow foreign exchange market. In response to the volatility, the Bank of Mozambique introduced a temporary band in both the foreign exchange auctions and the interbank market (MCI) in November 2005, limiting variation both in the weekly auction rates and in day-to-day increases in the exchange rates. The new guidelines restricting demand and price movements, combined with much larger auction sales, halted the depreciation of the currency and the exchange rate has remained relatively stable since. The deepening of the MCI was also supported by a code of conduct for banks and measures to facilitate firm quotation. The band restricting the day-to-day increases in the exchange rate was loosened from 0.25 percent to 1 percent in December 2006 and abolished in June 2007. The authorities reiterated their commitment to a flexible exchange rate regime, which will help improve competitiveness.

Demand for Mozambique's Exports

The analysis in the previous section does not provide clear evidence of a decline in competitiveness. However, the performance of Mozambique's export sector also depends on the demand for the products that Mozambique exports to world markets. Mozambique is particularly vulnerable to changes in demand, given its high level of export concentration. As shown in Table 10.4, megaproject exports (aluminum, electric current, and natural gas) accounted for more than 70 percent of total exports in 2005. In 1995, these commodities accounted for 0.2 percent of total exports. Thus, while it is clear that megaprojects have raised the contribution of the export sector to economic growth in Mozambique, they have also contributed to an increase in export concentration.

With the notable exception of aluminum, natural gas, fruits and nuts, and sugar and molasses, the average growth in exports (in U.S. dollars) of the products that Mozambique exports was below the overall average growth of total world exports during 2000–05 (Figure 10.6).[14] For some products, notably crustaceans and mollusks, tobacco, and cotton, this has been accompanied by relatively low average price increases. These two factors suggest a decline in world demand rather than in world supply for these products. For other products, notably fruits and nuts, the analysis suggests an expansion of world supply.[15]

The above analysis suggests that whereas world demand for megaproject exports has typically been increasing (in the case of aluminum, this would have been even clearer if 2006 were included, given the dramatic rise in world aluminum prices), it has been declining for traditional exports. Given that the previous section showed that Mozambique's competitiveness has remained relatively stable, the declining world demand faced by many of Mozambique's traditional exports may help explain why the contribution of the traditional export sector to growth in Mozambique has been relatively stagnant instead of increasing in line with megaproject

[14]Figure 10.6 shows that most of Mozambique's export products are positioned to the right of the vertical line that represents the average growth in world exports (8.6 percent) during 1995–2005. Some of Mozambique's exports are positioned below the horizontal line that represents the average rate of increases in the prices of world exports (1.7 percent). The combination of relatively low growth in export volumes and in prices implies that demand for these products has been expanding less rapidly than demand for world exports. The size of the bubbles represents the importance of each export commodity in total exports.

[15]Exports of electric current are not included in this analysis as these are governed by fixed price contracts with South Africa.

Table 10.4. Composition of Exports
(In percent of total exports)

	1995	2000	2001	2002	2003	2004	2005
Aluminum	0.2	16.5	54.5	44.6	54.4	60.9	57.3
Electric current	n.a.	18.4	8.2	13.3	10.9	6.8	8.0
Natural gas	n.a.	n.a.	n.a.	n.a.	0.0	2.2	6.2
Crustaceans, mollusks, etc.	45.6	26.4	13.4	14.5	7.6	6.4	4.5
Tobacco, raw and waste	0.6	2.1	1.3	3.0	2.1	2.7	2.4
Heavy petrol/bitum oils	1.8	2.4	1.2	3.5	2.1	3.2	0.8
Sugar/molasses/honey	4.2	1.2	1.1	2.2	1.6	2.2	0.4
Fruit/nuts, fresh/dried	8.0	5.8	2.0	2.2	1.0	2.0	1.4
Cotton	10.8	7.1	0.9	2.0	3.6	1.9	2.0

Source: United Nations Comtrade database.

exports. It also suggests that diversifying Mozambique's export base should be part of a strategy to raise the contribution of the traditional export sector and to move toward products that are more dynamic in the marketplace, such as manufacturing exports.

The Equilibrium Real Exchange Rate and Exchange Rate Overvaluation

The previous section argued that the REER in Mozambique has remained relatively stable, suggesting that the level of competitiveness is relatively unchanged. The analysis suggests that declining world demand for many of Mozambique's exports, rather than a deterioration in competitiveness, might have contributed to the disappointing performance of the traditional export sector. The analysis thus far has not made clear, however, whether the current level of the REER is appropriate or an equilibrium (in a sense that will be made clear below) for Mozambique. To the extent that the current level of the REER is higher than the underlying equilibrium level, Mozambique's export sector may be not performing as well as it might have, had the REER been closer to its equilibrium.

Moreover, the appropriate policies to improve competitiveness depend on whether or not the REER is aligned with the underlying equilibrium rate or not. Sustained departures of the REER from equilibrium imply the existence of macroeconomic imbalances that need to be corrected through macroeconomic adjustment. On the other hand, if the REER is in line with the EREER, structural reforms aimed at improving the competitiveness of the export sector may be a more appropriate strategy for increasing the contribution of the export sector to the Mozambican economy.

Figure 10.6. Export Performance by Product, 2000–05
(In percent)

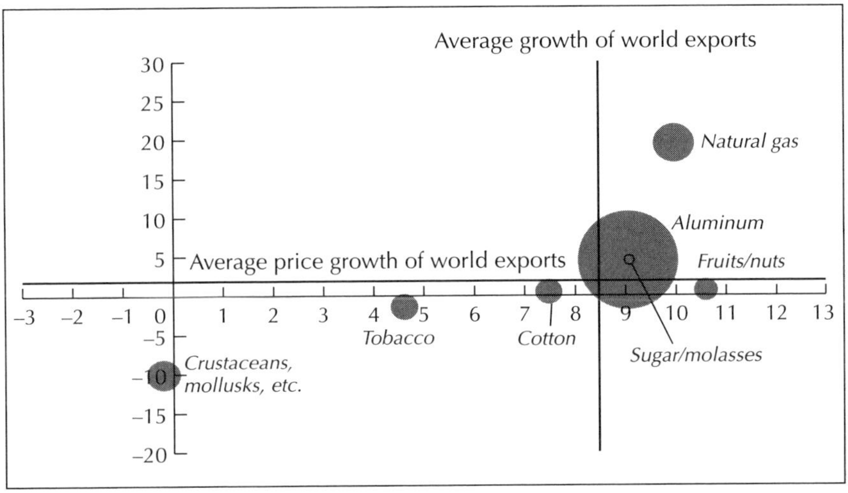

Source: IMF staff estimates.

There are a number of methodologies that have been used to estimate the EREER, each with its own strengths and weaknesses. To increase the robustness of our findings, we estimate the EREER for Mozambique using two different methodologies: first, using the relative purchasing-power-parity (PPP) approach modified to take into account the Balassa-Samuelson effect; second, using the fundamental equilibrium exchange rate (FEER) framework.[16]

Relative PPP Approach

The first approach for estimating the EREER defines the equilibrium exchange rate as the one that is consistent with relative PPP, modified to take into account the Balassa-Samuelson effect. Mozambique's *absolute* PPP exchange rate is defined as the nominal exchange rate consistent with the law of one price and implies that the real exchange rate is equal to one. *Relative* PPP is said to hold when the rate of depreciation of a bilateral

[16]Other concepts of the EREER include the traditional uncovered interest parity (UIP) and more recent approaches such as the underlying internal-external balance (UIEB) and the behavioral equilibrium exchange rate (BEER) approach.

nominal exchange rate matches the inflation differential between the two countries. When relative PPP holds, the real exchange rate is constant so that movements in the real exchange rate can be interpreted as deviations from relative PPP, or exchange rate disequilibria. Although few economists would argue that PPP holds continuously, "most instinctively believe in some variant of purchasing power parity as an anchor for long-run real exchange rates" (Rogoff, 1996). Indeed, as Sarno and Taylor (2003) point out, many of the key results in international macroeconomics rely on some form of PPP holding as a long-run relationship.

Despite the theoretical attractiveness of relative PPP, the empirical evidence remains inconclusive, although some recent evidence suggests that "PPP might be viewed as a valid long-run international parity condition when applied to bilateral exchange rates obtaining among major industrialized countries. . . ." (Sarno and Taylor, 2003). Its usefulness for developing and emerging countries appears limited, however.

Within the context of developing and emerging market countries, a particular challenge is to rationalize the existence of long-run deviations from PPP. A promising approach in this regard is the Harrod-Balassa-Samuelson model, which modifies relative PPP to take into account productivity differentials between the tradables and the nontradables sectors (the Balassa-Samuelson effect). The Balassa-Samuelson effect is based on the argument that in fast-growing economies such as Mozambique, productivity growth will be concentrated in the tradables sector. This will lead to wage increases in the tradables sector but, because tradable prices are determined in the world market, not to comparable increases in prices. However, higher wages in the tradables sector will put upward pressure on wages in the nontradables sector, which, in turn, will put upward pressure on the prices of nontradables, resulting in the appreciation of the real exchange rate. Given that higher productivity growth in the traded goods sector is likely to be a key feature of most fast-growing developing countries, including Mozambique, it makes sense to modify our measure of the EREER based on relative PPP to take this effect into account.

In the absence of reliable data on sectoral productivity, the Balassa-Samuelson hypothesis is usually tested by regressing the real exchange rate on the overall productivity differential.[17] Output and employment data for the tradables and nontradables sectors tend to be unavailable for most developing countries, however, and are difficult to compare across

[17]See, for example, De Gregorio, Giovannini, and Wolf (1994); Rogoff (1996); Kravis and Lipsey (1988); and Frankel (2005).

Figure 10.7. Real Exchange Rate and Per Capita GDP, 2005

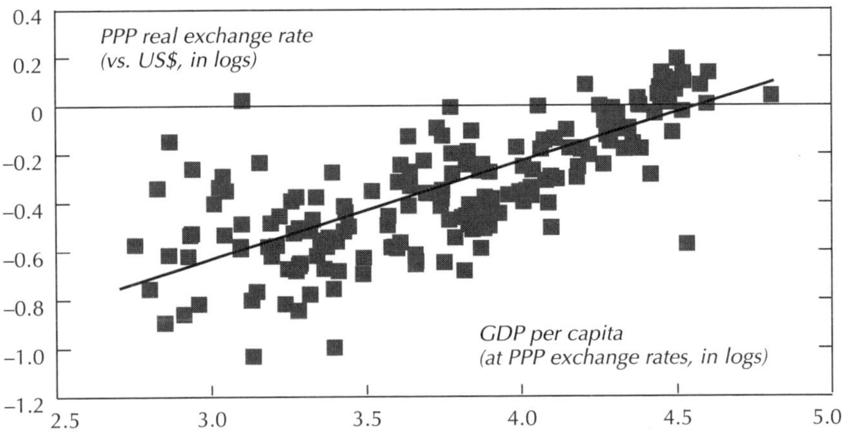

Source: IMF, World Economic Outlook database.
Note: PPP = purchasing power parity.

countries. It is therefore common to use per capita GDP as a proxy for productivity in the tradables sector.

Figure 10.7 plots the relationship between the real exchange rate (calculated using the PPP conversion factor) against GDP per capita at PPP exchange rates for 180 countries in 2005. As predicted by the Balassa-Samuelson hypothesis, there exists a clear positive relationship between the real exchange rate and productivity. Our estimates suggest that, on average, a 1 percent increase in PPP GDP per capita is associated with a real appreciation of 0.39 percent, which is consistent with the results from earlier studies. For example, Rogoff (1996) found a slope of 0.37 for a sample of 100 countries in 1990. De Broeck and Sløk (2001) repeated this estimate for a sample of 149 countries in 1999 and found a slope of 0.41. Frankel (2005) found a slope of 0.38 for a sample of 118 countries in 2000.

Based on the estimated equilibrium relationship between the real exchange rate and productivity differentials, we can obtain an estimate of the extent to which the Mozambican exchange rate has been undervalued or overvalued. The thick solid line in Figure 10.8 indicates the estimated equilibrium relationship between the real exchange rate and productivity, while the two thinner solid lines add or subtract 1.96 standard deviations from the estimated relationship—equivalent to a 95 percent confidence interval—to include some measure of the uncertainty surrounding the

Figure 10.8. PPP Equilibrium Exchange Rates, 1990–2005

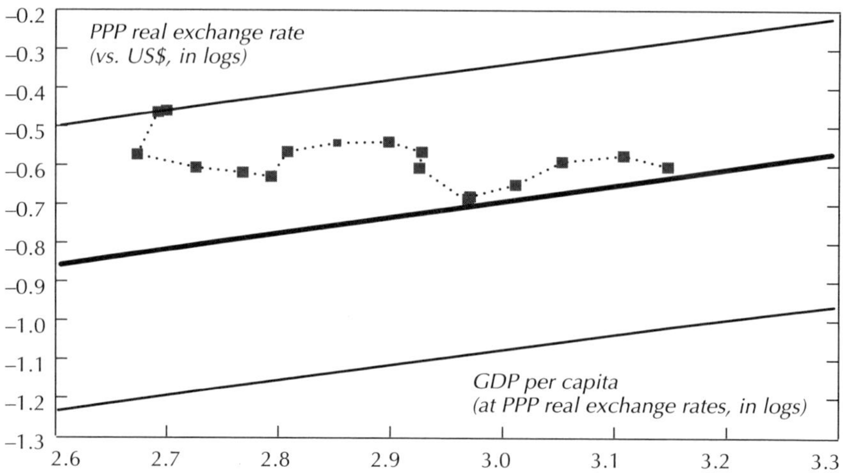

Sources: IMF, World Economic Outlook database; and IMF staff estimates.
Note: PPP = purchasing power parity.

estimate of the EREER. The dashed line plots the actual evolution of Mozambique's PPP real exchange rate against Mozambique's GDP per capita. The difference between the dashed and dotted lines can thus be interpreted as a measure of real exchange rate misalignment.

The results suggest that the Mozambican real exchange rate has been approaching equilibrium but may still be slightly overvalued. Figure 10.9 plots the percentage difference between the actual and equilibrium real exchange rates together with one standard error bands. These estimates suggest that the real exchange rate may have been overvalued at the beginning of the 1990s (during the civil war), moved toward convergence with the equilibrium exchange rate in 2000, and then been undervalued by about 10 percent in 2001. During 2002–04, the metical moved back toward convergence with the equilibrium exchange rate as a result of a real appreciation. In 2004, however, the exchange rate was once again overvalued, this time by about 5 percent, in response to unexpectedly high foreign exchange inflows that were not fully sterilized. Most of this overvaluation was undone in 2005, with the introduction of the foreign exchange auction system, although there is evidence that the real exchange rate may still be slightly overvalued. However, given the high degree of statistical

Figure 10.9. Estimated Real Exchange Rate Misalignment, 1990–2005

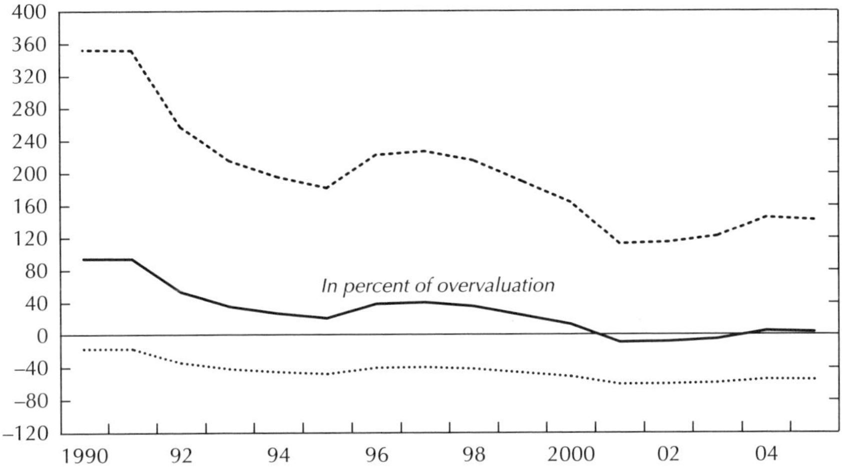

Sources: IMF, World Economic Outlook database; and IMF staff estimates.
Note: Dotted lines are standard error bands.

uncertainty, the level of misalignment is far outside the 95 percent confidence interval and is therefore not statistically significant.

These results are subject to a number of important caveats. First, the data used for this analysis, in particular the data on per capita GDP and the price data used for calculating PPP exchange rates, are subject to significant uncertainty. Second, this approach implicitly assumes that the only determinant of the equilibrium real exchange rate is GDP per capita (productivity), which may be too simplistic. Finally, the equilibrium real exchange rate path is estimated for a large number of countries and does not take into account country-specific factors that may lead to different equilibrium exchange rate paths for different countries. The next section will attempt to deal with some of these caveats.

The Fundamental Equilibrium Exchange Rate

The aim of this section is to analyze the EREER for Mozambique using the FEER framework estimated using the Johansen approach to cointegration (Johansen, 1988, 1991, 1995). The underlying equilibrium real exchange rate is the value of the REER that results in simultaneous attainment of internal and external equilibrium in the economy. Internal equilibrium is achieved when the nontradable goods market clears in the present period and is expected to clear in future periods. External equilibrium is achieved when the current account balance is at a sustainable level consistent with long-run capital flows.

The FEER approach addresses some of the weaknesses of the relative PPP methodology applied in the previous section. While there is not much we can do about measurement errors in the data, the inclusion of more variables that researchers have argued are determinants of the EREER will help us obtain a more precise estimate of the equilibrium real exchange rate path and thus enable us to analyze with more precision the extent to which the REER in Mozambique is misaligned. Moreover, by using a time-series rather than a cross-section approach, our results will incorporate country-specific information about the EREER.

The analysis was carried out using the trade-weighted REER constructed using the inflation rate based on the consumer price index (CPI) in Maputo. The analysis is based on the following long-run relation between the REER and its fundamentals:

$$\ln(REER) = \alpha_0 + \alpha_1 \ln(TOT) + \alpha_2 \ln(GOV) + \alpha_3 \ln(INV) + \ln(PROD) + \alpha_5 \ln(OPEN) + FDI + \varepsilon_t,$$

where

- *ln* denotes the natural logarithm and ε_t is an error term with the usual properties.
- *TOT* is defined as the terms of trade of goods.[18] An increase in the terms of trade will increase the demand for domestic goods, resulting in an increase in the relative price of nontradables. Hence, the expected sign is *positive*.
- GOV is defined as the share of government current expenditure in GDP.[19] An increase in government current expenditure will lead to either an increase or a decrease in the EREER, depending on the share of government current expenditure on tradable and nontradable goods. The expected sign is therefore *ambiguous*.
- *INV* is defined as the ratio of credit to the private sector to GDP.[20] A rise in the ratio of credit to the private sector to GDP will shift spending toward tradable or nontradable goods depending on the

[18]The measurement and plots of each variable, together with data sources, are given in the appendix.

[19]This is a proxy for government demand for nontradables.

[20]This is a proxy for investment.

import content of investment and thus cause either a depreciation or an appreciation. Hence, the expected sign is *ambiguous*.

- *PROD* is a measure of technological progress and is proxied by the real GDP per capita in Mozambique relative to its trading partners. The inclusion of technological progress captures the Balassa-Samuelson effect. Hence, an increase in productivity will lead to an appreciation of the EREER and the expected sign is *positive*.
- *OPEN* is a measure of the degree of capital controls and restrictions and is measured as the sum of exports and imports as a share of GDP. A reduction in controls will tend to increase the total amount of trade. The equilibrium response of the REER will depend on whether this leads to a deterioration or an improvement in the current account.[21] If the current account deteriorates, a depreciation of the REER is required, whereas the reverse is true if the current account improves. Hence, the expected sign is *ambiguous*.
- *FDI* is defined as the ratio of foreign direct investment to GDP and is used as a proxy for capital inflows. An increase in capital inflows would be expected to appreciate the REER. Hence, the expected sign is *positive*.

Unit root tests provide evidence that most of the variables are nonstationary in levels but stationary in first-differences, which is a precondition for cointegration to exist between the level variables. In particular, we are unable to reject the null hypothesis of a unit root for any of the variables apart from the ratio of FDI to GDP at the 5 percent level. ADF (augmented Dickey-Fuller) tests on the first-differenced variables reject the null hypothesis of a unit root for all variables with the exception of the terms of trade, which show some evidence of being integrated of order two.

The cointegration analysis suggests that there exists a long-run relationship between the REER and the underlying fundamentals. The starting point for this analysis was a (vector autoregression) VAR with 3 lags, estimated on data from the first quarter of 1998 to the third quarter of 2006.[22] Statistical tests suggest that the model can be reduced to 2 lags but that any further reduction in the number of lags is rejected statistically

[21]Given that most of the trade liberalization has been done by developed countries, not by developing countries, it is likely that the effect of increased trade will be an improvement in the current account.

[22]It is worth noting that because GDP is only available on an annual basis, quarterly data on GDP in Mozambique were constructed from annual GDP using a methodology similar to that of Adam (1999).

at the 5 percent level. Hence, we proceed with the analysis using a VAR with 2 lags.[23]

The existence of one cointegrating relation is confirmed by the Maximum Eigenvalue test at the 1 percent level and the Trace test at the 5 percent level. Table 10.5 reports the results from rewriting the VAR as a Vector Error Correction Model (VECM) with one cointegrating vector. The estimated parameters are broadly consistent with the predictions from economic theory. In particular, our results suggest that the REER has appreciated in response to

- Relative productivity growth (the Balassa-Samuelson effect). In particular, a 1 percent increase in productivity is associated with a 0.53 percent appreciation of the REER.
- Improvements in the terms of trade. A 1 percent improvement in the terms of trade is associated with a 0.67 percent appreciation in the REER.
- Increases in the share of government current expenditure in GDP. In particular, a 1 percent improvement in the ratio of government current expenditure to GDP is associated with a 0.85 percent appreciation of the REER.
- Increases in the share of FDI in GDP. In particular, a 1 percentage point increase in the ratio of FDI to GDP is associated with a 0.03 percentage point increase in the REER.
- A decrease in the openness of the economy. In particular, a 1 percentage point decrease in the measure of openness is associated with a 0.71 percent depreciation of the REER.

With the exception of FDI and private sector investment, which are statistically significant at the 5 and the 10 percent levels, respectively, the effect of all the fundamentals is significant at the 1 percent level.[24] Finally, the coefficient on the cointegrating vector in the VECM implies that in the absence of further shocks, half of the disequilibrium would be eliminated in about 1.8 years.

Measuring the degree of misalignment requires constructing an unobserved variable, the EREER, which requires decomposing the fundamentals into permanent and transitory components. In particular, the EREER

---

[23]After the inclusion of three impulse dummies, which can be justified on statistical and economic grounds, the VAR appeared well specified.

[24]As a rule of thumb, the parameter is significant at the 10 percent level when the *t*-statistic is above 1.8, at the 5 percent level when the *t*-statistic is above 2, and at the 1 percent level when the *t*-statistic is above 3. The exact thresholds depend on the degrees of freedom.

Table 10.5. Estimates of FEER Long-Term Relation[1]

Constant	–0.59
Terms of trade	0.65
	[4.76]
Government consumption	0.85
	[6.77]
Investment	0.11
	[1.85]
Productivity	0.53
	[7.26]
Openness	–0.71
	[–12.06]
FDI	0.03
	[2.51]
Half-life of deviation[2]	7.22

Source: Author's estimates.
Note: FEER denotes fundamental equilibrium exchange rate.
[1]Numbers in brackets refer to *t*-statistics.
[2]The half-life of deviation is derived from the error correction model. A half-life of 1 implies that 50 percent of any misalignment will be corrected in one quarter.

is defined as that value of the REER which is consistent in the long run with the *equilibrium* value of the fundamentals. As is common in the literature, we construct a measure of the equilibrium by extracting the permanent component of each fundamental. In this paper we apply the Hodrick-Prescott (HP) filter, which has become a popular choice among business cycle analysts.[25] We also assess whether the implied misalignments are significantly different from zero by plotting the 95 percent confidence interval as in the previous section. Figure 10.10 plots the estimated equilibrium rate together with the actual REER. The results show that Mozambique's REER has remained broadly in line with fundamentals during much of the sample but may also have experienced periods of misalignment. In particular, the REER appears to have been slightly overvalued in 1998 and 1999 at a time when the EREER was appreciating rapidly in response to increases in productivity relative to Mozambique's main trading partners. This appears to have been followed by a period of undervaluation in 2001 and in 2003. As noted previously, the exchange rate was tightly managed in 2003, which may have contributed to exchange rate misalignment. There is some evidence that the appreciation at the end of 2004 resulted in overvaluation at the end of 2004 and beginning of 2005. As noted previously, the new auction mechanism in January 2005 led to a sharp depreciation of the REER, which appears to have led to a realign-

[25]A smoothing coefficient of 1600 was used, as is common for quarterly data.

Figure 10.10. Equilibrium Real Exchange Rate, 1998–2006

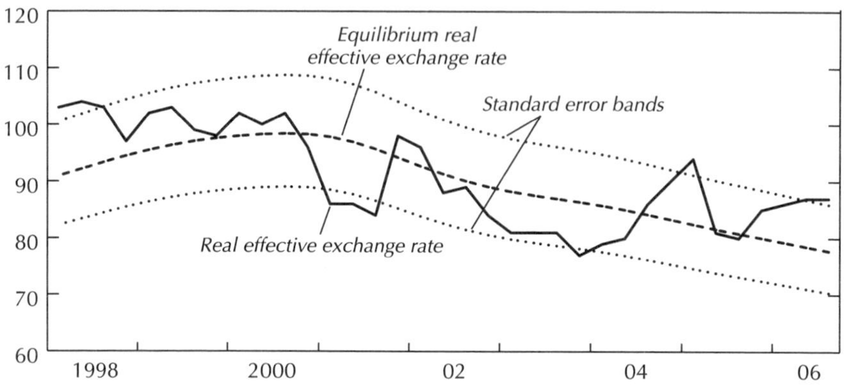

Source: IMF staff estimates.

ment with the EREER in the second half of 2005. Until June 2007, when the exchange rate bands were abolished, the REER had started to appreciate while the EREER continued to depreciate. As a result, the analysis provides some indication that Mozambique's REER may have been slightly more appreciated than its underlying equilibrium.

Figure 10.11 plots the degree of misalignment in percentage terms together with standard error bands and suggests that the REER may have been overvalued by 11 percent at end-2006. Because of statistical uncertainty, however, the actual misalignment may have been as little as 1 percent. Taken together with the results from the previous section on the EREER constructed using PPP, these results provide some evidence to suggest that the economy may have been less competitive than is implied by its economic fundamentals. In other words, Mozambique's export performance may have been weaker than it could have been if the REER had been aligned with its underlying equilibrium rate.

Causes Underlying the Possible Misalignment of the REER in Mozambique

The results in the previous section suggest that Mozambique's REER may have been slightly overvalued until the exchange rate bands were removed. As noted previously, such departures of the REER from equilibrium, to the extent that they are more than temporary phenomena, may

Figure 10.11. Equilibrium Real Exchange Rate, 1998–2006

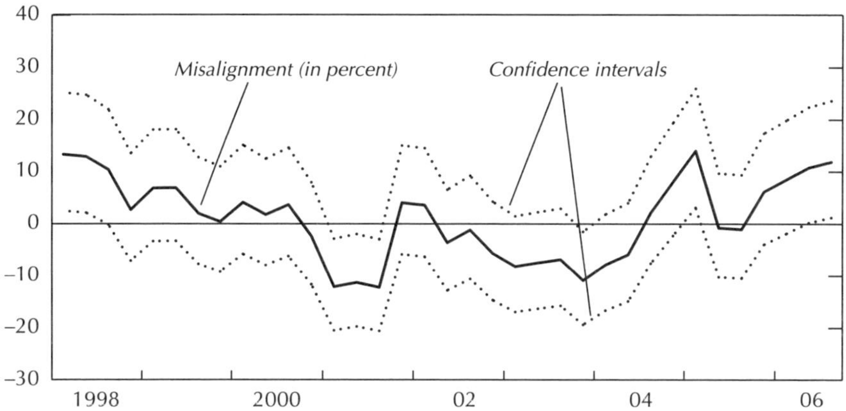

Source: IMF staff estimates.

imply the existence of imbalances in the economy that need to be corrected through macroeconomic adjustment. In the case of Mozambique, the emergence of significant overvaluation from the end of 2005 onward coincides with the introduction of new regulations limiting the daily variation in exchange rates. This suggests that the exchange rate restrictions that were in place until June 2007 may have partly explained why the REER appeared to be slightly misaligned. The aim of this section is to examine the nature of these exchange rate restrictions and to evaluate to what extent they may help explain why the REER appears to have been somewhat overvalued.

As noted previously, the Bank of Mozambique introduced a temporary band in both the foreign exchange auctions and the interbank market in November 2005 in response to volatility in the foreign exchange market. Initially, the band in the auction market led to a widening of the spread between the auction rate and the rate charged by banks to customers and foreign exchange bureaus (see Figure 10.12). The band in the interbank market also discouraged transactions between banks at quoted rates in the interbank market, although transactions continued outside the interbank market (see Figure 10.13).

In mid-December 2006, the Bank of Mozambique moved to increase the band limiting the daily variation in the interbank market exchange rate from 0.25 percent to 1 percent. As Figure 10.14 shows, this coincided with an increase (depreciation) of 2 percent in the interbank market quotation

Figure 10.12. Exchange Rate Spreads over Auction Rate
(In percent)

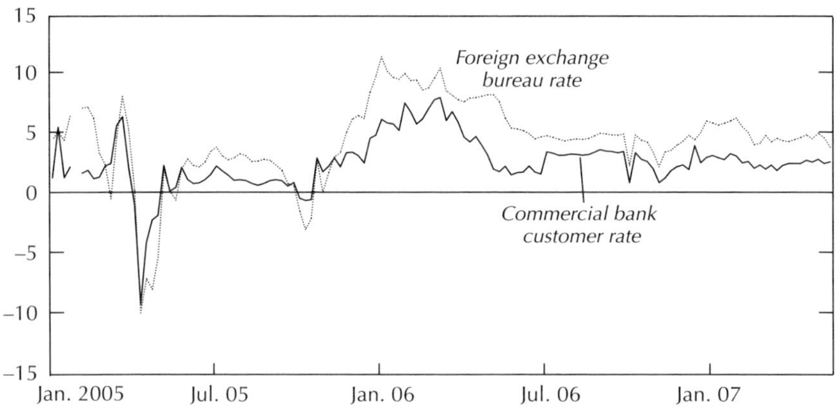

Source: Mozambican authorities.

rate, while the spread between the quotation rate and the rate outside the interbank market declined. Hence, the loosening of the band appears to have led to a depreciation of the nominal exchange rate, suggesting that prior to that the nominal exchange rate might have been slightly overvalued. The depreciation of the interbank market quotation rate also led to transactions taking place in the interbank market (see Figure 10.13), since on-screen quotations by banks could move closer to the rate outside the interbank market (see Figure 10.14).

At the same time, Figure 10.14 shows that actual on-screen transactions are taking place very close to the upper level of the band, while off-screen transactions are conducted at an even higher rate. As the Bank of Mozambique has pointed out, the primary interbank market rate and the secondary rate outside the interbank market should not be expected to converge completely since there is typically a shortage of foreign exchange that enables banks to sell foreign exchange at a higher rate. However, the fact that interbank market transaction rates are at the upper level of the band suggests that the band may still be binding and, thus, that there may still be pressure on the exchange rate to depreciate further.[26] The analysis

[26]Figure 10.14 includes error bars around the interbank market quotation rate showing the width of the band and thus the maximum deviation of interbank market transaction rates from the quotation rate.

Figure 10.13. Developments in the MCI Interbank Market

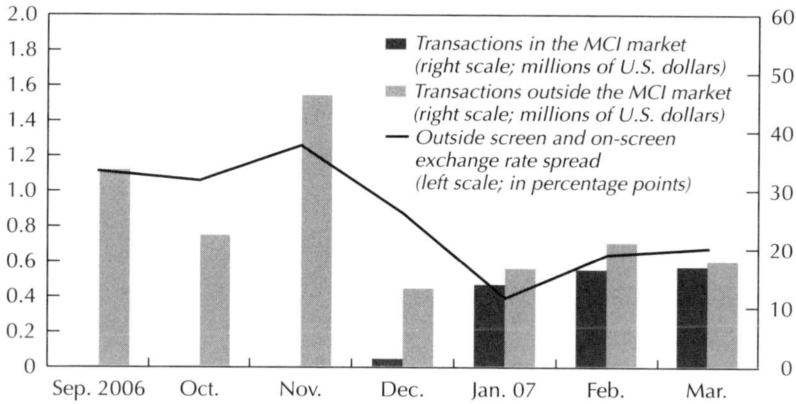

Source: Bank of Mozambique.
Note: MCI denotes Mozambique's exchange rate interbank market.

therefore suggests that the authorities were right to loosen the exchange rate band in order to bring on-screen and off-screen quotes in line with each other. The abolition of the band should contribute to bringing the REER in line with the underlying equilibrium rate.

Improving Mozambique's Trade Environment[27]

The previous sections have argued that a key strategy for promoting the competitiveness of the export sector in Mozambique is to maintain a flexible exchange rate. Such a strategy does not, however, eliminate the need for structural reforms aimed at improving competitiveness or measures to diversify the traditional export sector in Mozambique. This follows straightforwardly from the fact that the apparent overvaluation of the REER is a relatively recent phenomenon, whereas we have seen that the relatively unimpressive performance of the traditional export sector has been a feature of the Mozambican economy for at least two decades. The aim of this section is to investigate the potential for undertaking structural reforms with the aim of improving competitiveness, and the extent to which there is scope for increasing Mozambique's market access as a strategy for improving the performance of the traditional export sector.

[27]This section draws heavily on material in Kvintradze (2007).

Figure 10.14. Nominal Exchange Rates
(In percent)

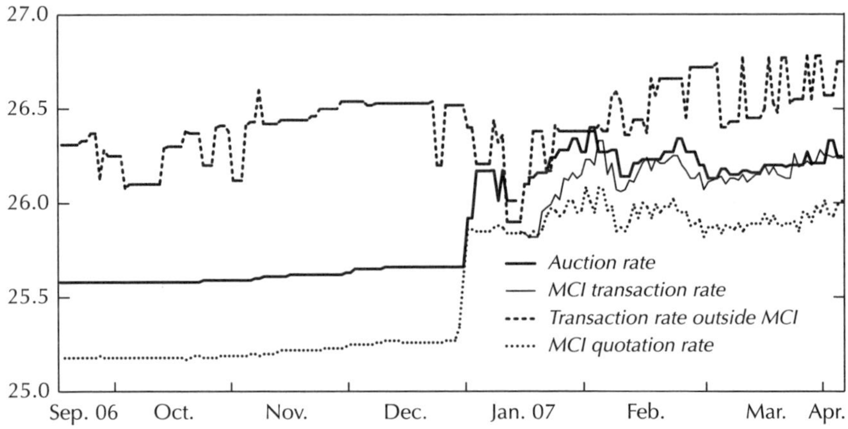

Source: Bank of Mozambique.
Note: MCI denotes Mozambique's exchange rate interbank market.

Competitiveness

As noted previously, it is common to use the REER to draw inferences about the competitiveness of the economy. The previous section showed that while the REER appeared to be overvalued until June 2007 relative to the underlying equilibrium rate, the EREER had depreciated by 24 percent since the fourth quarter of 2000, implying that the underlying fundamentals indicate an economy that is substantially more competitive today than it was six years ago. The fact that this has not been associated with an improvement in the performance of the traditional export sector may be due partly to the past overvaluation, but it may also be a sign that the CPI-based REER is an imperfect measure of competitiveness.[28]

The literature on competitiveness often highlights the importance of the business environment in which firms operate, including the importance of tariff and nontariff barriers. A reduction in tariffs and nontariff barriers to imports reduces input costs and improves allocative efficiency

[28]Other measures of competitiveness include the REER calculated using unit labor costs in the manufacturing sector. Data on unit labor costs and wholesale prices are unfortunately not available for Mozambique. Estimates using nonfood CPI inflation yielded results similar to those reported in this chapter.

among firms.[29] Tokarik (2006) even suggests that tariff reductions work as an "export-promotion" strategy that countries such as Mozambique should pursue independently of the policy stance of other countries.

Table 10.6 suggests, however, that Mozambique's trade barriers are among the lowest in the region and are lower than those in several ASEAN countries, in part because of its lower nontariff barriers.[30] In addition, Mozambique's trade-weighted average tariff is low in comparison with several others in southern Africa. However, given that the simple average tariff remains relatively high (see Table 10.7), there may be still some scope for further tariff reductions.[31]

Data on export-tax equivalents of tariff barriers computed by Tokarick (2006) provide further evidence for the fact that there may be scope for reducing tariff rates in Mozambique. As Table 10.8 shows, Mozambique's tariff structure (using 2001 data) imposes an effective tax of between 9.6 and 10.8 percent on exports, depending on methodology.[32] This is substantially higher than the tariffs of other fast-growing countries in sub-Saharan Africa, such as Botswana, but lower than those of many Asian countries. Results from the same study suggest that Mozambique could raise the value of its exports by 8.7 percent if import tariffs were reduced by 100 percent. This provides strong arguments for further tariff reductions.[33]

---

[29]Low tariff barriers provide part of the explanation for the rapid rise of megaprojects in Mozambique. As a result of their classification as export-processing zones, megaprojects benefit from, among other things, duty-free entry of goods, on-site customs facilities, and various tax incentives.

[30]It should be noted, however, that this may simply reflect better information on nontariff barriers in the ASEAN countries.

[31]Trade-weighted average tariffs may be more useful as a measure of protectionism if imports are concentrated in a few product categories. However, they may also be misleading if high tariffs discourage imports of some products, which therefore have a low weight in the calculation of the trade-weighted tariff. Mozambique started to gradually reduce its maximum tariff in 1999. The maximum tariff is currently 20 percent, down from a pre-1999 level of 35 percent.

[32]The first approach calculates the export tax necessary to keep real income constant if import tariffs are eliminated, while the second approach keeps export volumes constant.

[33]Further trade liberalization must also be weighed against the cost of lower tariff revenues. Alfieri, Rawlinson, and Cirera (2006) estimate that Mozambique's tax revenues may fall between 28 and 30 percent as a result of further trade liberalization in the Southern African Development Community and unilateral most-favored-nation liberalization. These results underline the importance of ongoing efforts to expand Mozambique's revenue base. However, reducing tariffs will also help reduce smuggling, which, according to anecdotal evidence reported by Arndt (2005), may be important in Mozambique. This

Table 10.6. Trade Restrictiveness Index

	Overall (1–10)	Tariff barriers (1–5)	Nontariff barriers (1–3)
Comparators in sub-Saharan Africa			
Mozambique	**2**	**2**	**1**
Angola	1	1	1
Congo, Dem. Rep. of	2	2	1
Madagascar	2	2	1
Zambia	2	2	1
Mauritius	4	1	2
Botswana	5	2	2
Lesotho	5	2	2
Namibia	5	2	2
South Africa	5	2	2
Swaziland	5	2	2
Tanzania	5	2	2
Zimbabwe	6	3	2
Comparators in Asia			
Indonesia	4	1	2
Malaysia	4	1	2
Thailand	5	2	2

Source: IMF.

Some progress has already been made in improving the business climate in Mozambique. However, there is increasing recognition of the need for a strategy to improve Mozambique's rankings in terms of the ease of doing business (140th out of 175 countries; World Bank, 2006) and competitiveness (128th out of 131 countries in the Global Competitiveness Index; World Economic Forum, 2007). However, the distance between Mozambique's ranking in the World Bank's index and the rankings of India (134), China (93), and some of the ASEAN countries (the lowest ranking was 135) is much smaller. The fact that these countries have been successful in dramatically improving the performance of their export sectors suggests that a business environment conducive to private sector development and export growth may be within Mozambique's reach if a well-targeted strategy for improving the business climate can be implemented. This may be particularly true for the manufacturing sector, which is especially reliant on a conducive business environment and which we have argued previously is often viewed as the engine of export-led growth.[34]

is consistent with large discrepancies between export data reported by Mozambique and import data reported by neighboring countries.

[34]Cadot and Nasir (2001) report some results that suggest that production costs in Mozambique's garment industry (a typical manufacturing industry) are among the lowest in sub-Saharan Africa. Despite this, Mozambique's garment export industry is significantly

Table 10.7. Average Tariff

	Trade-weighted average tariff	Simple average tariff
Comparators in sub-Saharan Africa		
Mozambique	**9.1**	**12.1**
Mauritius	2.2	3.1
Angola	5.4	7.2
South Africa	5.8	7.7
Tanzania	8.1	12.7
Madagascar	9.2	13.5
Namibia	9.6	7.7
Swaziland	9.6	7.7
Zambia	9.6	13.4
Botswana	11.1	7.7
Lesotho	16.8	7.7
Zimbabwe	18.0	16.2
Congo, Dem. Rep. of	n.a.	12.0
Comparators in Asia		
Indonesia	6.2	7.0
Malaysia	4.2	7.3
Thailand	6.2	11.9

Source: IMF Trade Restrictiveness Index.

The main elements of such a strategy, which is being formulated by the Ministry of Industry and Commerce with assistance from the World Bank, are summarized in Chapter 9 and will therefore not be discussed further here. It seems clear, however, that the successful implementation of such a strategy will be one of the main priorities for improving the performance of the traditional export sector, and manufacturing exports in particular, in Mozambique.

Market Access

In addition to implementing measures to improve competitiveness, a key determinant of Mozambique's export performance is the access Mozambique's exporters have to foreign markets. Mozambique exports mainly to countries where it enjoys preferential market access, in particular the countries of the Southern African Development Community (SADC) and the European Union (EU), and the United States (see Table 10.9). Mozambique has preferential market access to Southern African countries under the SADC Trade Protocol, to the EU under the Cotonou

less successful than those in Lesotho and South Africa, which have higher production costs but operate in a significantly better business environment.

Table 10.8. Export-Tax Equivalents of Import Tariffs
(In percent; based on 2001 data)

	Real income constant	Export volume constant
Comparators in sub-Saharan Africa		
Mozambique	**10.8**	**9.6**
Malawi	9.8	9.8
Zambia	8.6	8.4
South Africa	6.2	6.1
Tanzania	14.1	13.2
Botswana	3.7	3.3
Comparators in Asia		
India	31.0	28.5
Vietnam	12.7	12.6
China	12.1	12.0
Philippines	9.7	5.4
Malaysia	5.0	4.4
Thailand	16.5	11.5

Source: Tokarick (2006).

Agreement and Everything But Arms (EBA) initiative, and to the United States under the African Growth and Opportunity Act (AGOA).

Mozambique benefits, in particular, from its close proximity to South Africa. Under the SADC Trade Protocol, Mozambique's exports have preferential access to the lucrative South African market, which absorbs more than 15 percent of Mozambique's exports. Moreover, South Africa accounted for more than 11 percent of FDI in Mozambique in 2005. The importance of FDI from South Africa is likely to continue in the future following the South African central bank's relaxation of capital controls on investments in the SADC.

Until recently, a key difference between East Asia and sub-Saharan Africa was the former's emphasis on liberalizing trade relations on a broad multilateral basis, following the most-favored-nation (MFN) principle underlying successive rounds of trade negotiations under the aegis of the World Trade Organization (WTO), whereas the expansion of exports from sub-Saharan Africa has typically been based on regional or bilateral preferential trading arrangements. In observing the MFN principle, countries levy tariffs or impose other restrictions without consideration for the origin of the goods or services imported, extending equal access to their markets to all exporting countries. Regional or bilateral trading agreements, on the other hand, extend preferential access only to goods and services from the countries participating in the agreements.

Vamvakidis (1998) and the World Bank (2004) are among several studies that have argued that economies grow faster after broad-based

Table 10.9. Destination of Mozambique's Exports
(In percent of total exports)

	1991–2001	2002–05
Exports to industrial countries	57.50	66.16
United States	7.86	1.47
European Union	40.09	63.86
Exports to Africa	29.38	23.10
South Africa	16.23	15.75

Source: IMF, Direction of Trade Statistics database.

multilateral liberalization than after discriminatory liberalization. This conclusion reflects the widespread view that regional or bilateral trade arrangements can lead to welfare-reducing trade diversion in addition to welfare-improving trade creation if trade is diverted from a more efficient exporter to a less efficient one. Other studies have argued that overlapping trade agreements—sometimes referred to as the noodle bowl of bilateral and regional trade agreements—increase the complexity of the world trading system and might impose administrative costs on trade. As a result, the World Bank (2004) has estimated that sub-Saharan Africa would stand to lose 0.7 percent of its GDP if all the countries in the region negotiated bilateral free trade agreements on manufacturing products with Australia, Canada, the European Union, Japan, New Zealand, and the United States. Yang and Gupta (2005) argue that the costs could be even higher because (1) not all countries want to negotiate bilateral free trade agreements with African countries; (2) complex rules of origin can be and have been used to restrict market access; and (3) sub-Saharan countries trying to negotiate and implement multiple bilateral free trade agreements are hampered by capacity constraints.

Mozambique has been more successful than most other sub-Saharan African countries in simplifying its trading arrangements. It is a member of only one regional trade arrangement (SADC) and has thus been able to avoid the confusion associated with participating in overlapping trade agreements. This was one of the rationales for Mozambique's decision to suspend its participation in the Common Market for Eastern and Southern Africa (COMESA) in 1995. However, given developments in Mozambique's traditional export sector and taking into account the other arguments made above, it is not clear that preferential trade arrangements have made an unambiguously positive contribution to Mozambique's export performance. Moreover, because of further trade liberalization, whether through an increasing number of regional or bilateral free trade agreements or through further multilateral liberalization stemming from, for example, the WTO Doha Round of trade negotiations, African countries are likely to experience the erosion of trade preferences, which may hurt their export sectors.

The preceding discussion on market access has a number of implications for policies that may improve the performance of Mozambique's export sector in the medium term.[35] First, Mozambique should strive to ensure that African countries contribute to making the Doha Round a success. Numerous studies and the experience of many Asian countries suggest that African countries stand to make substantial gains from further multilateral trade liberalization. Second, Mozambique should work toward reducing trade barriers against countries that are not members of existing or future free trade agreements to avoid the trade-diverting effect inherent in these agreements. Third, Mozambique should undertake structural reforms to improve competitiveness and diversify its export base so as to minimize the effect of preference erosion on its export sector.

Conclusions and Policy Implications for Mozambique

This chapter has analyzed the performance and competitiveness of Mozambique's export sector and discussed possible strategies for increasing the impact of the export sector on the economy. Our analysis suggests that although exports have been growing rapidly during the past few years, this is due largely to developments in the megaproject export sector, especially aluminum. While megaprojects have clearly had a positive effect on the Mozambican economy, it was noted in the introduction to this chapter that their importance should not be overstated. In particular, diversifying the export base to include non-megaprojects appears to be a precondition for translating Mozambique's impressive growth into employment generation and poverty reduction.

While the CPI-based REER does not suggest that Mozambique's competitiveness has been deteriorating, our results do suggest that the REER may have been slightly overvalued and thus that there is scope for competitiveness to improve. We have argued that evidence of real exchange rate misalignment in the past has often coincided with periods when the exchange rate was tightly managed. In addition, there is some evidence that many of Mozambique's traditional exports may be facing declining world demand. This, coupled with the concentration of exports in

[35]See Yang and Gupta (2005) and IMF (2007) for detailed discussions on the policy implications of regional trade arrangements in Africa.

the megaproject sector, suggests that Mozambique should make efforts to diversify its export base, especially toward manufacturing exports, which are thought to be particularly important for export-led growth.

While a possible overvaluation of the REER is a fairly recent phenomenon, the relatively disappointing performance of Mozambique's traditional export sector is not. This suggests that revitalizing Mozambique's traditional export sector requires structural reforms to improve competitiveness and address the lack of export diversification, in particular the lack of non-megaproject manufacturing exports. A cornerstone of the drive toward increasing competitiveness is the development of a strategy to improve the business climate in Mozambique, which is discussed in Chapter 9. In addition, Mozambique should endeavor to play a positive role in the move toward further broad-based MFN trade liberalization while striving to make existing and future regional trade arrangements less discriminatory toward nonmembers and promoting liberal rules of origin. The implementation of these measures will be key to increasing the contribution of the non-megaproject export sector to economic growth and helping Mozambique achieve its ambitious growth and poverty reduction targets.

Lessons for Sub-Saharan Africa

While focusing on Mozambique, this chapter contains a number of conclusions with clear policy implications for other sub-Saharan countries. First, while export growth is important, efforts should be made to ensure that export growth in sub-Saharan Africa makes a positive contribution to income levels, job creation, and poverty reduction. Given that many sub-Saharan African countries are rich in natural resources, this requires putting in place a regime that balances the need to attract foreign direct investment against the aim of maximizing each country's returns from its resource endowments. As discussed in Chapter 8, Mozambique is making important strides in this regard by putting in place a fiscal regime for the mining and petroleum sectors.

Second, expanding the contribution of the export sector requires a broadening of the export base beyond capital-intensive natural resource projects while diversifying into products that are dynamic in the world marketplace. This requires putting in place a strategy to improve competitiveness and the business climate, and reducing trade barriers.[36] With

[36]The lessons for the rest of sub-Saharan Africa with respect to the business climate are discussed in Chapter 9.

respect to the latter, Mozambique's experience suggests that sub-Saharan African countries may benefit from reducing their participation in overlapping and conflicting regional trade arrangements and instead focusing on further MFN liberalization.

With respect to competitiveness, Mozambique's experience underlines the importance of careful monitoring of the real exchange rate to ensure that it does not become overvalued. This is particularly true for countries in sub-Saharan Africa, which, because of increases in capital inflows that are due to the scaling up of aid and to the exploitation of natural resources, are prone to Dutch disease effects and possible exchange rate overvaluation.[37] In that regard, Mozambique's experience suggests that misalignment of the real exchange rate is typically associated with an exchange rate that is tightly managed. This provides some justification for greater exchange rate flexibility in the face of sharp increases in capital inflows.

Appendix. Variable Definitions and Sources

The dataset used for estimation purposes consists of quarterly observations for 1996–2004. The "foreign" variable (used for the calculation of the productivity proxy) was calculated as the renormalized weighted average of the five trading partners based on the Information Notice System (INS) weights for the real effective exchange rate. For Mozambique the partner countries (weights) were South Africa (0.46), Portugal (0.11), France (0.07), the United States (0.06), Japan (0.05), Germany (0.04), Spain (0.04), the United Kingdom (0.04), Italy (0.03), Canada (0.02), the Netherlands (0.02), Belgium (0.02), Korea (0.02), and Thailand (0.01). Quarterly GDP for Mozambique was constructed from annual data using an approach similar to that in Adam (1999).

The definitions and sources for the variables are as follows:

The real effective exchange rate

Source: Information Notice System (INS) and IMF staff calculations.

Ratio of public current consumption expenditure to GDP

Source: IMF staff estimates.

Terms of trade

Source: IMF, World Economic Outlook database.

Ratio of domestic credit to the private sector to GDP

Source: IMF staff estimates.

---

[37]See Chapter 9 for details.

Real per capita GDP relative to main trade partners, normalized to 1 in 2000 with weights as discussed above

Source: IMF, World Economic Outlook database and staff estimates.

Ratio of sum of exports and imports to GDP

Source: IMF, World Economic Outlook database.

Ratio of net foreign direct investment (current prices) to GDP

Source: IMF staff estimates.

Bibliography

Adam, C.S., 1999, "Financial Liberalisation and Currency Demand in Zambia," *Journal of African Economies*, Vol. 8 (October), pp. 268–306.

———, and D.L. Bevan, 2003, "Aid, Public Expenditure and Dutch Disease," CSAE Working Paper 2003-02 (Oxford: Centre for the Study of African Economies, University of Oxford).

Agénor, P.-R., 2004, *The Economics of Adjustment and Growth* (Cambridge, Massachusetts: Harvard University Press).

Alfieri, Andrea, Alexis Rawlinson, and Xavier Cirera, 2006, "Estimating Tax and Trade Impacts of Alternative Trade Reform Scenarios on Mozambique," Discussion Paper No. 29E (Maputo, Mozambique: National Directorate of Studies and Policy Analysis, Ministry of Planning and Development). Available via the Internet: http://www.mpd.gov.mz/gest/documents/29E%20Estim%20impact.pdf

Arndt, Channing, 2005, "The Doha Trade Round and Mozambique," Discussion Paper No. 9E (Maputo, Mozambique: National Directorate of Studies and Policy Analysis, Ministry of Planning and Development). Available via the Internet: http://www.mpd.gov.mz/gest/documents/9E_Doha_Trade.pdf

———, and Finn Tarp, 2005, "Trade Policy Reform and the Missing Revenue: An Application to Mozambique," Discussion Paper No. 1E (Maputo, Mozambique: National Directorate of Studies and Policy Analysis, Ministry of Planning and Development). Available via the Internet: http://www.mpd.gov.mz/gest/documents/1E_Trade-Policy.pdf

Bigsten, A., and M. Söderbom, 2006, "What Have We Learned from a Decade of Manufacturing Enterprise Surveys in Africa?" *World Bank Research Observer*, Vol. 21 (Autumn), pp. 241–65.

Brenton, Paul, Frank Flatters, and Paul Kalenda, 2005, "Rules of Origin and SADC: The Case for Change in the Mid Term Review of the Trade Protocol," Africa Region Working Paper No. 83 (Washington: World Bank). Available via the Internet: http://www.worldbank.org/afr/wps/wp83.pdf

Bulíř, A., and T. Lane, 2002, "Aid and Fiscal Management," IMF Working Paper 02/112 (Washington: International Monetary Fund).

Cadot, O., and J. Nasir, 2001, "Incentives and Obstacles to Growth: Lessons from Manufacturing Case Studies in Madagascar," Regional Program on Enterprise Development Discussion Paper No. 17 (Washington: World Bank).

Corden, W.M., and J.P. Neary, 1982, "Booming Sector and De-Industrialisation in a Small Open Economy," *The Economic Journal*, Vol. 92 (December), pp. 825–48.

de Broeck, M., and T. Sløk, 2001, "Interpreting Real Exchange Rate Movements in Transition Countries," IMF Working Paper 01/56 (Washington: International Monetary Fund).

De Gregorio, J., A. Giovannini, and Holger Wolf, 1994, "International Evidence on Tradables and Nontradables Inflation," *European Economic Review*, Vol. 38 (June), pp. 1225–44.

Flatters, Frank, 2002, "Trade Policy Strategies for Mozambique" (Washington: United States Agency for International Development).

Frankel, J., 2005, "On the Renminbi: The Choice Between Adjustment Under a Fixed Exchange Rate and Adjustment Under a Flexible Rate," NBER Working Paper No. 11274 (Cambridge, Massachusetts: National Bureau of Economic Research).

Hinkle, L.E., and P.J. Montiel, 1999, *Exchange Rate Misalignment: Concepts and Measurement for Developing Countries* (Washington: Oxford University Press for the World Bank).

International Monetary Fund, 2005, "Dealing with the Revenue Consequences of Trade Reform" (Washington: IMF Fiscal Affairs Department). Available via the Internet: http://www.imf.org/external/np/pp/eng/2005/021505.pdf

———, 2006, "Integrating Poor Countries into the World Trading System," IMF Economic Issues No. 37 (Washington). Available via the Internet: http://www.imf.org/external/pubs/ft/issues/issues37/ei37.pdf

———, 2007, *Regional Economic Outlook: Sub-Saharan Africa*, April 2007 (Washington).

———, and World Bank, 2002, "Market Access for Developing Country Exports—Selected Issues (Washington). Available via the Internet: http://www.imf.org/external/np/pdr/ma/2002/eng/092602.pdf

Johansen, S., 1988, "Statistical Analysis of Cointegration Vectors," *Journal of Economic Dynamics and Control*, Vol. 12 (June–September), pp. 231–54.

———, 1991, "Estimation and Hypothesis Testing of Cointegration Vectors in Gaussian Vector Autoregressive Models," *Econometrica*, Vol. 59 (November), pp. 1551–80.

———, 1995, *Likelihood-Based Inference in Cointegrated Vector Autoregressive Models* (Oxford: Oxford University Press).

Johnson, Simon, Jonathan David Ostry, and Arvind Subramanian, 2007, "The Prospects for Sustained Growth in Africa: Benchmarking the Constraints," IMF Working Paper 07/52 (Washington: International Monetary Fund).

Kravis, I., and R. Lipsey, 1988, "National Price Levels and the Prices of Tradables and Nontradables," *American Economic Review, Papers and Proceedings*, Vol. 78 (May), pp. 474–78.

Kvintradze, E., 2007, "Trade Policy in Mozambique: An Overview," in *Republic of Mozambique: Selected Issues*, IMF Staff Country Report No. 07/258 (Washington: International Monetary Fund).

Nkusu, M., 2004, "Aid and the Dutch Disease in Low-Income Countries: Informed Diagnoses for Prudent Prognoses," IMF Working Paper 04/49 (Washington: International Monetary Fund).

Oomes, N., 2006, "Aid and the Equilibrium Exchange Rate: The Case of Mozambique" (unpublished; Washington: International Monetary Fund).

Rajan, R.G., and A. Subramanian, 2005, "What Undermines Aid's Impact on Growth?" IMF Working Paper 05/126 (Washington: International Monetary Fund).

Rogoff, K., 1996, "The Purchasing Power Parity Puzzle," *Journal of Economic Literature*, Vol. 34 (June), pp. 647–68.

Sarno, L., and M.P. Taylor, 2003, *The Economics of Exchange Rates* (Cambridge, United Kingdom: Cambridge University Press).

Tokarick, S., 2006, "Does Import Protection Discourage Exports?" IMF Working Paper 06/20 (Washington: International Monetary Fund).

United States Agency for International Development (USAID), 2004, *Removing Obstacles to Economic Growth in Mozambique: A Diagnostic Trade Integration Study* (Washington).

———, 2006a, "Inside Southern African Trade," Southern African Global Competitiveness Hub, Issue 7 (Washington, December).

———, 2006b, "Mozambique: Globalization and Domestic Policy Choices" (Washington).

———, 2006c, "Mozambique's Integration into Global Markets" (Washington).

Vamvakidis, Athanasios, 1998, "Regional Trade Arrangements Versus Broad Liberalization: Which Path Leads to Faster Growth? Time-Series Evidence," IMF Working Paper 98/04 (Washington: International Monetary Fund).

World Bank, 2004, *Global Economic Prospects 2005: Trade, Regionalism and Development* (Washington).

———, 2006, "Doing Business 2007: How to Reform" (Washington).

World Economic Forum, 2007, *Global Competitiveness Report 2007–2008* (Davos).

Yagci, Fahrettin, and Enrique Aldaz-Carroll, 2004, "Salient Features of Trade Performance in Eastern and Southern Africa," Africa Region Working Paper No. 76 (Washington: World Bank).

Yang, Yongzheng, 2005, "Africa in the Doha Round: Dealing with Preference Erosion and Beyond," IMF Policy Discussion Paper No. 05/08 (Washington: International Monetary Fund).

———, and S. Gupta, 2005, "Regional Trade Arrangements in Africa: Past Performance and the Way Forward," IMF Working Paper 05/36 (Washington: International Monetary Fund).

Younger, S.D., 1992, "Aid and the Dutch Disease: Macroeconomic Management When Everybody Loves You," *World Development*, Vol. 20 (November), pp. 1587–97.

Abbreviations and Acronyms

ASEAN	Association of Southeast Asian Nations
ASEAN-4	Indonesia, Malaysia, the Philippines, and Thailand
ATM	Autoridade Tributária Moçambicana (central revenue authority of Mozambique)
BdPES	Balanço do Plano Económico e Social (evaluation of social economic plan or evaluation of annual Poverty Reduction Strategy)
BOP	Balance of payments
CFMP	Cenario Fiscal de Medio Prazo (medium-term fiscal framework)
CGE	Conta Geral do Estado (final state accounts)
CPF	Central processing facility
CPIA	Country Policy and Institutional Assessment
CUT	Conta Única do Tesouro (single treasury account)
DFID	U.K. Department for International Development
EITI	Extractive Industries Transparency Initiative
FDI	Foreign direct investment
e-SISTAFE	Sistema Integrado da Administração Financeira do Estado Eletronico (the government's electronic integrated system for financial administration)
GCI	Global Competitiveness Index
GBS	General budget support
H&A	Harmonization and alignment
ICA	Investment climate assessment
MDG	Millennium Development Goal
MF	Ministry of Finance
MOU	Memorandum of understanding
MPD	Ministry of Planning and Development
MTEF	Medium-term expenditure framework
ODAMOZ	Official Development Aid Mozambique (database)
OE	Orçamento do Estado (annual state budget)
OECD-DAC	Organization for Economic Cooperation and Development–Development Assistance Committee
PAF	Performance Assessment Framework

PAP	Program Aid Partner
PARPA	Plano de Acção para a Redução da Pobreza Absoluta (Poverty Reduction Strategy, or PRS)
PARPA I	Poverty Reduction Strategy for 2001–05
PARPA II	Poverty Reduction Strategy for 2006–09
PEFA	Public Expenditure and Financial Accountability
PES	Plano Económico e Social (social economic plan, or annual Poverty Reduction Strategy
PFM	Public financial management
PIU	Project Implementation Unit
PPA	Petroleum production agreement
PRS	Poverty Reduction Strategy
PRSP	Poverty Reduction Strategy Paper
PSA	Production sharing agreement
REER	Real effective exchange rate
SADC	Southern African Development Community
SIDA	Swedish International Development and Cooperation Agency
SMEs	Small and medium-size enterprises
SPA	Strategic Partnership with Africa
SSA	Sub-Saharan Africa
SWAP	Sector-wide approach
TFP	Total factor productivity